Managing the Aerospace System with Lean Six Sigma

Lean Six Sigma entered the aviation and aerospace industries in 1993 in response to significant changes affecting these industries. Since then, Lean Six Sigma has made monumental contributions to the aerospace system. A robust Lean Six Sigma program serves the aviation and aerospace industry well because it gives managers and frontline workers a common language to unite their efforts to improve overall performance and quality. Lean Six Sigma management practices have provided tailor-made solutions that address a multitude of problems experienced by the aviation and aerospace industries alike. *Managing the Aerospace System with Lean Six Sigma: A Roadmap to Success* is designed to provide those with a desire to practice the art of Lean Six Sigma – in any industry, but specifically in the aviation and aerospace sector – the tools and knowledge to ensure success. Each part is designed to guide the student/candidate through a Lean Six Sigma structured Body of Knowledge (BoK). Each chapter is designed to support the BoK elements that are aligned with that part topic and ordered so that they progressively build the student/candidate's mastery of the skills needed to progress from "Yellow Belt", through "Green Belt", to "Black Belt". Filled with illustrative examples of how Lean Six Sigma is currently being employed in the aviation and aerospace industries, and how it can be expanded, this book will be a required textbook for teaching Lean Six Sigma. The book is designed for lectures and application in the classroom, for use with students and candidates at all levels of the Lean Six Sigma certification process.

John Longshore is a Master Black Belt in Lean and Six Sigma and a Professor Emeritus in the David B. O'Maley College of Business at Embry Riddle Aeronautical University's Daytona Beach Campus. His many years of industry experience include projects for the military and private organizations focused on continuous improvement. His academic teaching responsibilities include systems engineering management, project management, production and operations management, quantitative methods in business, logistics, Lean Six Sigma, and other related business courses.

Angela Cheatham is an associate professor of management at Embry Riddle Aeronautical University, teaching supply chain management from a logistics perspective, Lean Six Sigma, project management, logistics management for aviation and aerospace, and transportation. She holds a Black Belt in Six Sigma and has participated in FAA and industry projects focusing on commercial space integration, supply chain, project management, and lean processes.

Managing the Aerospace System with Lean Six Sigma

A Roadmap to Success

John Longshore and Angela Cheatham

Routledge
Taylor & Francis Group
LONDON AND NEW YORK

Designed cover image: imaginima © Getty Images

First published 2026
by Routledge
4 Park Square, Milton Park, Abingdon, Oxon OX14 4RN

and by Routledge
605 Third Avenue, New York, NY 10158

Routledge is an imprint of the Taylor & Francis Group, an informa business

British Library Cataloguing-in-Publication Data
A catalogue record for this book is available from the British Library

ISBN: 978-1-032-65050-0 (hbk)
ISBN: 978-1-032-65047-0 (pbk)
ISBN: 978-1-032-65053-1 (ebk)

DOI: 10.4324/9781032650531

Typeset in Minion
by Apex CoVantage, LLC

Contents

Part I

The Origins of Lean Six Sigma

1
The Nature and Purpose of Lean Six Sigma

LEARNING OBJECTIVES

Upon completion of this chapter the student should be able to:

1. Understand the components of Lean and Six Sigma and their role in fostering a culture of continuous improvement within organizations.
2. Describe and discuss the six key concepts of Lean and Six Sigma.
3. Explain the notation Y = F(X) and its significance in Lean Six Sigma.
4. Understand the business case rationale for Lean Six Sigma, especially within the aviation and aerospace industry.
5. Gain insight into thought process mapping and its role in enhancing critical thinking and problem-solving.

LEAN SIX SIGMA DEFINED

Lean Six Sigma is a business management methodology that combines the principles of Lean manufacturing and Six Sigma to improve efficiency, quality, and overall performance within an organization. The aim is to eliminate waste, reduce variation, and enhance customer satisfaction by systematically identifying and eliminating process defects and inefficiencies.

Lean Six Sigma revolves around two key components: Lean and Six Sigma

Lean principles focus on minimizing waste and non-value-added activities in processes. It emphasizes the elimination of activities that do not contribute to delivering value to the customer. Lean aims to streamline operations, improve flow, and enhance productivity by identifying waste such as overproduction, waiting time, excess inventory, unnecessary movement, defects, and unused employee creativity.

Six Sigma focuses on reducing process variation and thus defects through a data-driven methodology. It uses a structured problem-solving phased approach entitled DMAIC, which stands for Define-Measure-Analyze-Improve-Control. These phases lead a team

DOI: 10.4324/9781032650531-2

logically from defining a problem through implementing solutions to underlying causes and then establishes best practices to ensure solutions stay in place.

The purpose of Lean Six Sigma is to create a culture of continuous improvement within an organization. It does this via Lean Six Sigma principles and techniques that:

1. *Improve quality* – by reducing defects and errors, organizations enhance the quality of products and services and increase customer satisfaction and loyalty.
2. *Increase efficiency* – by eliminating waste and optimizing processes, organizations improve efficiency and reduce cost, which enables task accomplishment with fewer resources in less time with minimal, near-zero error.
3. *Enhance customer satisfaction* – with a laser focus on understanding and meeting customer needs, Lean Six Sigma keeps products and processes in optimal alignment to consistently meet customer expectations.
4. *Drive profitability* – maximizing return on invested capital, increasing productivity with fewer defects, and increasing customer satisfaction via improved quality and response time.

This is made possible by an organization adopting a robust Lean Six Sigma program.

THE INTEGRATION OF LEAN AND SIX SIGMA

The integration of Lean and Six Sigma is a powerful approach which combines the principles and methodologies of both Lean and Six Sigma to achieve operational excellence, process improvement, and enhanced quality in organizations. Lean focuses on eliminating waste and improving process flow, while Six Sigma aims at reducing process variation and defects. By integrating these two approaches, organizations leverage their complementary strengths and drive significant improvements across various aspects of their operations. Figure 1.1 provides a graphic representation of six key principles and concepts of Lean Six Sigma.

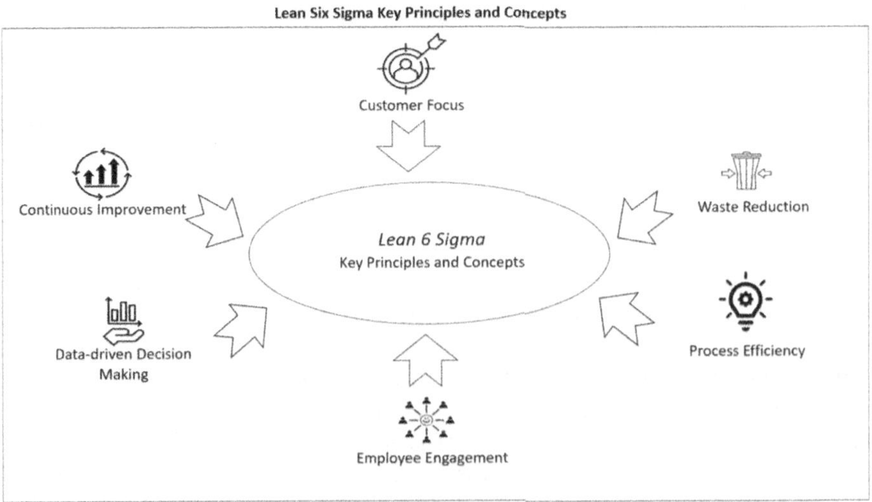

Figure 1.1 Lean Six Sigma Key Principles and Concepts

Customer Focus: Both Lean and Six Sigma emphasize the importance of understanding and meeting customer requirements and expectations. Customer feedback and data analysis play a vital role in identifying improvement opportunities and driving process optimization.

Process Efficiency: Lean techniques, such as value stream mapping, help identify and eliminate non-value-added activities, reduce cycle times, and improve overall process efficiency. Six Sigma tools, such as statistical process control (SPC), assist in measuring and monitoring process performance and identifying and reducing process variation.

Waste Reduction: Lean principles focus on identifying and eliminating different types of waste, including overproduction, waiting time, unnecessary transportation, excess inventory, overprocessing, defects, and underutilized talent. By reducing waste, organizations can improve productivity, lead times, and resource utilization.

Data-Driven Decision Making: Six Sigma emphasizes the use of data and statistical analysis to make informed decisions and solve complex problems. Data collection, measurement systems analysis, hypothesis testing, and root cause analysis are integral parts of the Lean Six Sigma approach.

Continuous Improvement: Both Lean and Six Sigma promote a culture of continuous improvement. Using Lean tools like Kaizen events and Six Sigma's DMAIC methodology, organizations strive for incremental and sustainable improvements in their processes.

Employee Engagement: Engaging employees at all levels of the organization is crucial for the successful implementation of Lean Six Sigma. Empowering employees to identify improvement opportunities, participate in problem-solving, and providing them with the necessary training and tools fosters a culture of ownership and accountability.

Process Velocity: The integration of Lean and Six Sigma also enables organizations to achieve a balance between process velocity and quality in both focus and approach as they progress on the path to operational excellence. While each has a different focus and approach, both are of vital importance to organizational success.

- *Focus* – process velocity refers to the speed at which a process can be completed. The focus of process velocity is reducing the time it takes to complete that process to increase efficiency and thus productivity. Quality refers to the degree to which a product or service meets customer expectations. Its focus is on ensuring that the product or service is delivered with high levels of quality consistently to increase satisfaction and loyalty.
- *Approach* – the approach to improving process velocity is to identify and eliminate any steps in a process that add unnecessary time and delay. This means streamlining the process, removing bottlenecks, and optimizing resources. The approach to improving quality is to identify and eliminate defects or errors in the product or service early in the development or delivery process. This means implementing quality control measures, conducting inspections, audits, and training employees.
- *Benefits* – improving process velocity leads to increased productivity, faster turnaround times, reduced cost and, yes, quality! Improving quality leads to increased customer satisfaction and loyalty, improved reputation, and increased revenue through repeat business and positive word-of-mouth.

WHAT DOES "Y = F(X)" MEAN IN LEAN SIX SIGMA

The notation "Y = F(X)" shows the relationship between two variables, where "X" is the input and "Y" is the output. The function "F" explains how "X" is transformed to produce "Y". In this case, "X(s)" is the Laplace transform of the input, and "Y(s)" is the transform of the output, with "s" being the complex frequency variable.

In Lean Six Sigma, "Y = F(X)" represents how inputs (X) affect outputs (Y). "Y" often stands for a key performance indicator like product quality, process efficiency, or customer satisfaction. "F(X)" is the process that transforms inputs into outputs.

Examples include:

- Poor hamburger taste (Y) due to an uncalibrated grill (X).
- Low employee morale (Y) because of a bad time-off approval system (X).
- Long customer wait times (Y) caused by employees distracted by technology (X).
- Aircraft component failures (Y) linked to part shortages (X).

The goal in Lean Six Sigma is to optimize this relationship to improve performance and reduce defects, using statistical tools to identify the key inputs that most affect the output.

THE BUSINESS CASE FOR LEAN SIX SIGMA

Implementing Lean Six Sigma can provide several compelling business benefits and a strong business case for organizations. Some of the key reasons organizations adopt Lean Six Sigma are depicted in Figure 1.2.

Cost Reduction: Lean Six Sigma helps identify and eliminate waste, inefficiencies, and defects in processes. By streamlining operations, reducing defects, and improving resource utilization, organizations can achieve significant cost savings. This includes savings from reduced rework, lower scrap rates, decreased inventory levels, improved productivity, and optimized use of resources.

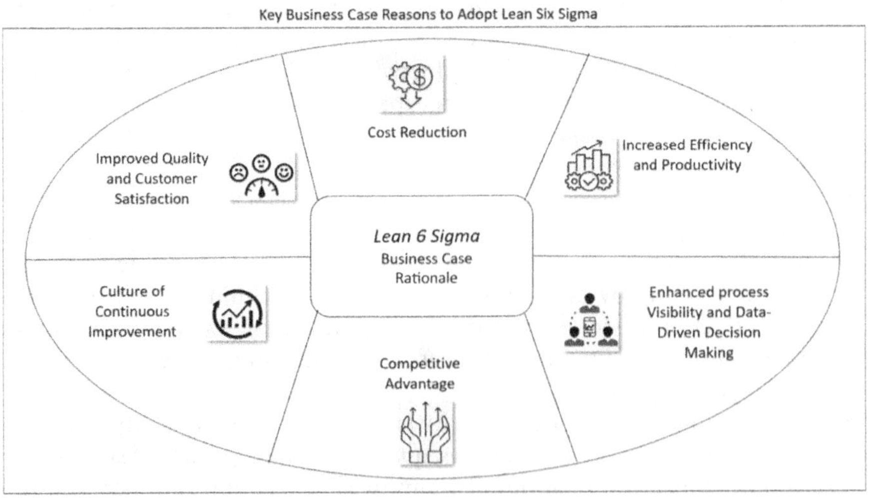

Figure 1.2 Key Business Case Reasons to Adopt Lean Six Sigma

Improved Quality and Customer Satisfaction: The focus on reducing process variation and defects in Six Sigma, combined with Lean's emphasis on customer value, helps organizations enhance product and service quality. By delivering higher-quality products or services that meet or exceed customer expectations, organizations can improve customer satisfaction, loyalty, and retention.

Increased Efficiency and Productivity: Lean Six Sigma eliminates non-value-added activities, streamlines process flows, and improves process efficiency. By reducing process cycle times, eliminating bottlenecks, and enhancing resource utilization, organizations can achieve higher productivity levels and throughput. This leads to increased capacity, faster delivery times, and improved responsiveness to customer demands.

Enhanced Process Visibility and Data-Driven Decision Making: Lean Six Sigma promotes the use of data and metrics to drive decision making and process improvement. By implementing robust measurement systems, organizations gain better visibility into process performance and can identify improvement opportunities based on data analysis. This leads to informed decision making, better problem-solving, and a focus on addressing root causes.

Culture of Continuous Improvement: Lean Six Sigma fosters a culture of continuous improvement, where employees are encouraged to identify and implement process enhancements. By engaging employees at all levels, organizations tap into their expertise, creativity, and problem-solving abilities. This empowers employees to contribute to process improvement initiatives, leading to a culture of ownership and continuous learning.

Competitive Advantage: Lean Six Sigma enables organizations to deliver higher-quality products or services with shorter lead times and at lower costs. This can give them a significant competitive advantage in the market. By continuously improving processes, organizations stay ahead of competitors, adapt to changing customer needs, and drive innovation.

It is important to note that achieving these benefits requires proper implementation, training, and ongoing commitment to Lean Six Sigma principles. Organizations need to invest in training employees, establishing effective measurement systems, and creating a supportive infrastructure for continuous improvement. However, the potential returns on these investments, in terms of improved performance, cost savings, and customer satisfaction, make Lean Six Sigma a compelling business case for many organizations.

LEAN SIX SIGMA: DID YOU KNOW?

The Lean Six methodology focuses on customer knowledge by translating customer needs, wants, and expectations into areas for improvement. The Lean Six Sigma methodology concentrates effort on improving critical business activities. Lean Six Sigma focuses attention on the process and processes to make sure that they deliver value directly to the customer consistently.

The backbone of a Lean Six Sigma effort is improvement projects, chosen based on their ability to contribute to the organization's bottom line and being connected to the strategic objectives of that organization. Good projects improve productivity, reduce costs, and increase quality. Since Lean Six Sigma projects seek to remove waste in any form and reduce un-natural variation in processes, projects are easy to identify. Project teams seek out sources of waste and variation, investigate production backlogs or areas in need of more capacity, and focus squarely on the customers and environmental issues. Regardless of project orientation, all Lean Six Sigma efforts originally consisted of eight essential broad phases: Recognize, Define, Measure, Analyze, Improve, Control, Standardize, and Integrate.

This cycle is now expressed as DMAIC: define, measure, analyze, improve, and control. We will be examining this process in depth starting in Chapter 4.

GUIDING CRITICAL THINKING: THOUGHT PROCESS MAPPING

Thought process mapping is a technique used to visually represent and organize the steps involved in critical thinking and problem-solving. It helps individuals or teams understand and communicate their thinking process, identify potential gaps or biases, and improve the overall quality of their decision-making. Figure 1.3 illustrates a step-by-step guide to thought process mapping.

Define the Problem: Clearly articulate the problem or issue you are trying to address. This provides a clear focus for your thought process mapping.

Identify the Goal: Determine the desired outcome or goal you want to achieve through your critical thinking. This helps keep your thinking process aligned with the desired result.

Brainstorm Ideas: Generate a list of possible solutions, alternatives, or approaches to the problem. Encourage open and creative thinking without evaluating ideas at this stage.

Organize Ideas: Arrange the brainstormed ideas into logical groupings or categories. Look for common themes or connections between ideas to create a structured overview.

Evaluate Ideas: Assess the feasibility, potential risks, and benefits of each idea or approach. Consider factors such as resources required, time constraints, and potential impact on stakeholders.

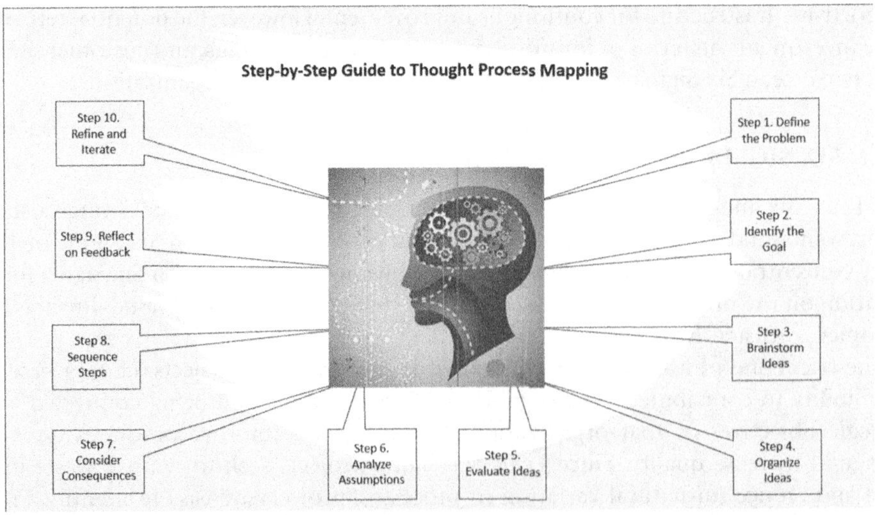

Figure 1.3 Step-by-Step Guide to Thought Process Mapping

Analyze Assumptions: Reflect on the assumptions or beliefs underlying each idea. Challenge these assumptions and critically evaluate their validity. Consider alternative perspectives and potential biases.

Consider Consequences: Think through the potential consequences or implications of each idea or decision. Identify potential risks, unintended consequences, or trade-offs associated with different options.

Sequence Steps: Determine the logical sequence of steps or actions required to implement each idea or decision. Identify dependencies between steps and consider any potential constraints.

Reflect on Feedback: Seek input and feedback from others, if possible. Consider different viewpoints, expertise, or experiences that can enhance your thought process and decision-making.

Refine and Iterate: Review and refine your thought process map as you gain additional insights or information. Iterate through the previous steps to ensure a thorough and well-rounded analysis.

Examples of how thought process mapping techniques are illustrated and used in Lean Six Sigma efforts are illustrated in Figure 1.4.

Flowchart: A flowchart is a visual representation of a process that shows the sequence of steps or actions and decision points. It uses symbols and arrows to depict the flow of information, materials, or activities. Flowcharts help analyze and improve processes by identifying bottlenecks, redundancies, and opportunities for optimization.

Concept Map: A concept map visually represents the relationships between concepts or ideas. It uses nodes or boxes to represent concepts and lines or arrows to connect them, indicating relationships or associations. Concept maps help organize and clarify complex information, facilitate understanding, and promote critical thinking.

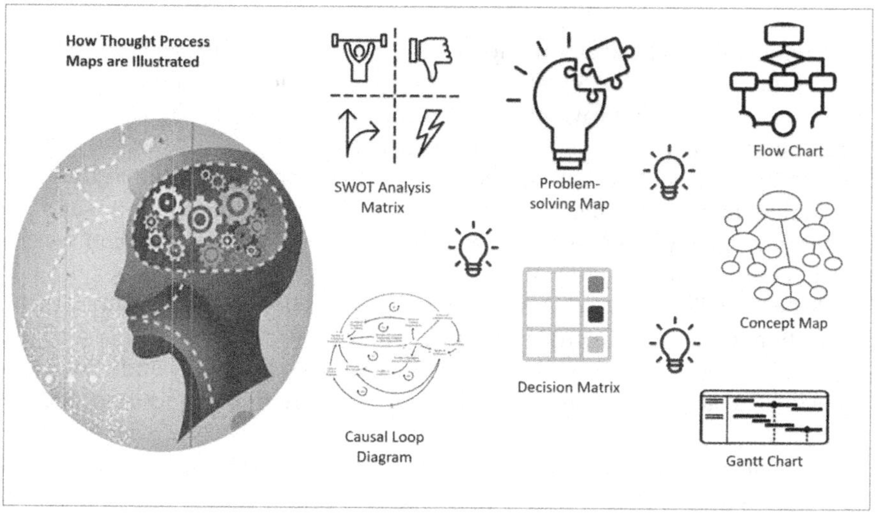

Figure 1.4 Examples of How Thought Process Maps are Illustrated

Problem-Solution Map: A problem-solution map visually represents a problem or challenge and potential solutions. It identifies the root causes or factors contributing to the problem and maps out potential solutions or strategies to address them. This mapping technique helps analyze alternatives, evaluate their feasibility, and choose the most effective solution.

Decision Matrix: A decision matrix is a tool for evaluating multiple options against predefined criteria. It uses a grid format where each option is assessed based on its performance against each criterion. The matrix helps compare and rank different options objectively, facilitating decision making.

Gantt Chart: A Gantt chart is a visual representation of a project schedule. It shows tasks or activities as horizontal bars along a timeline, indicating their start and end dates. Gantt charts help plan and track progress, identify dependencies, and manage resources in project management.

Causal Loop Diagram: A causal loop diagram (CLD) represents the causal relationships between different variables or factors. It uses arrows and feedback loops to indicate how changes in one variable affect others. CLDs help understand complex systems, identify feedback mechanisms, and analyze the dynamics of cause and effect.

SWOT Analysis Matrix: A SWOT analysis matrix visually represents the strengths, weaknesses, opportunities, and threats associated with a business, project, or decision. It uses a grid format to categorize and analyze internal and external factors, providing an overview of the current situation.

By visually mapping out your thought process, you gain a clearer understanding of the logical flow and connections between the stages of critical thinking. This approach helps identify potential biases, uncover hidden assumptions, and ensure a comprehensive and systematic analysis of the problem at hand.

WHY FOCUS ON THE AVIATION AND AEROSPACE INDUSTRY?

Lean Six Sigma efforts are having a significant impact on the aviation and aerospace industry today. Figure 1.5 presents some of the more compelling reasons for this trend.

Safety and Quality: The aviation and aerospace industry prioritize safety and quality as paramount. Lean Six Sigma methodologies help identify and eliminate defects, reduce errors, and improve process controls, which directly aligns with the industry's commitment to safety and high-quality standards.

Complex Operations: Aviation and aerospace operations involve intricate processes, including manufacturing, maintenance, supply chain management, and service delivery. Applying Lean Six Sigma principles helps streamline these complex operations, eliminate waste, and enhance efficiency.

Cost Reduction: The aviation and aerospace industry faces cost pressures, with high operational expenses, complex supply chains, and stringent regulatory requirements. Lean Six Sigma provides tools and techniques to identify and eliminate non-value-added activities, reduce cycle times, optimize resource utilization, and achieve cost savings.

Customer Satisfaction: The aviation industry is customer-centric, focusing on passenger experience, on-time performance, and service reliability. Lean Six Sigma aids in improving processes, reducing delays, enhancing customer satisfaction, and addressing issues that impact the overall customer experience.

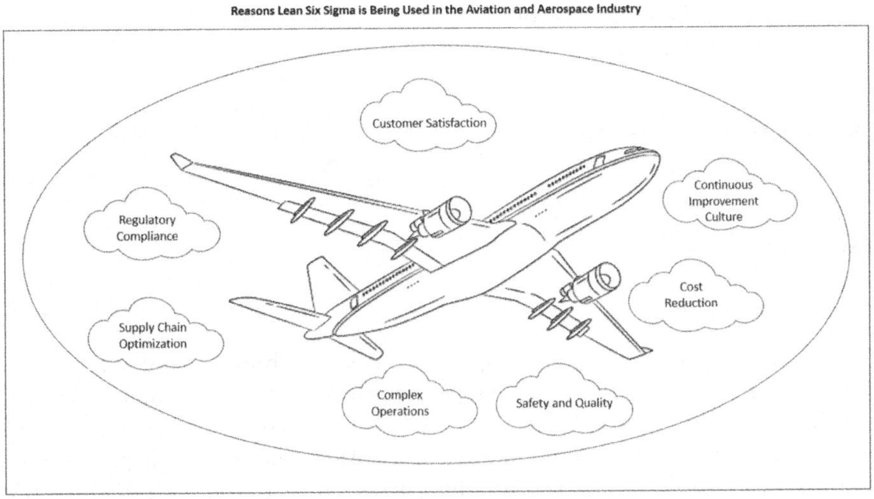

Figure 1.5 Reasons Lean Six Sigma Is Being Used in the Aviation and Aerospace Industry

Continuous Improvement Culture: Lean Six Sigma promotes a culture of continuous improvement, which is crucial for maintaining and enhancing competitiveness in the aviation and aerospace industry. By embracing Lean Six Sigma, organizations can foster a mindset of innovation, problem-solving, and proactive identification of improvement opportunities.

Regulatory Compliance: The aviation and aerospace sectors operate under strict regulatory frameworks to ensure safety, security, and adherence to industry standards. Lean Six Sigma methodologies enable organizations to meet regulatory requirements, maintain compliance, and proactively address potential risks or non-conformities.

Supply Chain Optimization: The aviation industry relies on extensive and complex supply chains involving various suppliers, vendors, and service providers. Implementing Lean Six Sigma principles helps optimize supply chain management, reduce lead times, improve inventory management, and enhance overall coordination and efficiency.

Considering these factors, Lean Six Sigma becomes an essential approach for the aviation and aerospace industry to improve safety, quality, efficiency, customer satisfaction, and cost-effectiveness while maintaining regulatory compliance. It aligns with the industry's core values and supports the pursuit of operational excellence in a challenging and safety-critical environment.

SUMMARY

Chapter 1 began by defining Lean and Six Sigma and discussing the nature and purpose of each and how they are joined to form a powerful toolset. It then dove into a short historical perspective of Lean and Six Sigma and provided perspective on their evolution. The reader was then provided with a discussion as to how they are currently integrated for maximum effectiveness. It then addressed the equation "Y = F(X)" and explained that it is this breakthrough equation that is used to find out which inputs will send the optimal or best output. The chapter then guided critical thinking using thought process mapping and provided illustrative examples. Elaboration was then provided on why the focus of this book is on the aviation and aerospace industry and reasons and examples of why and how it is currently beginning employed and can be expanded.

LEAN SIX SIGMA AT WORK

Lean Six Sigma at Work!

AJ Inc., an aeronautical job shop specializing in machining wing spar forgings into finished products, utilizes three separate inspections as its primary method of ensuring the quality of its products. The first inspection occurs following the initial machining operations (grinding, milling, and boring) and before the part is sent to a subcontractor for heat treating. After the part is returned from heat treatment, key dimensions are checked at the second inspection. A final inspection is conducted before the finished part leaves the plant.

With these three inspections, discrepancies between actual part dimensions and the specifications are found only after the part has completed several machining operations. This approach results in significant scrap and rework costs. If the forgings pass incoming inspection and begin to progress through the machining operations, for a typical part, four of six operations will have been completed before any errors are caught during the in-process inspection that occurs before the part is shipped out for heat treatment. The work done after the operation where the error occurred is wasted because each subsequent machining operation is performed on a faulty part.

A Lean Six Sigma team studied the inspection method and determined that process improvements could be made to improve incoming forging consistency and reduce variation. Operators at each step in the process are now responsible for checking actual part dimensions against specifications. The team also initiated a corrective action for each non-conformance to standards. Corrective action plans prevent future errors.

As a result of its efforts, AJ Inc. has seen an improvement of one sigma, which translates to a tenfold reduction in the number of defects.

At three sigma, it could expect 66,807 defects per million. At an average cost of $10/piece to fix, the costs incurred were $668,007. Now that AJ Inc. is operating at four sigma, it expects 6,210 defects per million. At $10/piece to fix, its cost is $62,100. Further improvement activities are planned to reduce variation and improve performance to five sigma.

BIBLIOGRAPHY

Akbulut-Bailey, Asli Yagmur, Jaideep Motwani, and Everett M. Smedley. "When lean and six sigma converge: A case study of a successful implementation of lean six sigma at an aerospace company." *International Journal of Technology Management* 57.1/2/3 (2012): 18–32.

Arnheiter, E. D., and J. Maleyeff. "The TQM magazine." *The TQM Magazine* 17.1 (2005): 5–18. https://doi.org/10.1108/09544780510573020.

Breyfogle, F. W. *Implementing Six Sigma*, John Wiley & Sons, Inc., 1999. Copyright 2003 by Forrest W. Breyfogle III. All rights reserved.

Byrne, G., D. Lubowe, and A. Blitz. "Strategy & leadership." *Strategy & Leadership* 35.2 (2007): 5–10. ISSN 1087–8572.

Drohomeretski, Everton, Sergio E. Gouvea da Costa, Edson Pinheiro de Lima, and Paula Andrea da Rosa Garbuio. "Lean, six sigma, and lean six sigma: An analysis based on operations strategy." *International Journal of Production Research* 52.3 (2014): 804–824. https://doi.org/10.1080/00207543.2013.842015.

Ericson, Jonathan D. "Mapping the relationship between critical thinking and design thinking." *Journal of the Knowledge Economy* 13.1 (2022): 406–429.

Foster Jr., S. Thomas. "Does six sigma improve performance?" *Quality Management Journal* 14.4 (2007): 7–20. https://doi.org/10.1080/10686967.2007.11918043.

Hoerl, R. W., and M. M. Gardner. "International journal of lean six sigma." *International Journal of Lean Six Sigma* 1.1 (2010): 30–38. https://doi.org/10.1108/20401461011033149.

Johnson, M. E., and S. I. Dubikovsky. "Incorporating lean six sigma into an aviation technology program." In *Proceedings of SEFI 2008 Annual Conference*. West Lafayette, IN, 2008.

Maleyeff, J., E. A. Arnheiter, and V. Venkateswaran. "The TQM journal." *The TQM Journal* 24.6 (2012): 542–555. https://doi.org/10.1108/17542731211270124.

O'Connell, Roxanne M. "Mind mapping for critical thinking." In *Cases on Teaching Critical Thinking Through Visual Representation Strategies*. IGI Global, 2014, pp. 354–386.

Panayiotou, Nikolaos A., Konstantinos E. Stergiou, and Nikolaos Panagiotou. "International journal of quality & reliability management." *International Journal of Quality & Reliability Management* 2022. ISSN 0265–671X.

Prabhushankar, G. V., et al. "The origin, history, and definition of six sigma: A literature review." *International Journal of Six Sigma and Competitive Advantage* 4.2 (2008): 133–150.

Psychogios, Alexandros G., and Loukas K. Tsironis. "Towards an integrated framework for lean six sigma application: Lessons from the airline industry." *Total Quality Management & Business Excellence* 23.3–4 (2012): 397–415.

Ruben, R. B., S. Vinodh, and P. Asokan. "Lean six sigma with environmental focus: Review and framework." *The International Journal of Advanced Manufacturing* 94 (2018): 4023–4037.

2
Selecting Lean Six Sigma Projects Within Aviation and Aerospace

LEARNING OBJECTIVES

Upon completion of this chapter the student should be able to:

1 Explain the organizational preparedness checklist areas and key questions for Lean Six Sigma projects.
2 Describe the steps involved in creating a business case and project charter for a Lean Six Sigma project.
3 Apply the Balance Score Card matrix to assess the balance of cost, schedule, and quality in a Lean Six Sigma aviation/aerospace project.
4 Differentiate between Lean Six Sigma projects and standard projects in terms of tracking and performance measurement.
5 Evaluate stakeholder needs and influence using the RACI (responsible, accountable, consulted, and informed) chart and Power Action grid and develop contingency plans tailored to the aviation/aerospace MRO industry.

ORGANIZING FOR SUCCESS

Dwight D. Eisenhower said, "Plans are nothing; planning is everything." Certainly, he was not talking about Lean Six Sigma projects, but this statement applies 100 percent to any process improvement efforts an organization plans to undertake.

The act of properly planning a project and preparing an organization for executing the plan virtually ensures success because it is a continual team effort of evaluation, organization, and communication by all its members. The teams that do these things well with the focus on end results produce successful Lean Six Sigma project outcomes.

Before committing to executing a Lean Six Sigma project within an organization, assessing that preparedness on a range of key implementation aspects helps with identifying if that organization is in fact ready for a Lean Six Sigma journey (Figure 2.1).

DOI: 10.4324/9781032650531-3

Ten Key Aspects of Organizational Preparedness for a Lean Six Sigma Project

	Yes	No	Partial	
1. Leadership Support and Commitment			✓	a. Does the organization have strong support and commitment from top-level management?
			✓	b. Do leaders across the organization actively sponsor initiatives, collaborative allocate resources and promote a culture of continuous improvement throughout the organization?
2. Project Selection and Scope				a. Are organizational projects selected that align with strategic objectives and measured by their impact of customer satisfaction, quality, and efficiency?
			✓	b. Is project scope clearly defined with objectives and expected outcomes clearly focused with clarity?
3. Cross Functional Teams				a. Are cross-functional teams with representatives from various departments and functions used in executing organization-wide projects?
				b. Do team members possess the necessary skills and knowledge to contribute effectively if cross-functional teams are used?
				c. Is there collaboration and effective communication among team members evident if cross-functional teams are used?
4. Roles and Responsibilities				a. Are roles and responsibilities for team members and project stakeholders clearly defined?
				b. Is there collaboration and effective communication among team members evident if cross-functional teams are used?
5. Project Management				a. Are project management practices planned, executed and monitored and used on organizational projects?
				b. If project plans are used, are defined timelines, milestones, and deliverables used?
				c. If project plans are used, are regular progress reviews conducted and issues or roadblocks dealt with expeditiously and adjustment to plan made?
6. Data Collection and Analysis				a. Does the organization use robust data collection methods to gather accurate and relevant data?
				b. Are statistical tools and techniques used to analyze the data and identify root causes for any process variation and opportunities for improvement?
7. DMAIC Methodology				a. Does the organization use a structured problem-solving approach such as the DMAIC (Define, Measure, Analyze, Improve, Control) to guide projects?
				b. If DMAIC is used, does each phase use specific activities and tools to systematically drive improvement?
8. Change Management				a. How does the organization recognize and address resistance to change within the organization?
				b. How does the organization implement change management strategies to gain buy-in from employees and stakeholders?
				c. How would the organization communicate the benefits of a Lean Six Sigma project and provide training/support to facilitate successful implementation?
9. Communication and Stakeholder Engagement				a. How does the organization maintain regular communication with project stakeholders, sponsors, leaders, team members, and impacted employees?
				b. How are project updates, progress, and success communicated to keep stakeholders informed and engaged in the process?
10. Continuous Learning and Sustainability				a. Does the organization foster a culture of continuous learning and improvement? How?
				b. Does the organization capture and share lessons learned from the project to promote knowledge transfer?
				c. If a Lean Six Sigma project were executed would the organization implement controls and monitoring mechanisms to sustain the improvements achieved by the project?

Figure 2.1 Sample Checklist: Ten Key Aspects of Organizational Preparedness for a Lean Six Sigma Project

Here are ten key aspects of organizational preparedness:

1 Leadership support and commitment:
   a Does the organization have strong support and commitment from top-level management?
   b Do leaders across the organization actively sponsor initiatives, collaboratively allocate resources and promote a culture of continuous improvement?
2 Project selection and scope:
   a Are organizational projects selected that align with strategic objectives and are measured by the impact on customer satisfaction, quality, and efficiency?
   b Is project scope clearly defined with objectives and expected outcomes clearly focused on with clarity?
3 Cross-functional teams:
   a Are cross-functional teams, with representatives from various departments and functions, used in executing organization-wide projects?
   b Do team members possess the necessary skills and knowledge to contribute effectively if cross-functional teams are used?
   c Are collaboration and effective communication among team members evident if cross-functional teams are used?
4 Roles and responsibilities:
   a Are roles and responsibilities for team members and project stakeholders clearly defined?
   b Are expectations clearly communicated to team members so that everyone understands their contribution to the project success?
5 Project management:
   a Are project management practices planned, executed, and monitored in organizational projects?
   b If project plans are used, are defined timelines, milestones, and deliverables used?
   c If project plans are used, are regular progress reviews conducted and issues or roadblocks dealt with expeditiously and adjustments made to the plan?
6 Data collection and analysis:
   a Does the organization use robust data collection methods to gather accurate and relevant data?
   b Are statistical tools and techniques used to analyze the data and identify root causes for any process variation and opportunities for improvement?
7 DMAIC methodology:
   a Does the organization use a structured problem-solving approach such as DMAIC (define, measure, analyze, improve, control) to guide projects?
   b If DMAIC is used, does each phase use specific activities and tools to systematically drive improvement?
8 Change management:
   a How does the organization recognize and address resistance to change within the organization?
   b How does the organization implement change management strategies to gain buy-in from employees and stakeholders?
   c How would the organization communicate the benefits of a Lean Six Sigma project and provide training and support to facilitate successful implementation?
9 Communication and stakeholder engagement:
   a How does the organization maintain regular communication with project stakeholders, sponsors, leaders, team members, and impacted employees?

   b How are project updates, progress, and success communicated to keep stakeholders informed and engaged in the process?
10 Continuous learning and sustainability:
   a Does the organization foster a culture of continuous learning and improvement? How?
   b Does the organization capture and share lessons learned from the project to promote knowledge transfer?
   c If a Lean Six Sigma project were executed, would the organization implement controls and monitoring mechanisms to sustain the improvements achieved by the project?

This simple checklist can be used for in-depth discussions with organizational members during the organizational assessment process. It can act as confirmation that the organization is ready to proceed with a Lean Six Sigma project or as a catalyst for change before proceeding.

By planning and organizing for success with these preparedness data points, a "go or no-go" can be effectively reached to be all parties. If that decision is to "go", then a successful Lean Six Sigma initiative can be virtually ensured with substantial improvements in quality, efficiency, and customer satisfaction.

Project Characteristics and Selection

Once it is confirmed that the organization is ready for a Lean Six Sigma project, the next step is selecting the right project. It is a critical step in maximizing the benefits of the methodology and ensuring a successful outcome.

Of vital importance initially is strategic alignment. Projects should align with the strategic goals and priorities of the organization. Areas that have a significant impact should be identified, such as customer satisfaction, financial performance, operational efficiency, or compliance. There should be a laser focus on projects that directly contribute to the organization's key objectives. There should next be an assessment of the process's importance. Critical processes that have a high impact on overall business performance, customer experience, or operational efficiency should be targeted. Also, target processes that cause bottlenecks, delays, errors, or excessive waste. Consider the availability and quality of data related to the process being considered. Projects that have reliable and accessible data enhance analyses and improvement measurement.

Evaluate the project's potential impact in terms of cost savings, revenue generation, customer satisfaction, and/or process gain efficiency. Assess the project's feasibility in availability and resource skillsets, timeframe, and technical complexity. This examination should also assess overall project management capabilities and any dependencies or constraints that may affect the project's successful execution. Stakeholder buy-in should be ascertained and engaged, as well as that of process owners and affected managers, during the project selection process. Aggressively seek their input, support, and commitment to ensure that selected projects receive the necessary resources and cooperation for successful project implementation. Encourage a culture of continuous improvement through employee involvement in the selection process. Seek their insight for process improvement ideas. This fosters a clear sense of ownership by the organization's rank and file, critical to project success.

If multiple projects are being evaluated, consider using prioritization techniques such as an impact–effort matrix or cost-benefit type or return on invested capital type of analysis approach to evaluate a project's suitability for execution. The former can be more of a qualitative evaluating tool, while the latter provides a more straightforward dollars and cents quantitative assessment.

On several projects, organizations use internal rate of return (IRR) as a benchmark instead of the net present value (NPV) approach. When you use NPV to rank investments, the outcome can depend upon the interest rate. It is often the nature of financial folks to want to boil everything down to a single number. The IRR is simply the interest rate that makes the NPV of a project equal to 0. This type of evaluation method also allows for several projects to be evaluated based on their respective cashflow over time. Additionally, this engages those who want hard dollar numbers used as criteria on which to base a decision. Figure 2.2 provides an illustration of the basic Excel program data structure used.

The impact–effort matrix (Figure 2.3) is a prioritization tool that can be used to visually capture and assess project execution potential.

Internal Rate of Return Rating Model

	A	B	C	D	E	F	G	H	I	J	K
1		Time	1	2	3	4	5	6	7	NPV r=.2	NPV r=.01
2	Project 1		-400	200	600	-900	1900	250	230	$268.54	$918.99
3	Project 2		-200	150	150	200	300	100	80	$297.14	$741.07
4	Project 1	IRR Proj 1 No Guess	IRR Proj 2 No Guess								
5	no guess	47.5%	80.1%								
6											
7	guess	Guess Proj 1	Guess Proj 2								
8	-0.9	47.5%	80.1%								
9	-0.7	47.5%	80.1%								
10	-0.5	47.5%	80.1%								
11	-0.3	47.5%	80.1%								
12	-0.1	47.5%	80.1%								
13	0.1	47.5%	80.1%								
14	0.3	47.5%	80.1%								
15	0.5	47.5%	80.1%								
16	0.7	47.5%	80.1%								
17	0.9	47.5%	80.1%								
18											

Figure 2.2 Internal Rate of Return Rating Model

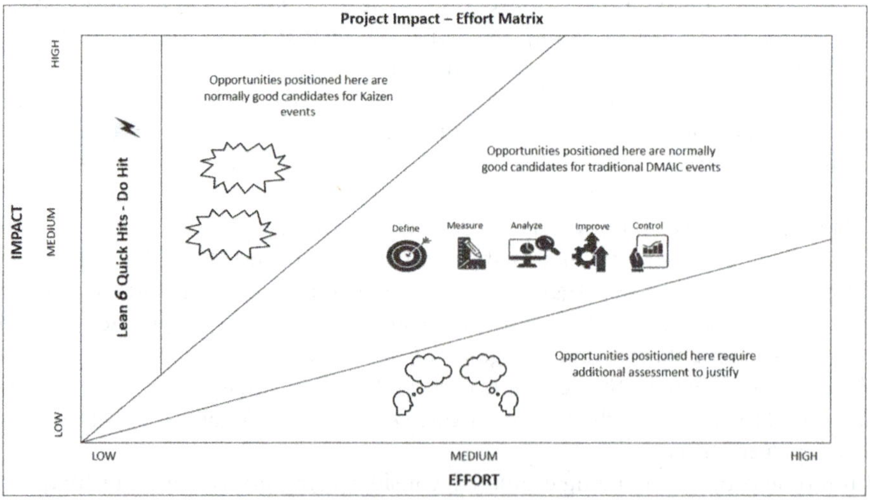

Figure 2.3 Project Impact–Effort Matrix

The matrix assesses the two main dimensions of impact and effort on scales of low and high impact. By using a quadrant layout and positioning those projects in the four quadrants, an effective visual map is developed. Quadrant 1 contains projects that can be classified as quick hits; they lend themselves to projects that can be executed without extensive planning and can show immediate return on investment. Quadrant 2 contains potential projects that are assessed as ready for execution; kaizen ready. Quadrant 3 requires a more prolonged effort where a standard DMAIC process is deemed necessary, and Quadrant 4 requires in-depth research before being justified for execution.

Aviation and aerospace Lean Six Sigma projects share certain characteristics unique in project assessment. When evaluating project characteristics for potential execution in this context, there are certain factors that should be considered.

- Does the project have a current or potential safety focus? Projects that prioritize safety enhancements, risk reduction, and compliance with regulatory requirements should be considered.
- Does the project have a quality improvement focus? If the project focus is on reducing defects, minimizing rework and waste, improving product or service quality, and enhancing customer satisfaction. It may be a candidate for a quick hit project or Kaizen event.
- Does the project deal directly with regulatory compliance? If projects are oriented towards ensuring compliance with industry-specific regulations and standards such as those related to maintenance, operations, safety management systems, or environmental requirements, they should be assessed closely.
- Does the potential project address efficiency and cost reduction? Lean Six Sigma projects in aviation and aerospace that target process efficiency, cost reduction, and resource optimization are prime for potential quick hits. This may involve streamlining operational workflows, optimizing fuel consumption, reducing turn-around time, or enhancing supply chain management services.
- Does the project address the customer experience? If a potential project focuses on improving customer satisfaction, loyalty, and service delivery, it should be deemed a worthy candidate. Examples to look for are enhancement in on-time performance, reducing customer complaints, or improving the boarding process.
- Does the project involve technology and innovation? Look for projects that embrace innovation and technology that drives improvement in all the aforementioned areas. Examples like optimizing software systems or leveraging data analytics for performance monitoring and decision making are prime candidates.

Keep in mind as you are going through the selection process that all Lean Six Sigma projects need to be manageable in scope and have a laser focus on process improvement. Start project execution with something small in scale to ensure that experience can be gained and demonstrated tangible results can be achieved early on.

Balancing Cost, Schedule, and Quality

Balancing cost, schedule, and quality are critical dimensions of any Lean Six Sigma project and crucial to its success. Because of their laser focus on process optimization and removal of waste in a brief period, allowing just one of these attributes to affect execution alignment can mean trouble.

Along with balancing the three critical dimensions of cost, schedule, and quality of our Lean Six Sigma Project, we must also consider what type of high-level metrics will be used to present a comprehensive representation of performance across those critical dimensions.

The adaptation of a balanced score card dimensional format works well and is understood by almost all stakeholders. The same dimensions are used: financial, customer, internal process, learning, and growth, with one addition, overall project performance. Each of these is aligned with suggested metric categories with recommended measurement criteria. Table 2.1 illustrates high-level Lean Six Sigma project metrics across dimensions.

Table 2.1 High-Level Lean Six Sigma Project Metrics Across Dimensions

Financial Dimension	**Cost Savings**: Measure the financial impact of process improvements by tracking the cost savings achieved through waste reduction, improved efficiency, or increased productivity. **Revenue Growth**: Track the revenue generated as a result of improved product/service quality, customer satisfaction, or market share.
Customer Dimension	**Customer Satisfaction**: Measure customer satisfaction through surveys, feedback, or net promoter scores to assess the level of customer experience and loyalty. **Customer Complaints**: Track the number of customer complaints or resolution time to ensure improvements in addressing customer concerns.
Internal Process Dimension	**Cycle Time Reduction**: Measure the time taken to complete a process from start to finish to gauge how process improvements are taking hold. **Defect Rate**: Monitor the number of defects and errors in the production process to ensure alterations made in processes are effective.
Learning and Growth Dimension	**Employee Training and Certification**: Track the number of employees trained in Lean Six Sigma methodologies and their certification levels to assess the growth of skills and knowledge within the organization. **Innovation Rate**: Measure the number of innovative ideas or improvements generated by employees, encouraging a culture of continuous improvement.
Overall Project Performance Dimension	**Project Completion Time**: Measure the time taken to complete the Lean Six Sigma project from initiation to completion, ensuring timely execution of activities. **Project ROIC**: Calculate the return on invested capital of the project by comparing the financial benefits gained against the project costs.

Table 2.2 Lean Six Sigma Dimensional Status Report

	A	*B*	*C*	*D*	*E*	*F*	*G*	*H*	*I*	*J*	*K*
1		Time	1	2	3	4	5	6	7	NPV r = .2	NPV r = .01
2	Project 1		–400	200	600	–900	1000	250	230	$268.54	$918.99
3	Project 2		–200	150	150	200	300	100	80	$297.14	$741.07
4	Project 1	IRR Proj 1 No Guess	IRR Proj 2 No Guess								
5	No Guess	47.5%	80.1%								
6											
7	Guess	Guess Proj 1	Guess Proj 2								
8	–0.9	47.5%	80.1%								
9	–0.7	47.5%	80.1%								
10	–0.5	47.5%	80.1%								
11	–0.3	47.5%	80.1%								
12	–0.1	47.5%	80.1%								
13	0.1	47.5%	80.1%								
14	0.3	47.5%	80.1%								
15	0.5	47.5%	80.1%								
16	0.7	47.5%	80.1%								
17	0.9	47.5%	80.1%								
18											

Table 2.2 provides an example of a dimensional status report developed for an aviation/aerospace organization. The report was reviewed daily by the Lean Six Sigma implementation team during scheduled "drive" meetings and weekly with team managers during scheduled "project status" meetings.

Project Tracking

After the "authorization to proceed" has been formally issued, the Lean Six Sigma (LSS) project can begin. Once this occurs, project management tracking practices are essential to keeping the dimensional attributes of cost, schedule, and quality in balance and progressing on schedule. During project execution, these same project tracking practices monitor and track the status of the project in terms of the "project triad fundamentals" of time, money, and resources and compare that status with the original project plan.

Because LSS projects and standard projects have some differences in their approach, methodology, and objectives, there are some key distinctions and focus elements that should be considered when designing a project tracking process for LSS projects. Table 2.3 presents six areas of distinction between Lean Six Sigma projects and standard projects. Each of these areas is further assessed by approach, methodology, and objective.

In addition to highlighting the distinction between a Lean Six Sigma–focused project and a standard project, the project tracking process should be able to accommodate and

Table 2.3 Differences Between Lean Six Sigma Projects and Standard Projects

Distinction	*Approach, Methodology, and Objective*
Methodology	• **Lean Six Sigma Projects:** Structured and data-driven methodology that combines principles from Lean (focus on waste reduction and process efficiency) and Six Sigma (focus on reducing defects and process variation). It utilizes DMAIC or DFSS as the problem-solving framework. • **Standard Projects:** Standard projects may lack a defined methodology or follow a more general project management framework. There is generally not a specific focus on process improvement or waste reduction.
Focus	• **Lean Six Sigma Projects:** Lean Six Sigma projects focus on process improvement, defect reduction, and minimizing waste to enhance overall process performance and customer satisfaction. • **Standard Projects:** Standard projects can vary significantly in their objectives, ranging from new product development to organizational change, and may not have a specific emphasis on process improvement.
Data-Driven Approach	• **Lean Six Sigma Projects:** Data analysis and statistical tools play a central role in Lean Six Sigma projects. The decision-making process is based on objective data and metrics to identify root causes and drive improvements. • **Standard Projects:** While data analysis might still be used in standard projects, it might not be as extensively employed as in Lean Six Sigma projects, and the decision-making process relies more on subjective judgement.
Problem-Solving Focus	• **Lean Six Sigma Projects:** Lean Six Sigma projects are usually geared towards solving specific process-related problems, reducing variability, and improving quality. • **Standard Projects:** Standard projects can address a wide range of issues, not necessarily limited to process improvement or quality enhancement.
Roles and Expertise	• **Lean Six Sigma Projects:** Lean Six Sigma projects involve individuals with specific training (e.g. Green Belts, Black Belts) who are well versed in the methodology and statistical tools. • **Standard Projects:** Standard projects may involve project managers and team members with diverse skill and backgrounds, depending on the nature of the project.

(*Continued*)

Table 2.3 (Continued)

Distinction	*Approach, Methodology, and Objective*
Continuous Improvement	• **Lean Six Sigma Projects:** Lean Six Sigma is built on the principle of continuous improvement, where organizations strive for ongoing enhancements in processes and performance. • **Standard Projects:** While continuous improvement can be a goal for any project, it might not be as ingrained in the culture and methodologies of standard projects as it is in Lean Six Sigma.

present the right types of metrics to ensure that cost, schedule, and quality are accurately assessed. Here are eight key elements to consider.

One, define key performance indicators (KPIs). Identify and establish relevant KPIs that align with the project objectives. These KPIs should be specific, measurable, achievable, relevant, and time bound. Some examples are cycle time; defect rates, cost savings, customer satisfaction scores, and process yields. Two, develop a project tracking plan. Create a detailed plan outlining how the project progress will be tracked, including frequency and methods of data collection, responsible parties, and reporting mechanisms. Determine the tools and systems to be used for tracking, such as project management software, spreadsheets, or visual management boards. Three, hold regular progress reviews. Schedule regular progress review meetings or checkpoints to assess the project's status. These meetings allow the project team to share updates, discuss challenges, and make necessary adjustments. During these reviews, compare actual progress against the original project timeline, milestones, and KPIs to identify any deviations or areas requiring corrective action. Four, rigorously enforce data collection and analysis. Continuously collect and analyze relevant data to track project performance. Ensure that data is accurate, reliable, and aligned with the selected KPIs. Use statistical tools and techniques to analyze the data and identify trends, patterns, and areas for improvement. Five, visually manage the project. Implement visual management techniques to provide a clear and concise representation of project status. Utilize visual tools such as Gantt charts, dashboards, or project boards that display key project information, milestones, and progress. Use network diagrams sparingly. Most find those difficult to interpret. Six, adhere to rigorous problem-solving and root cause analysis methodologies. If the project encounters challenges or deviations from the desired outcomes, apply problem-solving methodologies such as the DMAIC process to identify, isolate, and address root causes. Document all corrective actions taken to get the project back on track. Seven, maintain open and effective communication channels with all stakeholders, ensuring that progress updates and project status reports are shared regularly. These reports should include relevant metrics, accomplishments, challenges, action plans, and any changes to the project scope or timeline. Tailor the communication to suit the needs of different stakeholders, providing the appropriate level of detail. Eight, live continuous improvement. Embrace a culture of continuous improvement throughout the project tracking process. Encourage the project team to identify opportunities for further optimization, process enhancements, and efficiency gains. Capture lessons learned and best practices that can be applied to future Lean Six Sigma projects.

Contingency Plans and Change Control

In all projects, contingency planning and change control are of the utmost importance. However, when executing Lean Six Sigma projects and especially those dealing with aviation and aerospace, each presents unique challenges.

Contingency planning refers to the process of identifying potential risks and developing strategies to address them proactively. The goal is to be prepared for unexpected events or obstacles that could hinder the successful completion of the project. When developing contingency plans for Lean Six Sigma projects, follow the nine key–step process to yield satisfactory results. Figure 2.4 illustrates a nine-step plan for a maintenance, repair, and overhaul (MRO) customer where a Lean Six Sigma effort was performed. The steps are in the order of execution.

The first step in the process is to ensure that a portion of the budget has been allocated for the contingency planning process. This is generally performed during the initial project planning phase and is a topic addressed in the project charter document.

The next step is to identify potential risk that may arise during the project. Each project activity line item should be assessed as to the degree of risk. This involves brainstorming and gathering inputs for team members, stakeholders, and subject matter experts (SMEs). Examples of general risk identified and planned for during this process are resources, technology, data, scope, timelines, or any other aspect that might adversely impact the project's progress.

Once a risk is identified, it is analyzed in terms of its likelihood of occurrence and its potential to adversely impact the project's objectives. Risks are then prioritized based on their level of severity and likelihood of occurrence. An excellent tool to use in this process in a failure modes and effects analysis (FMEA). FMEA provides a systematic approach that helps teams proactively analyze risk and their failure modes, their causes, and the effects they may have on the process or project. Based on the risk analysis and FMEA ranking, an

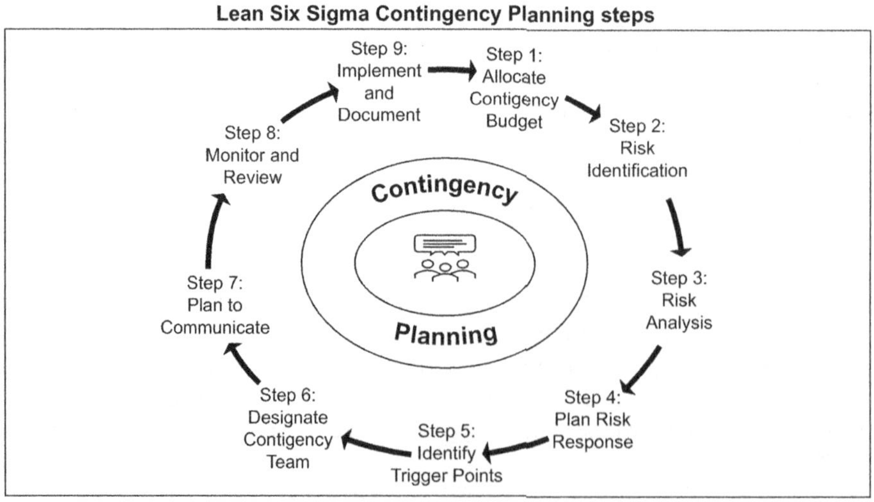

Figure 2.4 Lean Six Sigma Contingency Planning Steps

appropriate response plan is then developed for each significant risk. Response strategies can include risk avoidance, risk migration, risk transfer, or risk acceptance.

The next step is to identify trigger points. These are indicators or thresholds that signal when a specific risk is about to materialize. I have found that having a specific step in the contingency planning process that aids in the timely activation of the contingency plan before the risk escalates and adversely affects the project is of great help.

The next step is to designate a contingency response team composed of project SMEs that can respond to the risk threat effectively. While the contingency response team is being formed and charged, communication should be engaged with all relevant stakeholders and team members. I have always used a RAIC matrix to target who gets notified and when this occurs.

The monitor and review step should be considered a "continuous agile improvement" process event that allows the team to actively monitor the progress and continuously the risk landscape. This ongoing effort allows the contingency team to adjust contingency plans if necessary or create new ones for emerging risk.

The last step, implementing and documenting, is a crucial step. If a risk materializes, the contingency plan is put into action promptly and works. It is essential that all documentation pertaining to all actions taken, the results, and any lessons learned from the experience be cataloged and retained for auditing purposes.

Partnering With Stakeholders

Recognizing stakeholders, understanding their needs, identifying conflicts or resistance, and planning and communicating accordingly are crucial aspects of managing stakeholders in a Lean Six Sigma project. Because of its critical nature, how you navigate this process could well determine whether your project succeeds or fails! Over the years, in leading Lean Six Sigma projects in both domestic and international environments, I have used a step-by-step approach to recognize the stakeholders that has been found effective. It first starts with stakeholder identification.

You should identify all individuals, groups, or organizations who have a vested interest in or are affected by the Lean Six Sigma project. This includes internal stakeholders such as employees, managers, and executives, as well as external stakeholders like customers, suppliers, regulatory bodies, and shareholders. The next step is the needs assessment.

An analysis of each stakeholder's needs and expectations should be performed. This information will guide your planning and communications efforts. Next, a stakeholder analysis is performed.

Each stakeholder should be evaluated as to their level of influence, power, and potential impact on the project. Their attitudes, perspectives, and potential resistance to change should be observed and weighed. Potential conflicts of interest should be noted among the stakeholders and then assessed as to how this may have a negative impact on project success. Development of a stakeholder engagement plan is next.

A stakeholder engagement plan that outlines strategies and action to effectively engage and manage all stakeholders throughout the project should be developed. Consideration of the specific needs and concerns of each stakeholder group should be observed. A determination of the level of involvement and communication required for each stakeholder should be based on their potential influence and impact on the project. Putting together a communication plan is next.

A comprehensive communication that addresses the information needs of the different stakeholders throughout the project should be developed. Key messages, channels, and frequency of communications for stakeholder groups should the clearly defined. All communications should be clear, consistent, and tailored to the specific needs and preferences of the target stakeholder. The next step is managing conflict.

You should anticipate potential conflict or resistance among stakeholders and develop strategies to address them proactively. Areas of potential disagreement should be identified and then addressed so that common ground and mutually beneficial solutions are found. Open dialogue, active listening, and transparency to mitigate conflicts should be fostered continuously. Regular updates and feedback mechanisms are next.

A regular update mechanism to keep stakeholders informed about the project's progress, achievements, and challenges should be established. Feedback from stakeholders should be sought and their concerns or suggestions addressed promptly. This is an excellent mechanism for continuous improvement and stakeholder engagement as well. The last step is that of adjustments and adaptation.

Stakeholder dynamics should be continuously monitored, and you should be prepared to adjust the engagement plan and communications plan as needed. Stay flexible and responsive to changes in stakeholders' needs, project requirements, or external factors that may influence stakeholder relationships.

Effective stakeholder management in a Lean Six Sigma project requires active engagement, empathy, and continuous proactive communications. By recognizing all stakeholders, understanding their needs, addressing conflicts or resistance, and planning and communicating, you can foster stakeholder buy-in, support, and collaboration throughout the project lifecycle.

Learning about the wants and needs of the stakeholder is of course the first step in ensuring a partner relationship with them throughout the execution of a Lean Six Sigma project. The next step is to put in place a stakeholder analysis process. This will allow you, the project team, and all vested stakeholders to have confidence the project is being executed professionally.

Stakeholder analysis identifies all the individuals and groups who have influence over the progress of the Lean Six Sigma project and will be affected by its result. It provides a way for identifying the current level of support for change among these individuals and groups and the degree of influence that they have upon the change process. Stakeholder analysis should be client specific. Each organization has its own set of influencers to deal with. In one aviation/aerospace organization where I performed numerous Lean Six Sigma projects, the union played a major role in how the project was to be executed.

A valuable starting point for the stakeholder analysis is in the development of the *communication plan*. Once the stakeholder analysis is completed, a targeted integrated suite of communication strategies can be designed that ensures concerns and interest are addressed to the individual stakeholder and stakeholder group. It is important that stakeholder analysis be performed on a scheduled basis. I had mine embedded into the project plan.

I have found that two methods of portraying stakeholder analysis seem to work best in Lean Six Sigma projects: a *RAIC matrix framework* and *power interest grid.*

For the project team, a RACI type matrix was used because of its project activity granularity and organizational functional alignment. Figure 2.5 illustrates an example of one used in the aviation/aerospace project previously mentioned.

Here is how each category was defined:

R – Responsible: This category represents stakeholders responsible for the project or its outcomes. They have a high-level of influence and can directly impact on the project's success.

A – Accountable: These stakeholders are those who are ultimately answerable for the project's success. They may not be directly involved in day-to-day activities but have authority to make critical decisions.

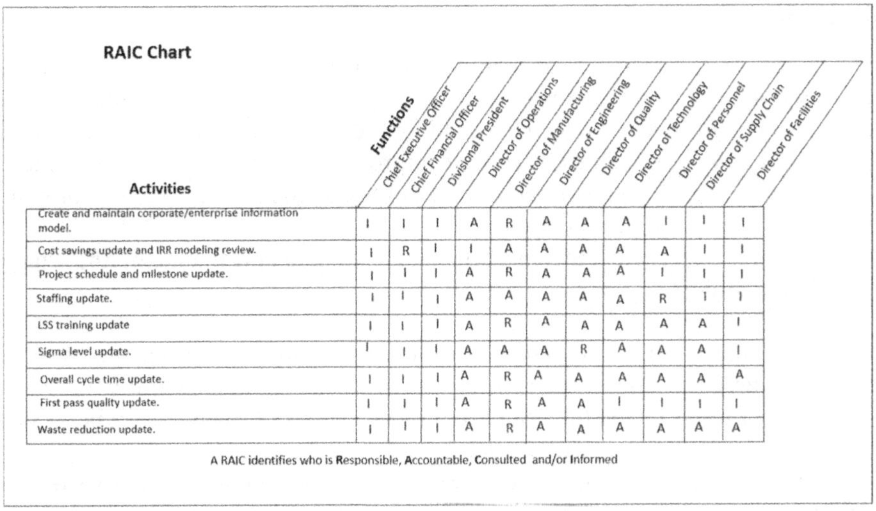

RAIC Chart

Activities / Functions	Chief Executive Officer	Chief Financial Officer	Divisional President	Director of Operations	Director of Manufacturing	Director of Engineering	Director of Quality	Director of Technology	Director of Personnel	Director of Supply Chain	Director of Facilities
Create and maintain corporate/enterprise information model.	I	I	I	A	R	A	A	A	I	I	I
Cost savings update and IRR modeling review.	I	R	I	I	A	A	A	A	A	I	I
Project schedule and milestone update.	I	I	I	A	R	A	A	A	I	I	I
Staffing update.	I	I	I	A	A	A	A	A	R	I	I
LSS training update	I	I	I	A	R	A	A	A	A	A	I
Sigma level update.	I	I	I	A	A	A	R	A	A	A	I
Overall cycle time update.	I	I	I	A	R	A	A	A	A	A	A
First pass quality update.	I	I	I	A	R	A	A	I	I	I	I
Waste reduction update.	I	I	I	A	R	A	A	A	A	A	A

A RAIC identifies who is Responsible, Accountable, Consulted and/or Informed

Figure 2.5 RAIC Chart

I – Informed: these stakeholders are those who need to be kept informed about the project's progress and outcomes. They have an interest in the project but may not have direct decision-making authority.

C – Consulted: These stakeholders are those whose input and expertise are sought during the project. They may not have direct authority but possess valuable knowledge or insight.

The *power interest grid* would be used during the stage of DMAIC stage gate reviews. The audience for these types of project reviews normally consisted of project charter board members and other interested executives. Figure 2.6 is an example of one used for the aviation/aerospace project previously mentioned.

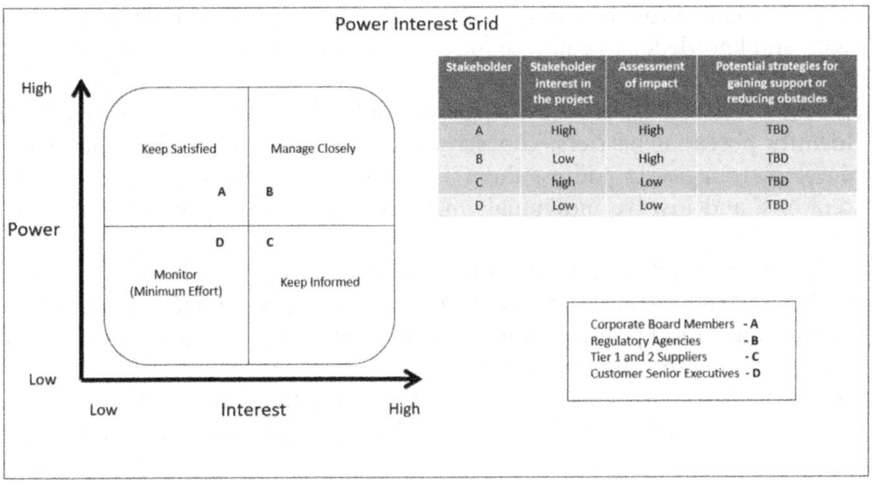

Stakeholder	Stakeholder interest in the project	Assessment of impact	Potential strategies for gaining support or reducing obstacles
A	High	High	TBD
B	Low	High	TBD
C	high	Low	TBD
D	Low	Low	TBD

Figure 2.6 Example of Power Interest Grid

Leading Change

Leading change and change management are critical aspects of any Lean Six Sigma project. Lean Six Sigma projects focus on process improvements and reducing waste, while change management involves effectively guiding individuals and team members through the transition that comes with those process improvement initiatives. I have found this to be one of the most challenging aspects of a Lean Six Sigma project, and, if not managed properly, it can lead to project failure.

Here are ten key steps effective in both leading change and managing that change in Lean Six Sigma projects.

Step 1: Establish a sense of urgency – Communicate the need for change and create a sense of urgency among the project team and stakeholders. Clearly articulate the reasons for undertaking the Lean Six Sigma project and the potential benefits it can bring to them and the organization.

Step 2: Create a compelling vision – Develop a clear and compelling vision for the future state that aligns with the organization's strategic objectives.

Step 3: Secure leadership support – Obtain visible and active support from senior leaders and executives. Engage them as champions of the change initiative to provide guidance, resources, and support. Their endorsement will lend credibility to the project and help overcome resistance.

Step 4: Communicate effectively – Develop a robust communication plan to keep stakeholders informed about the project's progress, goals, and benefits. Tailor the communication to different audiences and address their concerns and questions. Use multiple channels, such as town halls, email updates, and project newsletters, to ensure widespread understanding and engagement.

Step 5: Build a strong coalition – Identify key stakeholders and build a coalition of individuals who are influential and supportive of the Lean Six Sigma project. Involve representatives from different departments or functions to ensure diverse perspectives and broad support. This coalition can help drive change, overcome resistance, and advocate for the project's success.

Step 6: Empower and engage employees – Involve employees at all levels in the change process. Encourage their active participation, engagement, and ownership of the improvements. Provide training and support to help them develop the necessary skills and knowledge to embrace the changes brought about by the Lean Six Sigma project.

Step 7: Address resistance – Anticipate and address resistance to change head-on! Identify potential barriers, concerns, or fears that stakeholders may have and develop strategies to address them. Communicate the benefits, address misconceptions, and involve individuals in the decision-making process to gain their buy-in.

Step 8: Implement pilots and quick wins – Implement small-scale pilots or quick wins to demonstrate the effectiveness of the Lean Six Sigma project. Showcase tangible improvements and positive results to build momentum and create a culture of success and continuous improvement.

Step 9: Provide resources and training – Ensure that the necessary resources, such as training, tools, and technology, are available to support the change effort. Provide targeted training to employees on Lean Six Sigma methodologies and tools to enable them to actively contribute to the project's success.

Step 10: Monitor and celebrate progress – Continuously monitor the progress of the change initiative and celebrate milestones and achievement. Celebrating successes will reinforce the importance of the change effort and motivate others to embrace Lean Six Sigma principles.

By following these ten steps, you can effectively lead change in a Lean Six Sigma project. You will also create a supportive environment and successfully drive adoption of improvements throughout the organization. Remember that change takes time, and consistent leadership, communications, and engagement are critical for long-term success.

SUMMARY

Chapter 2 began by providing insight on how to organize for success when selecting Lean Six Sigma projects within the aviation and aerospace industry. It then detailed common project characteristics and selection criteria. A discussion then ensued that stressed the need to balance cost, schedule, and quality by vigilant project tracking. It then illustrated how contingency planning and change control processes and procedures are central to project success. Partnering and stakeholder management was then addressed, followed by a discussion on the importance of leading change and change control.

LEAN SIX SIGMA TOOLS AT WORK!

Lean *6* Sigma Tools at work!

Global competition! Increasing fuel costs! Labor shortages! The aviation and aerospace industry is facing such challenges and is racing to improve their operational methods and processes. Airlines have implemented quality and Lean tools to make improvements in the way they do their daily business. Here is an example of a Lean Six Sigma project worked a major airlines.

To find the most efficient and consistent way to safely "turn a plane", bring it in, clean it, load it, and push it out again, Airlines XX wanted to apply the principles of Lean orderliness, communications, and standardization of the task involved to optimize their turn-around times. Industry average for the long-haul systems they were targeting was between 90 and 120 minutes. Although they were on the lower end of the scale, 88-108 minutes average, they wanted to reach a average of ~91 minutes consistently. Since the average in-gate cost per minute was -$101.81, their cost savings were estimated to be substantial.

Using ideas from automobile pit crews, we started by removing wasteful steps and activities, then embarked on redesigning processes with a cycle time reduction focus. Improvement teams also attacked the seven forms of waste, removed unnecessary movements of people and activities, and made sure that the tools required for each programmed event were on hand where they were needed, when they were needed. Numerous maneuvers required a choregraphed approach for the teams to meet this goal; ramp crews needed to work with baggage carts, belt loaders, tow bars and push tractors operators. When last checked, the goal of obtaining an average of 91 minutes consistently was within reach, with ~93 minutes average.

Figure 2.7 Lean Six Sigma Tools at Work!

CHAPTER 2 DISCUSSION QUESTIONS

1 Select five of the ten key aspects of organizational preparedness you think are the most critical to a Lean Six Sigma project's success and support your selection with rationales for selection.
2 Compare and contrast the internal rate of return rating and model and the project impact–effort matrix. Which of the two methodologies do you think is superior? Support your answer.
3 Briefly describe why the building of a Lean Six Sigma business case and formulating a formal project charter are critical to a LSS project's success.
4 Describe why the balancing of cost, schedule, and quality is considered critically important during execution of a Lean Six Sigma project.
5 Compare and contrast the processes of contingency planning and change control in the context of Lean Six Sigma project execution.

BUSINESS CASE STEP BY STEP

Creating a Business Case and Project Charter

Crafting a business case and project charter for a Lean Six Sigma project involves clearly articulating the rationale, objectives, scope, and expected benefits of the proposed project. I have learned that this plays a key role in setting the tone of the project and ensures that all individuals who should and will be involved with it understand what the objective is, what their share of supporting the project will be, and the expected outcome.

Here is an 11-step guide to building a Lean Six Sigma business case I have used on past projects which you might find useful.

- Step 1 – Provide a concise overview of the project, highlighting its importance, potential impact, and alignment with the organization's strategies and goals.
- Step 2 – Clearly state the problem or opportunity that the project aims to address. Describe the current challenges, inefficiencies, or areas for improvement in context to the industry.
- Step 3 – Define the goals and objectives of the project. These should be measurable, achievable, and aligned with the organization's priorities. Some examples with an aviation focus might include improving safety metrics, reducing defects, enhancing operational efficiency, or optimizing resource utilization.
- Step 4 – Define the scope of the project by specifying the boundaries, limitations, and areas of focus. Describe the expected deliverables and outcomes. Ensure that the scope is realistic and manageable within the defined project timeframe.
- Step 5 – Identify key stakeholders and their roles and interests in the project. Assess their level of influence, support, and potential impact on the project's success. Describe how stakeholders' engagement and communication will be managed to ensure their buy-in and support.
- Step 6 – Outline the Lean Six Sigma approach and methodologies that will be applied in executing the project. Describe the tools and techniques that will be used for data collection, analysis, problem-solving, and process improvement. Ensure it is understood that steps in the DMAIC methodology will be followed.
- Step 7 – Identify the resources required to execute the project successfully. This includes personnel, budget, technology, data, and any other necessary resources. Specify responsibility for resources and potential constraints or dependencies.

- Step 8 – Provide a high-level project timeline to include key milestones and major activities. This helps set expectations and sends the message that project progress will be monitored and managed effectively.
- Step 9 – Identify potential risks and uncertainties associated with the project and its implementation. Assess the potential impact of these risks and develop mitigation strategies to minimize their effects. This demonstrates proactive risk management, shows preparedness, and builds confidence in the team.
- Step 10 – Clearly articulate the expected benefits of the project. Use examples such as improve safety, quality, and efficiency. Mention cost savings and how it will be enhanced. Remember to mention enhancing the customer experience. Quantify benefits when and wherever possible and estimate the projected return on invested capital.
- Step 11 – Seek approval from relevant stakeholders, to include the project sponsors, executives, or governance bodies. Ensure that the business case and project charter are reviewed, understood, and signed off on by all relevant parties.

A project charter is a formal document that outlines the shared understanding of a project's scope development and project objectives while also defining the roles and responsibilities of each party involved. The goal of creating a project charter is to get your stakeholders to agree on why you are doing the project, what's in scope (at a high level), and who's doing what. Some organizations require a signed project charter before allocating resources, including funding, to your project.

Here is an example of a Lean Six Sigma project charter developed for a client in aviation and aerospace that was used for a major builder of aeronautical systems.

- Executive Summary:

  The *Derivative Rotary Systems Lean Six System project* aim is to develop innovative solutions and technologies that advance systems architecture and advance the aviation and aerospace industry. The project will be conducted by a cross-functional integrated process team composed of subject matter experts and recognized professionals, led by Dr. John Longshore, a Lean Six Sigma Master Black Belt, and will be carried out under the auspices of the Research and Development arm of the Advanced Development Programs (ADP) Rotary System Division. The primary objective of this project is enhancing safety, process efficiency and effectiveness, and manufacturing technologies; promoting sustainability within the ADP Division; and driving economic growth.
- Project Objectives:
  1. Develop innovative technologies and solutions to improve safety standards within the ADP Rotary System Division aerospace operations.
  2. Enhance the efficiency and performance of rotary system vehicles through advanced engineering design and production.
  3. Promote sustainable practices within the ADP Rotary Systems Division to minimize environmental impact.
  4. Foster research and development activities within the ADP Rotary Systems Division by organizing and leading a quality functional development (QFD) workshop to spur innovation and drive economic growth in the division.
  5. Strengthen collaboration and knowledge sharing among ADP divisions by organizing Kaizen workshops that engage cross-functional personnel.
  6. Enhance adherence to regulatory standards and compliance throughout the project.

- Scope:

  The *Derivative Rotary Systems Lean Six System project* scope will encompass the following key areas:

  1 Advanced rotary systems design and development.
  2 Next-generation propulsion system and development.
  3 Innovative avionics and electronics.
  4 Smart materials and composites for enhanced performance and stability.
  5 Cockpit management and control systems for improved efficiency.
  6 Sustainable biofuels and alternative propulsion sources.
  7 Research and development of next-generation rotary systems.
  8 Collaborative platforms for sharing best practices and knowledge within the ADP Division.

- Deliverables:

  The *Derivative Rotary Systems Lean Six System project* will produce the following deliverables:

  1 Comprehensive research reports and technical documentation.
  2 Prototypes and proof-of-concept reports for innovative technologies.
  3 Sustainable ADP Rotary Systems Division practices guidelines.
  4 Enhanced safety protocols and standards.
  5 Knowledge-sharing platforms and resources for ADP Rotary Systems Division stakeholders.
  6 Policy recommendations and regulatory guidelines.

- Timeline:

  The *Rotary Systems Lean Six System project* is scheduled to commence on (start date) and is expected to be completed by (end date). The detailed project timeline, including milestones and phases, will be outlined in the master project management plan.

- Budget:

  The estimated budget for the *Rotary Systems Lean Six System project* is (total pro forma budget). Allocation of funds will be determined and managed by the project manager and the finance team, ensuring responsible stewardship throughout the entire project lifecycle. Earned value management will be observed.

- Stakeholders:

  1 ADP Rotary Systems Division personnel.
  2 Project team members.
  3 Industry experts and consultants.
  4 Aviation and aerospace companies.
  5 Research institutions and academia.
  6 General public and environmental organizations.

- Risks:

  Potential risks and challenges associated with the *Rotary Systems Lean Six System project* will be identified and assessed during the project planning phase and delineated in the risk management plan. Risk mitigation strategies and contingencies will be put into place to minimize any negative impact of the project's success.

- Project management approach:

  The master project plan will be designed around a structured project management approach. Agile and critical chain methodologies will be considered on sub-projects and decided on a case-by-case basis. Scheduled progress reports, milestone reviews, and stakeholders will be factored into the master schedule. The project manager will be responsible for coordinating activities and ensuring effective communications among team members and all stakeholders.

- Approval:
  The project chapter is approved and authorized by the *Advanced Development Programs (ADP) Rotary System Division* and serves as the foundational document for the *Rotary Systems Lean Six System project.* Any changes or deviations for this charter must be approved by the *Advanced Development Programs (ADP) Rotary System Division* and communicated to all relevant stakeholders.
- Signature of project sponsor
- Name of project sponsor
- Date
- Signature of project manager
- Name of project manager
- Date

Change control planning in a Lean Six Sigma project refers to the formalized process of managing and controlling any proposed changes to a project's scope, schedule, resources, or any other aspect that could impact its success. The primary goal of change control planning is to ensure that all changes are evaluated, approved, and implemented in a structured manner to minimize disruptions and maintain project quality and objectives.

Using the same example of a past MRO customer, here are seven key change control planning components put into place before that Lean Six Sigma project started.

- Component #1, Change identification: Any proposed change, whether it comes from team members, stakeholders, or external factors, will be identified and documented. This includes changes to project requirements, scope, timelines, resources, or any other significant aspect of the project.
- Component #2, Impact analysis: Once a change is identified, a thorough impact analysis will be conducted to assess how the proposed change will affect the project. This analysis should consider factors such as project objective, cost, timeline, resource availability, risks, and potential benefits.
- Component #3, Change review and approval: The impact analysis is presented to the project leadership and relevant stakeholders for review and approval. The decision-makers evaluate the potential impact of the change and decide whether to approve, reject, or modify it based on its alignment with the project's goals and objectives.
- Component #4, Change implementation: If the change is approved, it is incorporated into the project plan and executed in a controlled manner. The project team ensures that all necessary adjustments are made, and relevant stakeholders are informed of the change.
- Component #5, Change documentation: Throughout the change control process, all steps, decisions, and outcomes are thoroughly documented. This documentation helps in maintaining a clear record of all changes, the reasons behind them, and their impacts.
- Component #6, Change risk management: Change control is closely related to risk management. When evaluating proposed changes, the team will also consider potential risks and develop appropriate risk mitigation strategies.

- Component #7, Continuous improvement: In the context of Lean Six Sigma, change control also aligns with the principles of continuous improvement. The project team will be open to feedback and lessons learned from change control activities, and this information will be used to improve future projects and enhance overall performance.

Like the contingency planning process, there are several steps that should be followed in change control organizing and planning. In Figure 2.8, 12 steps are presented that were used to establish this for the MRO customer.

The first step is to establish a change control board (CCB). It should be composed of key stakeholders, experts, and decision-makers from various relevant departments. The CCB will be responsible for evaluating and approving proposed changes. The second step is to define change categories. Changes should be categorized based on their impact and criticality. For aviation and aerospace organizations, changes are classified as either minor, major, safety related, regulatory, or operational. The third step is standardizing change request documentation. A standardized change request process needs to be implemented where anyone can submit a change request. The request should be documented and include details such as the reason for the change, proposed solution, potential impact on safety, cost, schedule, and any other relevant factors.

The fourth step is assessing impact. This requires a thorough impact assessment of each change request. The assessment should cover safety implications, regulatory compliance, schedule adjustments, resource allocation, cost estimates, and any other relevant factors. The fifth, risk analysis, evaluates identified risks associated with the proposed change. This analysis should identify any new risks introduced by the change and assess their severity and likelihood of occurrence.

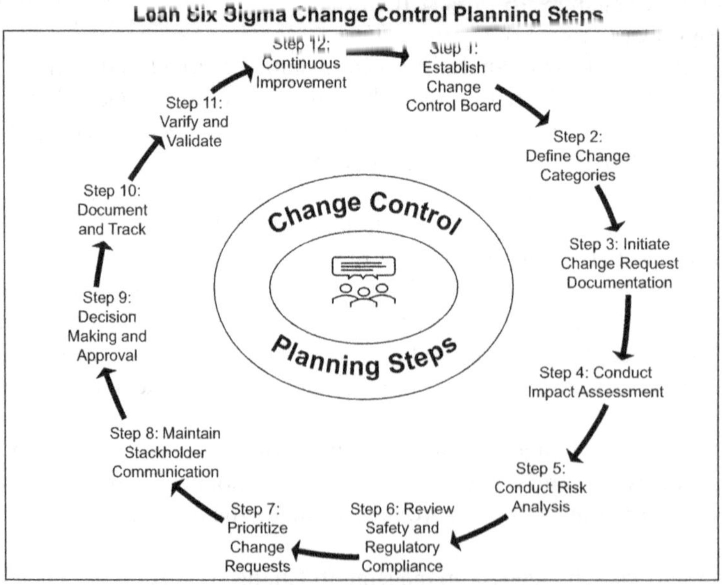

Figure 2.8 Lean Six Sigma Change Control Planning Steps

Step six deals with safety and regulatory compliance. For aviation and aerospace organizations, this step is of paramount importance. Proposed changes must align with safety standards, regulations, and certification requirements. The seventh step is change prioritization. Change requests are prioritized based on their impact, urgency, and alignment with the project's objectives. The CCB uses this prioritization to make informed decisions about which changes to approve first. Step eight deals with stakeholder communications. It is critical to maintain transparent communication with all stakeholders throughout the change control process. Keep them informed of proposed changes, their status, and the reasons behind approval or rejection decisions.

Decision-making and approval is step nine. The CCB will review all change requests and make informed decisions on whether to approve, reject, or defer each change. The decision must consider the impact on safety, project schedule, costs, and any other relevant factors. Step ten, documentation and tracking, ensures that all approved changes are properly documented and tracked throughout their implementation. This documentation should include details of the change, rationale for approval, and the responsible parties for executing the change.

Step eleven, verification and validation, ensures that all approved changes are successfully implemented and that desired outcomes are achieved and safety and regulatory requirements are adhered to. The final step, continuous improvement, assesses the effectiveness of the overall change control process and ensures that improvements are made and evaluated so efficiency and effectiveness are enhanced.

Change control ensures that a Lean Six Sigma project remains on track, adheres to its original objectives, and delivers the intended results. By managing changes in a structured manner, the project team can maintain control over potential disruptions and deliver successful outcomes.

BIBLIOGRAPHY

Amrani, Aicha, and Yves Ducq. "Lean practices implementation in aerospace based on sector characteristics: Methodology and case study." *Production Planning & Control* 31.16 (2020): 1313–1335.

Antony, Jiju, et al. "Ten commandments of lean six sigma: A practitioners' perspective." *International Journal of Productivity and Performance Management* 67.6 (2018): 1033–1044.

Carreira, Bill, and Bill Trudell. *Lean Six Sigma That Works: A Powerful Action Plan for Dramatically Improving Quality, Increasing Speed, and Reducing Waste*. Amacom Books, 2006.

Cudney, Elizabeth A., and Rodney Kestle. *Implementing Lean Six Sigma Throughout the Supply Chain: The Comprehensive and Transparent Case Study*. CRC Press, 2018.

Douglas, Jackie, et al. "The role of organizational climate in readiness for change to lean six sigma." *The TQM Journal* 29.5 (2017): 666–676.

Drohomeretski, Everton, et al. "Lean, six sigma and lean six sigma: An analysis based on operations strategy." *International Journal of Production Research* 52.3 (2014): 804–824.

Elias, Arun Abraham. "Stakeholder analysis for lean six sigma project management." *International Journal of Lean Six Sigma* 7.4 (2016): 394–405.

Franco, Paulo Cesar, Fernando A. S. Marins, and Messias Borges Silva. "The key success factors in choosing and conducting a lean six sigma project." In *Proceeding of the 21st Annual Conference POMS*, 2010. https://pomsmeetings.org/confproceedings/015/fullpapers/015-0738.pdf

Gabriele, Nico Costantino, and Kai Yang. "The AMSE lean six sigma governance model." *International Journal of Lean Six Sigma* 7.3 (2016): 233–266.

Galli, Brian J. "Can project management help improve lean six sigma?" *IEEE Engineering Management Review* 46.2 (2018): 55–64.

Gellis, Corey. "Assessment of leadership styles and lean six sigma critical success factors in the aerospace and defense industry." 2021. https://stars.library.ucf.edu/etd2020/867/

George, Mark O. *The Lean Six Sigma Guide to Doing More with Less: Cut Costs, Reduce Waste, and Lower Your Overhead*. John Wiley & Sons, 2010.

Gerger, Atakan, and Ali Rıza Firuzan. "Use of six sigma method as a process improvement technique: A case study in aerospace industry." *Academic Journal of Science* 6.1 (2016): 191–202.

Hill, Jonathan, et al. "The implementation of a lean six sigma framework to enhance operational performance in an MRO facility." *Production & Manufacturing Research* 6.1 (2018): 26–48.

Klochkov, Yury, Albina Gazizulina, and Kunnummal Muralidharan. "Lean six sigma for sustainable business practices: A case study and standardisation." *International Journal for Quality Research* 13.1 (2019): 47.

Kumar, Maneesh, Jiju Antony, and Byung Rae Cho. "Project selection and its impact on the successful deployment of six sigma." *Business Process Management Journal* 15.5 (2009): 669–686.

Laureani, Alessandro, and Jiju Antony. "Leadership–a critical success factor for the effective implementation of lean six sigma." *Total Quality Management & Business Excellence* 29.5–6 (2018): 502–523.

Lavin, Patricia, and Mary Jo Vetter. "Using lean six sigma to increase the effectiveness of an evidence-based quality improvement program." *Journal of Nursing Care Quality* 37.1 (2022): 81–86.

Lazarz, Sara. "Change management through a lean six sigma lens." 2021. https://minds.wisconsin.edu/bitstream/handle/1793/82135/Lazarz%2C%20Sara.pdf?sequence=1&isAllowed=y

Lertwattanapongchai, S., and F. W. Swierczek. "Assessing the change process of lean six sigma: A case analysis." *International Journal of Lean Six Sigma* 5.4 (2014): 423–443.

Mahato, Satyajit, Amit Rai Dixit, and Rajeev Agrawal. "Application of lean six sigma for cost-optimized solution of a field quality problem: A case study." *Proceedings of the Institution of Mechanical Engineers, Part B: Journal of Engineering Manufacture* 231.4 (2017): 713–729.

Marzagão, Daniela Santana Lambert, and Marly M. Carvalho. "Critical success factors for six sigma projects." *International Journal of Project Management* 34.8 (2016): 1505–1518.

Netland, Torbjørn H. "Critical success factors for implementing lean production: The effect of contingencies." *International Journal of Production Research* 54.8 (2016): 2433–2448.

Null, Gary, Jennifer A. Cross, and Charles Brandon. "Effects of lean six sigma in program management." *Journal of Manufacturing Technology Management* 31.3 (2020): 572–598.

Pickrell, Gary, Harry J. Lyons, and Judy Shaver. "Lean six sigma implementation case studies." *International Journal of Six Sigma and Competitive Advantage* 1.4 (2005): 369–379.

Reed, Victoria. *Strategies for Improving the Success Rates of Lean Six Sigma Projects*. Diss. Walden University, 2020.

Sarwar, Jawad, et al. "Impact of stakeholders on lean six sigma project costs and outcomes during implementation in an air-conditioner manufacturing industry." *Processes* 10.12 (2022): 2591.

Singh, Bikram Jit, and Dinesh Khanduja. "Perspectives of control phase to manage six sigma implements: An empirical study." *International Journal of Business Excellence* 7.1 (2014): 88–111.

Sunder M, Vijaya. "Lean six sigma project management–a stakeholder management perspective." *The TQM Journal* 28.1 (2016): 132–150.

Tetteh, Erdem Gerard, and Benedict M. Uzochukwu, eds. *Lean Six Sigma Approaches in Manufacturing, Services, and Production*. IGI Global, 2014.

Thomas, Andrew J., et al. "Implementing lean six sigma to overcome the production challenges in an Aerospace company." *Production Planning & Control* 27.7–8 (2016): 591–603.

Treviño-Garza, Claudia L. "Learning to define lean six sigma projects with cases." In *IIE Annual Conference. Proceedings*. Institute of Industrial and Systems Engineers (IISE), 2012.

Vijayan, Devika, and Minu Anna Johny. "A study of implementing lean & fast tracking in construction project management." *International Research Journal of Engineering and Technology (IRJET)* 6.6 (2019): 1454–1458.

Vivekananthamoorthy, Natarajan, and S. Sankar. "Lean six sigma." In *Six Sigma Projects and Personal Experiences*. IntechOpen, 2011.

3

Designing Lean Six Sigma Teams

Leadership Characteristics and Strategies

LEARNING OBJECTIVES

Upon completion of this chapter the student should be able to:

1. Explain the leadership characteristics and strategies needed for the successful implementation of Lean Six Sigma projects.
2. Differentiate between leadership characteristics in general Lean Six Sigma projects and those specific to the aviation/aerospace industry.
3. Develop strategies for building and planning a high-performing Lean Six Sigma team.
4. Identify key leadership elements essential for leading a Lean Six Sigma team effectively.
5. Describe the roles, tasks, and responsibilities of Lean Six Sigma team members, along with the team's goals, objectives, and ground rules.

Designing Lean Six Sigma teams requires careful consideration of leadership characteristics and strategies to ensure successful implementation of projects. Leading general Lean Six Sigma projects and leading Lean Six Sigma projects in aviation and aerospace share many similarities in terms of methodology and tools. However, there are certain nuances and considerations specific to the aviation and aerospace industry that are key to a project's success.

Let us first look at leadership characteristics shared by both types of Lean Six Sigma projects.

First, both leaders should have technical expertise. Lean Six Sigma teams should be led by individuals with a strong understanding of the methodology and its tools. The leader should possess deep knowledge of Lean Six Sigma principles, statistical analysis, and process improvement techniques.

Second, they should understand how to handle change management. Lean Six Sigma implementations involve significant changes to existing processes and cultures. Leaders should have strong change management skills to effectively communicate the need for change, manage resistance, and guide teams through the transformation process.

DOI: 10.4324/9781032650531-4

Third, both leaders require vision and an understanding of strategy. Each leader should be able to articulate a clear vision for the project and align it with the organization's strategic goals. They should have a deep understanding of the business context and be able to guide the team in selecting projects that deliver the most value.

Fourth, each leader should be able to build a cohesive team. Each requires leaders who can build high-performance teams by creating an environment of trust, collaboration, and accountability. They should be able to foster a culture of continuous improvement and empower team members to contribute their expertise and ideas.

Fifth, each leader should be skilled at communicating and influencing. Strong communication skills are essential for Lean Six Sigma leaders to effectively convey complex concepts and ideas to team members and stakeholders. They should be adept at influencing and persuading others to adopt Lean Six Sigma principles and embrace process improvement initiatives.

Sixth, be able to coach and mentor. Both leaders should be able to provide guidance, coaching, and mentorship to team members, helping them develop their skills in Lean Six Sigma methodologies. This includes providing constructive feedback, recognizing achievements, and fostering a learning culture within the team.

Seventh, each leader must be results oriented. Both should possess a strong focus on results and be able to drive the team towards achieving project initiatives. They should establish key performance metrics and regularly monitor progress, adjusting as necessary to ensure success.

Eighth, each must be a continuous learner. Because Lean Six Sigma is a very dynamic field, both leaders must be committed to their own ongoing learning and professional development. They should stay updated on industry trends, new tools, and methodologies to continuously enhance their leadership skills.

Now, let us review some of the leadership skills that are considered necessary for those Lean Six Sigma project leaders that are focused on the aviation and aerospace industry.

First, possess industry knowledge. Leaders of aviation and aerospace Lean Six Sigma team should possess a deep understanding of the industry's regulations, safety, standards, and unique challenges. They should be familiar with aeronautical manufacturing processes, maintenance and repair operations, and the specific needs of the aviation industry.

Second, have a safety focus. Safety is paramount in the aviation and aerospace industry. Leaders should prioritize safety and ensure that Lean Six Sigma initiatives align with safety standards and regulations. They should also integrate best practices into process improvement projects, emphasizing risk assessment and mitigation.

Third, observe regulatory compliance. The aviation and aerospace community operates under a strict regulatory framework. Leaders should have a comprehensive understanding of these regulations and compliance requirements. They should ensure that Lean Six Sigma projects comply with applicable regulations and work closely with regulatory bodies when necessary.

Fourth, understand reliability and maintenance. Reliability is critical in aviation and aerospace. Leaders should have a solid understanding of reliability and maintenance concepts, including preventive and predictive maintenance techniques. They should be able to guide teams in implementing Lean Six Sigma methodologies to optimize maintenance processes and enhance equipment reliability.

Fifth, understand supply chain management. Aviation and aerospace involve complex global supply chains. Leaders should possess supply chain management knowledge to effectively identify and address process bottlenecks, reduce lead times, and improve supplier quality. They should collaborate with suppliers to implement Lean Six Sigma principles within their own respective tier.

Sixth, be able to manage risk. Leaders in aviation and aerospace Lean Six Sigma teams should be skilled in risk management. They should be able to identify and mitigate risks associated with process changes, equipment reliability, and safety. They should guide teams in conducting comprehensive risk assessments and developing appropriate risk mitigation strategies.

Seventh, be able to collaborate with engineering and design. In aviation and aerospace, engineering and design play a crucial role. Leaders must be able to collaborate closely with engineering teams to incorporate Lean Six Sigma principles into product design and development processes. They should also be able to facilitate cross-functional collaboration and ensure effective communications between engineering, operations, and quality teams.

Eighth, be knowledgeable in maintenance, repair, and overhaul (MRO) activities. MRO operations are integral to the aviation and aerospace industries. Leaders should focus on Lean Six Sigma strategies that optimize MRO processes, reduce downtime, enhance efficiency, and improve turn-around times for maintenance related tasks.

Ninth, be proficient at crisis management. The aviation and aerospace industry can face unexpected crises or emergencies. Leaders should possess crisis management skills and be prepared to respond swiftly and effectively to crisis situations. They should guide Lean Six Sigma teams in adapting to changing circumstances while maintaining process improvement initiatives.

Tenth, be proficient at industry benchmarking. Leaders should be familiar with industry best practices and benchmarks in aviation and aerospace. They should promote benchmarking activities to identify areas for improvement, learn from industry leaders, and drive continuous improvement efforts within their respective teams.

It is crucial to adapt Lean Six Sigma principles to the specific needs and challenges for both those efforts considered general industry focused and those that are oriented to the aviation and aerospace industry. By selecting leaders with the necessary industry knowledge and leveraging tailored strategies, organizations can maximize the impact of Lean Six Sigma teams and achieve significant improvements.

Figure 3.1 provides a leadership characteristics listing for general industry focused Lean Six Sigma leaders and those focused on the aviation and aerospace industries.

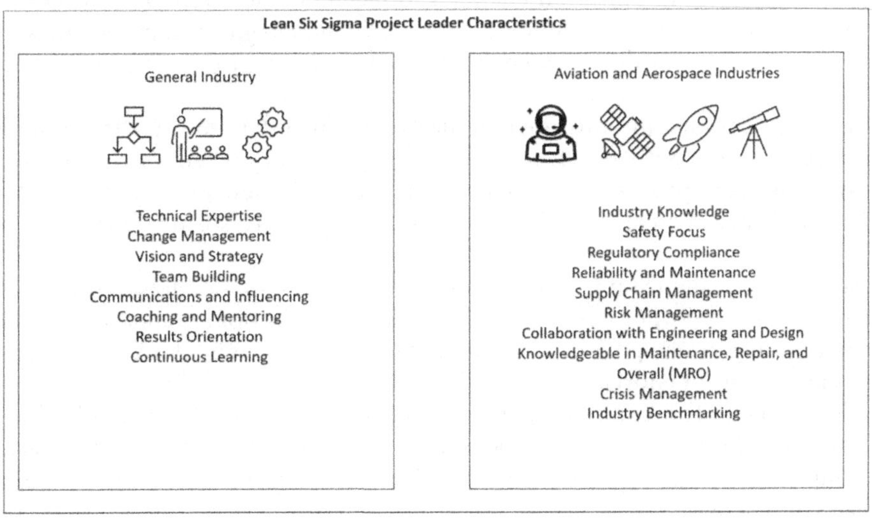

Figure 3.1 Lean Six Sigma Leader Characteristics

Designing a Lean Six Sigma team regardless of industry focus requires careful planning and consideration. Here are some strategies found to be beneficial to building high-powered teams for general focused projects and those focused on the aviation and aerospace industries.

Clearly identify who will lead the team, who will be responsible for the data analysis, process improvement, project management, and any other key task peculiar to your project. Build your team with members who possess diverse skills sets and expertise. Include individuals with analytical thinking, problem-solving abilities, and keen communication skills. This diversity will enhance the team's ability to tackle various challenges.

Ensure team members receive adequate training in Lean Six Sigma methodologies, especially those you will use on the project. This training can come in the form of certification programs, workshops, and on-the-job mentoring. Doing this will equip the team with the necessary knowledge and tools to identify and address process inefficiencies effectively.

Create a culture that encourages continuous improvement within the project organization. This involves promoting a mindset that embraces change, values data-driven decision-making, and supports experimentation and risk-taking. Ensure you recognize and reward team members' contributions to the project.

Define clear goals and objectives for the team. These goals should be aligned with the project's organizational strategic objectives and focus on measurable improvements in key performance indicators (KPIs) such as cost or cycle time reduction, quality improvement, and customer satisfaction.

Identify and prioritize improvement projects based on their potential impact on business objectives. Use data-driven analysis to identify areas of improvement. Select projects that have a high likelihood of success and align with the organization's strategic priorities.

Because Lean Six Sigma teams work across different departments and functions, encourage cross-functional collaboration and communication between team members and stakeholders. This will help identify process dependencies and ensure a holistic approach to process improvement.

Set up regular communication channels to facilitate effective information sharing within the team and with stakeholders. This can include regular team meetings, progress reports, and visual management tools such as dashboards and project tracking boards.

Implement a robust monitoring and measurement system to track the progress of the project. Use the KPIs developed when the goals and objectives were defined to effectively measure process improvements. Regularly review project status, identify barriers, and take corrective actions as required to ensure steady progress is being made.

Last, encourage the team to learn from both successes and failures. Capture lessons learned and share best practices across the project organization. Emphasize the importance of adapting to changing circumstances and evolving methodologies to sustain continuous improvement efforts.

Building an effective Lean Six Sigma team takes time and effort. It is essential to support the team throughout the building journey and provide them with the necessary leadership and resources needed for success. Figure 3.2 provides an illustration of these strategies for reference.

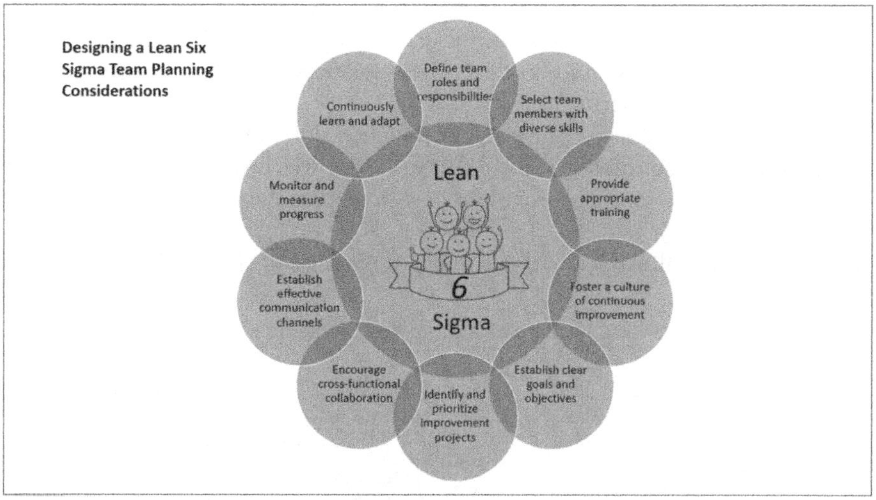

Figure 3.2 Designing a Lean Six Sigma Team Planning Considerations

AMAZING LEADERSHIP

Amazing leadership within the context of leading an organization's Lean Six Sigma project can be characterized by the ability to inspire, empower, and guide that organization and the team towards achieving its goals and objectives. It involves utilizing a combination of skills, qualities, and behaviors to influence and motivate others to perform at their best. Here are key elements that set apart those with amazing leadership skills.

- Has a clear vision of the future and can articulate it to others in a manner they can understand. They inspire and motivate others as well by communicating a compelling purpose that aligns with the organization's values and goals. They conduct themselves ethically with integrity and act with honesty, transparency, and fairness, thus gaining the trust and respect of their team members. This fosters a culture of trust and accountability throughout the team structure.
- Understand and empathize with the emotions and perspectives of others. They listen actively, show concern, and consider the feelings and needs of their team members, fostering strong relationships and a supportive work environment. They are skilled communicators, both in one-on-one interactions and in addressing larger groups. They encourage open dialogue, active challenging discussions, and provide constructive feedback.
- Possess strategic thinking abilities, enabling them to analyze complex situations, anticipate challenges, and make informed decisions. They consider the big picture while also paying attention to details, ensuring that their actions align with long-term goals. They adapt to change well and navigate through uncertainty with ease. They remain agile and open-minded, embracing change, new ideas and encouraging innovation within their teams.
- Empower their team members by entrusting them with responsibilities and authority. They delegate effectively, providing guidance and support while allowing individuals to grow, learn and make decisions. Great leaders inspire and motivate their team members by setting high standards, encouraging creativity and innovation, and recognizing and celebrating achievements.

- Are continuous learners and developers. They understand the importance of personal growth and encourage continuous learning within their team and support it with investment of time and funding. They seek opportunities to develop themselves and their team members.
- Demonstrate the behaviors and values they expect from others. They model integrity, resilience, accountability, and a strong work ethic, inspiring their team members to follow suit and perform above and beyond expectations.

Figure 3.3 provides an illustration of key amazing leadership elements.

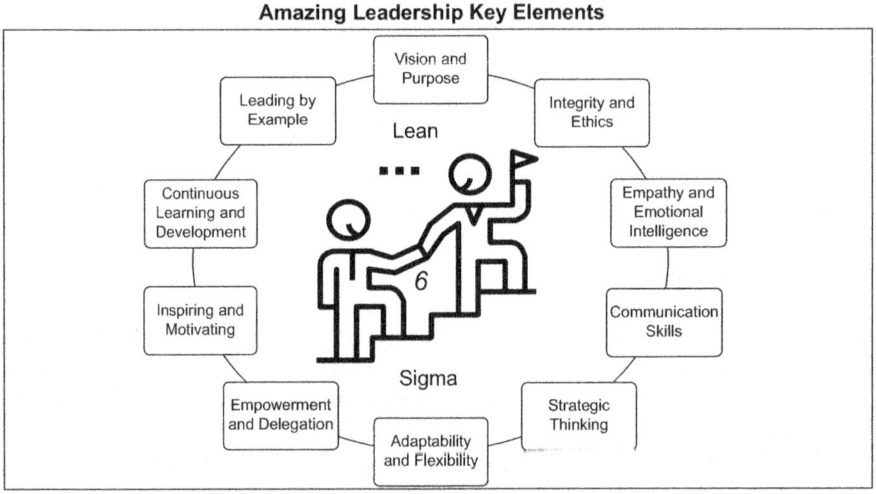

Figure 3.3 Amazing Leadership Key Elements

FOCUSED GOALS AND OBJECTIVES

Goals and objectives play a crucial role in Lean Six Sigma projects. Because the Lean Six Sigma methodology's overarching aim is to improve process efficiency and reduce defects or errors, goals and objectives provide direction and focus. They help align the Lean Six Sigma project with the overall strategy of the organization by setting specific targets that contribute directly to the organization's success.

Clearly defined goals and objectives provide what may be called "clarity of purpose", meaning they provide a clear understanding of what the project aims to achieve. This clarity helps team members stay focused, prioritize their efforts, and work towards a common purpose. They also ensure that everyone involved understands the expected outcome.

Goals and objectives provide measurable targets against which progress, and success can be assessed through measurement and performance evaluation. They enable the use of data-driven approaches to measure process performance and track improvements over time. This measurement aspect is fundamental to the Lean Six Sigma DMAIC (define, measure, analyze, improve, control) framework.

Well-defined goals and objectives create a sense of purpose and motivate project team members to actively participate in the improvement efforts. When individuals understand how their work contributes to achieving specific goals, they are more engaged and committed to the project and the organization.

Because Lean Six Sigma projects are driven by the desire to achieve continuous improvement, goals and objectives provide a target for improvement efforts and help identify areas that require attention. They also ensure that the project team remains focused on driving sustainable change and achieving measurable results.

By establishing goals and objectives, organizations can prioritize projects and allocate resources effectively. Clear goals help identify the most critical areas for improvement, allowing the organization to allocate limited resources effectively to where they have the greatest impact.

As a communication tool, goals and objectives enable effective communication with stakeholders. When the objectives are well defined and clearly communicated, it helps organizational members understand the purpose and benefits of the Lean Six Sigma project. This in turn fosters support and cooperation at all levels of the organization.

Understanding the critical role of well-designed goals and objectives play in a Lean Six Sigma project is a first step in building a team that will execute them. The next is to ensure that those same goals and objectives are focused and align with the organization's strategic priorities and that of the project. As described in the discussion on leadership characteristics, there are similarities as well as differences between goals and objectives developed for Lean Six Sigma projects of a general nature and those that are directly oriented towards aviation and aerospace Lean Six Sigma teams. Figure 3.4 shows general focused goals and objectives and those focused more on aviation and aerospace.

Starting with general focused goals, the Lean Six Sigma team's main goal is to identify and eliminate waste, reduce variation, and optimize processes. The objective is to achieve measurable improvements in efficiency, quality, and customer satisfaction. Reduction of cycle time is a general goal of a team, either by streamlining processes, eliminating bottlenecks, or improving flow. The objective is to accelerate the speed of delivering products or services to customers, enhancing responsiveness and agility.

A common objective of general projects is cost reduction. This is done by eliminating non-value-added activities, improving resource utilization, minimizing defects and rework. The goal should focus on identifying cost-saving opportunities and implementing solutions that lead to significant financial benefits.

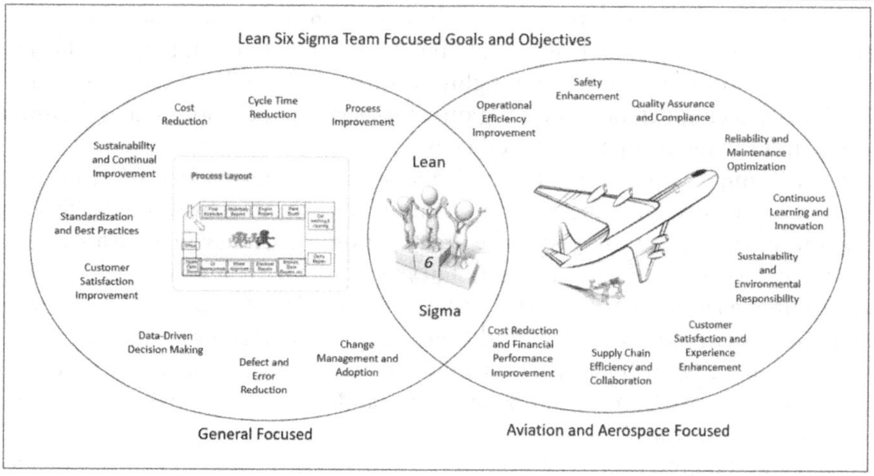

Figure 3.4 Lean Six Sigma–Focused Goals and Objectives

Enhancing customer satisfaction is a critical objective. Teams must understand customer requirements and expectations, identify ways to exceed them, and implement process improvements that directly impact the customer. Often the goal is to minimize defects, errors, and customer complaints. The team should focus on identifying root causes for any defects identified, implementing error-proofing measures where required and improving quality control processes to ensure high quality product or service reliability.

An important goal is to foster a culture of continuous improvement and engage employees in Lean Six Sigma initiatives. Objectives may include increasing employee involvement, providing training and development opportunities, and recognizing and rewarding employee contributions to process improvement efforts.

Lean Six Sigma teams should, as a goal, establish a culture of data-driven decision making. Objectives may include improving data collection and analysis capabilities, implementing statistical process control techniques, and using data to guide problem solving and improvement efforts. The team should also, as a goal, establish standardized processes and best practices across the organization. The objective is to create consistency, reduce variation, and facilitate continuous improvement. The team can document and then share best practices to ensure knowledge transfer and replication for success across departments and locations.

Successful implementation of Lean Six Sigma requires change management. The goal is to effectively communicate the need for change, gain buy-in from management, and ensure smooth adoption of new processes and practices. Teams should focus on objectives related to change readiness, communications, training, and overcoming resistance to change. Along with the change process, the team must lead the sustainability and continual improvement initiative. The team should have an objective for sustainable improvements and building a foundation for ongoing progress. This might include developing systems for monitoring and sustaining improvements, conducting periodic reviews and audits, and fostering a mindset of continual learning and improvement.

Because of the unique challenges and priorities of the aviation and aerospace sectors, goals and objectives targeted for the industry are recommended for Lean Six Sigma team building. The first of these is safety enhancement.

The team has a clear understanding that the primary goal in aviation and aerospace is to enhance safety. Objectives may include reducing safety incidents, improving safety processes, and implementing proactive measures to identify and mitigate risks.

Improving operational efficiency would be the next objective on the list. The aviation and aerospace industry operates in a highly complex and regulated environment. Goals may include reducing delays, improving on-time performance, optimizing maintenance processes, and enhancing operational efficiency.

Along with improving the efficiency of operations, the team must be attuned to the importance of quality assurance and its compliance. An objective may be to enhance quality control processes throughout the organization. Goals may include a reduction in defects and errors and achieving and maintaining regulatory compliance.

Because the aviation and aerospace industry are under continuous cost pressures, a focused objective of cost reduction and financial performance improvement should be emphasized during team building. Goals may include reducing operational costs, optimizing resource utilization, minimizing waste, and improving financial performance using Lean Six Sigma tools.

Reliability and maintenance optimization would be the next unique focus area for the team. Both reliability and maintenance are essential for aviation and aerospace operations.

As an objective for the team, increasing the time a fleet of aircraft are in full operational status might be a goal. Objectives might include improving equipment reliability, reducing maintenance cycle times, optimizing preventive and predictive maintenance, and maximizing operational uptime.

The aviation and aerospace industries rely on a complex global supply chain network therefore, its efficiency is paramount to its survival. A Lean Six Sigma team should understand well that a focused objective must be to improve its efficiency, effectiveness, and collaboration. Goals may include improving supply quality, reducing lead times, enhancing inventory management, and fostering collaboration and communications with suppliers for better overall supply chain performance.

Airworthiness and regulatory compliance would be another focus area that should be emphasized by the Lean Six Sigma team. As an objective, the overall team guidance on the adherence to all applicable airworthiness regulations. Goals may include enhancing airworthiness standards and implementing Lean Six Sigma practices to drive continuous improvement in regulatory compliance processes.

Customer experience and stakeholder satisfaction should be earned daily by the organization and the Lean Six Sigma team. Objectives to accomplish this may be improving on-time performance, enhancing their experience, reducing their complaints, and implementing customer-centric improvement across points.

Because the aviation and aerospace industries are increasingly focused on sustainability and environmental responsibilities, the Lean Six Sigma team should understand the role they play when providing a service to the customer. As an objective, a shared responsibility consciousness between the team and the customer is critical. Goals may include reducing carbon emissions, implementing sustainable practices, or optimizing fuel efficiency by using Lean Six Sigma initiatives.

Rapid technological advances and evolving best practices foster an innovative and continuous learning environment within the aviation and aerospace industry. A Lean Six Sigma team should have a focused objective way for collaboration and to fully support the customer to ensure their continued success as they evolve. Goals may include promoting a culture of continuous learning and innovation, encouraging employees to embrace new technologies and methodologies, and fostering collaboration and knowledge sharing among team members and the customer.

Regardless of Lean Six Sigma project type, it is essential to align all team goals and objectives with the organization's overall strategy and ensure that the team contributes to the achievement of the broader organizational objectives. Progress should be tracked regularly, performance measured against established goals, and adjustments made as needed to ensure the team's efforts drive tangible outcomes.

GROUND RULES

Ground rules for project teams are essential guidelines and principles that team members agree to follow throughout a project. These rules help maintain order, promote effective collaboration, and ensure that all team members are aligned with the project's objectives.

Ground rules help define how and when team members should communicate. They also emphasize the importance of treating all team members with respect and courtesy. Responsibilities and roles are clarified by ground rules and how time management will be approached, ensuring project milestones and deliverables are met. Quality standards are set to ensure standardization of deliverables.

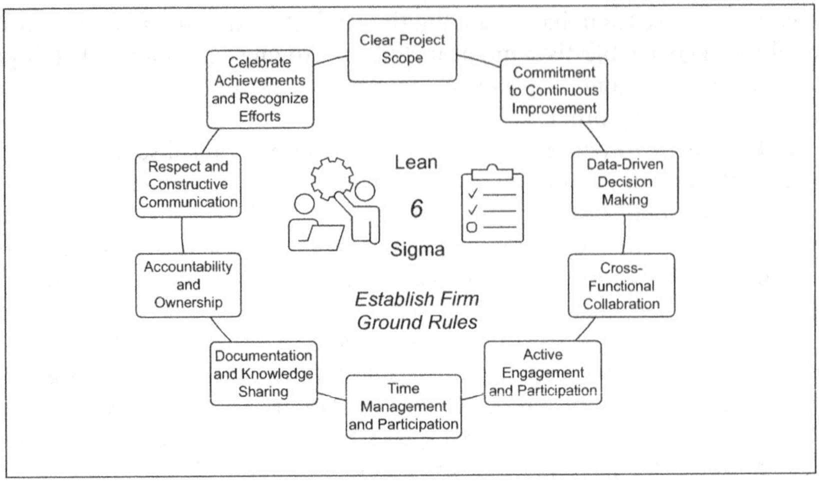

Figure 3.5 Lean Six Sigma Team General Ground Rules

Constructive discussions to address disagreements are defined by ground rules, thus establishing a process for conflict resolution.

Team involvement is addressed by establishing rules that define acceptable behavior for attendance, discussion, constructive criticism, feedback, and punctuality. They define and determine how decisions will be made within the team.

Critical to the project, scope of work is defined and adherence enforced. Project status updates are scheduled, too, and accountability for tasks individually and collectively is defined by ground rules. Team achievements and milestone accomplishment are earmarked in ground rules as rationales for team celebration and positive reinforcement for team morale and motivation.

Figure 3.5 illustrates ground rules that should be considered regardless of project orientation.

Remember that ground rules should be agreed upon by the entire team. They should be revisited periodically to ensure they remain relevant and effective throughout the project's life. The establishment of team ground rules should be linked to team norms that drive team focus and cohesiveness.

Respect and courtesy – Treat all team members with respect, courtesy, and professionalism, regardless of their role or position.

Active listening – Practice active listening during team discussions, allowing everyone to express their thoughts and ideas fully.

Constructive feedback – Provide feedback in a constructive and supportive manner, focusing on the issue at hand rather than personal attacks.

Timeliness and punctuality – Be punctual for meetings and deadlines to ensure effective time management and show respect for others' time.

Confidentiality – Maintain confidentiality of sensitive team discussion, data, or information shared within the team.

Responsibility and accountability – Take responsibility for assigned tasks and be accountable for the work's outcome.

Participation – Actively participate in team activities, discussions, and decision-making processes.
No blame culture – Avoid blaming individuals for failure or mistakes; instead, focus on learning from them and finding solutions.
Conflict resolution – Address conflicts openly and constructively, seeking resolution through dialogue and compromise.
Goal orientation – Keep the team's goals and objective at the forefront of all discussions and decisions.
Equality and inclusivity – Promote equality and inclusivity by valuing diverse perspectives and ensuring everyone can contribute.
Open communication – Encourage open and transparent communication among team members.
Support and collaboration – Offer support to team members when needed and foster a collaborative environment where knowledge and resources are shared.
Use of technology – Define guidelines for the appropriate use of technology during meetings to minimize distractions.
Decision-making process – Establish a clear decision-making process, such as voting or consensus building, to avoid ambiguity and ensure everyone's input is considered.
Continuous improvement – Encourage a culture of continuous improvement, where team members are open to feedback and constantly seek ways to enhance their performance.
Work–life balance – Recognize and respect the importance of work-life balance for all team members.
Show adaptability – Be open to change and demonstrate flexibility in response to evolving circumstances.
Recognition and appreciation – Acknowledge and appreciate the efforts and contributions of team members.

Remember that team norms are guidelines for how the team members will interact and communicate. Norms help to clarify the expected behavior of individuals on the team and prevent unnecessary conflict. Norms matter to a team because they lead to the establishment of effective ground rules.

CLEAR UNDERSTANDING OF ROLES, TASKS, AND TEAM MEMBER RESPONSIBILITIES

In Lean Six Sigma projects, regardless of project focus, it is crucial for team members to have a clear understanding of their tasks and responsibilities. This ensures efficient project execution and increases the chances of a successful project outcome. Table 3.1A, B, and C lists a typical staffing and role mix for a Lean Six Sigma team in both general and aviation and aerospace–focused projects.

Regardless of project focus, Lean Six Sigma team members must clearly understand their roles, responsibilities, and industry-specific considerations within the project. This fundamental clarity promotes effective collaboration, minimizes confusion, and enables each team member to contribute to the project's success. Regular communications and training are essential to maintain a shared understanding throughout the project lifecycle.

Table 3.1A Lean Six Sigma Staffing and Role Mix

Team Role	*General Focused*	*Aviation/Aerospace Focused*
Project Champion/ Sponsor	This individual is responsible for providing overall project support, securing necessary resources, and ensuring alignment with organizational goals. They play a crucial role in removing obstacles and promoting project success.	The project champion or sponsor in aviation and aerospace is typically a senior leader within the organization who provides support, resources, and guidance for the project. They ensure the project aligns with organizational goals and strategic objectives. They actively engage with stakeholders to promote project success.
Project Leader/ Manager	The project leader oversees the entire Lean Six Sigma project. They coordinate team activities, manage timelines, monitor progress, and ensure adherence to project goals and objectives. The project leader also facilitates communication among team members and stakeholders.	The project manager/leader oversees the entire Lean Six Sigma project in the aviation and aerospace industry. They are responsible for coordinating team activities, managing timelines, monitoring progress, and ensuring adherence to project goals and objectives goals and objectives. The project manager/leader also interfaces with stakeholders, manages risks, and facilitates communication among team members.
Lean Six Sigma Team Members	These individuals actively participate in the project and are responsible for specific tasks and deliverables. They may have expertise in Lean Six Sigma methodologies and contribute their knowledge and skills to problem-solving, data analysis, process improvement, and implementation efforts.	Team members actively participate in the project and are assigned specific task and responsibilities. They have expertise in Lean Six Sigma methodologies, aviation regulations, and background in systems development. Team members contribute their knowledge and skills to data analysis, process improvement, root cause analysis, and the implementation of solutions.

Table 3.1B Lean Six Sigma Staffing and Role Mix

Team Role	*General Focused*	*Aviation/Aerospace Focused*
Data Analyst	SMEs possess in-depth knowledge of specific processes or areas within the organization. They provide insights, data, and expertise to support project analysis, improvement recommendations, and implementation plans. These team members are responsible for collecting, analyzing, and interpreting data to identify process bottlenecks, root causes, and improvement opportunities. They use statistical tools and techniques to extract meaningful insights and drive data-based decision-making.	SMEs in aviation and aerospace projects possess specialized knowledge and experience related to aviation operations, safety, maintenance, and improvement recommendation plans. SMES help ensure that solutions align with industry regulations and best practices Data analysts play a critical role in aviation and aerospace projects. They are responsible for collecting, analyzing, and interpreting data from various sources, such as maintenance records, flight data, or safety reports. They use statistical tools and techniques to identify trends, patterns, and areas for improvement, which helps derive evidence-based decisions.

Table 3.1C Lean Six Sigma Staffing and Role Mix

Team Role	*General Focused*	*Aviation/Aerospace Focused*
Process Owners	Process owners are responsible for the day-to-day management and improvement within the organization. They collaborate with the project team, provide necessary process information, and contribute to the development and implementation of improvement initiatives.	Process owners in aviation and aerospace projects are responsible for specific processes or functions within the industry. They collaborate with the project team, provide necessary process information, and contribute to the development and implementation of improvement initiatives. They also ensure project outcomes align with operational requirements and industry standards.
Change Management Specialist	In Lean Six Sigma projects, change management is crucial for successful implementation. Change management specialists	Change management specialist in aviation and aerospace projects help mange the transition and integration of

(*Continued*)

Table 3.1C (Continued)

Team Role	*General Focused*	*Aviation/Aerospace Focused*
	help identify potential resistance, develop communication strategies, and facilitate organizational buy-in for process improvement.	process improvements within the organization. They facilitate stakeholder engagement, communicate the benefits of the changes, and address potential resistance to change. Change management specialists ensure that improvements are effectively implemented while considering regulatory compliance and safety considerations.

SUMMARY

Chapter 3 began by first defining the characteristics of great leadership and of the leader who possesses them. It then addressed the need for strong overall leadership skills when leading a Lean Six Sigma project and the requirement to build a team composed of strong leaders as individual team members. The reader was then exposed to the importance of having focused goals and objectives for team members and the overarching need for ground rules of engagement as the team begins its Lean Six Sigma journey. The chapter then presented a comparison of the leadership skills deemed necessary to lead Lean Six Sigma projects of a general nature and those deemed necessary to lead projects within the aviation and aerospace industries. The chapter concluded with a discussion on task and team staffing and their respective roles and responsibilities in Lean Six Sigma projects.

LEAN SIX SIGMA AT WORK!

Lean Six Sigma at Work – Contact Leadership

Effective leaders understand how important it is to get to know employees. At AJ, leadership makes it a point to talk personally and make eye contact with each employee regularly. This means greeting employees while walking through the plant or offices, stopping to exchange a few words, and being present for both shifts. These meetings create an opportunity for interaction and enable leaders to hear employees' ideas and concerns. To get the employees' thoughts, they ask questions.

AJ owners see their job as making sure that work, in terms of quality production, gets into the shop and that their employees are responsible for making quality products. As leaders, they want to buy in on their vision for the organization: grow the company. To do this, their employees will have to grow themselves, obtaining new skills and performing new jobs. These one-on-one meetings provide them with the opportunity to motivate employees, set performance expectations, provide feedback and encouragement, and track progress. They can also clarify any questions their employees may have. Lots of changes have been taking place over the past two years, and their one-on-one meetings have reduced the resistance to change.

AJ owners also serve as decision makers. By walking through the plant and interacting with employees on a regular basis, they can see what is working and what is not. As they assess the situation and analyze problems, they can adjust AJ strategy, goals, and objectives. They involve employees in designing the solutions to the issues that arise. In many cases, they just ask questions to get them started. If there are signs of frustration, they step in and provide guidance and direction. This ensures that their employees feel good about the changes they helped put into place and the accomplishments they achieved.

CHAPTER 3 DISCUSSION QUESTIONS

1 Compare and contrast the Lean Six Sigma (LSS) project leader characteristics for general industry and those required for the aviation and aerospace industries.
2 Using the amazing leadership key elements presented in Figure 3.3, select the top five you would consider the most important. Support your answer with the rationale used for their selection.
3 Why are establishing essential guidelines and principles for Lean Six Sigma team members considered critical before initiating a project?
4 Briefly describe how the following quality tools help a Lean Six Sigma team collect data, visualize problems, observe trends, and contribute to informed decision making.

a Process Mapping
b Value Stream Mapping
c Pareto Charts
d Cause and Effect Diagrams
e Control Charts
f Histograms
g Scatter Diagrams
h 5 Whys
i Statistical Process Control
j Kaizen Events
k Failure Modes and Effects Analysis
l Fault Tree Analysis
m Root Cause Analysis
n Design of Experiments
o Poka-Yoke
p Standard Work
q 5S
r Human Factors Analysis
s Failure Modes and Effect and Criticality Analysis
t Lean Six Sigma Visual Management

BIBLIOGRAPHY

Aghili, Shaun. "A six sigma approach to internal audits." *Strategic Finance* 90.8 (2009): 38–44.

Al-Dosary, Abdullah A. "Application of lean six-sigma methodology to reduce the failure rate of valves at oil field." In *World Congress on Engineering and Computer Science 2014, WCECS 2014*. Newswood Limited, 2014.

Andersen, Bjorn, and Tom Fagerhaug. *Root Cause Analysis*. Quality Press, 2006.

Anderson, Mark J., and Patrick J. Whitcomb. "Design of experiments." *Kirk-Othmer Encyclopedia of Chemical Technology* (2000): 1–22.

Antony, Jiju. *Design of Experiments for Engineers and Scientists*. Elsevier, 2023.

Antony, Jiju, et al. "Ten commandments of lean six sigma: A practitioners' perspective." *International Journal of Productivity and Performance Management* 67.6 (2018): 1033–1044.

ArunKumar, G., and R. Dillibabu. "Design and application of new quality improvement model: Kano lean six sigma for software maintenance project." *Arabian Journal for Science and Engineering* 41.3 (2016): 997–1014.

Ashok Sarkar, Shri, Arup Ranjan Mukhopadhyay, and Sadhan Kumar Ghosh. "Root cause analysis, lean six sigma and test of hypothesis." *The TQM Journal* 25.2 (2013): 170–185.

Assarlind, Marcus, Ida Gremyr, and Kristoffer Bäckman. "Multi-faceted views on a lean six sigma application." *International Journal of Quality & Reliability Management* 30.4 (2013): 387–402.

Bahensky, James A., Janet Roe, and Romy Bolton. "Lean sigma – will it work for healthcare." *Journal of Healthcare Information Management* 19.1 (2005): 39–44.

Berntzen, Marthe, and Sut I. Wong. "Autonomous but interdependent: The roles of initiated and received task interdependence in distributed team coordination." *International Journal of Electronic Commerce* 25.1 (2021): 7–28.

Borgovini, Robert, Stephen Pemberton, and Michael Rossi. "Failure mode, effects and criticality analysis (FMECA)." In *Reliability Analysis Center*, 1993. https://s3vi.ndc.nasa.gov/ssri-kb/static/resources/a278508.pdf

Brenig-Jones, Martin, and Jo Dowdall. *Lean Six Sigma for Leaders: A Practical Guide for Leaders to Transform the Way They Run Their Organization*. John Wiley & Sons, 2018.

Brunozzi, Jeffrey R. *A Quantitative Study Examining the Relationship Between Management's Leadership Style and Lean Six Sigma Implementation Results*. Northcentral University, 2016.

Cavazzuti, Marco, and Marco Cavazzuti. "Design of experiments." In *Optimization Methods: from Theory to Design Scientific and Technological Aspects in Mechanics*. Springer, 2013, pp. 13–42.

Chakhrit, Ammar, and Mohammed Chennoufi. "Failure mode, effects and criticality analysis improvement by using new criticality assessment and prioritization based approach." *Journal of Engineering, Design and Technology* 21.5 (2023): 1545–1567.

Chen, Joseph C., Ye Li, and Brett D. Shady. "From value stream mapping toward a lean/sigma continuous improvement process: An industrial case study." *International Journal of Production Research* 48.4 (2010): 1069–1086.

Cheng, Lang Jung. "Implementing six sigma Within kaizen events, the experience of AIDC in Taiwan." *The TQM Journal* 30.1 (2018): 43–53.

Crowdle, Mary Margaret, Olivia McDermott, and Anna Trubetskaya. "A benefit costing process for lean six sigma programs." *The TQM Journal* 35.9 (2023): 369–387.

De Oliveira, Ualison Rebula, Henrique Martins Rocha, and Fernando Augusto Silva Marins. "Failure mapping through combination of process mapping, EPCA, FTA, and FMEA techniques." Chapter 3. https://www.researchgate.net/publication/325477346_Failure_mapping_through_combination_of_process_mapping_EPCA_FTA_and_FMEA_techniques

Devane, Tom. *Integrating Lean Six Sigma and High-Performance Organizations: Leading the Charge Toward Dramatic, Rapid, and Sustainable Improvement*. Vol. 4. John Wiley & Sons, 2004.

Doggett, A. Mark. "Root cause analysis: A framework for tool selection." *Quality Management Journal* 12.4 (2005): 34–45.

Doshi, Jigar, and Darshak Desai. "Application of failure mode & effect analysis (FMEA) for continuous quality improvement-multiple case studies in automobile SMEs." *International Journal for Quality Research* 11.2 (2017): 345.

Dudek-Burlikowska, Marta, and D. Szewieczek. "The Poka-yoke method as an improving quality tool of operations in the process." *Journal of Achievements in Materials and Manufacturing Engineering* 36.1 (2009): 95–102.

Eriksson, L., E. Johansson, N. Kettaneh-Wold, C. Wikström, and S. Wold. "Design of experiments." In *Principles and Applications*. Learnways AB, 2000.

Febriana, Tubagus Hendri, and Hasbullah Hasbullah. "Analysis and defect improvement using FTA, FMEA, and MLR through DMAIC phase: Case study in mixing process tire manufacturing industry." *Journal Européen des Systèmes Automatisés* 54.5 (2021).

Feng, Peter P., and Glenn Ballard. "Standard work from a lean theory perspective." *Annual Conference of the International Group for Lean Construction* 16 (2008).

Fisher, Michael. "Process improvement by Poka-yoke." *Work Study* 48.7 (1999): 264–266.

Fisher, Ronald Aylmer. "The design of experiments." In *The Design of Experiments*. Oliver & Boyd, 1960 xiv, 7th ed., p. 245.

Franchetti, Matthew, and Megan Yanik. "Continuous improvement and value stream analysis through the lean DMAIC six sigma approach: A manufacturing case study from Ohio, USA." *International Journal of Six Sigma and Competitive Advantage* 6.4 (2011): 278–300.

Galli, Brian J. "What risks does lean six sigma introduce?" *IEEE Engineering Management Review* 46.1 (2018): 80–90.

Gangidi, Prashant. "A systematic approach to root cause analysis using 3× 5 why's technique." *International Journal of Lean Six Sigma* 10.1 (2018): 295–310.

Gapp, Rod, Ron Fisher, and Kaoru Kobayashi. "Implementing 5S within a Japanese context: An integrated management system." *Management Decision* 46.4 (2008): 565–579.

Gargama, Heeralal, and Sanjay Kumar Chaturvedi. "Criticality assessment models for failure mode effects and criticality analysis using fuzzy logic." *IEEE Transactions on Reliability* 60.1 (2011): 102–110.

Gellis, Corey. "Assessment of leadership styles and lean six sigma critical success factors in the aerospace and defense industry." 2021. https://stars.library.ucf.edu/etd2020/867/

George, Mark O. *The Lean Six Sigma Guide to Doing More with Less: Cut Costs, Reduce Waste, and Lower Your Overhead.* John Wiley & Sons, 2010.

Ghaleb, Abdulrakeeb A., Mahmoud A. El-Sharief, and Mohamed G. El-Sebaie. "Study of tools, techniques and factors used in lean six sigma." *International Journal of Scientific Engineering and Research* 5.12 (2014): 1652–1658.

Gibbons, Paul Martin, et al. "The development of a value improvement model for repetitive processes (VIM) combining lean, six sigma and systems thinking." *International Journal of Lean Six Sigma* 3.4 (2012): 315–338.

Gokilakrishnan, G., et al. "Implementation of lean six sigma (LSS) techniques for tyre manufacturing in small and medium-sized enterprises." *International Journal of System Assurance Engineering and Management* (2023): 1–10.

Guerrero, Héctor H., and James R. Bradley. "Failure modes and effects analysis: An evaluation of group versus individual performance." *Production and Operations Management* 22.6 (2013): 1524–1539.

Gupta, Neha. "An overview on six sigma: Quality improvement program." *International Journal of Technical Research and Application* 1.1 (2013): 29–39.

Gupta, Shaman, and Sanjiv Kumar Jain. "The 5S and kaizen concept for overall improvement of the organisation: A case study." *International Journal of Lean Enterprise Research* 1.1 (2014): 22–40.

Haekal, Jakfat. "Quality control with failure mode and effect analysis (FMEA) and fault tree analysis (FTA) methods: Case study Japanese multinational automotive corporation." *International Journal of Scientific Advances (IJSCIA)* 3.2 (2022): 227–234.

Hardy, Daniel Lee, Saikat Kundu, and Muhammad Latif. "Productivity and process performance in a manual trimming cell exploiting lean six sigma (LSS) DMAIC–a case study in laminated panel production." *International Journal of Quality & Reliability Management* 38.9 (2021): 1861–1879.

Hon, Alice H. Y., and Wilco W. H. Chan. "Team creative performance: The roles of empowering leadership, creative-related motivation, and task interdependence." *Cornell Hospitality Quarterly* 54.2 (2013): 199–210.

Hu, Guiping, et al. "A multi-objective model for project portfolio selection to implement lean and six sigma concepts." *International Journal of Production Research* 46.23 (2008): 6611–6625.

Indrawati, Sri, and Muhammad Ridwansyah. "Manufacturing continuous improvement using lean six sigma: An iron ores industry case application." *Procedia Manufacturing* 4 (2015): 528–534.

Jing, Gary G. "Is this a six sigma project or kaizen event?" *Lean & Six Sigma Review* 14.2 (2015): 5.

Jordan, Wallace E. "Failure modes, effects and criticality analyses." In *Annual Reliability and Maintainability Symposium*. Springer, 1972. https://link.springer.com/book/10.1007/978-1-84628-498-4

Kaissi, Abdul-Karim Hosni. *Leadership Influence Styles: Investigating Their Effect on Six Sigma Change Program Implementation in a High-Tech Industry*. University of Phoenix, 2004.

Kiggundu, Moses N. "Task interdependence and job design: Test of a theory." *Organizational Behavior and Human Performance* 31.2 (1983): 145–172.

Klimecka-Tatar, Dorota. "Analysis and improvement of business processes management-based on value stream mapping (VSM) in manufacturing companies." *Polish Journal of Management Studies* 23.2 (2021).

Koshy, George P., and A. George Koshy. "Project management using statistical control chart." In *ASQ World Conference on Quality and Improvement Proceedings*. Vol. 58. American Society for Quality, 2004.

Kumar, Sameer, and Michael Sosnoski. "Using DMAIC six sigma to systematically improve shop-floor production quality and costs." *International Journal of Productivity and Performance Management* 58.3 (2009): 254–273.

Laureani, Alessandro, and Jiju Antony. "Standards for lean six sigma certification." *International Journal of Productivity and Performance Management* 61.1 (2011): 110–120.

Laureani, Alessandro, and Jiju Antony. "Leadership characteristics for lean six sigma." *Total Quality Management & Business Excellence* 28.3–4 (2017): 405–426.

Laureani, Alessandro, and Jiju Antony. "Leadership and lean six sigma: A systematic literature review." *Total Quality Management & Business Excellence* 30.1–2 (2019): 53–81.

Lazarevic, Milovan, et al. "A systematic literature review of Poka-yoke and novel approach to theoretical aspects." *Strojniski Vestnik/Journal of Mechanical Engineering* 65.7–8 (2019): 454–467.

Lee, Ming-Chang, and To Chang. "Combination of theory of constraints, root cause analysis and six sigma for quality improvement framework." *International Journal of Productivity and Quality Management* 10.4 (2012): 447–463.

Lertwattanapongchai, Suriya, and Fredric William Swierczek. "Assessing the change process of lean six sigma: A case analysis." *International Journal of Lean Six Sigma* 5.4 (2014): 423–443.

Linderman, Kevin, Roger G. Schroeder, and Adrian S. Choo. "Six sigma: The role of goals in improvement teams." *Journal of Operations Management* 24.6 (2006): 779–790.

Lu, Jiunn-Chenn, and Taho Yang. "Implementing lean standard work to solve a low work-in-process buffer problem in a highly automated manufacturing environment." *International Journal of Production Research* 53.8 (2015): 2285–2305.

Mariz, Renato Nunes, et al. "A review of the standardized work application in construction." In *Proceedings of the IGLC 20th Annual Conference of the International Group for Lean Construction, San Diego, CA, USA*, 2012. https://www.researchgate.net/publication/282297192_A_review_of_the_standardized_work_application_in_construction

Markarian, Jennifer. "Six sigma: Quality processing through statistical analysis." *Plastics, Additives and Compounding* 6.4 (2004): 28–31.

Martin, James William. *Lean Six Sigma for the Office: Integrating Customer Experience for Enhanced Productivity*. Productivity Press, 2021.

Marzagão, Daniela Santana Lambert, and Marly M. Carvalho. "The influence of project leaders' behavioral competencies on the performance of Six Sigma projects." *Revista Brasileira de Gestão de Negócios* 18 (2016): 609–632.

Matusova, Dominika. "The improvement of logistics processes through kaizen and six sigma." *Transport & Logistics* 16 (2016).

Men, Chenghao, and Ruiqian Jia. "Knowledge-oriented leadership, team learning and team creativity: The roles of task interdependence and task complexity." *Leadership & Organization Development Journal* 42.6 (2021): 882–898.

Michael Gnanaraj, S., S. R. Devadasan, and P. R. Shalij. "Current state maps on the implementation of lean and Six-Sigma paradigms and an exclusive model for deploying Lean Six-Sigma in SMEs." *International Journal of Productivity and Quality Management* 5.3 (2010): 286–309.

Michalska, Joanna, and Danuta Szewieczek. "The 5S methodology as a tool for improving the organization." *Journal of Achievements in Materials and Manufacturing Engineering* 24.2 (2007): 211–214.

Mishra, Aatish Kumar, et al. "Development of sustainable value stream mapping (SVSM) for unit part manufacturing: A simulation approach." *International Journal of Lean Six Sigma* 11.3 (2020): 493–514.

Montella, Emma, et al. "The application of lean six sigma methodology to reduce the risk of healthcare –associated infections in surgery departments." *Journal of Evaluation in Clinical Practice* 23.3 (2017): 530–539.

Moorthy, Krishna, et al. "A human factors analysis of technical and team skills among surgical trainees during procedural simulations in a simulated operating theatre." *Annals of Surgery* 242.5 (2005): 631.

Morais, Valter Rocha, Sérgio Sousa, and Isabel da Silva Lopes. "Implementation of a lean six sigma project in a production line." IANEG, 2015.

Muchsinin, Muchammad Yusuf, and Wiwik Sulistiyowati. "Quality control analysis to reduce product defects with the lean six sigma method and fault tree analysis." *Procedia of Engineering and Life Science* 3 (2022).

Nagi, Ayman, and Safwan Altarazi. "Integration of value stream map and strategic layout planning into DMAIC approach to improve carpeting process." *Journal of Industrial Engineering and Management (JIEM)* 10.1 (2017): 74–97.

Nemeth, Christopher P. *Human Factors Methods for Design: Making Systems Human-Centered.* CRC Press, 2004.

Pearce, Jone L., and Hal B. Gregersen. "Task interdependence and extrarole behavior: A test of the mediating effects of felt responsibility." *Journal of Applied Psychology* 76.6 (1991): 838.

Pereira, Ana, et al. "Reconfigurable standardized work in a lean company–a case study." *Procedia Cirp* 52 (2016): 239–244.

Petcu, Andreea Jenica, Sorin Anagnoste, and Mihai Draghici. "Lean six sigma-a challenge for organizations focused on business excellence." *The Romanian Economic Journal* 14.41 (2011): 147–158.

Pötters, Patrick, Robert Schmitt, and Bert Leyendecker. "Effectivity of quality methods used on the shop floor of a serial production–how important is Poka yoke?" *Total Quality Management & Business Excellence* 29.9–10 (2018): 1200–1212.

Pukelsheim, Friedrich. *Optimal Design of Experiments.* Society for Industrial and Applied Mathematics, 2006.

Rahani, A. R., and Muhammad Al-Ashraf. "Production flow analysis through value stream mapping: A lean manufacturing process case study." *Procedia Engineering* 41 (2012): 1727–1734.

Randhawa, Jugraj Singh, and Inderpreet Singh Ahuja. "5S–a quality improvement tool for sustainable performance: Literature review and directions." *International Journal of Quality & Reliability Management* 34.3 (2017): 334–361.

Ray, Sanjit, and Boby John. "Lean six-sigma application in business process outsourced organization." *International Journal of Lean Six Sigma* 2.4 (2011): 371–380.

Rooney, James J., and Lee N. Vanden Heuvel. "Root cause analysis for beginners." *Quality Progress* 37.7 (2004): 45–56.

Santos, Diego Michael Cornelius dos, Bruna Karine dos Santos, and César Gabriel dos Santos. "Implementation of a standard work routine using lean manufacturing tools: A case study." *Gestão & Produção* 28 (2021).

Sarwar, Jawad, et al. "Impact of stakeholders on lean six sigma project costs and outcomes during implementation in an air-conditioner manufacturing industry." *Processes* 10.12 (2022): 2591.

Senvar, Ozlem, and Hakan Tozan. "Process capability and six sigma methodology including fuzzy and lean." 2010. https://doi.org/10.5772/10389, https://www.intechopen.com/chapters/12326

Shahada, T. M., and I. Alsyouf. "Design and implementation of a lean six sigma framework for process improvement: A case study." In *2012 IEEE International Conference on Industrial Engineering and Engineering Management.* IEEE, 2012.

Shamsuzzaman, Mohammad, et al. "Using lean six sigma to improve mobile order fulfilment process in a telecom service sector." *Production Planning & Control* 29.4 (2018): 301–314.

Shappell, Scott A., and Douglas A. Wiegmann. "The human factors analysis and classification system – HFACS." United States Department of Transportation, 2000. https://rosap.ntl.bts.gov/view/dot/21482

Shappell, Scott A., and Douglas A. Wiegmann. "Applying reason: The human factors analysis and classification system (HFACS)." *Human Factors and Aerospace Safety* 1.1 (2001): 59–86.

Shimbun, Nikkan Kogyo. *Poka-yoke: Improving Product Quality by Preventing Defects.* CRC Press, 1989.

Simanová, Ľubica, Andrea Sujová, and Pavol Gejdoš. "Improving the performance and quality of processes by applying and implementing six sigma methodology in furniture manufacturing process." *Wood Industry/Drvna Industrija* 70.2 (2019).

Singh, Jagdeep, et al. "Managing industrial operations by lean thinking using value stream mapping and six sigma in manufacturing unit: Case studies." *Management Decision* 58.6 (2020): 1118–1148.

Singh, Jaspreet, Sanjeev Singh, and Amanpreet Singh. "Distribution transformer failure modes, effects and criticality analysis (FMECA)." *Engineering Failure Analysis* 99 (2019): 180–191.

Singh, Mahipal, et al. "A toolset for complex decision-making in analyze phase of lean six sigma project: A case validation." *International Journal of Lean Six Sigma* 14.1 (2023): 139–157.

Socconini, Luis, and Carlo Reato. *Lean Six Sigma Management System for Leaders*. Marge Books, 2019.

Sony, Michael. "Lean six sigma in the power sector: Frog into prince." *Benchmarking: An International Journal* 26.2 (2019): 356–370.

Sreedharan V, Raja, and Vijaya Sunder M. "A novel approach to lean six sigma project management: A conceptual framework and empirical application." *Production Planning & Control* 29.11 (2018): 895–907.

Stamatis, Diomidis H. *Failure Mode and Effect Analysis*. Quality Press, 2003.

Stanton, Neville A., et al. *Human Factors Methods: A Practical Guide for Engineering and Design*. CRC Press, 2017.

Stephen, Philip. *Application of DMAIC to Integrate Lean Manufacturing and Six Sigma*. Diss. Virginia Tech, 2004.

Sunder M, Vijaya. "Lean six sigma project management–a stakeholder management perspective." *The TQM Journal* 28.1 (2016): 132–150.

Sutrisno, Agung, and T. J. Lee. "Service reliability assessment using failure mode and effect analysis (FMEA): Survey and opportunity roadmap." *International Journal of Engineering, Science and Technology* 3.7 (2011): 25–38.

Tufail, Muhammad Mutasim Billah, et al. "Implementation of lean six-sigma project in enhancing health care service quality during COVID-19 pandemic." *AIMS Public Health* 8.4 (2021): 704.

Uluskan, Meryem. "Analysis of lean six sigma tools from a multidimensional perspective." *Total Quality Management & Business Excellence* 30.9–10 (2019): 1167–1188.

Vanzant-Stern, Terra. *Lean Six Sigm: International Standards and Global Guidelines*. Fultus Corporation, 2012.

Venkateswaran, N., and P. N. Padmanaban. "Impact of six sigma methodological practices in manufacturing unit–an experimental study." *Arabian Journal of Business and Management Review (Oman Chapter)* (2018): 1–11.

Veres, Cristina, et al. "Case study concerning 5S method impact in an automotive company." *Procedia Manufacturing* 22 (2018): 900–905.

Wald, Heidi, and Kaveh G. Shojania. "Root cause analysis." In *Making Health Care Safer: A Critical Analysis of Patient Safety Practices*. Vol. 51. Agency for Healthcare Research and Quality, 2001.

Wang, Peng, et al. "Adopting lean thinking in virtual reality-based personalized operation training using value stream mapping." *Automation in Construction* 119 (2020): 103355.

Wiegmann, Douglas A., and Scott A. Shappell. *A Human Error Approach to Aviation Accident Analysis: The Human Factors Analysis and Classification System*. Routledge, 2017.

Williams, Brent A. *Standard Work–Lean Tools and Techniques*. No. 2001-01-2598. SAE Technical Paper, 2001.

Williams, Patricia M. "Techniques for root cause analysis." *Proceedings (Baylor University. Medical Center)* 14.2 (2001): 154.

Wu, Albert W., Angela K. M. Lipshutz, and Peter J. Pronovost. "Effectiveness and efficiency of root cause analysis in medicine." *Jama* 299.6 (2008): 685–687.

Zhang, Abraham. "Quality improvement through Poka-yoke: From engineering design to information system design." *International Journal of Six Sigma and Competitive Advantage* 8.2 (2014): 147–159.

Zhao, Deyong, Weimin Ye, and Cuijuan Gao. "Research on process optimization for equipment maintenance based on lean six sigma management." In *2012 International Conference on Quality, Reliability, Risk, Maintenance, and Safety Engineering*. IEEE, 2012.

4

The Lean Six Sigma Improvement Process – Applying the DMAIC Methodology

LEARNING OBJECTIVES

1. Define the DMAIC methodology and its purpose in problem-solving.
2. Identify key characteristics of each phase of the DMAIC methodology.
3. Describe the criteria for selecting appropriate projects for applying DMAIC.
4. Explain various implementation options and when phases of the DMAIC process can be omitted.
5. Analyze the impact of DMAIC on both the general industry and the aviation/aerospace sectors.

DMAIC DEFINED

DMAIC is a problem-solving and improvement methodology used in various ways, particularly in the context of Lean Six Sigma. It stands for define, measure, analyze, improve, and control. DMAIC provides a structure approach for identifying and resolving problems, improving processes, and achieving measurable results.

The DMAIC methodology is a Lean Six Sigma methodology used to improve existing processes that are not meeting performance requirements or are experiencing issues. It is best suited for situations where a process is already in place but needs optimization and improvement. Later in the text we will address another Lean Six Sigma methodology, used for new products or processes from the outset of development, Design for Lean Six Sigma (DFSS).

Figure 4.1 provides an illustration of the five phases of the DMAIC methodology and some of the key elements of each phase.

In the first phase, Define, the problem or improvement goal is clearly defined. The focus is on understanding the specific issue(s), finding the impact on the process or organization, and defining what success looks like. Key elements of this phase include:

- Defining the problem statement – clearly articulate the problem or improvement goals.
- Identifying the customers and their requirements – understand who the stakeholders are and what they expect from the process or product.
- Creating a project charter – establish the scope, objectives, team members, and timeline for the DMAIC project.

DOI: 10.4324/9781032650531-5

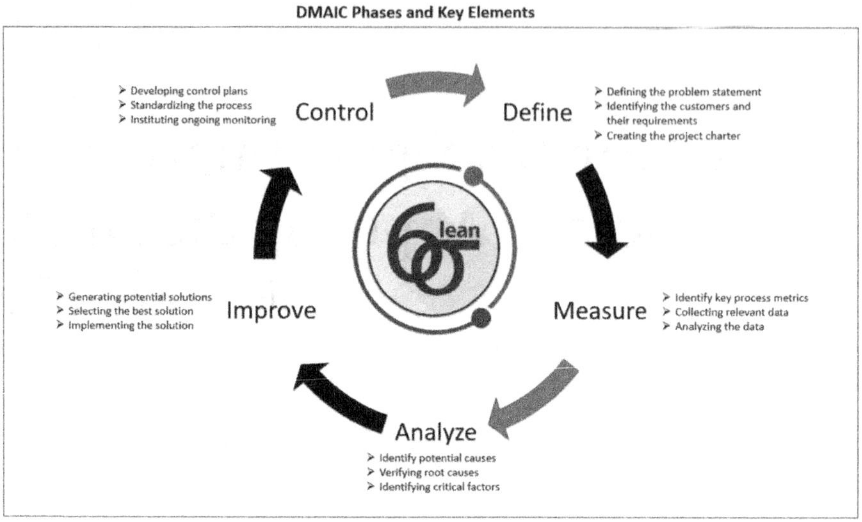

Figure 4.1 DMAIC Phases and Key Elements

In the second phase, Measure, data is collected to quantify the problem and understand the current state of the process. Accurate measurements are critical to identifying the root causes of the issue. Key steps in this phase include:

- Identifying key process metrics – determine which factors influence the problem and need to be measured.
- Collecting relevant data – gather data related to the process and the problem at hand.
- Analyzing the data – use statistical tools to interpret and summarize the data, identifying trends and variations.

In the third phase, Analyze, the team examines the data to identify the root causes of the problem. This step requires deeper investigation and hypothesis testing. Key activities in this phase include:

- Identifying potential causes – brainstorm reasons for the problem and create cause-and-effects diagrams to visualize the relationships.
- Verifying root causes – use data analysis and experiments to confirm or disprove the suspected root causes.
- Identifying critical factors – determine which factors have the most significant impact on the problem.

In the fourth phase, Improve, the focus is on developing and implementing solutions to address the root causes identified in the previous phase. Key activities in this phase include:

- Generating potential solutions – brainstorm and evaluate different ideas for addressing the root causes.

- Selecting the best solution – choose the most promising solution based on the data and analysis.
- Implementing the solution – put the selected solution into action on a small scale (pilot) and then gradually expand to the full process.

In the fifth phase, Control, ensuring the improvements are sustained over time and that the process remains stable is the main goal. Key actions in this phase include:

- Developing control plans – establish procedures and monitoring systems to track the process performance.
- Standardizing the process – create standard operating procedures (SOPs) to maintain consistency and prevent deviations.
- Instituting ongoing monitoring – continuously monitor the process to detect and address any deviations or issues that may arise.

As depicted in Figure 4.1, DMAIC is a cyclical process, meaning that once the Control phase is completed, the team can loop back to the Define phase to start the improvement process again or address other issues. This cycle allows organizations to continuously improve their processes and achieve higher levels of quality and efficiency.

When to Use DMAIC

I am often asked by organizational stakeholders if the DMAIC methodology is suitable for other types of projects within the organization. The short answer is yes! Because the DMAIC methodology at its core is a problem-solving and improvement methodology, it is particularly well suited for situations where there is a need to identify, analyze, and resolve complex problems or optimize processes. Here are some scenarios where the DMAIC methodology is beneficial:

- Process improvement – DMAIC is widely used to improve existing processes that are not meeting performance targets or customer requirements. It helps organizations identify root causes of process inefficiencies, defects, or variations and implement data-driven improvements.
- Quality management – when an organization aims to enhance product or service quality and reduce defects or errors, DMAIC is a valuable approach. It assists in understanding the sources of defects and implementing improvements to achieve higher quality standards.
- Customer complaints and feedback – if an organization receives frequent complaints or feedback about its products or services, DMAIC can be used to systematically investigate and address the underlying issues.
- Cost reduction – organizations seeking to reduce operational costs employ DMAIC to identify waste, inefficiencies, or non–value-added activities in their processes and implement cost-saving measures.
- Performance improvement – DMAIC can be applied to improve performance metrics, such as cycle time, productivity, throughput, customer satisfaction, and other key performance indicators (KPIs).

- Root cause analysis – when facing complex problems or recurring issues, DMAIC helps systematically uncover root causes, leading to more effective and sustained solutions.
- Data-driven decision making – DMAIC relies on data analysis to make informed decisions. It is ideal for organizations that have access to data and want to utilize it to drive improvements.
- Change management – for organizations undergoing significant changes or facing resistance to change, DMAIC provides a structured approach to managing and implementing improvements.
- Continuous improvement culture – DMAIC promotes a culture of continuous improvement within an organization. It encourages employees to identify and work on improvement projects, fostering a problem-solving mindset.

Note that DMAIC may not be the most appropriate approach for all situations. As mentioned earlier, for projects which require new processes to be developed Design for Six Sigma would be a better choice because of its developmental ground-up approach. For highly innovative projects or those that require creative solutions, other problem-solving methodologies, such as Design Thinking or Lean Start-up, may be more suitable. The decision to use DMAIC should be based on the specific context, the nature of the problem, and the organizations' objectives.

Selecting DMAIC Projects

Another question often asked by organizational stakeholders is: how do you select the right DMAIC projects? Since selecting the right DMAIC project is a critical step for the engagement team and the organization, careful consideration should be given to it. Figure 4.2 shows some helpful criteria for guiding the project decision-making selection process. Note there is no ranking of the criteria.

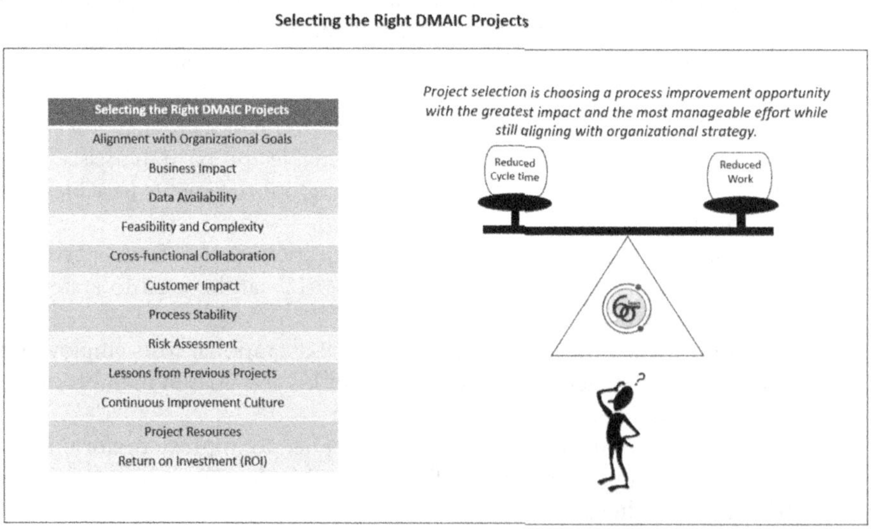

Figure 4.2 Selecting the Right DMAIC Projects

Explanation of each criterion is as follows:

- Alignment with organizational goals – choose projects that align with the organization's strategic goals. The selected projects should address issues or opportunities that have a significant impact on the organization's performance, customer satisfaction, or overall success.
- Business impact – prioritize projects based on their business impact. Consider the financial benefits, cost savings, customer satisfaction improvements, or other measurable outcomes that a project is expected to deliver.
- Data availability – ensure that sufficient data is available to support the DMAIC project. Data plays a crucial role in the measuring and analyzing phases, as it helps in understanding the current state of the process, identifying root causes, and measuring the impact of improvements.
- Feasibility and complexity – assess the feasibility of each project and consider the resources required for successful completion. Complex projects that involve multiple stakeholders or require extensive resources may need to be broken into smaller, more manageable sub-projects.
- Cross-functional collaboration – select projects that involve cross-functional teams or departments. By bringing together individuals with diverse expertise, it becomes easier to identify comprehensive solutions and implement changes effectively.
- Customer impact – projects that directly impact customer experience, satisfaction, and retention should be given high priority. Understanding and meeting customer requirements are crucial for business success.
- Process stability – prioritize projects where the underlying processes are relatively stable. Attempting to improve highly unstable or chaotic processes may lead to inconsistent results and difficulties in measuring improvements.
- Risk assessment – evaluate the potential risks associated with each project. Consider the consequences of failure and the likelihood of achieving the desired outcome.
- Lessons from previous projects – review the results of past DMAIC projects to learn from successes and failures. Apply these insights when selecting new projects to increase the chances of successful outcomes.
- Continuous improvement culture – look for projects that have a thread of continuous improvement woven into their culture. While this is no guarantee of project success, it does tell you that there is an environmental openness present within the organization that could foster heightened employee buy-in.
- Project resources – consider the availability of resources, including time, budget, and personnel, for each project. Ensure that the necessary support and commitment from management and stakeholders are in place.
- Return on invested capital (ROIC) – estimate the potential return on invested capital for each project. Prioritize projects that offer a significant return compared to the capital/resources invested.

By carefully considering these criteria, I have found that Lean Six Sigma teams and organizations can prioritize and select DMAIC projects that will lead to tangible and sustainable improvements in their processes and operations.

Implementation Options

Often the question arises as to the implementation options for projects using the DMAIC methodology. Here are some implementation options that I have used on past engagements that have worked well:

- In-house team – organizations can form an in-house DMAIC project team composed of employees from relevant departments. This team can be led by a trained Six Sigma Black or Seasoned Green belt or someone with experience in process improvement methodologies. Having an in-house team allows for better integration with the organization's culture and processes.
- External consultants – bringing in external consultants who are experts in DMAIC and Lean Six Sigma can be a viable option, especially for organizations that lack internal expertise or require additional support. Consultants can provide specialized knowledge and experience to accelerate the improvement process. The downside to using consultant is often the adaptation to the organization culture and employee buy-in.
- Cross-functional teams – for complex projects that involve multiple departments or processes, forming cross-functional teams is beneficial. These teams consist of individuals from different areas of the organization who collaborate to address the problem collectively. Cross-functional teams offer a diverse range of perspectives and skills, which can lead to a more comprehensive solution.
- Lean Six Sigma workshops and training – organizations can invest in training their employees in the Lean Six Sigma methodology od DMAIC. This approach empowers employees at all levels to identify improvement opportunities and work on small-scale projects within their own department.
- Pilot projects – starting with a pilot project is a practical way to implement DMAIC. Teams can choose a smaller, less complex process to apply DMAIC principles and test potential solutions before scaling up to larger projects.
- DMAIC competition – to foster a team-oriented atmosphere and one of continuous improvement, organizations often host DMAIC project competitions where employees and teams propose improvement projects, and the best ideas receive support and resources to be implemented.
- Kaizen events – kaizen events, also called rapid improvement events, are those short-term, intense improvement efforts focused on specific processes. They can be part of the DMAIC journey, especially for quickly identifying and implementing improvements.
- Online collaboration platforms – using online collaboration platforms and project management tools can help in organizing and tracking projects. The tools facilitate communication and data sharing among team members, even if they are in separate locations.
- Benchmarking and best practice replication – consider benchmarking against industry best practice to get ideas about how other organizations successfully used the DMAIC methodology. Learning from successful examples can provide valuable insights and ideas about what works and what does not.

The choice of implementation option depends on the organization's goals, available resources, and the complexity of the projects. Whatever approach is taken, it is essential to maintain focus on the continuous improvement element and ensure that the DMAIC projects are in alignment with the organization's overall strategy.

Execution of the DMAIC Methodology

While DMAIC is a structured problem-solving and effective improvement methodology, it is not mandatory to follow all phases for every improvement initiative. The extent to which you apply DMAIC can vary depending upon the specific situation, the complexity of the problem, available resources, and organizational goals. Here are some scenarios where you may or may not follow all the DMAIC phases:

- Small-scale improvements – for minor or straightforward process improvements, you may not need to go through the entire DMAIC process. In such cases, you might focus on the Define and Improve phases to identify the problem, set a clear goal, and implement a solution quickly.
- Quick fixes – when facing issues that require immediate attention, you might bypass some of the DMAIC phases and focus solely on identifying and implementing a quick fix or work around. However, that said, it is essential to revisit the issue later to ensure a more permanent solution is put into place.
- Known solution – if the root cause of the problem is already known, there might not be a need to go through extensive analysis in an Analyze phase. Instead, you can jump straight to the Improve phase and implement the known solution. Just ensure you are treating the problem and not the symptom.
- Ongoing continuous improvement – in organizations with a strong culture of continuous improvement, some projects might be ongoing and iterative. In such cases, the Control phase becomes critical to sustaining the improvements over time.
- Limited resources – in resource-constrained environments, you might prioritize projects and allocate resources accordingly. Some projects may receive more attention and follow all DMAIC phases, while others may be scaled back or deferred.
- Research and development – in research or innovation-focused projects, where the objective is to explore new ideas and solutions, DMAIC may not be the most suitable approach. Instead, other methodologies like Design Thinking or Agile might be more appropriate.
- Pre-defined solutions – for some projects, the solution might be pre-defined, and the focus could be on implementing it rather than going through the entire DMAIC process.

The decision to follow all DMAIC phases or to tailor the approach depends upon the context and objectives of the improvement initiative. While DMAIC provides a systematic framework for problem solving and process improvement, it is flexible enough to adapt to the unique needs of each project and organization. The key is to achieve meaningful and sustainable improvement, regardless of how closely you adhere to each DMAIC phase.

WHY DMAIC?

DMAIC is a methodology unto itself that can be, and should be, implemented in every organization that employs Lean Six Sigma as a critical component of continuous improvement. Nuances that are found in every organization influence how Lean Six Sigma, and the DMAIC methodology in particular, is executed. What is consistent across organizations using the DMAIC methodology is that it is recognized as a highly effective problem-solving and improvement methodology. As illustrated in Figure 4.3, it is considered by most practitioners the "ultimate" problem-solving tool.

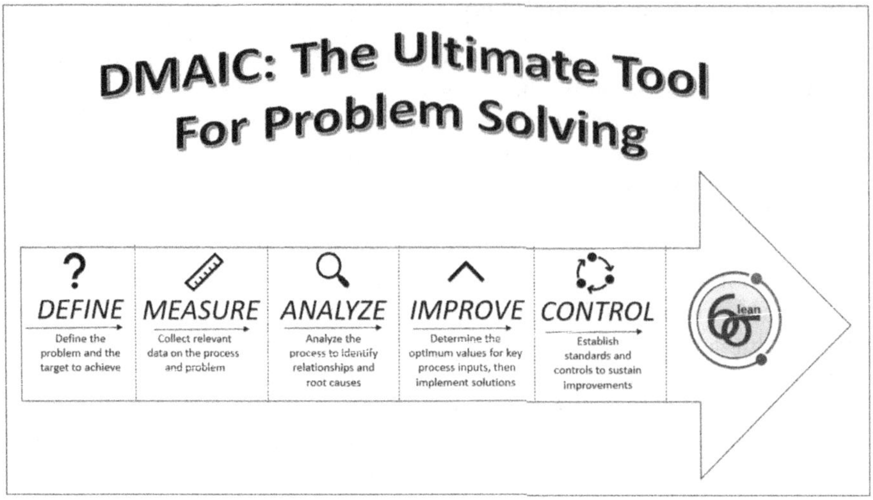

Figure 4.3 DMAIC: The Ultimate Problem-Solving Tool

Here are some key reasons this is true and it is so popular:

1. Structured approach – DMAIC provides a systematic and structured approach for problem-solving and process improvement. It guides the team through a well-defined sequence of steps, ensuring that all critical aspects are addressed.
2. Data driven decision making – DMAIC relies on data analysis to identify problems, measure process performance, and validate improvement. Data-driven decision making reduces guesswork and ensures that actions are based on objective evidence.
3. Focus on root cause analysis – the DMAIC process emphasizes identifying and addressing the root causes of problems rather than just treating the symptoms. This helps to implement more sustainable and stable solutions.
4. Customer-centric – DMAIC encourages organizations to consider customer requirements and feedback throughout the methodology execution process. This customer-centric approach ensures that improvement efforts align with customer needs and expectations.
5. Continuous improvement – implementing DMAIC fosters a culture of continuous improvement within the organization. It empowers employees and team members directly to identify opportunities for improvement and equips them with problem-solving skills.
6. Standardization and consistency – DMAIC encourages the development of standard operating procedures and best practices. By standardizing processes, organizations achieve greater consistency and predictability in the organization.
7. Problem prioritization – DMAIC helps organizations prioritize improvement projects based on their potential impact and alignment with strategic goals. This ensures that resources are directed to the most significant issues.
8. Accountability and ownership – DMAIC projects typically involve cross-functional teams and clear roles and responsibilities. This fosters accountability and ownership among members for the success of the project.

9 Performance measurement – through the Measure phase, DMAIC establishes baseline performance metrics, which are then used to measure the effectiveness of improvements in subsequent phases.
10 Lean Six Sigma integration – DMAIC is an essential component of Lean Six Sigma and ensures that the basic components of Lean and Six Sigma are maximized.
11 Continuous monitoring and control – the Control phase of DMAIC ensures that the improvements made are sustained over time. It establishes control plans and monitoring mechanisms to prevent the process from reverting to its previous state.
12 ROIC and business impact – DMAIC projects are typically selected based on their potential return on invested capital and overall business impact. This aligns improvement efforts with the organization's strategic objective and financial goals.

The DMAIC methodology provides a clear map for organizations to identify and address problems, optimize processes, and achieve measurable results. It enables them to continuously improve their operations, enhances customer satisfaction, reduces defects, and increases efficiency and profitability. Last, by its structured approach to problem-solving, the Define element tells the team what to measure, the Measure element shows the team what to analyze, the Analyze element shows the team what to improve, the Improve element shows the team what to control, and the Control element sets the organization's course for continuous improvement.

DMAIC: A ROADMAP FOR SUCCESSFUL LEAN SIX SIGMA DEPLOYMENT

The DMAIC methodology serves as a roadmap for a successful Lean Six Sigma deployment. It provides a structured and data-driven approach to identify and solve problems and achieve continuous improvement. Figure 4.4 illustrates a notional model of the path DMAIC follows from problem identification to Lean Six Sigma solution.

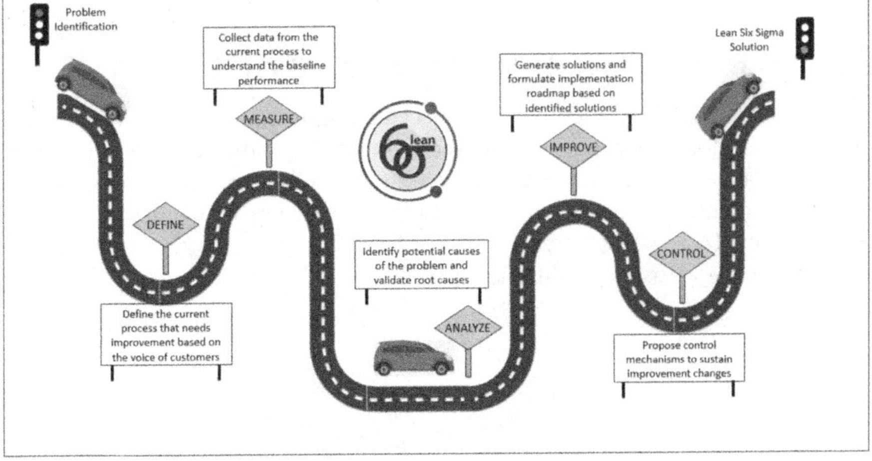

Figure 4.4 DMAIC: A Roadmap to Success

Here is how DMAIC contributes to a successful Lean Six Sigma deployment:

Define phase – in the Define phase, the project objectives and scope are clearly defined, aligning them with the organization's goals. This phase involves selecting improvement projects that have a significant impact on key performance metrics and customer satisfaction. The project charter is created to outline the project's scope, team members, timeline, and expected outcomes, ensuring clarity and accountability.

Measure phase – the Measure phase focuses on understanding the current state of the process, gathering relevant data, and establishing baseline performance metrics. Data collection plans and measurement systems are developed and validated to ensure accuracy. This phase sets the foundation for subsequent analysis and improvement activities.

Analyze phase – during the Analyze phase, data is thoroughly analyzed to identify the root causes of the problems and process variation. Tools such as Pareto charts, cause-and-effects diagrams, and statistical analysis are employed to pinpoint critical factors influencing process performance. A deeper understanding of the process helps in prioritizing improvement opportunities.

Improve phase – in the Improve phase, solutions are generated, evaluated, and implemented to address the identified root causes. Lean principles are incorporated to eliminate waste, streamline processes, and enhance efficiency. Improvement ideas are tested on a small-scale using pilot projects before full-scale implementation. This phase focuses on achieving the desired process improvements.

Control phase – the Control phase ensures that the improvements achieved in the Improve phase are sustained over time. Control plans are developed to monitor key performance metrics, and standard operating procedures are put into place to maintain process consistency. This phase establishes a system for ongoing monitoring and continuous feedback to prevent process regression.

By following the DMAIC roadmap, organizations can effectively deploy Lean Six Sigma principles throughout their operations. The DMAIC methodology provides a common language and framework for improvement projects, fostering a culture of continuous improvement. This structured approach helps organizations achieve tangible results, enhance customer satisfaction, reduce defects optimize processes, and drive positive bottom-line impact.

THE IMPACT OF THE LEAN SIX SIGMA DMAIC METHODOLOGY

The Lean Six Sigma DMAIC methodology has had a significant impact on various industries and organizations since its inception, including the aviation and aerospace industries. Because of its data-driven approach to problem solving, it has proved superior for improving quality by identifying and eliminating defects, reducing variability, and enhancing overall efficiency. Table 4.1 captures some key DMAIC impacts for general industries and for the aviation and aerospace industries as well.

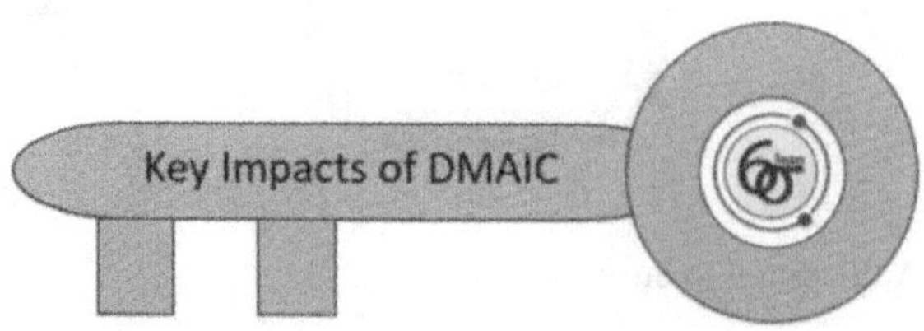

Table 4.1 Key Impacts of DMAIC

General Industries	• *Aviation and Aerospace Industries*
• Improved Process Efficiency and Quality	• Enhanced Safety
• Data-Driven Decision-Making	• Reduced Maintenance Costs
• Reduction in Variation	• Improved Supply Chain Management
• Increased Customer Satisfaction	• Optimized Fuel Efficiency
• Cultural Shift Towards Continuous Improvement	• Enhanced Quality Control
• Cost Reduction	• Efficient Project Management
• Employee Engagement and Empowerment	• Streamlined Certification Processes
• Standardization of Processes	• Enhanced Customer Satisfaction
• Support Strategic Objectives	• Innovation and Continuous Improvement
• Transferable Skills	• Human Factors and Training

The Lean Six Sigma DMAIC methodology has had a significant and positive impact on general industries as well as the aviation and aerospace industries by enhancing safety, reducing costs, improving efficiency, and fostering a culture of continuous improvement. It has aided these sectors in addressing complex challenges, optimizing processes, and delivering high-quality products and services to the customer. However, its impact can vary depending upon the organization's commitment to implementation, the complexity of the processes being addressed, and the skill level of the teams involved. Successful implementation of the Lean Six Sigma DMAIC methodology requires strong leadership, proper training, and a willingness to embrace a culture of continuous improvement.

SUMMARY

Chapter 4 served as a transition into Part II by introducing the reader to the Lean Six Sigma DMAIC (define, measure, analyze, improve and control) methodology used in the execution of Lean Six Sigma projects. It began by defining each DMAIC phase and addressed the question as to "why" to use DMAIC as a project execution methodology. It then addressed "when" to use the DMAIC methodology, "how" to select projects in which to use it, and implementation options. It then addressed the problem-solving attributes of the DMAIC methodology and guided the reader, by roadmap example, through the execution of a project and the different phases in which each step is executed. The chapter concluded with a discussion of the significant impacts the use of the Lean Six Sigma DMAIC methodology has had in the general industry and aviation and aerospace industry environments as the ultimate problem-solving tool.

CHAPTER 4 DISCUSSION QUESTIONS

1 Define and describe the five phases of the DMAIC process and elaborate on each phase's key elements.

2 Describe what you feel are five of the most important criteria that should be considered when selecting the right DMAIC project. Support your choices!
3 Describe why DMAIC is considered the "ultimate" problem-solving tool by Lean Six Sigma practitioners. Support your answer with an example.
4 Describe by phase how the DMAIC methodology serves as a roadmap for a successful Lean Six Sigma project deployment.
5 Select five of the key impacts of using the DMAIC methodology in the aviation and aerospace industries and describe by example how they contribute to success.

BIBLIOGRAPHY

Antony, Jiju, et al. "Using six sigma DMAIC for lean project management in education: A case study in a German kindergarten." *Total Quality Management & Business Excellence* 33.13–14 (2022): 1489–1509.

Basu, Ron. *Implementing Six Sigma and Lean*. Routledge, 2009.

Berardinelli, Carl F. "TO DMAIC or not to DMAIC?." *Quality Progress* 45.11 (2012): 72.

Chandel, Rohit, and Santosh Kumar. "Productivity enhancement using DMAIC approach: A case study." *International Journal of Enhanced Research in Science, Technology & Engineering* 5.1 (2016): 112–116.

Condé, Giovanni Cláudio Pinto, et al. "Defect reduction using DMAIC and lean six sigma: A case study in a manufacturing car parts supplier." *International Journal of Quality & Reliability Management* 40.9 (2023): 2184–2204. https://doi.org/10.1108/ijqrm-05-2022-0157

Daniyan, Ilesanmi, et al. "Application of lean six sigma methodology using DMAIC approach for the improvement of bogie assembly process in the railcar industry." *Heliyon* 8.3 (2022).

De Mast, Jeroen, and Joran Lokkerbol. "An analysis of the six sigma DMAIC method from the perspective of problem solving." *International Journal of Production Economics* 139.2 (2012): 604–614.

Flifel, Abdalhkeim F. A., Nebojša Zakić, and Aleksandra Tornjanski. "Identification and selection of six sigma projects." *Journal of Process Management and New Technologies* 5.2 (2017).

Furterer, Sandra L. *A Framework Roadmap for Implementing Lean Six Sigma in Local Governmental Entities*. University of Central Florida, 2004.

Girmanová, Lenka, et al. "Application of six sigma using DMAIC methodology in the process of product quality control in metallurgical operation." *Acta Technologica Agriculturae* 20.4 (2017): 104–109.

Hwang, Yeong-Dong. "The practices of integrating manufacturing execution systems and six sigma methodology." *The International Journal of Advanced Manufacturing Technology* 31 (2006): 145–154.

Jirasukprasert, Ploytip, et al. "A six sigma and DMAIC application for the reduction of defects in a rubber gloves manufacturing process." *International Journal of Lean Six Sigma* 5.1 (2014): 2–21.

Knapp, Susan. "Lean six sigma implementation and organizational culture." *International Journal of Health Care Quality Assurance* 28.8 (2015): 855–863.

Kumar, Maneesh, Jiju Antony, and Byung Rae Cho. "Project selection and its impact on the successful deployment of six sigma." *Business Process Management Journal* 15.5 (2009): 669–686.

Kumar, Sameer, and Michael Sosnoski. "Using DMAIC six sigma to systematically improve shopfloor production quality and costs." *International Journal of Productivity and Performance Management* 58.3 (2009): 254–273.

Kumaravadivel, A., and U. Natarajan. "Application of six-sigma DMAIC methodology to sand-casting process with response surface methodology." *The International Journal of Advanced Manufacturing Technology* 69.5–8 (2013): 1403–1420.

Lynch, Donald P., Suzanne Bertolino, and Elaine Cloutier. "How to scope DMAIC projects." *Quality Progress* 36.1 (2003): 37–41.

Mandal, Pathik. "Improving process improvement: Executing the analyze and improve phases of DMAIC better." *International Journal of Lean Six Sigma* 3.3 (2012): 231–250.

Nagi, Ayman, and Safwan Altarazi. "Integration of value stream map and strategic layout planning into DMAIC approach to improve carpeting process." *Journal of Industrial Engineering and Management (JIEM)* 10.1 (2017): 74–97.

Nowotarski, Piotr, Pawel Szymanski, and Patrycja Rzepecka. "DMAIC method of quality improvement of ground works processes: case study." In *IOP Conference Series: Earth and Environmental Science*. Vol. 221. No. 1. IOP Publishing, 2019.

Prabu, K., et al. "Six sigma implementation through DMAIC: A case study." *International Journal of Process Management and Benchmarking* 3.3 (2013): 386–400.

Rahman, Abdur, et al. "Application of six sigma using define measure analyze improve control (DMAIC) methodology in garment sector." *Independent Journal of Management & Production* 9.3 (2018): 810–826.

Rathi, Rajeev, Dinesh Khanduja, and S. Sharma. "A fuzzy MADM approach for project selection: A six sigma case study." *Decision Science Letters* 5.2 (2016): 255–268.

Ray, Sanjit, and Prasun Das. "Six Sigma project selection methodology." *International Journal of Lean Six Sigma* 1.4 (2010): 293–309.

Shokri, Alireza, and Gendao Li. "Green implementation of lean six sigma projects in the manufacturing sector." *International Journal of Lean Six Sigma* 11.4 (2020): 711–729.

Snee, Ronald D. "Use DMAIC to make improvement part of 'the way we work'." *Quality Progress* 40.9 (2007): 52–54.

Sreedharan V, Raja, and Vijaya Sunder M. "A novel approach to lean six sigma project management: A conceptual framework and empirical application." *Production Planning & Control* 29.11 (2018): 895–907.

Timans, Werner, et al. "Implementation of lean six sigma in small-and medium-sized manufacturing enterprises in the Netherlands." *Journal of the Operational Research Society* 63.3 (2012): 339–353.

Uluskan, Meryem. "A comprehensive insight into the six sigma DMAIC toolbox." *International Journal of Lean Six Sigma* 7.4 (2016): 406–429.

Part II

The Define Phase of DMAIC

5
The Process Mindset; Identifying the Value Streams

LEARNING OBJECTIVES

1 Distinguish between the different phases of the DMAIC methodology and describe the activities that occur during the Define phase.
2 Explain process thinking and define the elements of a SIPOC (suppliers, inputs, process, outputs, and customers) map, demonstrating its construction.
3 Differentiate between value-added and non–value-added activities in a value stream.
4 Construct a process activity flow chart and a swim lane chart and define their key elements.
5 Describe the "eight types of waste" and analyze the differences between physical and virtual flows using spaghetti charting.

Chapter 5 builds upon Chapter 4 introduction of the DMAIC methodology and takes a deep dive into each of the five phases, starting with the Define phase. Figure 5.1 shows a model that captures the essences of what is accomplished while using the DMAIC methodology. A breakout of the Define phase contains the activities/steps normally accomplished during phase execution. Each activity/step will be addressed as we move through the discussion, but first let us start with a discussion of obtaining the right mindset to start the DMAIC methodology.

Process Thinking and Value Stream Mapping

"Process thinking" and "value stream" are concepts often used within organizations to analyze and improve the efficiency and effectiveness of their processes. Both concepts emphasize a systematic and structured approach to understanding, analyzing, and optimization, and each is often used in the context of Lean Six Sigma projects and DMAIC methodology.

DOI: 10.4324/9781032650531-7

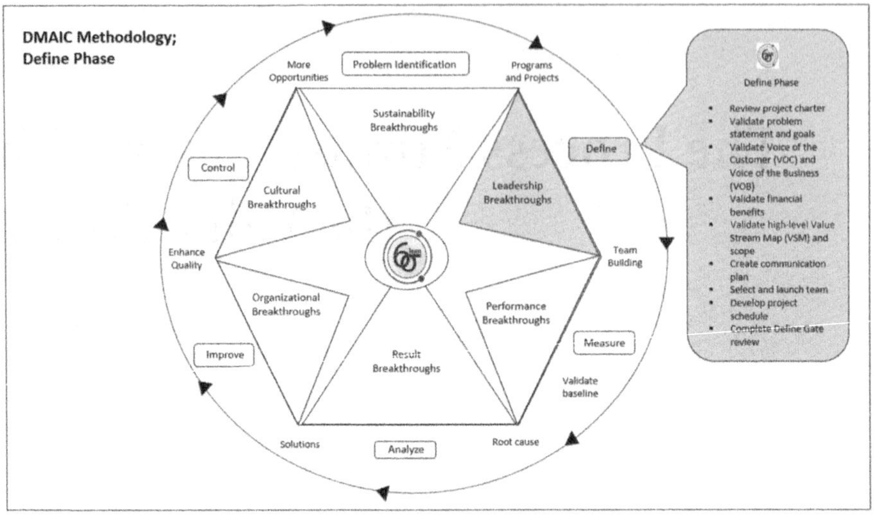

Figure 5.1 DMAIC Methodology: Define Phase

Process Thinking

Process thinking is an approach that focuses on understanding and optimizing the flow of work or activities within an organization. It involves viewing that organization as a series of interconnected processes rather than isolated functions. The key idea is to recognize that value is created by processes and that organizational performance can be enhanced by improving these processes. Principles upon which process thinking is built are:

- Focused on an end-to-end view – instead of focusing on individual tasks or departments, process thinking looks at the entire flow of work from start to finish. It emphasizes understanding how different tasks and activities are interconnected and contribute to achieving the overall goals of the organization.
- Focused on customer value – processes should be designed and improved with a focus on delivering value to the customer. By identifying and eliminating non-value activities, organizations can streamline their processes and enhance customer satisfaction.
- Focused on continuous improvement – process thinking encourages a mindset of continuous improvement. Organizations should regularly assess their processes, identify bottlenecks or inefficiencies, and seek ways to make incremental enhancements.
- Focused on collaboration – since processes often span different functions and departments, collaboration and communication between these areas are crucial for optimizing the flow of work.

Incorporating Relevant Elements Using SIPOC Mapping

SIPOC mapping is a valuable tool used in process improvement and management to clarify and document key elements of a process. The acronym SIPOC stands for SIPOC. It provides a structured framework for understanding the various components of a process and their relationships. Here is how each component of the SIPOC is assessed:

1 Suppliers – identify the entities or sources that provide the necessary inputs for your process. These could be individuals, departments, external vendors, or even other systems that contribute to the process being examined.

   As an example, if you are mapping the process of manufacturing a product, suppliers could include raw material suppliers, component manufacturers, and even internal departments that provide essential support.

2 Inputs list the specific items, data, or resources necessary to initiate and execute the process. Inputs are the materials and information that the process needs to transform into outputs.

   Still using the manufacturing example, inputs could encompass raw materials, design specifications, quality standards, and any other relevant data needed to create the product.

3 Process – detail the steps and activities involved in the process. This section outlines the sequence of actions that convert the inputs outputs. It helps provide clarity on how the process works.

   For the manufacturing example process, you would describe each step involved in transforming the raw materials and components into the final product. This could include tasks like assembly, testing, quality control, and packaging.

4 Outputs – define the end results or products that the process generates. Outputs are what the customers receive as value from the process.

   Using the manufacturing process example, outputs would refer to the finished products ready for distribution. This could include quantities produced, product specifications, and any accompanying documentation.

5 Customers – identify the recipients or stakeholders who receive the outputs of the process. Customers can be internal or external, and they are the ones who benefit from the process outputs.

   For the manufacturing process example, customers might include distributors, retailers, and end customers who purchase and use the products.

To incorporate relevant elements using SIPOC mapping, here are steps I have used that work well:

- Identify the process – choose the specific process you want to map, such as a manufacturing process, service delivery, information flow, or a call center escalation process.
- Gather the information – gather relevant data from various sources, to include documentation, stakeholders, and subject matter experts.
- Populate the SIPOC template – create a SIPOC table with columns for SIPOC. Each column should be filled with the relevant information you have gathered.
- Review and validate – review the completed SIPOC map with stakeholders and subject matter experts to ensure accuracy and completeness.
- Identify improvement opportunities – analyze the SIPOC map to identify potential areas for improvement, such as streamlining processes, reducing waste, or enhancing customer satisfaction.

Help Desk SIPOC Map

Suppliers	Inputs	Process	Outputs	Customer
Customer	Problem or issue	Call help desk	Open request information	Help desk level -1 support staff
Customer	Information request	Get requested information	Package requested information	Requested information received by customer
Level -1 support	Problem, issue, or request unknown	Request and save information	Register request and requester in Ll.xls	Status feedback to customer
Level -1 support	Problem, issue, or request known	E-mail request to level - 2 support	Known request	Status feedback to customer
Level - 2 support	Problem, issue, or request unknown	Get and evaluate request from level -1 support	Evaluated request	Status feedback to customer
Level - 2 support	Problem, issue, or request	Prioritize and save registration	Register request and requester in L2.xls	Requested information received by customer

Figure 5.2 Help Desk SIPOC Map

SIPOC mapping helps provide a comprehensive overview of a process and serves as a foundation for more in-depth process analysis and improvement initiatives. It enhances communications, highlights dependencies, and fosters a better understanding of how different elements contribute to an overall process. Figure 5.2 illustrates a SIPOC map developed for a help desk client. In this case, the SIPOC mapping process preceded the overall value stream mapping (VSM) development for the client.

Value Stream Mapping

A value stream is the sequence of activities that a product or service goes through from the beginning (customer demand) to the end (delivery to the customer). The concept is central to Lean Six Sigma process thinking, with its focus on minimizing waste (non–value-added) activities and maximizing (value-added) activities for customers. Through value stream mapping, the flow of materials, information, and other necessary activities can be visualized within a process flow. Principles upon which VSM is built are:

- Focus on value – the primary objective is to identify and enhance the value-added steps within a process. Value is defined from the perspective of the customer: any activity that directly contributes to meeting customer needs and requirements.
- End-to-end perspective – VSM looks at the entire value stream, from the initial raw materials to the delivery of the final product or service to the customer. It involves mapping the flow of materials, information, and actions across departments and functions.
- Current state mapping – this involves creating a visual representation of the current state of the value stream, including all the steps, activities, inputs, outputs, cycle times, and any bottlenecks or delays.
- Identify value-added and non–value-added activities – value-added activities directly contribute to meeting customer needs, while non–value-added activities do not. These can include waiting, unnecessary movement, overproduction, and defects. The goal is to minimize or eliminate non–value-added activities.
- Flow and lead time – VSM focuses on analyzing the flow of work through the value stream and the time it takes to complete the process (lead time). This analysis helps identify areas where work is piling up, causing delays, and where improvements can be made to streamline the flow.
- Continuous improvement – VSM is a tool for continuous improvement. It encourages ongoing efforts to identify and eliminate waste, improve efficiency, and enhance the value delivered to customers.
- Collaboration and cross-functional teams – VSM involve collaboration among various departments and functions that contribute to the value stream. Cross-functional teams work together to identify and solve problems, share insights, and develop solutions.
- Visual representation – VSM is typically created using symbols and icons to visually represent different process steps, materials, information flow, and other relevant aspects. Additionally, visual representation makes it easier to understand and communicate complex processes.
- Customer-centric approach – VSM is driven by the need to meet customer demands and expectations efficiently. The focus is on delivering value to the customer while minimizing waste and non–value-added activities.

By applying these principles, organizations can identify opportunities for improvement, optimize processes, and create more efficient and effective value streams, leading to increased customer satisfaction and organizational success.

Developing a Value Stream Map

Value streams can be evaluated by developing a value stream map. VSMs are a powerful tool used in Lean Six Sigma and process improvement to analyze and optimize the flow of materials, information, and activities within a process. A value stream map provides a holistic view of the current state of a process, highlights areas of waste and inefficiency, and guides efforts to design a future and in some cases a to-be state with improved performance. Here is a step-by-step guide on how to construct one:

First, identify the process – select the specific process or workflow that requires mapping. It could be a manufacturing process, service delivery, product development, or any other series of interconnected activities.

Second, define the scope – clearly define the boundaries of the process you are mapping. Determine where the process starts and ends and identify any major inputs and outputs.

Third, gather data – collect information about the process, including cycle times, lead times, workloads, process steps, and data related to inventory, demand, and performance.

Fourth, draw the current state map – use a large, blank sheet of paper or specialized software to draw your value stream map. The map typically consists of the following components:

- Customer – represents the customer or end user of the process on the right side of the map.
- Supplier – depict the supplier or source of input on the left side of the map.
- Value-added activities – draw rectangles to represent each value-added activity in the process. Label these rectangles with the activity name, cycle time, and quantity.
- Non–value-added activities (waste) – use triangles to represent each non–value-added activity. This would include one of the eight identified wastes that will be addressed later in this chapter.
- Information flow – include arrows to show the flow of information, materials, and products between process steps, departments, or functions.
- Data boxes – use data boxes to display relevant metrics, such as cycle times, lead times, and inventory levels, at each process step.
- Timeline – add a timeline at the bottom of the map to show the overall time taken for the process.

Fifth, analyze the current state – study the completed current state map to identify bottlenecks, inefficiencies, waste, and areas where improvements can be made. Calculate cycle times, lead times, and process efficiency metrics.

Sixth, design the future state – collaborate with a cross-functional team to brainstorm and design a future state that eliminates waste, reduces cycle time and lead times, and enhances overall efficiency. Focus on creating a more streamlined and optimized process.

Seventh, draw the future state map – create a new VSM that depicts the envisioned future state of the process. Incorporate changes and improvements based on your analysis and brainstorming.

Eighth, develop an ideal state map if needed – this map will describe changes to the process in a perfect world if there are no barriers or inhibitors in the process (the perfect process).

Ninth, develop an action plan – identify the specific action items, project, or initiatives needed to transition from the current state to either the future or ideal state. Assign responsibilities, set timelines, and establish key performance indicators (KIPs) to measure progress.

Tenth, implement and continuously improve – initiate the action plan and monitor the progress of improvement. Regularly review the value stream map and adjust as necessary. Continuously seek opportunities for further optimization.

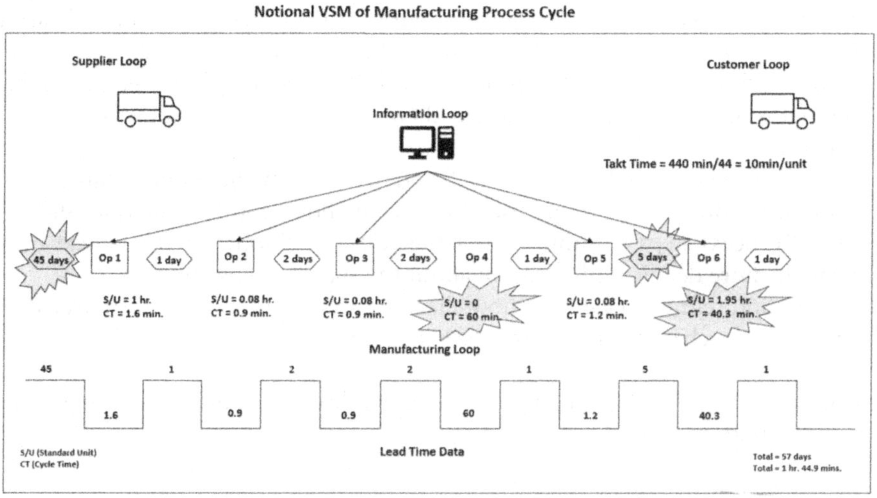

Figure 5.3 Notional VSM of Manufacturing Process Cycle

Creating a VSM is a collaborative effort that involves input from various stakeholders and team members. It provides a visual representation of the process, enabling a shared understanding of the current, future, and ideal states and guides efforts to eliminate waste and enhance value to the customer. Figure 5.3 provides a notional VSM of a manufacturing process measuring total and individual station cycle times.

It also integrates all respective layered loops to include supplier, information, manufacturing, and customer loops. While VSMs may vary in layout and icons used, one fundamental is consistent to each one developed: Each is designed to illustrate where bottlenecks exist and where non-valued activities are being performed.

Constructing Process Activity Flow Charts and Swim Lanes

Often when assessing process flows, process activity flow charts and swim line diagrams are effective visual tools for mapping and analyzing workflows, identifying bottlenecks, and improving processes.

Process Activity Flow Chart

A process activity flow chart visually represents the sequence of activities in a process, showing how inputs are transformed into outputs. It uses various symbols and shapes to depict different process steps. Typical steps that are followed when producing a process activity flow chart are:

- Identify the process – choose the process that requires mapping. Define the start and end points of the process.
- List the activities – break the process down into individual activities or tasks. These are the steps that contribute to the overall process. Rectangles are used to represent the flow of work.

- Sequence the activities – connect the activities in the order they occur, indicating the flow of work. Arrows are used to show the direction of the process.
- Add decision points – if the process involves decision-making points or branding paths, use diamonds to represent them. Label the diamonds with the decision criteria.
- Include inputs and outputs – for each activity, identify the inputs required and the outputs produced. Arrows are used to show the flow of inputs and outputs.
- Detail process steps – within each activity, use additional shapes or text boxes to provide more detailed information about the specific steps involved.
- Review and refine – review the flow chart for accuracy and clarity. Adjust as needed to ensure the chart accurately represents the process.

Figure 5.4 provides an example of a process activity flow chart for aircraft design effective in orienting program teams.

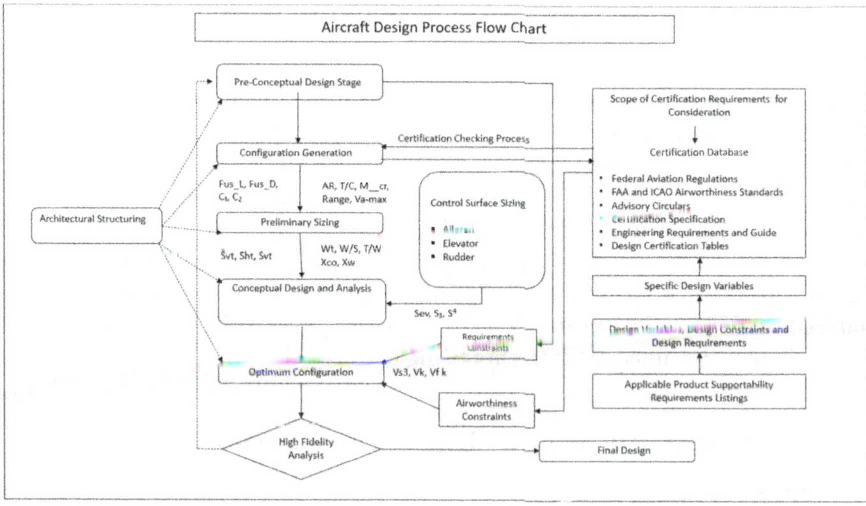

Figure 5.4 Aircraft Design Process Activity Flow Chart

Swim Lane Diagrams

A swim lane diagram, also called a cross-functional flowchart, also adds an additional layer of information by assigning process activities to specific roles, teams, or departments. Each "swim lane" represents a different entity responsible for specific tasks. Typical steps followed when developing a swim lane diagram are:

- Identify swim lanes – determine the categories or roles represented in the swim lane diagram. These might be departments, teams, individuals, external entities, or processes.
- Draw the swim lanes – draw horizontal lines across the diagram to create the swim lanes. Label each swim lane with the corresponding category or role.
- List activities – list the process activities in the appropriate swim lanes, based on the responsibilities of each category or role.

- Sequence activities – connect the activities within each swim lane to show the sequence of tasks. Use arrows to indicate the flow.
- Collaboration and handoffs – where activities involve multiple entities, show handoffs and collaboration by using arrows that cross swim lanes.
- Add decision points – like process flow activities, use diamonds to represent decision points.
- Collaboration and handoffs – where activities involve multiple entities, show handoffs and collaboration by using arrows that cross swim lanes.
- Add decision points – like process flow activities, use diamonds to represent decision points.
- Review and refine – review the swim lane diagram to ensure it accurately represents the process and interactions between activities.

Figure 5.5 provides an example of product ordering swim lane diagram that I have found effective in orienting project teams.

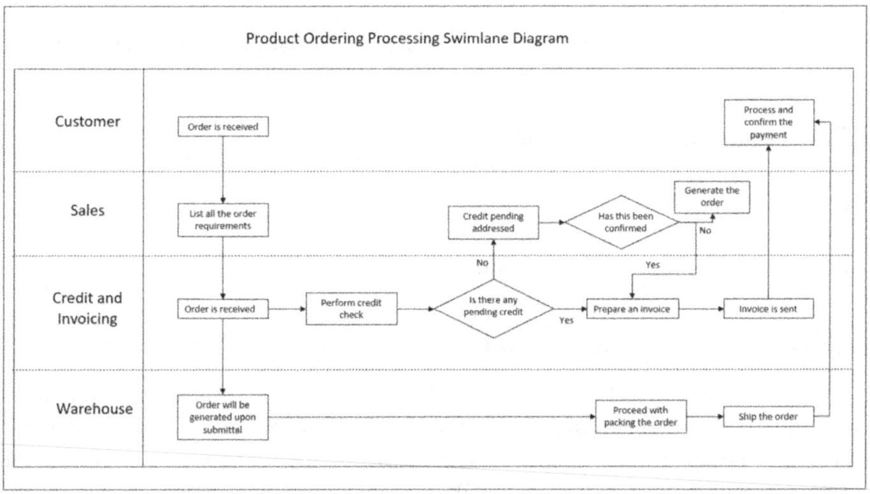

Figure 5.5 Product Ordering Processing Swim Lane Diagram

Both process activity flow charts and swim lane diagrams provide a clear visual representation of processes, helping team members and stakeholders understand the flow of work and responsibilities and provide areas for improvement. Depending on the complexity of the process and the level of detail needed, you can choose the most suitable diagramming approach. There are also various software tools available for creating the diagrams, such as Microsoft PowerPoint or Visio, Lucid chart, draw.io, and several others, which offer pre-made shapes and templates to facilitate the process.

Determining What Is Value Added and Non–Value Added

Determining what is value added and non–value added is a fundamental concept in process analysis and improvement, especially within Lean Six Sigma methodologies. Value-added activities contribute to the creation of value for the customer, while non–value-added activities are those that do not directly contribute to the product or service. Non–value-added activities are divided into two categories, one where they are classified as "waste" and one that, while activities do not directly enhance the product or service being provided, they are essential for compliance, risk management, or other legitimate reasons. We first examine value-added activities.

Value-Added Activities

Value-added activities are those that the customer is willing to pay for because they directly transform the product or service in a way that enhances its form, function, or quality. These activities move the process closer to delivering the final product to the customer. Basic characteristics of value-added activities include:

- Transformation – physically or logically alters the product or service. They change its shape, properties, or characteristics.
- Direct contribution – contribute directly to fulfilling customer requirements, needs, or expectations.
- Enhanced value – improves the perceived value of the product or service in the eyes of the customer.

Examples of value-added activities are:

1 Assembling parts to create a product like an aircraft.
2 Designing features that meet the customer's needs.
3 Performing quality checks to ensure product reliability.

Non–Value-Added Activities (Waste)

One of the key concepts in Lean Six Sigma thinking is the identification and elimination of the "Eight Wastes", which are common inefficiencies that can be found in processes. These wastes were originally identified as part of the Toyota production system and are often referred to using the acronym "DOWNTIME" with each letter corresponding to a waste. These non–value-added activities do not contribute to the creation of value for the customer. They do not alter the product or service in a meaningful way and can be eliminated or minimized to improve efficiency. Figure 5.6 provides an illustration of these eight wastes.

- Defects – errors or defects that require rework or corrections.
- Overproduction – creating more than is needed, leading to excess inventory.
- Waiting – idle time during which no value is being created.
- Non-utilized talent – not effectively using the skills of team staffing.
- Transportation – moving items between locations without changing their form or function.
- Inventory – storing excess materials, products, or information, tying up resources.
- Motion – unnecessary physical movement of people, equipment, or tools.
- Extra-processing – adding features or quality beyond what the customer requires.

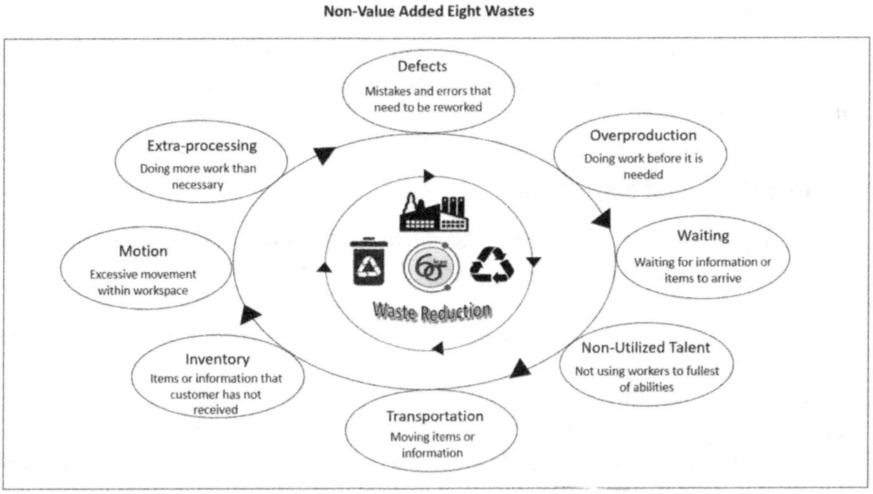

Figure 5.6 Non–Value-Added Eight Wastes

Examples of waste non–value-added activities are:

1 Waiting for approval.
2 Excessive inspections or testing.
3 Unnecessary paperwork or documentation.

Non–Value-Added Activities (Essential): while these activities may not directly enhance the product or service being provided, they are essential for compliance, risk management, and other legitimate reasons. Common types of these activities include:

- Regulatory compliance – certain industries, such as pharmaceuticals and aviation, must adhere to strict regulatory guidelines and documentation. While the documentation itself might not directly contribute to the product, it is necessary for legal compliance and customer safety.
- Safety procedures – manufacturing processes often include safety checks, protective gear, and other precautions. These measures might not directly contribute to product quality, but they are crucial for preventing accidents and ensuring worker safety.
- Quality assurance – while quality checks and inspections do not directly add value to the final product, they are necessary to ensure that the product meets the required standards and is free from defects.
- Documentation – keeping records, maintaining documentation, and archiving information might not add value to the product itself, but they are often necessary for traceability, auditing, and legal purposes.
- Redundancy and reliability – in critical aviation and aerospace systems or medical devices, redundancy and backup systems are often built in to ensure reliability and fail-safes. These redundancy measures might not add value from a customer's perspective but are necessary to prevent catastrophic failures.

- Administrative processes – administrative tasks like payroll, compliance reporting, and employee benefits management might not directly contribute to the core business operations, but they are essential for maintaining the organization's functionality.

Determining Value and Non-Value

When evaluating activities within a process, consider the following questions to determine if an activity is value added or non–value added:

1. Does the activity change the product? Does it alter the form, function, or properties of the product or service?
2. Is the customer willing to pay for it? Would the customer be willing to pay for this activity if they knew about it?
3. Does it fulfill a customer's need? Does the activity directly contribute to fulfilling customer requirements or expectations?
4. Does it enhance quality or functionality? Does the activity improve the quality, reliability, or functionality of the product?

By critically assessing each activity using questions such as these, you can better identify opportunities to eliminate or streamline non–value-added "waste" activities and focus resources on value-added tasks. For non–value-added "necessary" activities, efforts should still be made to streamline and optimize then. When engaged in waste reduction efforts, the focus should be on reducing the non–value-added activities while trying to increase the value-added activities. As illustrated in Figure 5.7, because a larger percentage of an activity is in fact waste, the return on invested time is greater when that portion of an activity is "attached" and reduced first; then value added activities can be worked on

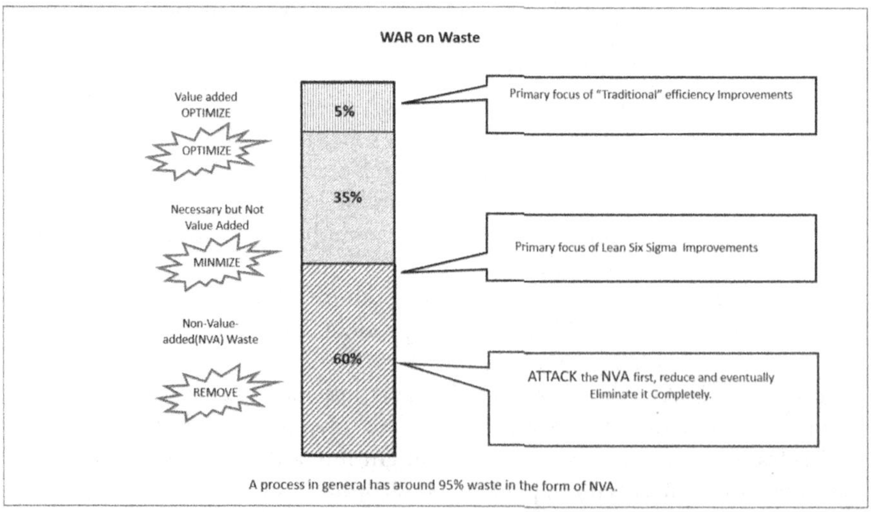

Figure 5.7 WAR on Waste

Using Spaghetti Charting to Map Physical and Virtual Flows

Spaghetti charting is a visual mapping technique used to analyze and improve the flow of materials, people, or information within a physical space. It is commonly employed in Lean Six Sigma and process improvement efforts to identify inefficiencies, redundances, and opportunities for optimization. While spaghetti charting is typically applied to physical flows, the concept can be adapted to map virtual flows as well. Here are the steps for spaghetti charting starting with the physical flow. Virtual flow spaghetti charting will follow.

Physical Flow Spaghetti Charting

- Select a process – choose a specific process or workflow that requires analysis. This could be a manufacturing line, a service delivery process, or any sequence of activities.
- Gather data – observe the actual movement of people, materials, or products involved in the chosen process. Record the paths taken by these elements.
- Analyze the chart – study the spaghetti chart to identify areas of congestion, unnecessary movement, bottlenecks, and long distances traveled.
- Identify improvement opportunities – based on your analysis, brainstorm ways to optimize the flow. Look for opportunities to reduce movement, streamline paths, and minimize inefficiencies.
- Implement changes – implement the identified improvements and monitor the impact on the flow. This could involve rearranging workstations, modifying layouts, or adjusting process sequences.

Figure 5.8 illustrates a physical flow spaghetti chart of a metal plating operation. It was developed to see how we could better design the flow of the product through the entire plating process.

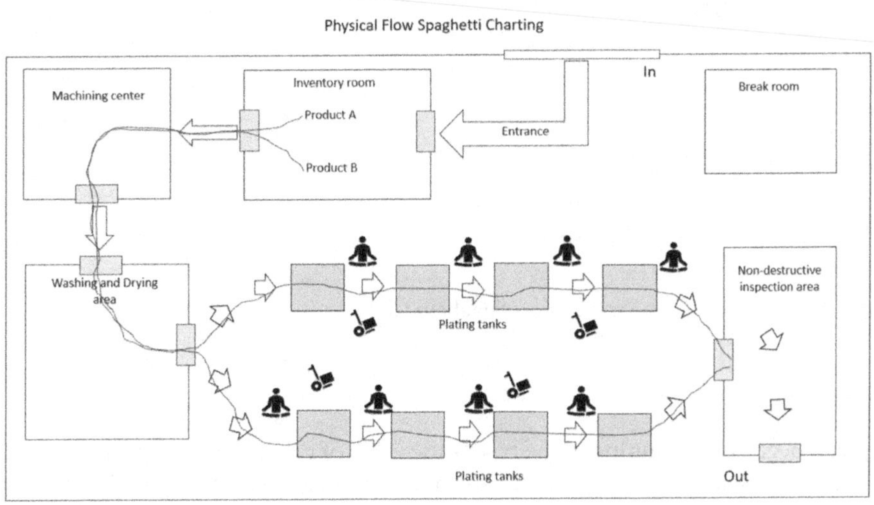

Figure 5.8 Physical Flow Spaghetti Chart

Virtual Flow Spaghetti Charting

- Select a virtual process – choose a virtual process or workflow that involves the movement of information or data. This could be an approval process, communication flows, or digital project management.
- Document information movement – record the sequence of steps, interactions, and handoffs that occur as information or data moves through the virtual process.
- Map information paths – create a visual representation of the information flow using diagrams, charts, or software tools. Use arrows and labels to illustrate the movement and interactions.
- Analyze and optimize – examine the virtual spaghetti chart to pinpoint delays, redundant steps, bottlenecks, and any other inefficiencies.
- Streamline the flow – propose changes to the virtual process to enhance efficiency. This could involve automating certain steps, simplifying decision-making, or clarifying communication channels.
- Implement and evaluate – put the improvements into practice and monitor the impact on the virtual flow. Regularly review and refine the process based on feedback and data.

Figure 5.9 illustrates a virtual flow spaghetti chart of a Hemming process that we were evaluating.

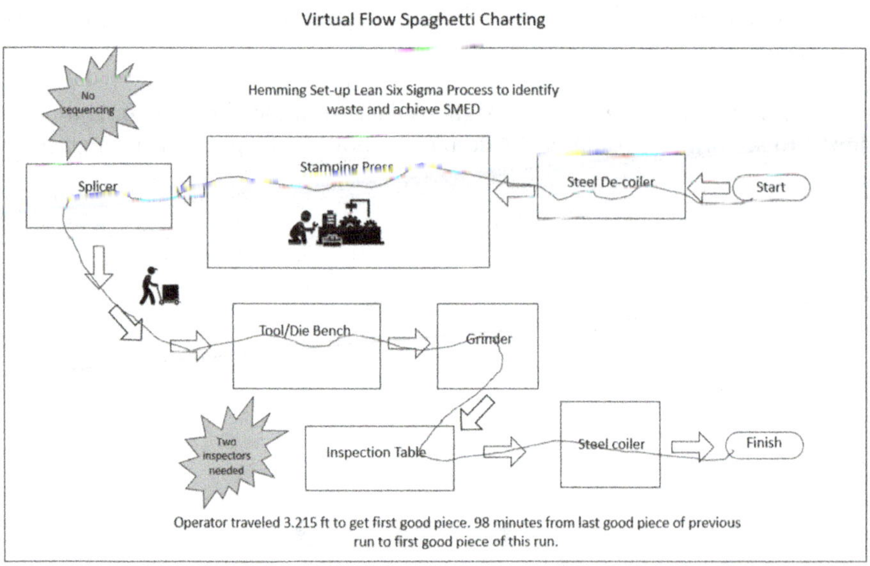

Figure 5.9 Hemming Setup Virtual Flow Spaghetti Chart

SUMMARY

Chapter 5 began by explaining to the reader the value of process thinking and the power of the value stream and described the process of developing one. It then detailed the process of developing a SIPOC mapping structure, along with the principal elements that should be assessed during its development. The reader was then presented the process by which a process activity flow chart is designed, along with swim lane charting. The chapter then addressed value-added and non–value-added activities and how they fit within the process mapping structure. This then led to a review of the classical eight waste elements and how non–value-added activities were broken down into "waste" and "necessary" categories. The subject of spaghetti charting for both physical and virtual flows was then reviewed to close the chapter.

LEAN SIX SIGMA AT WORK

Lean Six Sigma Tips

Problem solving is the isolation and analysis of a problem and the development of a permanent solution. The process followed in problem solving should be logical and systematic. The following are generally used Lean Six Sigma steps:

Step 1. Identify the problem and/or process.
Step 2. Define the requirements.
Step 3. Establish goals.
Step 4. Gather information about the current problem and/or process.
Step 5. Define and measure key process steps and inputs:

- Select appropriate metrics: key process output variables (KPOVs).
- Determine how these metrics will be tracked over time.
- Determine current baseline performance of problem and/or process.
- Determine the key process input variables (KPIVs) that drive the key process output variables.

Step 6. Identify potential root causes of the problem.
Step 7. Validate the cause-and-effect relationship.

- Determine what changes must be made to the key process input variables to positively affect input variables.

Step 8. Implement the solution to address the root causes of the problem.
Step 9. Test the solution(s).

- Determine whether the changes have positively affected the KPOVs.

Step 10. Measure results.
Step 11. Evaluate and monitor improvements.

- If the changes resulted in performance improvements, establish control of the KPIVs at the new levels.
- If the changes have not resulted in performance improvements, return to Step 5 and make appropriate changes.

CHAPTER 5 DISCUSSION QUESTIONS

1 Describe process thinking and elaborate on the principles upon which it is built.
2 Describe the purpose of the value stream map and how it is constructed.
3 Define and describe SIPOC mapping. How does it aid in clarifying key elements in a process?
4 Compare and contrast process activity flow charting and swim lane diagrams.
5 Define and give examples of value-added activities, non–value-added activities (waste), and non–value-added activities (essential).
6 Describe the differences between physical flow spaghetti charting and virtual flow spaghetti charting.

BIBLIOGRAPHY

Aggogeri, Francesco, and Marco Mazzola. "Combining six sigma with lean production to increase the performance level of a manufacturing system." *ASME International Mechanical Engineering Congress and Exposition* 48654 (2008).

Akinci, Burcu, Martin Fischer, and Todd Zabelle. "Proactive approach for reducing non-value adding activities due to time-space conflicts." In *Proceedings of the 6th Annual Conference of the International Group for Lean Construction*. Guaruja: IGLC, 1998.

Alwi, Sugiharto, Keith Hampson, and Sherif Mohamed. "Non value-adding activities: A comparative study of Indonesian and Australian construction projects." In *Proceedings of the 10th Conference of the International Group for Lean Construction*. Federal University of Rio Grande do Sul, 2002.

Al-Zubaidia, S. Q. D., E. Colib, and G. Fantonia. "Automating production process data acquisition towards spaghetti chart 4.0." *International Journal of Industrial Engineering & Management (IJIEM)* 13.3 (2022).

Andersen, Bjørn, Tom Fagerhaug, and Bjørnar Henriksen. *Mapping Work Processes*. Quality Press, 2002.

Armaya'u, Zango Umar, M. M. Gumel, and Hayat Suleiman Tuge. "Comparing flowchart and swim lane activity diagram for aiding transitioning to object-oriented implementation." *American Journal of Education and Technology* 1.2 (2022): 99–106.

Bakar, Noor Widasuria Abu, Shahrulniza Musa, and Abdul Hadi Mohamad. "A mini comparative study of requirements modelling diagrams towards swimlane: Evidence of enterprise resource planning system." *Journal of Physics: Conference Series* 1529.5 (2020). IOP Publishing.

Bayramzadeh, Sara, et al. "The impact of operating room layout on circulating nurse's work patterns and flow disruptions: A behavioral mapping study." *HERD: Health Environments Research & Design Journal* 11.3 (2018): 124–138.

Bogdan, Fleacă, and Corocăescu Mihai. "Process map to create added value to customer based on quality deployment function." *International Multidisciplinary Scientific GeoConference: SGEM* 17 (2017): 657–664.

Cantini, Alessandra, Filippo De Carlo, and Mario Tucci. "Towards forklift safety in a warehouse: An approach based on the automatic analysis of resource flows." *Sustainability* 12.21 (2020): 8949.

Capuano, Terry, et al. "Work flow analysis: Eliminating non–value-added work." *JONA: The Journal of Nursing Administration* 34.5 (2004): 246–256.

Carnaghan, Carla. "Business process modeling approaches in the context of process level audit risk assessment: An analysis and comparison." *International Journal of Accounting Information Systems* 7.2 (2006): 170–204.

Chiarini, Andrea. "Waste savings in patient transportation inside large hospitals using lean thinking tools and logistic solutions." *Leadership in Health Services* 26.4 (2013): 356–367.

Cuervo-Cazurra, Álvaro. "Sequence of value-added activities in the multinationalization of developing country firms." *Journal of international Management* 13.3 (2007): 258–277.

Deng, Jian, Bo Chen, and Jiazhi Zeng. "Model transformation method for compensation events and tasks from business process model to flowchart." In *Information Computing and Applications: Third International Conference, ICICA 2012, Chengde, China, September 14–16, 2012. Proceedings 3*. Berlin and Heidelberg: Springer, 2012.

Dettmer, H. William. *The Logical Thinking Process*. Quality Press, 2007.

Eisenreich, Anja, et al. "Toward a circular value chain: Impact of the circular economy on a company's value chain processes." *Journal of Cleaner Production* (2022): 134375.

Emblemsvåg, Jan, and Bert Bras. "Process thinking – a new paradigm for science and engineering." *Futures* 32.7 (2000): 635–654.

Emiliani, M. L., and D. J. Stec. "Using value-stream maps to improve leadership." *Leadership & Organization Development Journal* 25.8 (2004): 622–645.

Erlach, Klaus, and Klaus Erlach. *Value Stream Design*. Berlin and Heidelberg: Springer, 2013.

Falcone, Domenico, et al. "Material flow map and layout optimization: Action plan and software validation." *Proceedings of the XV Summer School "Francesco Turco" Impianti Industriali Meccanici, Porto Giardino, Monopoli, Italy* (2014): 14–18.

Fritzsche, Lars, et al. "Task-based digital human simulation with editor for manual work activities–industrial applications in product design and production planning." In *DHM and Posturography*. Academic Press, 2019, pp. 569–575.

Hadek, Amine, et al. "Sipoc model in Moroccan engineering education context: Lean approach." *International Journal of Education (IJE)* 7.1 (2019): 47–61.

Haekal, Jakfat, and Ibrahim Masood. "Lean manufacturing approach in pipe center cross production process." In *AIP Conference Proceedings*. Vol. 2680. No. 1. AIP Publishing, 2023.

Han, Sangwon, SangHyun Lee, and Feniosky Pena-Mora. "Identification and quantification of non-value-adding effort from errors and changes in design and construction projects." *Journal of Construction Engineering and Management* 138.1 (2012): 98–109.

Helmold, Marc. "Waste and value-added." In *Lean Management and Kaizen: Fundamentals from Cases and Examples in Operations and Supply Chain Management*. Cham: Springer International Publishing, 2020, pp. 31–44.

Hines, Peter, et al. "Value stream management." *The International Journal of Logistics Management* 9.1 (1998): 25–42.

Hines, Peter, Nick Rich, and Ann Esain. "Value stream mapping: A distribution industry application." *Benchmarking: An International Journal* 6.1 (1999): 60–77.

Holt, Robert R. *Primary Process Thinking: Theory, Measurement, and Research*. Jason Aronson, Inc., 2008.

Improta, Giovanni, et al. "Lean thinking to improve emergency department throughput at AORN Cardarelli hospital." *BMC Health Services Research* 18 (2018): 1–9.

Irani, Shahrukh A., and Jin Zhou. "Value stream mapping of a complete product." *Department of Industrial, Welding and Systems Engineering, The Ohio State University, Columbus, OH* 43210 (2011).

Jeyaraj, A., and Sauter, V. L. "Validation of business process models using swimlane diagrams." *Journal of Information Technology Management* 25.4 (2014): 27–37.

Jum'a, Luay. "The effect of value-added activities of key suppliers on the performance of manufacturing firms." *Polish Journal of Management Studies* 22.1 (2020): 231–246.

Keyte, Beau, and Drew A. Locher. *The Complete Lean Enterprise: Value Stream Mapping for Administrative and Office Processes*. CRC Press, 2004.

Kogut, Bruce. "Designing global strategies: Comparative and competitive value-added chains." *Sloan Management Review (pre-1986)* 26.4 (1985): 15.

Kuhlang, Peter, et al. "Systematic improvement of value streams–fundamentals of value stream oriented process management." *International Journal of Productivity and Quality Management* 12.1 (2013): 1–17.

Lacerda, António Pedro, Ana Raquel Xambre, and Helena Maria Alvelos. "Applying value stream mapping to eliminate waste: A case study of an original equipment manufacturer for the automotive industry." *International Journal of Production Research* 54.6 (2016): 1708–1720.

Langley, Ann. "Process thinking in strategic organization." *Strategic Organization* 5.3 (2007): 271–282.

Lovelle, Jared. "Mapping the value stream." *IIE Solutions* 33.2 (2001): 26–33.

McManus, Hugh, and Richard Millard. "Value stream analysis and mapping for product development." 2002. http://hdl.handle.net/1721.1/84146

Meng, Yudong, et al. "Improvement for oxidative stability and sensory properties of sunflower oil flavored by Huai Chrysanthemum× morifolium Ramat. Essential oil during accelerated storage." *Processes* 9.7 (2021): 1199.

Michalos, George, et al. "Workplace analysis and design using virtual reality techniques." *CIRP Annals* 67.1 (2018): 141–144.

Mishra, Pratima, and Rajiv Kumar Sharma. "A hybrid framework based on SIPOC and six sigma DMAIC for improving process dimensions in supply chain network." *International Journal of Quality & Reliability Management* 31.5 (2014): 522–546.

Ng, K. C., et al. "Elimination of waste through value Add/Non value add process analysis to improve cost productivity in manufacturing – A case study." In *2013 IEEE International Conference on Industrial Engineering and Engineering Management*. IEEE, 2013.

Noto, Guido, and Federico Cosenz. "Introducing a strategic perspective in lean thinking applications through system dynamics modelling: The dynamic value stream map." *Business Process Management Journal* 27.1 (2021): 306–327.

Nshirim, Ekechi Sixtus, and Urenna Nwagwu. "Integrated approach for process improvement: Value engineering, lean methodology, SIPOC, and value stream mapping." *International Journal of Applied and Natural Sciences* 1.1 (2023): 58–66.

Patkar, Vivek, Matthew South, and Richard Thomson. "From guidelines to careflows: Modelling and supporting complex clinical processes." *Computer-Based Medical Guidelines and Protocols: A Primer and Current Trends* 139 (2008): 44.

Pereira Librelato, Tatiane, et al. "A process improvement approach based on the value stream mapping and the theory of constraints thinking process." *Business Process Management Journal* 20.6 (2014): 922–949.

Rodrigues, Roberto W. S. "Formalising UML activity diagrams using finite state processes." In *Proceedinga of the 3rd International Conference on the Unified Modeling Language*. York, UK, 2000.

Rodrigues, Rosiane Pinheiro, et al. "Descriptor flowchart of the work process: Tool to strengthen primary health care." *Saúde em Debate* 43 (2020): 109–116.

Rother, Mike, and John Shook. *Learning to See: Value Stream Mapping to Add Value and Eliminate Muda*. Lean Enterprise Institute, 2003.

Royer, Jeffrey S. "Potential for cooperative involvement in vertical coordination and value-added activities." *Agribusiness* 11.5 (1995): 473–481.

Sabir, Brahim, et al. "Using the integrated management system and approach SIPOC in higher education for the evaluation and improving the quality of life of students." *The Online Journal of Quality in Higher Education* 2.3 (2015): 141.

Singh, Jagdeep, et al. "Evaluating lean thinking using value stream mapping in manufacturing industry-a case study." *International Journal of Productivity and Quality Management* 22.1 (2017): 101–116.

Singh, Paramdeep, and Harpuneet Singh. "Application of lean tool (value stream mapping) in minimisation of the non-value added waste (a case study of tractor industry)." *Applied Mechanics and Materials* 110 (2012): 2062–2066.

Stridh, Madeleine. "Material flow: An analysis of a production area for improved material flow." Independent Thesis from Lulea University of Technology, 2020. https://www.diva-portal.org/smash/record.jsf?pid=diva2%3A1452965&dswid=2518

Teichgräber, Ulf K., and Maximilian De Bucourt. "Applying value stream mapping techniques to eliminate non–value-added waste for the procurement of endovascular stents." *European Journal of Radiology* 81.1 (2012): e47–e52.

Thürer, Matthias, Ivan Tomašević, and Mark Stevenson. "On the meaning of 'waste': Review and definition." *Production Planning & Control* 28.3 (2017): 244–255.

Toivonen, Teemu, and Juha Siitonen. "Value stream analysis for complex processes and systems." *Procedia CIRP* 39 (2016): 9–15.

Tyagi, Satish, et al. "Value stream mapping to reduce the lead-time of a product development process." *International Journal of Production Economics* 160 (2015): 202–212.

Verdiyanti, Rizka Tri, and Rovilla El-Maghviroh. "The analysis of manufacturing cycle effectiveness (MCE) in reducing non added-value activities (Empirical study at PT. Bhirawa Steel Surabaya)." *The Indonesian Accounting Review* 3.2 (2013): 149–160.

Vinodh, S., et al. "Development of value stream map for an Indian automotive components manufacturing organization." *Journal of Engineering, Design and Technology* 13.3 (2015): 380–399.

Vinodh, S., M. Somanaathan, and K. R. Arvind. "Development of value stream map for achieving leanness in a manufacturing organization." *Journal of Engineering, Design and Technology* 11.2 (2013): 129–141.

Wahl, Terje, and Guttorm Sindre. "An analytical evaluation of BPMN using a semiotic quality framework." In *Advanced Topics in Database Research*. Vol. 5. IGI Global, 2006, pp. 94–105.

White, Stephen A. "Introduction to BPMN." *Ibm Cooperation* 2.0 (2004).

Wilson, Kristy J., and Bessie Rigakos. "Scientific process flowchart assessment (SPFA): A method for evaluating changes in understanding and visualization of the scientific process in a multidisciplinary student population." *CBE – Life Sciences Education* 15.4 (2016): ar63.

Winkelmann, Axel, and Burkhard Weiß. "Automatic identification of structural process weaknesses in flow chart diagrams." *Business Process Management Journal* 17.5 (2011): 787–807.

Wohed, Petia, et al. "On the suitability of BPMN for business process modelling." In *Business Process Management: 4th International Conference, BPM 2006, Vienna, Austria, September 5–7, 2006. Proceedings 4*. Berlin and Heidelberg: Springer, 2006.

Womack, Jim, and Dan Jones. *Seeing the Whole Value Stream*. Lean Enterprise Institute, 2011.

Yeung, Shirley M. C. "Integrating SIPOC into programme management for quality assurance." *International Journal of Management in Education* 4.2 (2010): 159–172.

Zhang, Feng, et al. "Flow chart generation-based source code similarity detection using process mining." *Scientific Programming* 2020 (2020): 1–15.

6 Understanding Customer Requirements

LEARNING OBJECTIVES

1. Explain the act of "active listening" to the voice of the customer and its importance in understanding customer needs.
2. Describe customer-driven activities and analyze how they impact customer satisfaction.
3. Apply Kano analysis to evaluate customer requirements and expectations, providing an example of its use.
4. Explain how data sources are used to gather customer requirements and analyze the process of deriving and using a sampling frame in the sampling process.
5. Describe how quality function deployment translates "critical to quality" requirements into specifications and explain the role of affinity diagramming in grouping customer data.

"LISTENING" TO THE VOICE OF THE CUSTOMER

"Listening" to the voice of the customer (VOC) refers to the process of actively gathering, understanding, and analyzing customer feedback, opinions, preferences, and concerns about a product, service, or brand. It is a crucial practice for organizations to better understand their customers' needs and expectations and to make informed decisions to improve their offerings. Figure 6.1 illustrates ten key points to consider when "listening" to the voice of the customer.

Here is an explanation as to how each of the ten points are employed and what they contribute to understanding the customers' wants and needs.

- Feedback channels – Collect customer feedback through various channels, including surveys, online reviews, social media, customer support interactions, and focus groups.
- Customer-centric approach – the focus should be on understanding the customer's perceptive rather than imposing assumptions. This involves actively seeking feedback and valuing customer opinions.

DOI: 10.4324/9781032650531-8

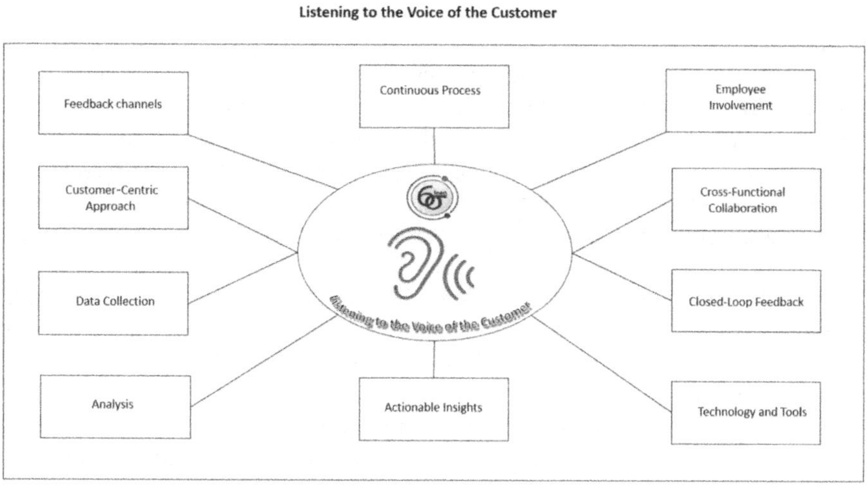

Figure 6.1 Listening to the Voice of the Customer

- Data collection – gather both qualitative and quantitative data. Qualitative data includes open-ended responses that provide insights into the customer's emotions, opinions, and experiences, while quantitative data involves numerical metrics and ratings.
- Analysis – analyze the collected data to identify patterns and common themes. This helps in uncovering both positive aspects that customers appreciate and areas that need improvement.
- Actionable insight – use the insights from customer feedback to drive meaningful changes. This might involve refining products, enhancing services, or addressing pain points.
- Continuous process – "listening" to the voice of the customer is an ongoing process. Customer preferences and needs can change over time; it is important to consistently gather and analyze feedback.
- Employee involvement – encourage employees to actively listen to customers. Customer-facing employees having direct contact with the customer can provide valuable and timely insights.
- Cross-functional collaboration – involves various departments such as marketing, product development, and customer service in the process. This ensures a holistic understanding and implementation of customer feedback.
- Closed-loop feedback – establish mechanisms to communicate back to customers about the actions taken based on their feedback. This enhances transparency and shows customers that their opinions are valued.
- Technology and tools – leverage technology, such as sentiment analysis tools and customer feedback platforms, to streamline the process of gathering and analyzing feedback.

"Listening" to the voice of the customer is not just about collecting feedback; it is about actively engaging with customers, understanding their needs, and using that information to drive improvements that can lead to increased customer satisfaction and loyalty.

Customer engagement necessitates that the voice of the customer be elevated within the organization so that customer feedback can be actively collected, analyzed, and incorporated into the organization's business processes to improve its produces and/or services. Table 6.1 provides five activities effective in voice of the customer elevation.

Tracking relationship activity involves understanding and interactions, feedback, and sentiments expressed by customers. This process is crucial for organizations to enhance their products, services, and overall customer experience. Numerous methods can be employed to accomplish this tracking. Some of the more effective ones I have found are:

- Feedback collection channels – various channels can be employed to capture customer feedback such as surveys, social media, online reviews, customer support interaction, and direct mail. These channels capture customer feedback from different touchpoints.
- Sentiment analysis – this analyzes the sentiment behind the feedback. It determines whether the feedback is positive, negative, or neutral. This provides insights into customer satisfaction and areas that need improvement.

Table 6.1 Elevations of Voice of the Customer

Activity	*What Happens*	*Why Done*
Track relationship	At regular intervals, survey customers about how they feel about the organization providing products or services.	• To set long-term goals and track overall progress. • To focus investments in key areas that align with improvements.
Monitor interaction	Determine how satisfied customers are with both results and process through surveys.	• Detect problematic trends • Provide feedback to customer-facing employees. • Catch/act on negative feedback from customer early.
Listen continuously	On a regular basis, sample customer interactions via monitoring communications via phone or e-mail or by visiting them.	• Detect early signs of potential problems. • Assess the emotional context of the customer's feelings.
Project alignment	Include definitions of target customer needs (design personas and customer requirements) in project plans.	• Ensure projects are laser focused on individual customer needs. • Align investment on core set of customer experiences.
Periodic leadership engagement	Encourage leadership to interact with customers and customer-facing employees often.	• Identify constraints encountered by employees. • Instill support confidence within employees.

- Text analytics – use natural language processing (NLP) techniques to extract valuable insights from the text-based feedback. Identify key words, recurring phrases, and patterns that provide deeper context to customer opinions.
- Customer journey mapping – map out the customer journey to understand where feedback is coming from in the lifecycle. This helps pinpoint specific touchpoints that need attention.
- Employee training and alignment – share customer feedback with employees who directly interact with customers. This helps in aligning their efforts with customer expectations.

By effectively tracking relationships within "listening to the voice of the customer", businesses can make informed decisions, enhance customer satisfaction, and drive growth.

Monitoring interaction activities involves actively tracking and analyzing the various ways customers provide feedback, share their opinions, and engage with your products and/or service. Numerous methods can be employed to accomplish this interaction monitoring; some of the more effective I have found are:

- Multi-channel tracking – identify the different channels through which customers interact and provide feedback. This may include social media platforms, online reviews, customer support calls, emails, surveys, feedback forms, and your website.
- Tagging and categorization – categorize interactions based on themes, topics, or issues. This makes it easier to identify common trends and areas of improvement.
- Alerts and notifications – set up alerts and notifications for specific keywords, phrases, or sentiments. This ensures that you are immediately alerted when important discussions arise.
- Customer support ticket analysis – monitor and analyze customer support tickets and interactions. Look for recurring issues, response times, and customer satisfaction levels.
- Competitor analysis – monitor customer interactions related to your competitors. This can provide insights into areas where your organization might have a competitive advantage or areas that need improvement.

By effectively monitoring interactions within "listening to the voice of the customer", you can gain valuable insights, enhance customer relationships, and drive positive changes throughout your organization.

The *listening continuously activity* refers to maintaining an ongoing, proactive approach to gathering and analyzing customer feedback and insights. This proactive approach ensures that you stay attuned to customer needs, preferences, and concerns in real time. Some of the most effective activities are:

- Social media listening – utilize social media monitoring tools to track mentions, comments, and discussions related to your products or services, engage with customers directly, and address their concerns promptly.
- Feedback loops – establish closed-loop feedback processes where you inform customers about how their feedback led to improvements or changes. These fosters trust and demonstrates your commitment to "listening".
- Customer segmentation – segment your customer base based on demographics, behaviors, or preferences. This enables you to tailor your "listening" efforts to specific groups and understand their unique needs.

- Iterative improvement – continuously acting on the feedback you receive. Implement changes, enhancements, and updates based on customer suggestions and concerns.
- Proactive outreach – initiate conversations with customers to gather feedback, even if they have not reached out first. Proactively seek their opinion on new features, improvements, or recent experiences.

Continuous listening is a dynamic and ongoing process that requires commitment to staying engaged with customers' evolving needs and expectations. By embracing this approach, you can build stronger customer relationships, drive innovation, and consistently improve your products and services.

The *project alignment activity* involves ensuring that the insights and feedback gathered from customers are effectively integrated into the projects and initiatives of your organization. This alignment ensures that customer needs and preferences drive decision-making and improvements. Here are several project alignment activities:

- Project kickoff meetings – when initiating a new project or initiative, include a discussion on relevant customer feedback and insights. This sets the tone for the project's alignment with customer needs.
- Design thinking – utilize design thinking to create solutions that directly address customer problems and align with their preferences.
- User stories – create user stories that encapsulate customer needs, behaviors, and desired outcomes. This ensures that the project team remains focused on delivering value to the customers.
- Prototyping and testing – develop prototypes or minimum viable products (MVPs) based on customer feedback. Test these with customers to validate whether they meet their expectations.
- Impact assessment – continuously assess the impact of customer driven changes. Measure how improvements in the project positively affect customer satisfaction and overall organizational goals.

By aligning your projects with the voice of the customer, you can enhance the relevance, value, and success of your initiatives, leading to improved customer satisfaction and business growth.

Periodic leadership engagement is essential for showing the leadership team's commitment to understanding and addressing customer needs. Here are some ways leadership engagement can effectively be exercised in the process:

- Leadership alignment – impress upon the leadership team the importance of listening to customer feedback and how it impacts the organization's overall strategy and success.
- Feedback presentations – have dedicated sessions where teams responsible for gathering and analyzing customer feedback present their findings to the leadership. This promotes transparency and accountability.
- Benchmarking – share customer feedback benchmarks with leadership to provide context on industry trends and competitive positioning.
- Leadership interaction – encourage leadership to directly interact with customers through feedback forums, focus groups, or customer advisory boards.
- Feedback-driven initiatives – present ongoing or upcoming initiatives that are directly influenced by customer feedback. Highlight the anticipated impact on customer satisfaction and business goals.

By engaging leadership periodically in "listening to the voice of the customer", you create a customer centric culture and a more aligned organization that actively seeks to improve customer experiences and meet their evolving expectations.

Customer-Driven Activities

Customer-driven activities refers to strategies, initiatives, and actions that are designed and executed based on a deep understanding of customer needs, preferences, and feedback. These activities place the customer at the center of decision-making processes and organizational operations. The goal is to create value for customers and enhance their overall experience with a product, service, or brand. Figure 6.2 provides a visual of some "customer-driven activities" that have been used to enhance customer engagement successfully.

Here is how these activities can be employed to successfully engage the customer:

- *Market research* – conducting thorough market research to understand customer demographics, behaviors, preferences, and pain points. This information helps in tailoring products and services to meet customer needs.
- *Product development* – designing and developing products or features based on customer input and demand. This ensures that the end product aligns with what customers genuinely want and need.
- *Personalization* – customizing products, services, and communications to cater to individual customer preferences. This can enhance the customer experience and foster loyalty.
- User friendly design – creating user-friendly interfaces and experiences that are intuitive and easy for customers to navigate. A well-designed user experience can influence customer satisfaction.
- Customer support and service – offering efficient and responsive customer support through various channels, including phone, chat, e-mail, and social media. Addressing customer issues promptly demonstrates a customer-focused approach.

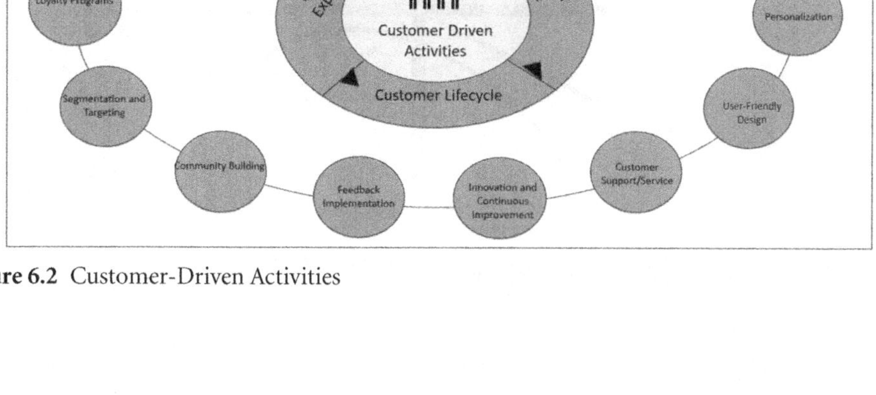

Figure 6.2 Customer-Driven Activities

- Innovation and continuous improvement – continuously innovating to stay ahead of customer expectations and market trends. Regularly updating products and services based on customer feedback ensures they remain relevant.
- Feedback implementation – actively using customer feedback to make improvements. Customers appreciate seeing their suggestions and concerns taken seriously.
- Community building – creating platforms, forums, or events where customers can interact with each other and the products and/or services being offered. This fosters a sense of community and leads to stronger customer loyalty.
- Loyalty programs – designing loyalty programs that award customers for their continued business. These programs encourage repeat business and brand advocacy.
- Post-purchase engagement – engaging with customers after a purchase to gather feedback, provide support, and offer additional value. This enhances the overall customer experience and encourages repeat business.

Customer-driven activities aim to establish strong customer relationships, increase their satisfaction, and create products and services that truly resonate with the target audience. Organizations that prioritize these activities are more likely to succeed in competitive markets by meeting and exceeding customer expectations.

A technique often used in Lean Six Sigma project to better understand customer preferences and prioritize features or attributes of products and services is Kano analysis. It categorizes customer preferences into different categories, helping organizations identify which features are essential, which are nice to have, and which might even have a negative impact if implemented. This helps in making informed decisions about product development and enhancements. Figure 6.3 provides an illustration of a Kano model developed for evaluating airline services.

In the aviation and aerospace industries, especially airlines, Kano analysis is employed to identify and prioritize the features and services they provide to customers. Here are some examples:

- Customer preference – airlines use Kano analysis to categorize various features or services they offer based on how customers perceive them.

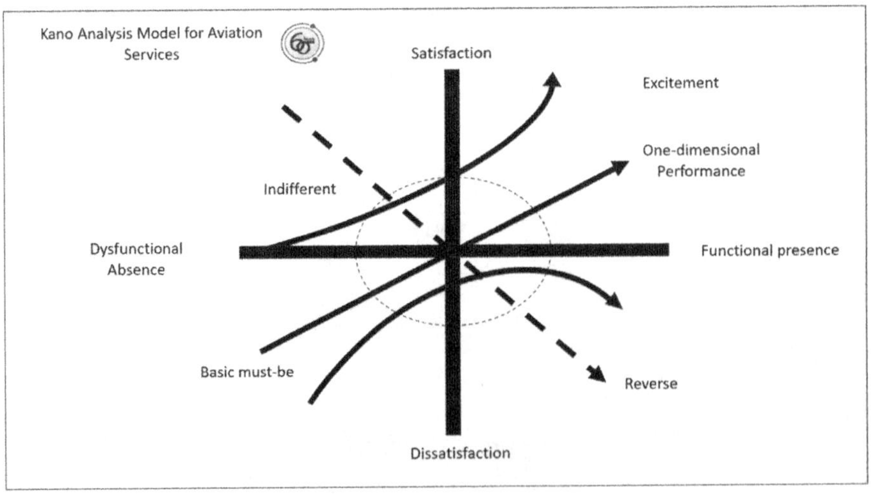

Figure 6.3 Kano Analysis Model for Aviation Services

- Service design and innovation – by identifying different types of features – basic (must-be) needs, performance (one-dimensional) needs, excitement needs, indifferent needs, and reverse needs – airlines can focus on designing and innovating their services accordingly. A detailed breakdown of how each these features is defined is as follows:
  - Basic (must-be) needs – these are essential features that customers expect as a baseline. In the aviation or airline industry, this could include safety features, comfortable seating, timely departures, and basic in-flight amenities.
  - Performance (one-dimensional) needs – these are features that directly correlate with customer satisfaction. Airlines focus on these features to gain a competitive advantage. These involve in-flight entertainment, quality meals, legroom, and individual customer service.
  - Excitement needs – these are unexpected or delightful features that can pleasantly surprise customers. For aviation, this might involve in-flight experiences, personalized services, exclusive lounges, and innovative entertainment options.
  - Indifferent needs – these are features that do not significantly impact customer satisfaction. Airlines might decide to include or exclude these features based on cost and offer feasibility.
  - Reverse needs – these are features that, if included, could lead to customer dissatisfaction. Identifying and avoiding these features is crucial for maintaining customer satisfaction.
- Resource allocation – Kano analysis helps airlines allocate resources more effectively by focusing on features that the customers truly value. It aids in making informed decisions about where to invest resources for maximum impact on customer satisfaction.
- Competitive advantage – by understanding the varying impact of different features on customer satisfaction, airlines can differentiate themselves from competitors. They can identify areas where they can excel and offer unique value to customers.
- Product development and enhancement – Kano analysis is not just for new features; it is also valuable for enhancing existing ones. Airlines can prioritize improvements to existing services based on customer preferences and satisfaction.
- Customer surveys and feedback – Kano analysis can be integrated into customer surveys to gather data on how customers perceive different features. The data can then be used to refine and tailor offerings.

Kano analysis allows aviation and aerospace organizations to make more informed decisions about their product or service offerings by aligning them with customer preferences. This can lead to higher customer satisfaction, improved loyalty, and a more competitive position for them among their competitors.

SOURCES OF CUSTOMER DATA

Customer data can come from various sources, both online and offline. It is important to handle and use this data responsibly and in compliance with privacy regulations. Figure 6.4 presents some of the more common types of data sources that are available to help understand customer requirements better.

- Website and e-commerce platforms – website analytics can provide insights into user behavior on your website. E-commerce platforms like Shopify, WooCommerce, or Magento can collect data on customer transactions, preferences and browsing history.

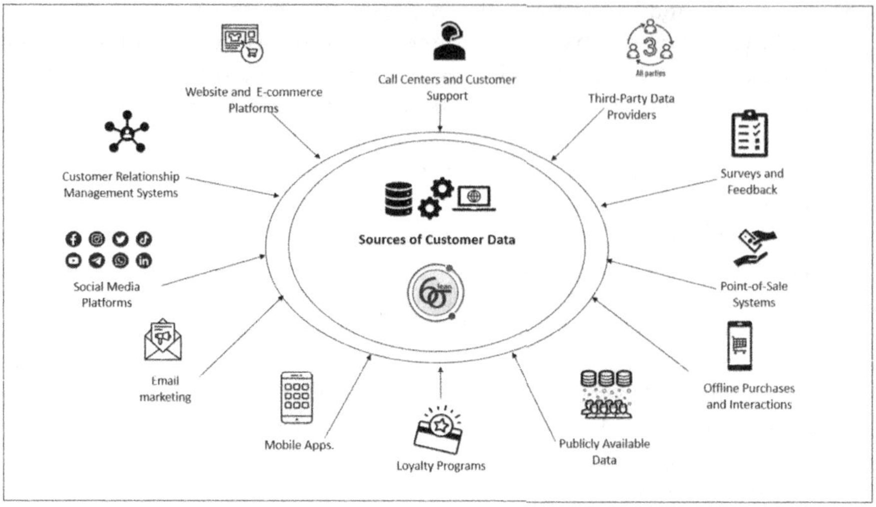

Figure 6.4 Sources of Customer Data

- Customer relationship management (CRM) systems – CRM software such as Salesforce, HubSpot, and Zoho CRM store customer contact information, interactions, purchase history, and communications preferences.
- Social media platforms – social media platforms like Facebook, Twitter (now X), and Instagram provide insights into customer demographics, engagement, and interests based on their interactions with your brand's social media profiles.
- Email marketing – Email marketing platforms like Mailchimp or Constant Contact can provide data on open rates, click-through rates, and customer preferences based on their interactions with your product or service social media profile.
- Mobile apps – you can collect data on user behavior, preferences, and interactions within the app.
- Point-of-sale (POS) systems – POS systems can capture purchase data, transaction history, and loyalty program interactions.
- Surveys and feedback – surveys, feedback forms, and customer reviews can provide direct insights into customer opinions, preferences, and satisfaction levels.
- Third-party data providers – data brokers and third-party providers offer data sets that can enrich your customer profiles with additional demographic and behavioral information.
- Call centers and customer support – interactions with call centers or customer support can provide valuable data on customer inquiries, issues, and preferences.
- Loyalty programs – data from loyalty programs can reveal customer spending patterns, preferences, and engagement levels.
- Offline purchases and interactions – data from in-store purchases and interactions can be collected through loyalty cards, receipts, and other tracking methods.
- Publicly available data – data from public sources like social media profiles, public records, and online directories can provide insights into customer interests and demographics.

Remember that while collecting customer data is essential for understanding and serving your audience better, it is crucial to follow data protection regulations like the General Data

Protection Regulation (GDPR) and California Consumer Protection Act (CCPA) and implement strong data security measures to safeguard this information. Always obtain proper consent when necessary and be transparent about how you intend to use customer data.

ACHIEVING REPRESENTATIVE SAMPLES BY USING SAMPLE FRAMES

Achieving a representative sample is crucial in research to ensure that the data collected accurately reflects the larger population you are interested in studying. An effective way to aid in the process is to use a "sampling frame". A sampling frame is a list or database for all potential elements (individuals, households, business, etc.), that could be included in your sample. Using a sampling frame helps you select a sample that closely mirrors the characteristics of the population you are studying. Figure 6.5 provides an illustration of how a sample frame works.

Here is how you can achieve a representative sample using a sampling frame:

- Define the population – clearly define the population you want to study. This could be a group of individuals, households, airlines, and so on. Make sure you understand the characteristics that define this population.
- Create or obtain a sampling frame – develop a comprehensive list or database of all the elements in your target population. This could be based on existing databases, directories, customer lists, or other relevant sources. The sampling frame should cover the ensure population without any gaps.
- Clean and update the sampling frame – ensure that the sampling frame is accurate and up to date. Remove duplicates, incorrect entries, and irrelevant records. This helps prevent bias and inaccuracies in your sample selection.
- Random sampling – use a random sampling method to select elements from the sampling frame. Simple random sampling involves each element having an equal chance of being selected. Random sampling helps ensure that your sample is unbiased and representative.
- Stratified sampling (optional) – if your population can be divided into sub-groups (strata) based on certain characteristics such as age, gender, or income, consider

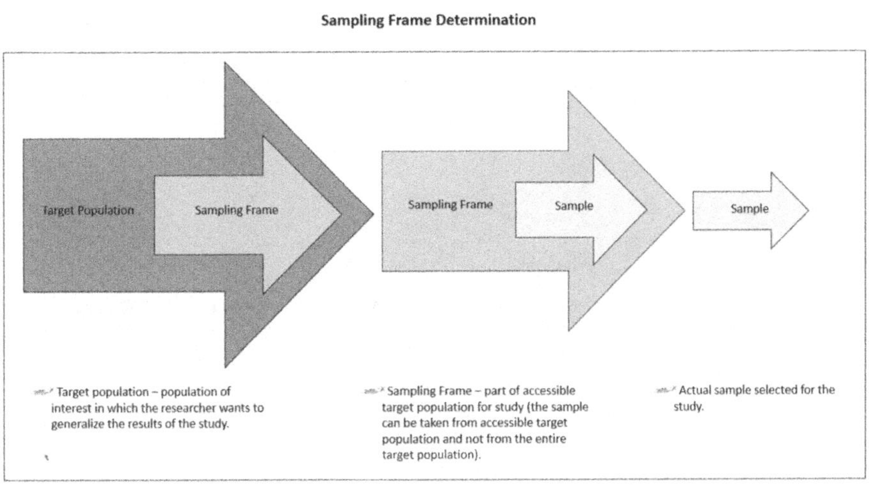

Figure 6.5 Sampling Frame Determination

using stratified sampling. This involves selecting random samples from each subgroup to ensure representation across all strata.

- Calculate sample size – determine the appropriate sample size for your study. This can be based on statistical calculations that consider factors like population size, confidence level, and desired margin of error.
- Select sample elements – using the random or stratified sampling approach, select the specific elements from the sampling frame that will make up your sample.
- Contact sample elements – reach out to the selected elements and invite them to participate in your study. This could involve sending surveys, conducting interviews, or any other data collection method.
- Monitor response rates – track how many of the selected elements respond to your study. If response rates are low, consider follow-up efforts to increase participation.
- Analyze and interpret results – once you have collected data from your sample, analyze and interpret the results. Keep in mind the characteristics of the population you are studying and how well your sample represents them.
- Account for non-response bias (if applicable) – if some selected elements do not respond, there is a potential for non-response bias. Compare the characteristics of the respondents and non-respondents to assess whether bias might be present.

Using a well-defined sampling frame is essential for achieving a representative sample that accurately reflects the population's characteristics. It helps you minimize bias and draw meaningful conclusions from your research.

USING AFFINITY DIAGRAMMING TO GROUP CUSTOMER DATA

Affinity diagramming, also known as the KJ method, is a collaborative technique used to organize and make sense of information or data by grouping related ideas or terms together. This method is often employed in brainstorming sessions, problem-solving, and data analysis. Figure 6.6 shows the use of affinity diagramming showing the four characteristics of an aircraft that require addressing during the system's development.

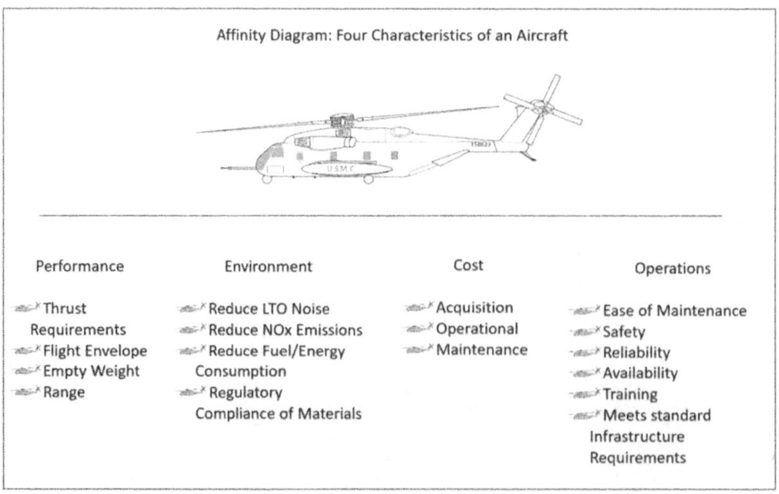

Figure 6.6 Affinity Diagram Showing the Four Characteristics of an Aircraft

Here is how you can use affinity diagramming to group customer data effectively:

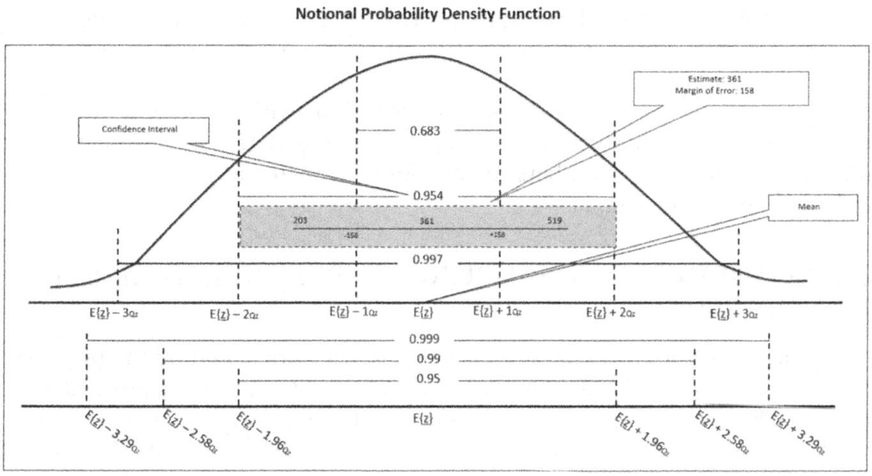

Figure 6.7 Notional Probability Density Function

- Gather customer data – collect various customer data points, such as feedback, suggestions, complaints, preferences, and any other relevant information. This data can come from surveys, interviews, reviews, and other sources you deem necessary.
- Prepare data cards – write each customer's data on separate sticky notes or cards. You can use different colors to represent the different categories if desired.
- Set up the workplace – find a space where you can lay out the notes or cards developed. This can be a wall, whiteboard, table, or, as in the case of Figure 6.7, a PowerPoint (.ppt) presentation.
- Generate themes – review the customer data and identify recurring themes, patterns, or simulations. These could relate to common concerns, preferences, problems, unique characteristics, or positive feedback.
- Grouping process – start grouping the data cards, sticky notes, or PowerPoint categories into clusters or categories based on their related themes. Arrange the clusters or categories in a way that makes sense to you and the team.
- Labeling – once you have the group process complete, label each cluster or category with a descriptive header that summarizes the theme or topic (e.g., performance, environment, etc.)
- Discuss and refine – as you work through the grouping and labeling process, engage in discussions with your team to ensure everyone agrees on the placement of cards and the labels for each group.
- Create categories – you might notice that some clusters or categories can be further grouped. If this is the case, use a work breakdown flow structuring and move the smaller clusters or categories into them.
- Iterate and organize – continue organizing and rearranging the clusters and categories until you feel that the groups accurately reflect the main themes in your customer data.
- Document and analyze – once you have finalized the grouping, record/document the affinity diagram for future reference. This diagram is a visual representation of the relationships within your customer data.

- Draw insights – analyze the affinity diagram to draw insights from the grouped data. This can help you identify priority areas for improvement, customer trends, or common pain points.
- Action items – based on the insights gained from the affinity diagram, develop action items or strategies to address the identified themes and improve customer satisfaction.

Affinity diagramming is particularly useful when dealing with a large amount of unstructured data and trying to make sense of complex system patterns. It is a collaborative process that encourages team members to contribute to their perspectives and collectively derive insights from the data.

ASSESSING THE DEGREE OF SAMPLING UNCERTAINTY; WHAT IS THE MARGIN OF ERROR?

Assessing the degree of sampling uncertainty involves understanding the potential variability or error that can arise due to using a sample to estimate characteristics of a larger population. This uncertainty is typically quantified using statistical measures like confidence intervals and margin of error. Figure 6.7 is a notional probability density function (PDF) example that highlights these areas.

Here are some ways you can assess the degree of sampling uncertainty:

Understand confidence intervals. A confidence interval (CI) is a range of values within which the true population parameter is likely to fall with a certain level of confidence. For example, a 95% confidence interval means that if you were to take many samples and calculate confidence intervals, about 95% of them would contain the true population parameter.

When you have collected your sample data, calculate the confidence interval for the parameter you are estimating (e.g., mean, proportion). The formula for the confidence interval depends on the parameter and the distribution of data. The confidence level represents the probability that the confidence interval will contain the true parameter. Common levels are 90%, 95%, and 99%. A higher confidence level widens the interval.

Consider the margin of error. This is the range above and below the sample estimate within which the true population parameter is likely to fall. It is half of the width of the confidence interval. For example, if the sample estimate is 361, and the margin of error is 158, then the confidence intervals would be 203 and 519, respectively (see Figure 6.7).

Consider the sample size and uncertainty. A larger sample size results in a smaller margin of error and a narrow confidence interval; the basis of the central limit theorem. Increasing the sample size can reduce sampling uncertainty.

Evaluate distribution assumptions. The choice of statistical test and the calculation of confidence intervals depend on the distribution of your data. Data must meet the assumptions for the chosen test. Higher variability in the sample data can lead to larger confidence intervals and increased uncertainty.

Create graphs and charts that show the confidence interval along with the sample estimate and clearly explain the concept of confidence intervals and the associated uncertainty in your findings when presenting your results.

Last, consider the practical significance. Practical significance refers to the magnitude of the difference, which is known as the effect size. Results are practically significant when the difference is large enough to be meaningful in real life. While statistical significance is important, also consider whether the observed effect or parameter estimate is practically meaningful.

DISCOVERING THE CUSTOMER'S "CRITICAL TO QUALITY" REQUIREMENTS

Critical to quality (CTQ) requirements refer to the specific characteristics of a product or service that are most important to customers and have a direct impact on their satisfaction. Discovering CTQ requirements is essential for delivering products and services that meet and exceed customer expectations. Figure 6.8 shows four overarching guiding themes generally observed during the CTQ discover process.

First, there should be a clear understanding of the customer's needs. This requires an acute "listening to the VOC" so there is clarity of customer needs/requirements. Second, those needs/requirements must be prioritized. As mentioned earlier in the chapter, Kano analysis is the tool of choice here. It can tell you what product/service attribute just satisfies the customer and what attribute "excites" that customer. Third, ensure the level of detail used during the prioritization process is sufficient for the same product or service being provided. Fourth, target the process to the individual customer.

Here is a list of suggested ways you can uncover customers' CTQ requirements for product and service of a general nature:

- Gather customer feedback – collect feedback from customers through surveys, interviews, focus groups, and social media. Ask open-ended questions about what features, aspects, or attributes are most important to them.
- Segment your customer base – divide your customer base into segments based on demographics, behaviors, preferences, and other relevant factors.
- Conduct surveys – develop target surveys that explicitly ask customers to rate the importance of various product or services features or attributes.
- Develop a customer journey map – creating a customer journey map is the process of forming a visual representation of customers' processes, needs, and perceptions throughout their interactions and relationship with an organization.

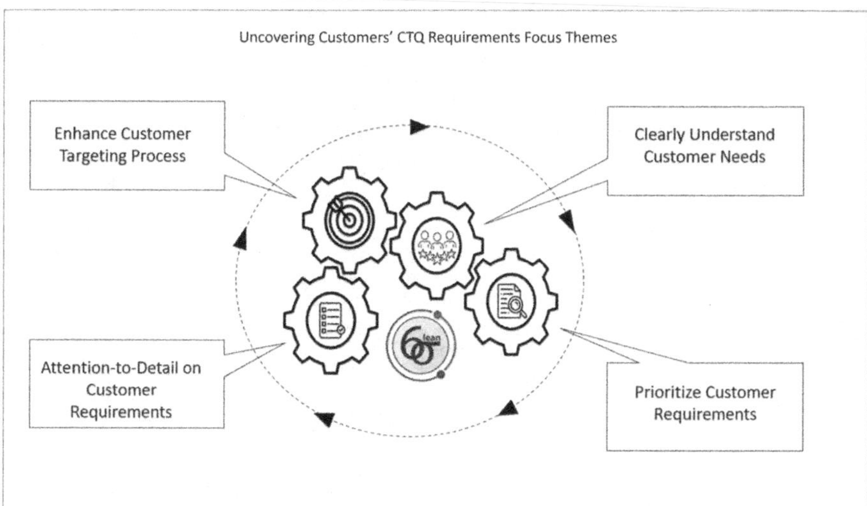

Figure 6.8 Uncovering Customers' CTQ Requirements: Focus Themes

- Engage with customer-facing teams – consult customer support, sales, and frontline employees who interact directly with customers. They often have valuable insight into customer preferences and pain points.
- Use quality function deployment (QFD) – QFD is a structured approach to translate customer needs into product features. It helps to systematically prioritize and align features with customer requirements. QFD will be addressed in the next section.

For the aviation and aerospace industries, while observing the major themes illustrated in Figure 6.8 remains applicable, CTQ requirements have specific characteristics and parameters that are crucial to ensuring the safety, reliability, and overall quality of their products and services that require focused effort to capture. Figure 6.9 lists some of the more critical areas that require focused consideration when gathering CTQ metrics.

- Safety standards – safety is paramount within the aviation industry. CTQ requirements include adherence to safety regulations, such as those established by the Federal Aviation Administration (FAA) or the European Union Aviation Safety Agency (EASA). These cover everything from the actual aircraft design and maintenance to flight operations and air traffic control.
- Aircraft design and manufacturing – ensuring the quality of aircraft design and manufacturing processes are crucial. CTQ requirements include structural integrity, material integrity, material quality, and adherence to engineering specifications. Components like wings, engines, and avionics must meet strict quality standards.
- Maintenance and inspection – aircraft must undergo regular maintenance and inspection to ensure they are safe to operate. CTQ requirements include rigorous maintenance schedules, detailed inspection procedures, and compliance with maintenance documentation.
- Flight crew training and certification – pilots and other flight crew members must meet specific training and certification standards. CTQ requirements include flight training programs, simulator training, and proficiency checks.

Aviation and Aerospace CTQ Requirements

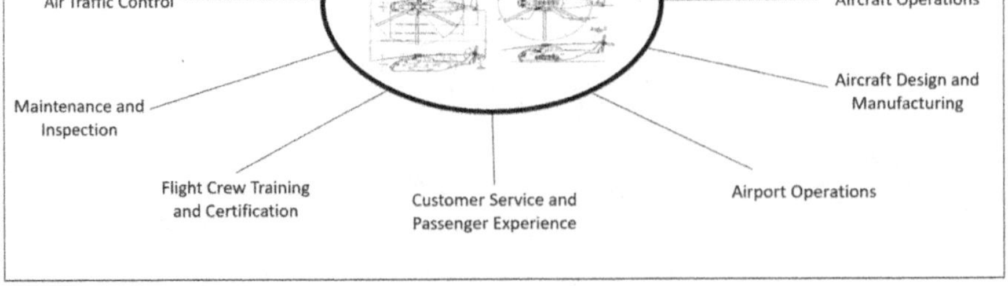

Figure 6.9 Aviation and Aerospace CTQ Requirements

- Air traffic control – air traffic controllers play a vital role in aviation safety. CTQ requirements for air traffic control include training, staffing levels, communications systems, and adherence to standardized procedures.
- Airport operations – ensuring the safety and efficiency of airport operations is essential. CTQ requirements encompass runway maintenance, security protocols, baggage handling systems, and passenger screening procedures.
- Quality management system – aviation organizations, including airlines, maintenance facilities, and airports, use quality management systems (QMSs) to meet CTQ requirements. These systems help ensure that processes are well documented, consistently followed, and subject to continuous improvement.
- Environmental regulations – with a growing emphasis on environmental sustainability, CTQ requirements in aviation include compliance with emissions standards and noise reduction measures.
- Customer service and passenger experience – while safety is the top priority, CTQ requirements also extend to customer service and the passenger experience for aviation and aerospace industries. Airlines must meet certain standards for in-flight services, passenger comfort, and responsiveness to passenger needs.
- Cyber-security – in today's digital age, protecting aviation systems from cyber threats is critical. CTQ requirements for cyber-security include measures to safeguard aircraft systems, air traffic control networks, and passenger data.
- Emergency response and contingency planning – the aviation and aerospace industry must have robust emergency response and contingency plans in place to address various scenarios, from aircraft emergencies to natural disasters.

Discovering CTQ requirements, regardless of business orientation, involves active listening, analyzing feedback, and a firm understanding of the customer. This understanding serves as a foundation for designing products and services that resonate with the customer, drive satisfaction, and, in the case of aeronautical systems, maintain the safety and reliability of systems for aviation operations.

TRANSLATING CTQ REQUIREMENTS INTO SPECIFICATIONS USING QUALITY FUNCTION DEPLOYMENT

Translating CTQ requirements into specifications involves turning customer-focused attributes and characteristics you have identified into specific, measurable, and actionable details that can guide product development, design, and quality control. Quality function deployment is a Lean Six Sigma method of choice for accomplishing this crucial step.

Quality function deployment is a planning and management quality process tool that drives optimal product and service development. It is a structured method of product or service planning that enables development teams to clearly specify a customer's needs. It then can be used to systemically evaluate the products or services capabilities in terms of impact on those identified needs. A key benefit of QFD, because of its structural design, is that it assists product development teams in communicating to decision makers exactly "what" needs to be developed and "how" it needs to be developed. It allows organizations to evaluate early in the conceptual stage of product or service development life cycle whether CTQs have been clearly understood and is worth the investment to proceed. Figure 6.10 illustrates a typical QFD house of quality matrices.

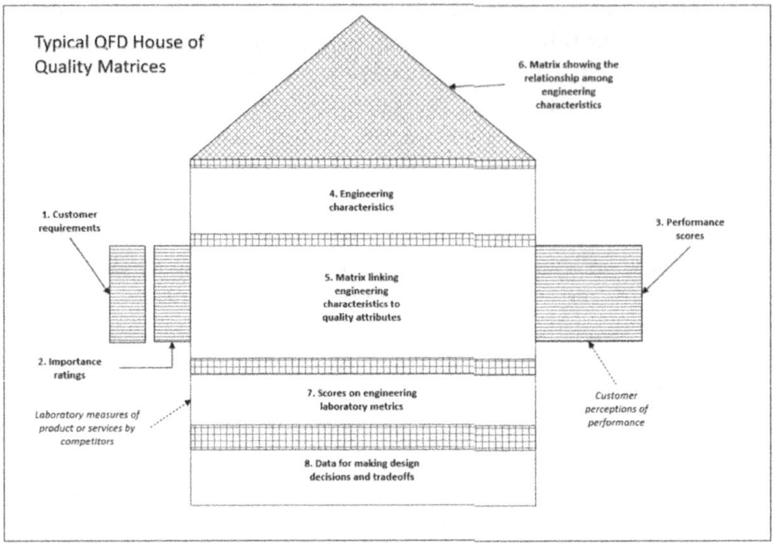

Figure 6.10 Typical QFD House of Quality Matrices

The matrix consists of several sections or sub-matrices joined together in various ways, each containing information that is related to the others.

Each of the labeled sections (1 through 8) shown in Figure 6.10 is a structured, systematic expression of a product or process development teams' perspective on an aspect of the overall planning for a new product, service, or process. The numbering suggests one logical sequence for populating the matrices.

The first section, titled "customer requirements", is a structured section of customer needs and wants. Generally, this structure is determined through qualitative research. Data is often presented in a tree diagram format.

The second section, titled "importance ratings", contains relative customer-driven importance ratings as determined by sampling the customer base for their priorities.

Section three, titled "performance scores", contains two main types of information:

- Quantitative market-oriented data, including customer satisfaction levels with the organization's product offering and its direct competitor's current offering.
- Strategic goals for the new product or service.

Section four contains the organization's technical language (generated from the customer's wants and needs recorded in section one) and a high-level description of the product or service planned for development.

Section five contains the linking of engineering characteristics with the customer's quality attributes rankings based of the development team's judgements of the strength of the relationship between each element of its technical response and each customer want and need.

Section six, "technical correlations", is half of a square matrix split along its diagonal and rotated 45°. This is the roof of the matrix, which led to the term "house of quality" becoming the standard designation for the entire QFD matrix structure. Section six contains the development team's assessment of the implementation interrelationships between elements of the technical characteristics.

Section seven contains a summary of the product or service metrics between the organization's current offering and that of the competitors.

Section eight provides the relative weighting of customer needs versus how well the organization's product or service is performing on the relevant product or services metrics. This section contains three types of information:

- The computer rank ordering of the technical responses, based on the rank ordering of the customer's wants and needs found in section two and the relationships found in section five.
- Comparative information on the competition's technical performance
- Technical performance targets

Understanding what the QFD methodology is and how its matrix is structured is, of course, a first step, but then CTQ requirements must be translated into technical specifications that can guide the product or service development process. A step-by-step process effective for performing the task is as follows:

- Identify CTQ requirements – begin by identifying and prioritizing CTQ requirements. These will have been determined through market research, customer feedback, and a deep understanding of "what" aspects of the product or service are most important to the customer.
- Creating the QFD matrix – a model, like that depicted in Figure 6.10, should then be developed as a central tool to link CTQs to technical specifications. CTQs should be reflected in the matrix rows, the technical specifications in the matrix columns.
- Assign importance ratings – assign an importance rating to each CTQ based on its relative significance to the customer. These ratings help prioritize the technical specifications that will address the CTQs effectively.
- Identify technical specifications – for each CTQ, work with cross-functional teams to identify the technical specifications needed to meet or exceed the customers' expectations and "how" they will be met. These specifications should be specific, measurable, and linked to the CTQs.
- Determine relationships – assess and determine the relationship between CTQs and technical specifications. The strength of these relationships can vary, with some technical specifications having a stronger impact on meeting CTQs than others. Use symbols or numerical values in the matrix to indicate the strength of these relationships.
- Set target values – define target values or tolerances for each specification. These values should be set in a way that ensures the CTQs are met or exceeded.
- Ensure alignment – ensure that technical specifications align with the CTQ and that they are realistic and achievable within the constraints of the organization and project.
- Develop action plans – based on the specifications and target values, develop action plans for product or service design and development. These plans should outline the steps necessary to achieve the specified technical characteristics.
- Review and iterate – continuously review and iterate on the QFD matrix as the product or service development progresses. It is important to adapt to changing customer needs and emerging technical insights.

By following these steps using a QFD methodology, you can ensure that CTQ requirements are effectively translated into specific technical specifications, providing clear guidance for product or service development teams and increasing the likelihood for meeting or exceeding customer expectations.

DEFINE STAGE: TOLLGATE REVIEW

Upon each stage of the DMAIC methodology, a review process is conducted to ensure the project has proper oversight, accountability, and a mechanism for course correction when needed. These are called "tollgates", and they help organizations achieve their goals for process improvement, quality enhancement, and overall performance optimization.

The Define phase tollgate review criteria are used to assess whether the project is ready to move forward to the Measure stage. These criteria help ensure that the project is well defined and has a clear focus. Review criteria for the Define stage include the following:

- Project charter – a project charter must be created that outlines the project's purpose, scope, objectives, team members, and high-level schedule.
- Problem statement – a clear and concise problem statement must be defined, describing the specific issue or challenge that the project aims to address. This problem statement should explain why this project is important to the organization.
- Project scope – the scope of the project must be well defined. What is included in the project, and what is not? Clear boundaries and limitations should be established as well.
- Project objectives – specific, measurable, achievable, relevant, and time-bound (SMART) objectives must be set for the project. These objectives should align with the problem statement.
- Stakeholder identification – all relevant stakeholders must be identified and their interests and expectations considered. This includes all internal and external stakeholders.
- High-level process map – A high-level process map or flowchart must be created to visualize the current process related to the problem. This will help understand the current process's context.
- Data availability – an assessment of whether the necessary data for the project is available and can be collected. Data is essential for the Measure and Analyze phases; this criterion is crucial.
- Team roles – the project must have the necessary resources, including people, time, and budget, to proceed to the next phase.
- Risks and assumptions – identification of potential risk and assumptions along with mitigation plans must be developed. Understanding these factors is crucial for risk management.
- Alignment with organizational strategy and goals – the project must align with the overall goals and strategies of the sponsoring organization.

The Define phase tollgate review is typically conducted by the project sponsor or a designated review team. Once all criteria are met, the project can proceed to Measure, where data is collected and analyzed to gain a deeper understanding of the issue or problem.

SUMMARY

Chapter 6 began with a discussion of "listening" to the voice of the customer to ensure requirements were clearly understood. It then moved into just how those requirements are understood. A discussion of how capturing customer information was conducted and reference made to how representative samples could be achieved using sampling frames. We then detailed the process for structuring survey questions and grouping data using affinity diagramming. The chapter then presented to the reader a process by which the degree of sampling uncertainty could be controlled by adjusting confidence level and the margin of error. It then outlined a procedure through which customer critical to quality attributes could be discerned and requirements could be identified and delineated. The chapter concluded by introducing to the reader the process of quality function deployment and emphasized how it could be employed during the Define phase process to ensure the mapping of customer requirements is in alignment with organizational capabilities to fulfill those requirements by understanding product and/or service specifications. This was followed by a Define phase tollgate review of the stage before proceeding into the Measure phase.

LEAN SIX SIGMA TOOLS AT WORK!

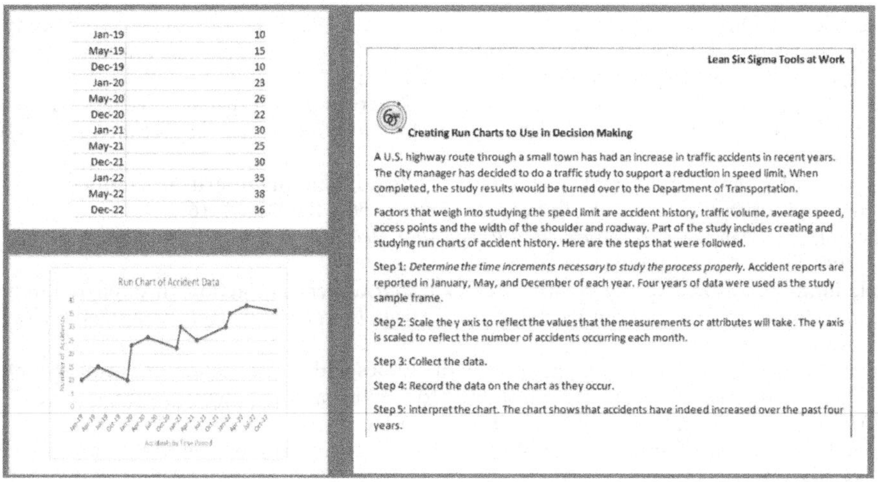

Figure 6.11 Lean Six Sigma Tools at Work

CHAPTER 6 DISCUSSION QUESTIONS

1 Describe the process of "listening" to the voice of the customer and elaborate on why is important when executing a Lean Six Sigma project.
2 Define and describe how customer-driven activities can help in understanding the voice of the customer.
3 Define and describe Kano analysis modeling. How does aid in understanding the voice of the customer?
4 Briefly describe the sources of customer data and elaborate on why it is important to capture this information for Lean Six Sigma project execution.
5 Define a sampling frame and describe how it is employed in Lean Six Sigma project execution.

BIBLIOGRAPHY

Aggarwal, Ashita. "Recipe for a great customer experience: The three voices–voice of customer (VoC), voice of employee (VoE) and voice of process (VoP)." In *Crafting Customer Experience Strategy: Lessons from Asia*. Emerald Publishing Limited, 2021, pp. 65–90.

Alghamdi, Mohammed. "An integrated design for six sigma-based framework to align strategy, new process development, and customer requirements in the airlines industry." University of Central Florida, 2016. https://ucf.digital.flvc.org/islandora/object/ucf%3A51079

Anderson, Andrew A. "Assessing statistical results: Magnitude, precision, and model uncertainty." *The American Statistician* 73.sup1 (2019): 118–121.

Anderson-Cook, Christine M., et al. "Quantifying reliability uncertainty from catastrophic and margin defects: A proof of concept." *Reliability Engineering & System Safety* 96.9 (2011): 1063–1075.

Bayus, Barry L., and S. Shane. "Understanding customer needs." *Handbook of Technology and Innovation Management* (2008): 115–142.

Beaman, Jay, and Jerry J. Vaske. "Structuring survey data to facilitate analysis and interpretation." *Human Dimensions of Wildlife* 13.5 (2008): 361–379.

Beatty, Paul C., Carol Cosenza, and F. J. Fowler. "Experiments on the structure and specificity of complex survey questions." In *Proceedings of the Survey Methods Research Section*. Alexandria, VA: American Statistical Association, 2006.

Brace, Ian. *Questionnaire Design: How to Plan, Structure and Write Survey Material for Effective Market Research*. Kogan Page Publishers, 2018.

Desouza, Kevin C., et al. "Customer-driven innovation." *Research-Technology Management* 51.3 (2008): 35–44.

D'Haen, Jeroen, Dirk Van den Poel, and Dirk Thorleuchter. "Predicting customer profitability during acquisition: Finding the optimal combination of data source and data mining technique." *Expert Systems with Applications* 40.6 (2013): 2007–2012.

Du, Xuehong, Jianxin Jiao, and Mitchell M. Tseng. "Understanding customer satisfaction in product customization." *The International Journal of Advanced Manufacturing Technology* 31 (2006): 396–406.

Dunn, Kate M., Kelvin Jordan, and Peter R. Croft. "Does questionnaire structure influence response in postal surveys?" *Journal of Clinical Epidemiology* 56.1 (2003): 10–16.

Dyché, Jill, and Evan Levy. *Customer Data Integration: Reaching a Single Version of the Truth*. Vol. 7. John Wiley & Sons, 2006.

Elliott, John, and Peter Raynor-Smith. "Achieving customer satisfaction through requirements understanding." In *European Workshop on Software Process Technology*. Berlin and Heidelberg: Springer, 2000.

Enticott, Joanne C., et al. "A systematic review of studies with a representative sample of refugees and asylum seekers living in the community for participation in mental health research." *BMC Medical Research Methodology* 17.1 (2017): 1–16.

Faugier, Jean, and Mary Sargeant. "Sampling hard to reach populations." *Journal of Advanced Nursing* 26.4 (1997): 790–797.

Fowler, Floyd J. *Improving Survey Questions: Design and Evaluation*. Sage, 1995.

Freeman, Graham, and N. Radziwill. "Voice of the customer (VoC): A review of techniques to reveal and prioritize requirements for quality." *Joqat–Journal of Quality Management Systems, Applied Engineering, and Technology Management* (2018): 1–29.

Gentili, Enzo, Francesco Aggogeri, and Marco Mazzola. "The effectiveness of the quality function deployment in managing manufacturing and transactional processes." *ASME International Mechanical Engineering Congress and Exposition* 42975 (2007).

Grijalvo, Mercedes, María Fernanda Eliopoulos, and Gustavo Morales-Alonso. "Closing gap between new development and voice of customer." *Economics and Business Letters* 9.4 (2020): 279–288.

Gupta, Mahima, and Charu Shri. "Understanding customer requirements of corrugated industry using Kano model." *International Journal of Quality & Reliability Management* 35.8 (2018): 1653–1670.

Hansen, Eric, and Robert J. Bush. "Understanding customer quality requirements: Model and application." *Industrial Marketing Management* 28.2 (1999): 119–130.

Harboe, Gunnar, and Elaine M. Huang. "Real-world affinity diagramming practices: Bridging the paper-digital gap." In *Proceedings of the 33rd Annual ACM Conference on Human Factors in Computing Systems*. Association for Computing Machinery, 2015. https://doi.org/10.1145/2702123.2702561.

Hart, Stephen D., Christine Michie, and David J. Cooke. "Precision of actuarial risk assessment instruments: Evaluating the 'margins of error' of group v. individual predictions of violence." *The British Journal of Psychiatry* 190.S49 (2007): s60–s65.

He, Lina, et al. "Understanding customer requirements through quantitative analysis of an improved fuzzy Kano's model." *Proceedings of the Institution of Mechanical Engineers, Part B: Journal of Engineering Manufacture* 231.4 (2017): 699–712.

Heen, Miliaikeala, Joel D. Lieberman, and T. D. Meithe. "A comparison of different online sampling approaches for generating national samples." *Center for Crime and Justice Policy* (2014). https://doi.org/10.13140/RG.2.2.24283.62243.

Hsiao, I.-Han, et al. "Survey sidekick: Structuring scientifically sound surveys." In *Intelligent Tutoring Systems: 12th International Conference, ITS 2014, Honolulu, HI, USA, June 5–9, 2014. Proceedings 12.* Springer International Publishing, 2014.

Hyman, William Albert. *Guide for Customer-Driven Benchmarking of Maintenance Activities.* Vol. 511. Transportation Research Board, 2004.

James, David E., Gregory Schraw, and Fred Kuch. "Using the sampling margin of error to assess the interpretative validity of student evaluations of teaching." *Assessment & Evaluation in Higher Education* 40.8 (2015): 1123–1141.

Jeong, Hong Jin, Chang Wook Kang, and Bo Hyun Kim. "Requirements development process for manufacturing information systems based on quality function deployment." *International Journal of Computer Integrated Manufacturing* 31.2 (2018): 164–174.

Liu, Jiali, and James Eagan. "ADQDA: A cross-device affinity diagramming tool for fluid and holistic qualitative data analysis." *Proceedings of the ACM on Human-Computer Interaction* 5.ISS (2021): 1–19.

Lucero, Andrés. "Using affinity diagrams to evaluate interactive prototypes." In *Human-Computer Interaction–INTERACT 2015: 15th IFIP TC 13 International Conference, Bamberg, Germany, September 14–18, 2015, Proceedings, Part II 15.* Springer International Publishing, 2015.

Macnamara, Jim. "Corporate listening: Unlocking insights from VOC, VOE and VOS for mutual benefits." *Corporate Communications: An International Journal* 25.3 (2020): 377–393.

Magnani, Robert, et al. "Review of sampling hard-to-reach and hidden populations for HIV surveillance." *Aids* 19 (2005): S67–S72.

Martinelli, Elisa Martina, Annalisa Tunisini, and Simone Guercini. "Customer-driven supply chains under IMP lens: A systematic literature review and conceptual framework." *IMP Journal* 11.2 (2017): 289–300.

Montelisciani, Gabriele, et al. "Ordering the chaos: A guided translation of needs into product requirements." *Procedia CIRP* 21 (2014): 403–408.

Nemeschansky, Ben, Tania von der Heidt, and Peter Beomcheol Kim. "Customer-driven menu analysis (CDMA): Capturing customer voice in menu management." *International Journal of Hospitality Management* 91 (2020): 102417.

Palmatier, Robert W., et al. "Understanding and valuing customer data." In *The Intelligent Marketer's Guide to Data Privacy: The Impact of Big Data on Customer Trust*, 2019, pp. 133–151. https://doi.org/10.1007/978-3-030-03724-6_7

Plangger, Kirk, et al. "Does (customer data) size matter? Generating valuable customer insights with less customer relationship risk." *Psychology & Marketing* 40.10 (2023): 2016–2028.

Puisa, Romanas, Jakub Montewka, and Przemyslaw Krata. "A framework estimating the minimum sample size and margin of error for maritime quantitative risk analysis." *Reliability Engineering & System Safety* 235 (2023): 109221.

Pula, Edith N., Merlin Stone, and Bryan Foss. "Customer data management in practice: An insurance case study." *Journal of Database Marketing & Customer Strategy Management* 10 (2003): 327–341.

Salah, Souraj, Abdur Rahim, and Juan A. Carretero. "Kano-based six sigma utilising quality function deployment." *International Journal of Quality Engineering and Technology* 1.2 (2009): 206–230.

Sawalakhe, Pranil Vijay. "A model for determining process-wise CTQs for testing laboratories." In *Quality Assurance in the Era of Individualized Medicine.* IGI Global, 2020, pp. 240–256.

Simonova, Stanislava, and Nikola Foltanova. "Implementation of quality principles for IT service requirements analyse." In *2017 International Conference on Information and Digital Technologies (IDT).* IEEE, 2017.

Smart, Karl L., and Matthew E. Whiting. "Using customer data to drive documentation design decisions." *Journal of Business and Technical Communication* 16.2 (2002): 115–169.

Stringfellow, Anne, Winter Nie, and David E. Bowen. "CRM: Profiting from understanding customer needs." *Business Horizons* 47.5 (2004): 45–52.

Terninko, John. *Step-by-Step QFD: Customer-Driven Product Design.* Routledge, 2018.

Toivanen, Miro. "Improving new product development through effective critical to quality process and supplier quality activity." 2022. https://www.theseus.fi/bitstream/handle/10024/747190/Toivanen_Miro.pdf?sequence=2&isAllowed=y

Wang, Ting, and Ping Ji. "Understanding customer needs through quantitative analysis of Kano's model." *International Journal of Quality & Reliability Management* 27.2 (2010): 173–184.

Westcott, Russ. "Your customers are talking, but are you listening?" *Quality Progress* 39.2 (2006): 22.

Widjaja, William, and Makoto Takahashi. "Distributed interface for group affinity-diagram brainstorming." *Concurrent Engineering* 24.4 (2016): 344–358.

Wu, Haoning, et al. "Neighbourhood representative sampling for efficient end-to-end video quality assessment." In *IEEE Transactions on Pattern Analysis and Machine Intelligence.* Vol. 45, Issue 12. IEEE Computer Society, 2023. https://doi.org/10.1109/TPAMI.2023.3319332

Part III

The Measure Phase of DMAIC

7
Problem Solving Using Statistics

LEARNING OBJECTIVES

1 Describe the purpose and key activities of the Measure phase of the DMAIC methodology.
2 Explain the role of measurements and basic statistics in the Measure phase.
3 Differentiate between descriptive and inferential statistics and summarize how inferential statistics are derived.
4 Distinguish between discrete and continuous data and summarize the types of measurement subjects and their groups.
5 Summarize the measures of central tendency, measures of dispersion, and the steps for organizing data for analysis.

INTRODUCTION

The Measure phase is the second step in the DMAIC problem-solving methodology. The primary purpose of the Measure phase is to gather data and establish a baseline to quantitatively assess the current state of the problem or process under study. Figure 7.1 provides an illustration of how the Measure phase fits into the overall DMAIC problem-solving process and associated activities.

Along with the activities conducted during this phase (see Figure 7.1), the Measure phase also serves several purposes which are critical to the overall DMAIC problem-solving methodology.

In the Measure phase, teams collect relevant data about the problem or process under investigation. This data would include process performance metrics, defect rates, cycle times, customer feedback, and any other data points that help with the understanding of the current process performance. By collecting this data, teams establish a baseline or benchmark for the process. This baseline provides a clear picture of how the process is currently performing and helps identify the magnitude of the problem or improvement opportunity.

The Measure phase also aims to identify sources of variation within the process. Variability can lead to defects or inconsistencies in the output. It does this by examining established metrics or key performance indicators (KPIs) that are then used to assess

DOI: 10.4324/9781032650531-10

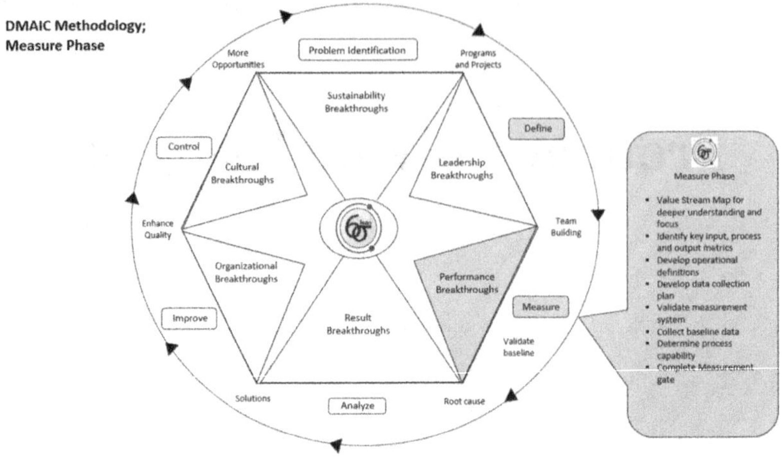

Figure 7.1 Measure Phase of the DMAIC Methodology

the performance throughout the DMAIC-driven project. These metrics must be specific, measurable, and relevant to the problem being addressed.

While detailed data analyses will occur in the subsequent Analyze phase, some initial data analysis takes place during the Measure phase to identify trends, patterns, and potential causes of problems. Process maps and flow charts are also created to visualize the current process and identify potential areas for improvement.

The Measure phase also provides an opportunity to ensure that all stakeholders have a shared understanding of the current state of the process and its performance issues. This allows project teams to refine plans and timelines based on data collected and insights gained. Thus, it helps set realistic expectations for the remainder of the project.

MEASUREMENTS, BASIC STATISTICS, AND RELATED TERMS

In a DMAIC-driven project, the Measure phase is a critical step where the current performance of a process is assessed in a systematic and objective manner. The role of measurements and basic statistics in this phase is to gather data, establish a baseline understanding of the process, and identify areas for improvement. Figure 7.2 illustrates some of these roles.

Here is a detailed description of these roles:

- Data collection – measurements and basic statistics play a pivotal role in data collection. The Measure phase involves defining what needs to be measured, selecting appropriate data sources, and gathering relevant data. The data collected must be accurate, consistent, and representative of the process under study.
- Establishing a baseline – measurements and basic statistics help establish a baseline for the process's current performance. This baseline serves as a reference point against which future improvements can be measured. Key metrics and indicators are calculated, such as mean (average), median (middle value), mode (most frequent value), range (difference between the maximum and minimum values), and standard deviation (a measure of data dispersion). These statistics provide a clear picture of the process's current state.

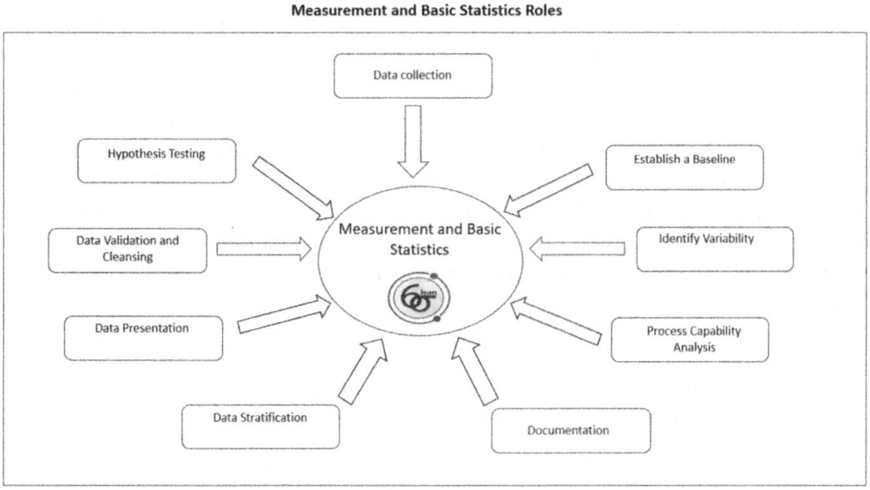

Figure 7.2 Measurement and Basic Statistics Roles

- Identifying variability – basic statistics, such as histograms, scatter plots, and control charts, are used to visualize data and identify patterns or variations in the process. Variability in the process is one of the main sources of defects, blemishes, or inefficiencies, and understanding it is crucial for process improvement.
- Process capability analysis – in the Measure phase, process capability studies are often conducted using statistical tools like capability indices, such as Cp and CpK, to assess whether the process can produce products or services within specified limits. This analysis helps determine if the process meets customer requirements and identifies areas where improvements are needed.
- Data validation and cleansing – measurements and basis statistics help identify and address data quality issues. Data outliers, missing values, or inaccuracies can distort the analysis and lead to incorrect conclusions. Data validation and cleansing techniques are applied to ensure data accuracy and reliability.
- Data stratification – stratifying data involves breaking it down into subgroups based on specific factors and characteristics. This can help identify patterns and root causes of variations within different subgroups of the process. Measurements and statistics are used to analyze and compare these subgroups.
- Hypothesis testing – basic statistics like t-tests, chi-squared tests, and analysis of variance (ANOVA) are employed in the Measure phase to test hypotheses about the process. This helps in identifying statistical significance and relationships that may exist within the data.
- Data presentation – clear and concise data presentation using charts, graphs, and visual representations of measurements and basic statistics is crucial for effective communication within the project team and stakeholders. Visualizations can make complex data more understandable.
- Documentation – measurements and basic statistics are documented rigorously in the Measure phase. This documentation serves as a basis for comparison throughout the DMAIC process and helps track progress and improvements over time.

The Measure phase of a DMAIC project relies heavily on measurements and basic statistics to guide, gather, analyze, and establish a comprehensive understanding of the current state of a process. The tools and techniques used help identify areas where the process falls short of expectations and provides a solid foundation for the subsequent phases of Analyze, Improve, and Control where targeted improvements are made and sustained.

In conjunction with an understanding of the roles that measurement and basic statistics play in the Measure phase, there are some key terms and concepts that are pivotal in how these roles are executed. Table 7.1 provides a list of common measurement and statistical key terms with the respective concepts used in DMAIC-driven, Lean Six Sigma projects.

Table 7.1 Measurement and Statistical Key Terms and Concepts

Key Term	*Concept*
Measurement	Measurement is the process of quantifying or assigning a value to an attribute of an object or phenomenon. It involves determining the size, length, quantity, or quality of something using standard units.
Data	Data refers to the information collected or recorded through measurements. Data can be numerical (quantitative) or categorical (qualitative).
Variable	A variable is a characteristic or attribute that can vary or take on different values in a dataset. It can be independent (predictor) or dependent (response) in statistical analysis.
Units of measurement	Units are standardized measures used to express the magnitude of a quantity. For example, meters for length, kilograms for mass, and seconds for time.
Measurement scale	Measurement scales categorize variables into different types based on the level of measurement. The four main scales are nominal, ordinal, interval, and ratio.
Descriptive statistics	Descriptive statistics involve methods for summarizing and describing data.
Mean	The mean is the average of a set of values. It is calculated by adding up all the values and dividing by the number of values.
Median	The median is the middle value in a dataset when it is arranged in ascending or descending order. It is less affected by outliers than the mean.
Mode	The mode is the most frequently occurring value in a dataset.
Range	The range is the difference between the maximum and minimum values in a dataset. It measures the spread or variability of data.

(*Continued*)

Table 7.1 (Continued)

Key Term	*Concept*
Variance	Variance measures how data points deviate from the mean. It quantifies the spread of data values.
Standard deviation	The standard deviation is a measure of how much individual data points vary from the mean. It is the square root of the variance.
Population vs. sample	In statistics, a population refers to the entire group of items or individuals of interest, while a sample is a subset of the population used to make inferences about the entire population.
Statistical inference	Statistical inference involves drawing conclusions or making predictions about a population based on data from a sample.
Probability	Probability is a measure of the likelihood of an event occurring. It ranges from 0 (impossible) to 1 (certain).
Probability distribution	A probability distribution describes how the probabilities of different outcomes are spread out in a random experiment. Common distributions include the normal distribution, binomial distribution, and Poisson distribution.
Hypothesis testing	Hypothesis testing is a statistical method used to make decisions about population parameters based on sample data. It involves formulating a null hypothesis and an alternative hypothesis and conducting tests to accept or reject the null hypothesis.
Confidence interval	A confidence interval is a range of values that is likely to contain the true population parameter with a specified level of confidence.

UNDERSTANDING THE TYPES OF MEASUREMENT SUBJECTS

Understanding the types of measurement subjects is essential when executing research and data collection in the Measure phase of a DMAIC-based project. Measurement subjects in this context refer to the entities or objects being measured or studied. Figure 7.3 lists the groupings and different types of categories commonly encountered when executing a Lean Six Sigma project.

These measurement subjects, referred to as "categories", are placed into three group types: individuals, objects or items, and events or occurrences, which make up the outer ring of Figure 7.3.

Individuals, or respondents, are living human beings who are the subjects of the measurement in many of the research studies you will conduct. Data in this grouping is typically gathered via surveys, interviews, psychological studies, and social research. Examples here would include observation of assembly line work or material flow, interviews with a sample of workers, or a phone center call script timing.

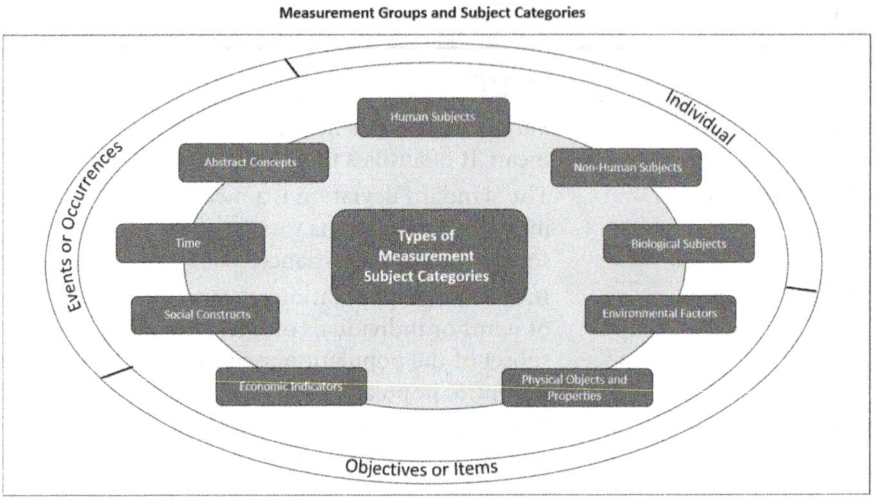

Figure 7.3 Types of Measurement Groups and Subject Categories

Objects or items refer to physical entities or inanimate articles measured or observed during research. These include products, materials, artifacts, or any other tangible items. Examples include measuring the dimensions of a sub-assembly sub-component, assessing the quality of a manufactured component, evaluating the durability of composite materials, or analyzing the chemical composition of plating solutions.

Events or occurrences refer to specific incidents, happenings, or phenomena, that are the subjects of measurement or observation. These events may be natural or engineered and require the gathering of data over time. An example here would be the validation of your measurement system via a Gage R&R (repeatability and reproducibility) exercise or the monitoring of temperature in plating tanks to ensure all chemicals are balanced.

Within each group, there are measurement subject categories, which are referred to as objects. Objects are what is being measured or studied in a research context. These measurement subject categories constitute the inner sphere of Figure 7.3.

Individual Groups

Human subject categories are of three types: individuals, groups or populations, and families. Individuals are the common type of measurement subject, where data is collected from individual human participants. When measuring the level of training, years on the job, or other associated work-based criteria, groups or populations are often assessed. The assessment of families generally assesses the measurement characteristics of family units, such as lots or batches, for quality control.

Non-human subject categories are also of three types: animals, plants, and inanimate objects. The most interesting one in this category and the one you will be dealing with when exercising the DMAIC process is the inanimate objects type. Here you will be measuring objects such as machines or materials for properties like weight, size, and conductivity.

An excellent example of this category would be a DMAIC project focused on plating variations performed during a production process.

Object or Item Groups

Environmental factor categories are of three types: climate, air quality, and geographical features. Climate parameters like temperature, precipitation, and humidity are measured when working with composite materials either for production or storage. Measurement of air quality based on pollutants is a common practice when performing projects involving painting. Geographical features are critical when planning for production layout effects and optimization of operating space.

The physical objects and properties category has two elements: physical measurements and chemical composition. In physical measurement, you will assess objects for properties like mass, length, velocity, and temperature. For chemical composition, you will be testing solutions such as those used for composite work, plating, painting, and general surface cleaning for the appropriate composition.

The economic indicators category branches into two groups: gross domestic product (GDP) and inflation rate. GDP, because it measures the economic output of a country or region, will be used repeatedly when you are working on a DMAIC-based project. An understanding of inflation rates will also prove beneficial when planning a DMAIC-based project.

Events or Occurrences

The social constructs category has three elements: gender, race, and ethnicity. These areas will be ones you will deal with when performing a DMAIC-driven project. They are integral to building a cohesive Kaizen team and understanding the human dynamics of leading such a team. Gender may be used to measure social constructs and its effects on various aspects of society and race and ethnicity to study and measure signs of discrimination.

The time category will be the subject of a measurement and is considered a DMAIC bedrock staple. Its use will be critical in all aspects of process understanding and alignment.

The abstract concepts category is divided into two branches: ideas or concepts and emotions, both of which are critical in a DMAIC-driven project. Using ideas and concepts, you might measure abstract attributes such as attitudes, beliefs, or ideologies using surveys or questionnaires. On assessing emotions, you may measure happiness, sadness, or stress using self-reporting and physiological indicators.

Understanding the type of groups and categories of measurement is crucial for selecting appropriate research methods when performing a DMAIC-driven project. Different subjects require different approaches to data collection and analysis. As a Lean Six Sigma candidate, you must carefully consider the nature of your subject when assessing processes and designing potential solutions.

DESCRIPTIVE AND INFERENTIAL STATISTICS: WHAT IS THE DIFFERENCE?

Descriptive statistics and inferential statistics are two fundamental branches of statistics used in Lean Six Sigma to analyze and interpret data. However, they serve different purposes and have different methods. Figures 7.4 and 7.5 provide illustrations of the types of descriptive statistics used in the Measure phase of a Lean Six Sigma–type project.

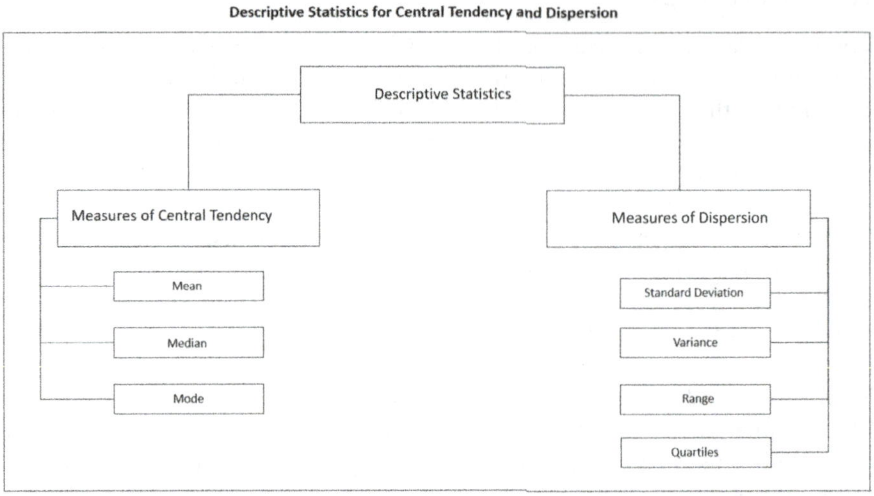

Figure 7.4 Descriptive Statistics for Central Tendency and Dispersion

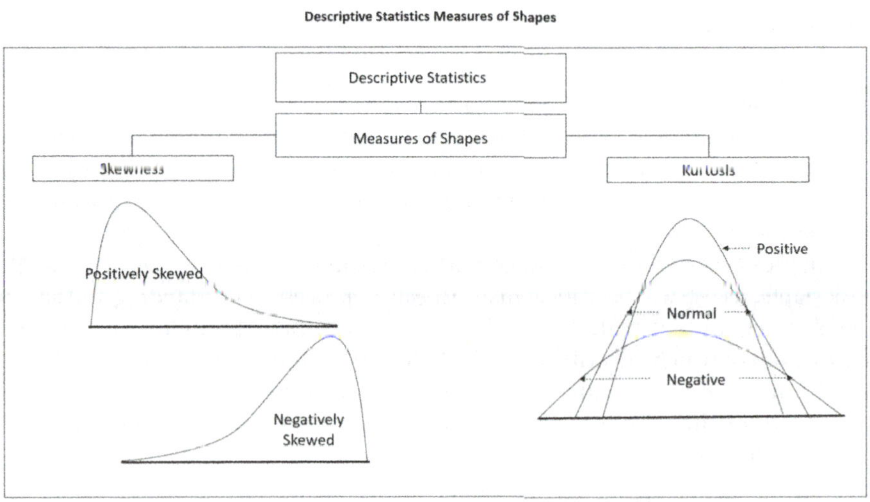

Figure 7.5 Descriptive Statistics Measures of Shapes

Descriptive Statistics

Descriptive statistics involve using various techniques to summarize and describe a dataset's main features. The primary goal is to provide a clear and concise summary of the data. Descriptive statistics are used to simplify and present data in an understandable way, making it easier to interpret and communicate with others.

Common measures in descriptive statistics include:

- Measures of central tendency – these include the mean (average), median (middle value), and mode (most frequent value) in the dataset.

- Measures of dispersion – these include:
  - Standard deviation – measures the dispersion of a dataset relative to its mean and is calculated as the square root of the variance.
  - Variance – the mean of square terms made up of the difference between each data item and the population mean. Variance is an indicator of the spread of the data.
  - Range – an ordered data set, it is the difference between the largest and the least value.
  - Quartiles – a division of observations into four defined intervals based on the data's values and how they compare to the entire set of observations.
- Measures of shape – these describe the distribution shape of the data. Two statistics used to describe shape are (see Figure 7.5):
  - Skewness – a distortion or asymmetry that deviates from the symmetrical bell curve, or normal distribution, in a dataset.
  - Kurtosis – a statistical measure used to describe the distribution of observed data around the mean.

Inferential Statistics

Inferential statistics involve making predictions, inferences, or generalizations about a population based on a sample of data. The primary goal is to draw conclusions about a population from a smaller representative subset. Figure 7.6 is an example of how inferential statistics are derived.

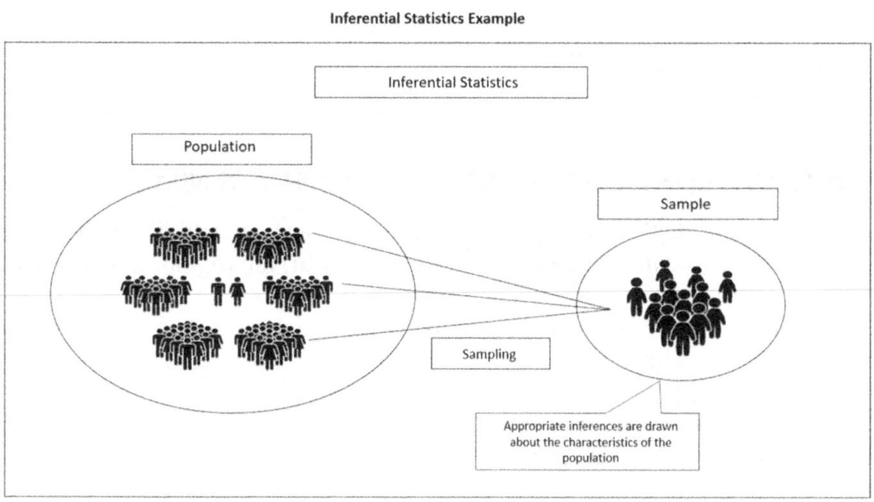

Figure 7.6 Inferential Statistics Example

Inferential statistics rely on probability theory and sampling techniques to make educated guesses about the population parameters, like the population mean and variance based on the sample statistics. Common methods in inferential statistics include hypothesis testing, confidence intervals, and regression analysis. You will often use inferential statistics to make a claim or test hypotheses about a population based on the data collected from your sample. This will involve assessing the likelihood of observed differences or relationships occurring by random chance or whether they are statistically significant.

Descriptive statistics are used to summarize and describe data, while inferential statistics are used to make inferences, predictions, and test hypotheses about a population based on a sample of data. Both branches of statistics play a crucial role in Lean Six Sigma project research and decision-making. They are used extensively in all DMAIC-driven initiatives. Each provides a different level of insight into data and helps researchers make informed judgements and decisions. Table 7.2 lists some of the main differences between descriptive and inferential statistics.

Table 7.2 The Difference Between Descriptive and Inferential Statistics

Descriptive Statistics	*Inferential Statistics*
It is the analysis of data that helps to describe, show, and summarize data under study.	It is the analysis of a random sample of data taken from a population to describe and make inferences about the population.
It organizes, analyses, and presents data in a meaningful way.	Used to compare, test, and make predictions.
It explains already-known data using population samples of a small size.	Used to explain the chance of occurrence of an event.
Results are shown with help of charts, graphs, and tables.	Uses estimation of parameters and testing of hypothesis.
Provides simple summaries about the sample and their measures.	Results shown as probability scores.
Includes calculating things such as the average of the data, its spread, and the shape it produces.	Used primarily when the dataset is large.

DISCRETE AND CONTINUOUS DATA: WHAT IS THE DIFFERENCE?

Data can be complicated! There is structured and unstructured data. Then, there is qualitative (or categorical) data and quantitative (or numerical) data. Quantitative data can be either "discrete" or "continuous".

Discrete data (often referred to as variables) take on countable and distinct values, whereas continuous data can take on any value within a data set (sample). When performing a Lean Six Sigma project and applying the DMAIC methodology, data analyses are performed continuously. The more you understand these data types, the more you will be able to identify opportunities for each.

Discrete data is a numerical type of data that includes whole, concrete numbers with specific and fixed values determined by counting. Continuous data includes complex numbers and varying data values over a particular time interval.

A simple way to describe how these can be used and the difference between the two is to visualize a scatter plot graph versus a line graph. Figure 7.7 illustrates how discrete and continuous type statistics are used in used together to manage a Lean Six Sigma project that dealt with cadmium plating.

Cadmium electroplating is used in application across a variety of industries, including:

- Aviation and aerospace – used because of its anti-corrosive qualities, natural lubricity, and adhesive bonding proprieties to make aluminum frames of aircraft and on landing gear struts.

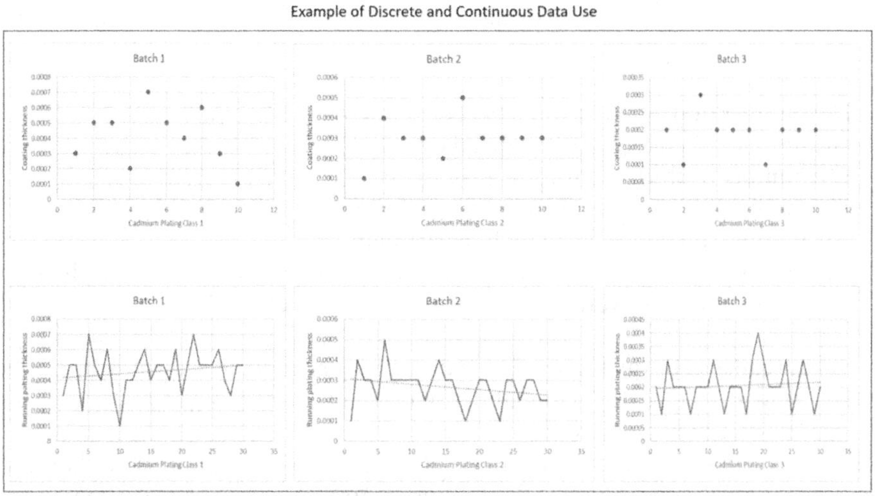

Figure 7.7 Example of Discrete and Continuous Data Use

- Transportation braking systems – because it has anti-corrosive ability.
- Marine – offers protection against salt-water corrosion.
- Consumer electronics – the conductivity of cadmium plating makes it ideal for use in connectors and relays and in batteries for cell phones and laptops.

The example illustrated in Figure 7.7 represents testing results of using first discrete data to examine the cadmium plating solution taking a random sample of mixture bases. Each batch is a different "type or classification" of plating mixture, and each has a different thickness (type 1.0005 in., type 2.0003 in., type 3.0002 in.). There is a +/−.000025 tolerance allowed for each type of coating.

Once the solution is declared stabilized and within specification, a "rough cut pilot" production process of artifacts for each type of coating is conducted to ensure plating thickness is consistent over the production run.

So now that the practical use of both discrete and continuous data has been illustrated by a real-world example, let us dive into some specifics of each.

What Is Discrete Data?

Discrete data refers to countable, individualized, and non-divisible figures in statistics. The data points exist only in set increments. Data analysis and statisticians visualize discrete data using bar graphs, line charts, histograms, and pie charts.

Discrete data typically involves counting rather than measuring, even if a computer or machine is doing the counting.

For example, if you track the number of pull-ups you do each day for a month, an underlying goal to evaluate your progress and the rate of improvement. With this said, your daily tally is a discrete, isolated number. So, the average number of pull-ups you did last week was 15 per day, 5 more per day than the previous week. The number of pull-ups is a whole number that you cannot break down into smaller parts.

Discrete data can be qualitative or quantitative. Examples of quantitative discrete data are:

- The number of defective products per production cycle run.
- The number of parts produced in a day.
- The number of students in your class.
- The number of employees in your organization.
- The number of computers in each department.
- The number of suppliers that are providing materials to build your product.
- The number of items you buy at the grocery store each week.

Discrete data can also be qualitative. The nationality you select on a form is a piece of discrete data. When grouped, the nationalities of everyone in your organization are valuable data that influence hiring practices.

Another example of discrete qualitative data is the data you collect using sliding scales. Imagine collecting product review data from users. You can create *ordinal* data points, such as "easy to use", "neutral", and "not easy". Visualizing this data helps quantify qualitative data.

Our national census consists of discrete data, both qualitative and quantitative. Counting and collecting this identifying information is how we understand the demographics of our population. It allows us to make predictions. The power of discrete data is great!

Discrete Data Characteristics

Discrete data is often used in simple statistical analysis because it is easy to summarize and compute. Other characteristics of discrete data are:

- Finite, countable, and non-divisible – discrete data includes discrete variables that are finite, numeric, and non-negative integers (e.g., 5, 10, 15, etc.).
- Easy to visualize – discrete data can be easily visualized and demonstrated using simple statistical methods such as bar charts, line charts, or pie charts.
- Can be categorical – discrete data can also be categorical, containing a finite number of data values, such as the gender of a person.
- Easy to distribute – discrete data is distributed discretely in terms of time and space. Discrete distributions make analyzing discrete values more practical.

WHAT IS CONTINUOUS DATA?

Continuous data typically involves fluctuating numbers between two presumed points. When these data points are connected on a graph, it will often result in a distinct line, like the line graphs illustrated in Figure 7.7.

These numbers are not always clean and tidy like those in discrete data, as they are usually collected from precise measurements. Over time, measuring a particular subject or article allows us to create a defined range where we can expect to collect more data.

Continuous data is all about accuracy. So, *continuous variables* often carry decimal points, with the number (base points) to the right stretched out as far as possible. This level of detail is paramount in Lean Six Sigma projects because Lean Six Sigma solutions are based on experiments and studies which involve constant measurement. If you have a number like "2.88290" anywhere on a spreadsheet, it is not a number you could derive quickly through measurement devices like stopwatches, scales, or thermometers.

Examples of continuous data are:

- Daily wind speed.
- Freezer temperature.
- Length of a customer service call.
- Product box measurements and weight.
- Plating production cycle runs.

Speaking of plating production runs, if we were to graph a production run of, say, 30 articles over a production run cycle, a histogram, which is often used to measure continuous data, could be developed to illustrate if the cycle run is "in control" or "out of control". Figure 7.8 illustrates a production run cycle of 30 articles on how the visualization of the data via histogram greatly aids the exploration.

Each histogram presented represents a continuous data run of information that paints a different picture of how the cadmium coating is being applied to the article under treatment. Batch runs 1 and 2 would be considered out of control based on the tolerance range and skew of the data. Batch run 3 would be considered in control but requires investigation because of outliers.

Continuous Data Characteristics

Unlike discrete data, continuous data can be either numeric or distributed over date and time. This data type normally uses rather advanced statistical analysis methods considering the infinite number of possible values it can assume. Some key characteristics of continuous data are:

- Changes over time – continuous data characteristically changes over time and thus can have different values at different time intervals.
- May or may not have decimals – continuous data is composed of random variables that may or may not be whole numbers.
- Visualized with line graphs or skews – continuous data is measured using data analysis methods such as graphs and skews, like those presented in Figures 7.7 and 7.8.

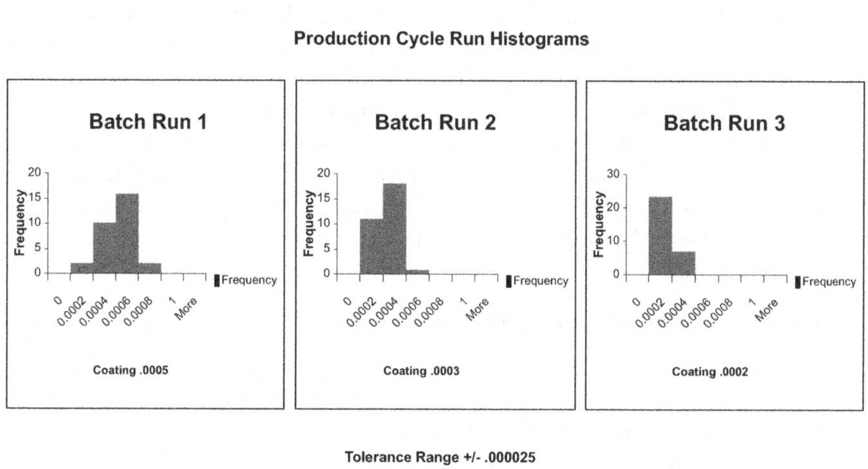

Figure 7.8 Production Cycle Run Histograms

Key Differences Between Discrete and Continuous Data

Both discrete and continuous data are important to statistical analysis. There are, however, some key differences between the two that should be understood before drawing conclusions or making assumptions about the data type. Table 7.3 illustrates some of the key differences between them based on attribute characteristics.

Table 7.3 Key Differences Between Discrete and Continuous Data

Attribute Characteristic	*Discrete*	*Continuous*
Value	Countable and finite	Any measured value within a specific range
Components	Ordinal and integer data values	Quantitative data points such as fractions, decimal numbers, and percentages
Countability and measurability	Counted on something as simple as a number line	Measured using in-depth measurement tools and methods like curves and skews
Divisibility	Non-divisible	Sub-divisible
Granularity	Less	More
Nature	Remains constant over a specific time interval	Varies over time and can have separate values at any given point
Common examples	Number of end items produced, number of parts that constitute the item, the size of each part	Height, weight, length, time, temperature, and age

Can Discrete Variables Be Treated as Continuous Variables and Vice Versa?

The short answer is "yes" to both. An example of discrete data being viewed as continuous is an everyday food staple such as "milk". While the grocery store knows the exact number of containers of milk sold by size, they order the milk to replenish stock by estimating the amount needed daily by forecast, which is based on continuous data.

An example of continuous data being viewed as discrete is age. You can accurately measure a person's age right down to the second, given that you know the time of birth. Age is a continuous variable in this case. However, we do not usually worry about someone's exact age. So age is treated as a discrete variable, counted in years.

The Importance of Discrete and Continuous Data

Both types of data are equally valuable to Lean Six Sigma data collectors. When executing a DMAIC-driven project, you will encounter countless instances in each phase that require measurement that leads to either type of data. A well-rounded research methodology is based on combining these two unique sets of data.

USING STATISTICAL SOFTWARE FOR DATA ANALYSIS

Using statistical software for data analysis is a common practice in various fields, including science, business, social sciences, and especially when performing a Lean Six Sigma project that is DMAIC driven. Statistical software helps researchers and analysts process, analyze, and interpret data efficiently.

Organizing Data for Analyses

The way we use that statistical software to derive meaningful insight through data analysis involves a series of steps. Figure 7.9 presents six general steps useful in organizing data for optimal analysis by statistical software.

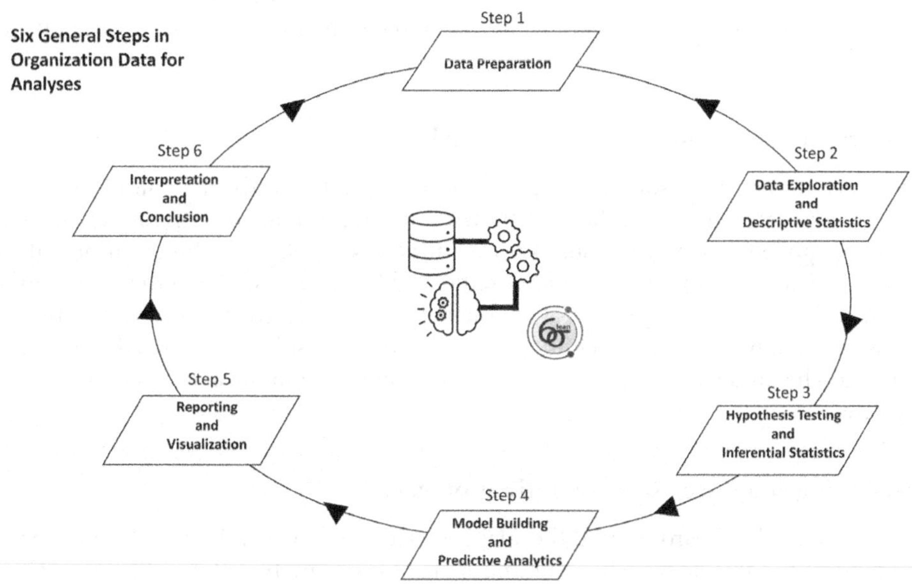

Figure 7.9 Six General Steps in Organizing Data for Analysis

Step 1 – Data Preparation – start by collecting and importing your data into the statistical software package selected. Data can come from various sources, including surveys, experiments, databases, or spreadsheets.

Step 2 – Data Preparation and Descriptive Statistics – use the selected statistical software to explore the data visually and through summary statistics. Generate descriptive statistics, such as means, medians, standard deviations, and frequency distributions, to understand the characteristics of the dataset.

Step 3 – Hypothesis Testing and Inferential Statistics – perform hypothesis tests to assess relationships and make inferences about the data. Common tests include t-tests, chi-squared tests, ANOVA, regression analysis, and correlation analysis. The selected software should provide tools to set up and execute these tests and interpret the results.

Step 4 – Model Building and Predictive Analytics – build statistical models, if necessary, to make predictions or gain a deeper understanding of your data. This could involve linear regression, logarithmic regression, decision trees, or machine learning algorithms. Most advanced analysis software offers model-building capabilities, with built-in model selection, evaluation, and validation capabilities.

Step 5 – Reporting and Visualization – create reports and presentations using the software to communicate your findings effectively. Most statistical software provides tools for generating tables, charts, and graphs for inclusion in reports. Most packages also allow you to export your results to other formats, such as Microsoft Word, PowerPoint, Excel, or PDF.

Step 6 – Interpretation and Conclusion – after conducting your analyses, interpret the results in the context of your research or problem. Explain the significance of your findings and whether they support your hypotheses or objectives. Draw meaningful conclusions and make recommendations based on your data analysis.

Choosing Statistical Software for Data Analysis

The choice of statistical software depends on the specific needs, the complexity of the analyses, your researcher's familiarity with the software, and the industry or field in which it is to be applied. It is not unusual for organizations to use a combination of software packages to meet various analytical requirements. I have done so before to take advantage of each package's strengths. Table 7.4 summarizes popular rated statistical software packages used by many industries, including manufacturing, healthcare, financial services, and academia. The ones with aircraft insets are commonly used in the aviation and aerospace industries.

Interpreting Graphical Representations of Data

All of us have either heard or used the adage "a picture is worth a thousand words". So, do we need to heed this adage when summarizing the information derived from statistical analyses from the software used?

How graphical representations are interpreted will influence what you will present and how you will present it. Since interpreting graphical representations of data is a fundamental skill in data analysis and research in general, knowledge of how you interpret the information derived from those representations is vital. Here are ten key steps on how to interpret the information conveyed by graphical representations of data:

Step 1 – Title and Labels – start by reading the title of the graph or chart. It often provides a brief description of what the graph represents. Check for axis labels (x-axis and y-axis) to understand what each axis represents. Labels should provide context for the data.

Step 2 – Data Points and Lines – examine the data points or lines on the graph. These represent the values or observations being plotted. Look for patterns, trends, or outliers in the data. Are there clusters of data, linear relationships, or irregularities?

Table 7.4 Summary of Popular Rated Statistical Software Packages

Software	*Key Features*	*Strengths*	*User Base*
Minitab	Minitab is user friendly and widely used in quality improvement and Lean Six Sigma projects. It offers a range of statistical tools for data analysis, quality control, and experimentation.	It excels in statistical analysis, hypothesis testing, regression analysis, and design of experiments.	Commonly used in academia and industries such as manufacturing, healthcare, and finance.
R	R is a free and open-source programming language and software environment for statistical computing and graphics. It has a vast library of packages for various statistical analyses and data visualization.	R is highly customizable, with a large and active user community. It is suitable for a wide range of statistical applications and advanced data analytics.	Widely used in academia, research, data science, and industries requiring advanced statical analysis, such as the design of aeronautical systems.
SAS	SAS (Statistical Analysis Software) is a comprehensive software suite for advanced analytics, business intelligence, and data management. It offers tools for data manipulation, statistical modeling, and reporting.	SAS is known for its data handling capabilities, advanced statistical modeling, and integration with other business intelligence tools.	Commonly used in industries such as healthcare, finance, government, and manufacturing in support of enterprise reporting planning (ERP) systems.
JMP	JMP is user-friendly statistical software with a focus on data exploration and visualization. It offers interactive tools for data analysis, experimentation, and modeling.	JMP is known for its dynamic and visual approach to data analysis, making in accessible to a broad audience, including non-statisticians.	Used in industries such as manufacturing, pharmaceuticals, and government.
SPSS	SPSS (Statistical Package for the Social Sciences) is a tried and proven software package for statistical analysis and data management. It provides a user-friendly interface for data entry, analysis, and reporting.	SPSS is widely used in social sciences, marketing research, and healthcare for basic statistical analysis, surveys, and reporting.	Commonly used in academia, social sciences, and market research.

(*Continued*)

Table 7.4 (Continued)

Software	*Key Features*	*Strengths*	*User Base*
Python	Python is free and open-source object-oriented software that is easy to code and read, with a robust standard library. It is an integrated and portable language, which adds to its usability.	Object-oriented language and GUI programming support, along with portability and extensible and embeddable features. Python is commonly used for developing websites and software, task automation, data analysis, and data visualization. Since it's relatively easy to learn, Python has been adopted by many non-programmers such as accountants and scientists for a variety of everyday tasks, like organizing finances.	Python is used by Intel, IBM, NASA, Pixar, Netflix, Facebook, JP Morgan Chase, Spotify, and a number of other massive companies. It's one of the four main languages at Google, while Google's YouTube is largely written in Python. The same goes for Reddit, Pinterest, and Instagram.
MATLAB	MATLAB is a high-performance programming language for technical computing. It integrates computation, visualization, and programming in an easy-to-use environment where problems and solutions are expressed in familiar mathematical notation. Typical uses include math and computation and algorithm development.	It provides a vast library of mathematical functions for linear algebra, statistics, Fourier analysis, filtering, optimization, numerical integration, and solving ordinary differential equations. It provides built-in graphics for visualizing data and tools for creating custom plots.	Engineers and scientists worldwide use MATLAB for a range of applications in industry and academia, including deep learning and machine learning, signal processing and communications, image and video processing, control systems, tests and measurements, computational finance, and computational biology.
Stata	Stata provides a range of nonparametric tests, nonparametric kernel regression, and nonparametric series regression. Access quantile regression, centiles, confidence intervals, resampling and simulations, smoothing, and ROC analysis.	Stata software uses artificial intelligence and machine learning to perform complex calculations; identify trends and patterns; and create charts, graphs, and tables accurately within minutes.	Stata software is primarily used by researchers in the fields of economics, biomedicine, and political science to examine data patterns.
Excel	Microsoft Excel, with its data analysis Toolpak add-in, offers basic statistical functions and tools for data analysis, making it accessible to many users.	Excel is readily available and familiar to many professionals, making it suitable for simple data analysis tasks.	Widely used in various industries and professions for basic statistical calculations.

Step 3 – Scale and Units – pay attention to the scale of the axes. Are they logarithmic? What are the units of measurement? Understand the ranges of values on each axis. This helps you gauge the magnitude of the data.

Step 4 – Data Representation – determine the type of graph being used. Common types include bar charts, line graphs, scatter plots, pie charts, and histograms. Different types of graphs are suited for different types of data. Analyze how the data is represented within the graph. For example, a bar chart might show comparisons between categories, while a line graph may illustrate trends over time.

Step 5 – Annotations and Legends – look for annotations, data labels, or a legend if applicable; these elements can provide additional context or explain specific data points. Legends are especially important for interpreting color-coded or symbol-coded data series.

Step 6 – Patterns and Trends – identify any patterns or trends in the data. Are values increasing, decreasing, or remaining relatively stable over time or across categories? Look for cyclical patterns, seasonality, or irregular fluctuations.

Step 7 – Outliers and Anomalies – be aware of outliers and anomalies in the data. These are data points that significantly differ from the majority and can have a substantial impact on interpretations. Consider whether outliers are due to errors or genuinely unique events.

Step 8 – Comparisons and Relationships – if there are multiple data series or categories on the graph, compare them. Are there differences or similarities between groups? Assess relationships between variables. Does one variable influence another?

Step 9 – Conclusion and Inference – based on your observations and analysis, draw conclusions or make inferences about the data. What can you deduce from the graph? Be cautious not to over-interpret the data; stick to what the graph shows.

Step 10 – Context and Background – consider the broader context of the data. Understand the purpose of the graph and any relevant background information. Be aware of any limitations or biases in the data collection process that may affect interpretation.

Interpreting graphical representations of data involves a combination of reading labels, assessing patterns, and drawing meaningful insights. Effective interpretation requires practice and a critical mindset to ensure that the information derived from the graph is accurate and useful for decision-making or further analysis.

SUMMARY

Chapter 7 began by first describing the Measure phase of the DMAIC methodology. It then addressed basic statistics, statistical measurements, and related terms commonly used in the Measure phase. The reader was then presented with a discussion on a process by which types of measurement subjects can be understood. This was followed by a discussion of descriptive and inferential statistics and how they differ. Discrete and continuous measurement was then presented, and a discussion was conducted on how they differ. Time was then devoted to how statistical software can be employed for data analysis, and recommendations were provided. The chapter concluded with a discussion of interpreting graphical summaries.

LEAN SIX SIGMA AT WORK!

Lean Six Sigma at Work

Based on the results of the Batch Production runs illustrated in **Figure 7-8**, further investigation was warranted to determine what causes were responsible for the out-of-control histogram readings on Plating Batches 1 and 2 and the outliers in batch 3.

An experiment was designed based on the sampling of a rough-cut production run spanning two shifts. The graph below describes the cause of rejection criteria selected along with frequency and percentage during the run.

Cause	Frequency	Cumulative Frequency	Percentage	Cumulative Frequency
Dirt in Solution	65	65	58.04	58.04
Imbalanced Solution	21	86	18.75	76.79
Cold Shuts	12	98	10.71	87.5
Pitting	5	103	4.46	91.96
Sharp Edges	4	107	3.57	95.54
Cleavage Points	2	109	1.79	97.32
Unclean article	2	111	1.79	99.11
Other	1	112	0.89	100

A Pareto chart was selected to illustrate the results of the experiment. A Pareto chart was chosen because it is a type of chart that contains bars and line graphs. Individual values are portrayed in descending order by bars, and the cumulative total is represented by the line. Pareto charts are often used to illustrate the famous *80-20 rule* that was first discovered by the great Italian economist Vilfredo Pareto (1848-1923). The *Pareto Rule* emphasizes the importance of few items in explaining a total. Below is the Pareto chart graph of the information presented above.

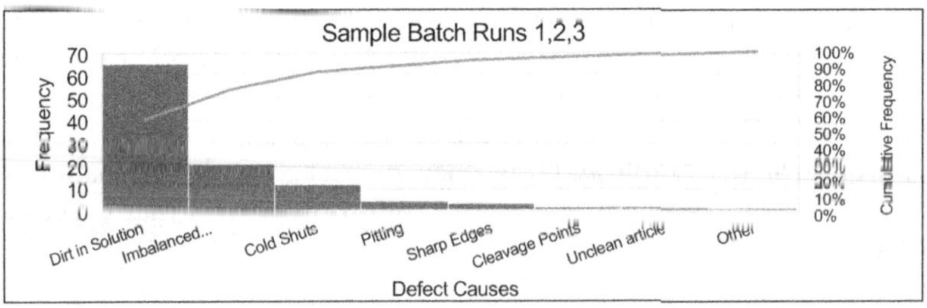

Based on the results from the experiment, all tanks were thoroughly cleaned and a shift change inspection instituted.

Figure 7.10

CHAPTER 7 DISCUSSION QUESTIONS

1. Select five of the roles measurements and basic statistics play during the Measurement phase of the DMAIC methodology and describe/discuss them.
2. Why is an understanding of measurement subjects essential for executing research and data collection in the Measurement phase? Select five of the types of measurement subject areas and describe/discuss them when providing your response.
3. Describe the differences between descriptive and inferential statistics.
4. Compare and contrast discrete and continuous data types. Give an example of each in your answer.
5. Briefly describe/discuss the six general steps in organizing data for analysis.

BIBLIOGRAPHY

Abatan, S. Matthew, and Michael Olayemi. "The role of statistical software in data analysis." *International Journal of Applied Research and Studies (iJARS) ISSN* (2014): 2278–9480.

Ali, Zulfiqar, and S. Bala Bhaskar. "Basic statistical tools in research and data analysis." *Indian Journal of Anaesthesia* 60.9 (2016): 662.

Alonso, Ricardo, and Odilon Camara. "Organizing data analytics." *Management Science* 70.5 (2024): 3123–3143.

Altman, Micah, and Michaell P. McDonald. "Choosing reliable statistical software." *PS: Political Science & Politics* 34.3 (2001): 681–687.

Arentze, Theo, and Harry Timmermans. "Parametric action decision trees: Incorporating continuous attribute variables into rule-based models of discrete choice." *Transportation Research Part B: Methodological* 41.7 (2007): 772–783.

Asadoorian, Malcolm O., and Demetrius Kantarelis. *Essentials of Inferential Statistics.* University Press of America, 2005.

Barnes, Sally, and Cathy Lewin. "An introduction to inferential statistics: Testing for differences and relationships." *Research Methods in the Social Sciences* (2005): 226–235.

Baumann, Peter. "Management of multidimensional discrete data." *The VLDB Journal* 3.4 (1994): 401–444.

Borenstein, Michael, et al. "Effect sizes for continuous data." *The Handbook of Research Synthesis and Meta-Analysis* 2 (2009): 221–235.

Bright, George W., and Susan N. Friel. "Graphical representations: Helping students interpret data." In *Reflections on Statistics.* Routledge, 2012, pp. 85–110.

Clark, Lee Anna, and David Watson. "Constructing validity: Basic issues in objective scale development." In A. E. Kazdin (Ed.), *Methodological Issues and Strategies in Clinical Research.* American Psychological Association, 2016, 4th ed., pp. 187–203. https://doi.org/10.1037/14805-012

Cope, Meghan, and Hilda Kurtz. "36 Organizing, coding, and analyzing qualitative data." In *Key Methods in Geography.* SAGE Publications, 2016, p. 647.

De Leon, A. R., A. Soo, and T. Williamson. "Classification with discrete and continuous variables via general mixed-data models." *Journal of Applied Statistics* 38.5 (2011): 1021–1032.

De Mast, Jeroen, and Joran Lokkerbol. "An analysis of the six sigma DMAIC method from the perspective of problem solving." *International Journal of Production Economics* 139.2 (2012): 604–614.

Diehl, Michael, and Wolfgang Stroebe. "Productivity loss in brainstorming groups: Toward the solution of a riddle." *Journal of Personality and Social Psychology* 53.3 (1987): 497.

Ebrahim, Shanil, et al. "Addressing continuous data for participants excluded from trial analysis: A guide for systematic reviewers." *Journal of Clinical Epidemiology* 66.9 (2013): 1014–1021.

Ebrahim, Shanil, et al. "Addressing continuous data measured with different instruments for participants excluded from trial analysis: A guide for systematic reviewers." *Journal of Clinical Epidemiology* 67.5 (2014): 560–570.

Erwig, Martin, et al. "Abstract and discrete modeling of spatio-temporal data types." In *Proceedings of the 6th ACM International Symposium on Advances in Geographic Information Systems.* Springer, 1998. https://link.springer.com/chapter/10.1007/978-3-662-09968-1_3

Fiske, Donald W. "Measuring to understand and understanding measuring." In *Applications of Interactionist Psychology: Essays in Honor of Saul B. Sells.* Routledge, 1988, pp. 121–143.

Galybin, A. N., and Sh A. Mukhamediev. "Determination of elastic stresses from discrete data on stress orientations." *International Journal of Solids and Structures* 41.18–19 (2004): 5125–5142.

George, Darren, and Paul Mallery. "Descriptive statistics." In *IBM SPSS Statistics 25 Step by Step.* Routledge, 2018, pp. 126–134.

Hanemann, W. Michael, and Barbara Kanninen. "The statistical analysis of discrete-response CV data." University of California, Berkeley, Department of Agricultural and Resource Economics, 1996.

Harry, Mikel J., et al. *Practitioner's Guide to Statistics and Lean Six Sigma for Process Improvements.* John Wiley & Sons, 2010.

Hazra, Avijit. "Descriptive and inferential statistics in biomedical sciences: An overview." In *The Quintessence of Basic and Clinical Research and Scientific Publishing.* Springer, 2023, pp. 461–478. https://doi.org/10.1007/978-981-99-1284-1_29

Heitjan, Daniel F. "Inference from grouped continuous data: A review." *Statistical Science* 4.2 (1989): 164–179.

Hirji, Karim F. *Exact Analysis of Discrete Data*. CRC Press, 2005.

Hollingshed, Melinda. "Standardizing six sigma green belt training: Identification of the most frequently used measure phase DMAIC tools." *International Journal of Lean Six Sigma* 13.2 (2022): 276–294.

Huang, Min-Wei, and Jasbir S. Arora. "Optimal design with discrete variables: Some numerical experiments." *International Journal for Numerical Methods in Engineering* 40.1 (1997): 165–188.

Joffe, Steven, et al. "Quality of informed consent: A new measure of understanding among research subjects." *Journal of the National Cancer Institute* 93.2 (2001): 139–147.

Kasperski, Adam. *Discrete Optimization with Interval Data*. Berlin: Springer, 2008.

Krippendorff, Klaus. "On the reliability of unitizing continuous data." *Sociological Methodology* (1995): 47–76.

Lavee, Gal, Ehud Rivlin, and Michael Rudzsky. "Understanding video events: A survey of methods for automatic interpretation of semantic occurrences in video." *IEEE Transactions on Systems, Man, and Cybernetics, Part C (Applications and Reviews)* 39.5 (2009): 489–504.

Leibovich, Tali, and Avishai Henik. "Comparing performance in discrete and continuous comparison tasks." *Quarterly Journal of Experimental Psychology* 67.5 (2014): 899–917.

Lunze, Jan, Bernhard Nixdorf, and Jochen Schröder. "Deterministic discrete-event representations of linear continuous-variable systems." *Automatica* 35.3 (1999): 395–406.

Marshall, Gill, and Leon Jonker. "An introduction to descriptive statistics: A review and practical guide." *Radiography* 16.4 (2010): e1–e7.

Marshall, Gill, and Leon Jonker. "An introduction to inferential statistics: A review and practical guide." *Radiography* 17.1 (2011): e1–e6.

Meletiou-Mavrotheris, Maria, and Despina A. Stylianou. "Graphical representation of data: The effect of the use of dynamical statistics technological tool." In *Information and Communication Technology*. Department of Educational Sciences, University of Cyprus, 2003. http://hdl.handle.net/10797/14686

Meyer, Patrick. *Understanding Measurement: Reliability*. Understanding Statistics, 2010.

Monteiro, Carlos Eduardo Ferreira, and Janet Mary Ainley. "The interpretation of graphs: Reflecting on contextual aspects." *Alexandria: Revista de Educação em Ciência e Tecnologia* 3.2 (2010): 17–30.

Nick, Todd G. "Descriptive statistics." *Topics in Biostatistics* (2007): 33–52.

Odukoya, Jonathan A., et al. "Item analysis of university-wide multiple choice objective examinations: The experience of a Nigerian private university." *Quality & Quantity* 52 (2018): 983–997.

O'Reilly III, Charles A., David F. Caldwell, and William P. Barnett. "Work group demography, social integration, and turnover." *Administrative Science Quarterly* (1989): 21–37.

Paykel, Eugene Stern. "Methodological aspects of life events research." *Journal of Psychosomatic Research* 27.5 (1983): 341–352.

Ready, Richard C., Jean C. Buzby, and Dayuan Hu. "Differences between continuous and discrete contingent value estimates." *Land Economics* (1996): 397–411.

Schöllhorn, W. I., et al. "Identification of individual walking patterns using time discrete and time continuous data sets." *Gait & Posture* 15.2 (2002): 180–186.

Schwendimann, René, et al. "The occurrence, types, consequences and preventability of in-hospital adverse events–a scoping review." *BMC Health Services Research* 18.1 (2018): 1–13.

Sestoft, Peter. "Organizing research data." *Acta Veterinaria Scandinavica* 53.1 (2011). BioMed Central.

Shokri, Alireza. "Quantitative analysis of six sigma, lean and lean six sigma research publications in last two decades." *International Journal of Quality & Reliability Management* 34.5 (2017): 598–625.

Simpson, Scot H. "Creating a data analysis plan: What to consider when choosing statistics for a study." *The Canadian Journal of Hospital Pharmacy* 68.4 (2015): 311.

Singh, Mahipal, et al. "A toolset for complex decision-making in analyze phase of lean six sigma project: A case validation." *International Journal of Lean Six Sigma* 14.1 (2023): 139–157.

Stapor, Katarzyna, and Katarzyna Stapor. "Descriptive and inferential statistics." In *Introduction to Probabilistic and Statistical Methods with Examples in R*. Springer, 2020, pp. 63–131.

Susac, Ana, et al. "Graphical representations of data improve student understanding of measurement and uncertainty: An eye-tracking study." *Physical Review Physics Education Research* 13.2 (2017): 020125.

Sutanapong, C., and P. I. Louangrath. "Descriptive and inferential statistics." *International Journal of Research & Methodology in Social Science* 1.1 (2015): 22–35.

Taghizadegan, Salman. *Essentials of Lean Six Sigma*. Elsevier, 2010.

Thomas, Len, and Charlies J. Krebs. "A review of statistical power analysis software." *Bulletin of the Ecological Society of America* 78.2 (1997): 126–138.

Tran, Dustin, et al. "Discrete flows: Invertible generative models of discrete data." *Advances in Neural Information Processing Systems* 32 (2019).

Tryon, Warren W., and David Bernstein. "Understanding measurement." *Understanding Research in Clinical and Counseling Psychology* (2003): 27–68.

Uluskan, Meryem. "Analysis of lean six sigma tools from a multidimensional perspective." *Total Quality Management & Business Excellence* 30.9–10 (2019): 1167–1188.

van Elst, Henk. "Foundations of descriptive and inferential statistics." *arXiv preprint arXiv:1302.2525* (2013).

West, Brady T., Kathleen B. Welch, and Andrzej T. Galecki. *Linear Mixed Models: A Practical Guide Using Statistical Software*. CRC Press, 2022.

Wilmut, J. "Objective test analysis: Some criteria for item selection." *Research in Education* 13.1 (1975): 27–56.

Winship, Christopher, and Robert D. Mare. "Structural equations and path analysis for discrete data." *American Journal of Sociology* 89.1 (1983): 54–110.

Zhan, Wei, and Xuru Ding. *Lean Six Sigma and Statistical Tools for Engineers and Engineering Managers*. Momentum Press, 2015.

8

Requirements of Measurement Systems

LEARNING OBJECTIVES

1 Describe the measures of central tendency, standard deviation, range, and variance.
2 Explain the elements of a control chart and analyze if a process is in control or out of control.
3 Articulate the importance of the normal distribution and explain capability indices in process capability analysis.
4 Describe the purpose of measurement system analysis (MSA), including gauge repeatability and reproducibility (gauge R&R) and the concepts of precision and accuracy.
5 Explain the significance of measurement system calibration, including bias, stability, and linearity.

MEASURING CENTRAL TENDENCY

Measuring central tendency is a fundamental aspect of descriptive statistics, which helps summarize a dataset by identifying a single value that represents the "center" or typical value of the data. There are several common measures of central tendency that Lean Six Sigma practitioners should be familiar with when executing a project using the DMAIC methodology.

- The first of these is the *arithmetic mean or just the mean* – the mean is the most common measure of central tendency. It is calculated by summing all the values in a dataset and then dividing them by the number of values. The formula of the mean $\langle I\rangle(\mu)\langle /I\rangle$ is:

$$\frac{\mu = \sum_{i=1}^{n} x_1}{n}$$

DOI: 10.4324/9781032650531-11

where:

(μ) is the mean.
(X_i) represents individual data points.
(n) is the total number of data points.

The mean is very sensitive to extreme outliers (exceeds two standard deviations when assessed in a probability density function (PDF)) in the data.

- The second of these is the *median* – the median is the middle value in a dataset when it is ordered from lowest to highest or vice versa. If there is an even number of data points, the median is the average of the two middle values. The median is less affected by extreme outliers than the mean.
- The third is the *mode* – the mode is the most frequently occurring value in a dataset. A dataset can have one mode (unimodal), more than one mode (multimodal), or no mode (all values occur with the same frequency). The mode is most useful for categorical data and can be used for numerical data as well.
- The fourth is the *geometric mean* – the geometric mean is used for data that represents ratios or multiplicative relationships. It is calculated by taking the *nth* root of the product of all values in the dataset, where *n* is the number of data points. The formula for the geometric mean *(G)* is:

$$G = \sqrt[n]{x_1 + x_2 + \cdots x_n}$$

where:

n^{th} √nth root of a number

The geometric mean is very useful for data focused on growth rates (forecasting) and financial returns.

- The fifth is the *harmonic mean* – the harmonic mean is most useful for data that represents rates or reciprocals. It is calculated by taking the reciprocal of the arithmetic mean of the reciprocals of the data points. The formula for the harmonic mean *(H)* is:

$$\overline{\;1 \quad 1 \qquad 1\;}$$
$$H = x_1 + x_2 + \cdots + x_n$$

The harmonic mean is most often used in Lean Six Sigma projects where the measuring of rates, speeds, or averaging time intervals is required.

The choice of which measure of central tendency to use depends upon the nature of the data and the research question being addressed. Often it is appropriate to use multiple measures to provide a more comprehensive understanding of the data's central tendency. Additionally, it is important to consider the distribution of the data and whether it is skewed or contains outliers when selecting the appropriate mean measurement tool.

QUANTIFYING PROCESS VARIABILITY

Quantifying process variability is an essential step in all Lean Six Sigma DMAIC-driven projects and is a critical factor in process improvement as well as quality control. It involves measuring and analyzing the degree of variation or dispersion in a process to understand its stability and performance. Some of the more common methods and techniques used to quantify process variability are:

- *Standard Deviation* – the standard deviation is a measure of how spread out the data points in a dataset are around the mean (average). A higher standard deviation indicates greater variability. It is often used to describe the variability in a normal distribution. The formula for the standard deviation is:

  $$(\sigma) = \sqrt{\sigma^2}$$

- *Range* – the range is the difference between the maximum and minimum values in a dataset. It provides a simple measure of dispersion but may not capture the full picture of variability, especially in the presence of outliers.
- *Variance* (σ^2) – variance is the square root of the standard deviation. It measures the average of the squared differences from the mean. It provides a measure of how individual data points deviate from the mean. The formula for variance is:

  $$\sigma^{2=(xi-\mu)2/(n-1)}$$

- *Coefficient of Variation (CV)* – the coefficient of variation is the ratio of the standard deviation to the mean. It is often used to express variability relative to the mean, making it useful for comparing the variability of different processes to different scales. The formula for the coefficient of variation is:

  $$CV = \frac{\sigma}{\mu}$$

- *Histogram* – histograms are graphical representations of data distribution. They can provide a visual insight into the shape and spread of data, allowing you to see patterns and identify potential sources of variability. An example of a histogram is shown as follows:

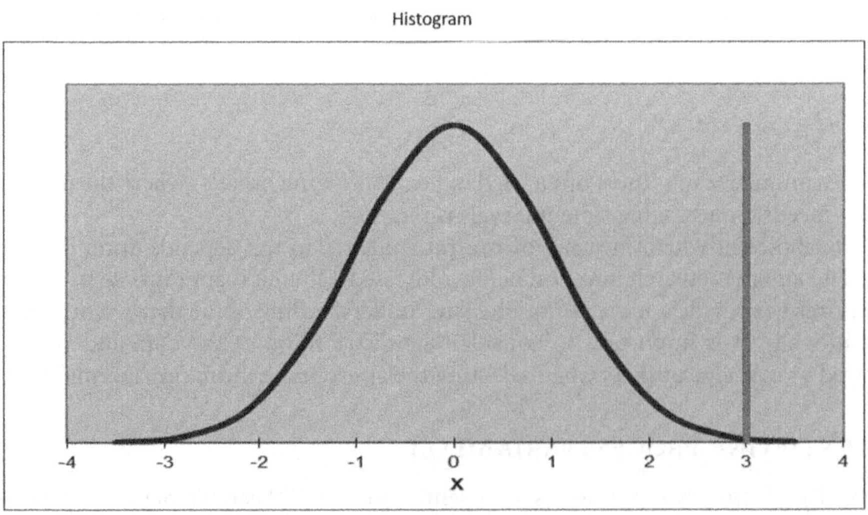

- *Control Charts* – control charts, such as the *X-bar and R-chart* or individual charts, are used in statistical process control (SPC) to monitor process variability over time. They help distinguish between common cause (random) and special cause (non-random) variation. Examples of the X-bar and R-chart are shown as follows:

Mean control chart and Range control chart

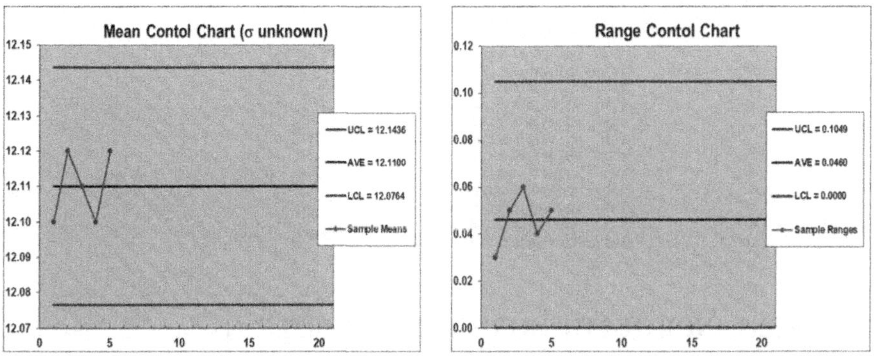

- *Analysis of Variance (ANOVA)* – is a statistical technique used to analyze the variation between multiple groups or treatments. It assesses whether the observed variability is due to differences between groups or if it can be attributed to random variation. Regression analysis can help identify relationships between variables and quantify the variability in the one variable explained by another. It is useful for understanding how changes in one variable affect another. An example of a multiple regression summary readout is provided as an example:

ANOVA Table

SUMMARY OUTPUT

Regression Statistics	
Multiple R	0.803398744
R Square	0.645449542
Adjusted R Square	0.57453945
Standard Error	1252.763898
Observations	19

ANOVA

	df	*SS*	*MS*	*F*	*Significance F*
Regression	3	42856229.89	14285410	9.102365	0.001126532
Residual	15	23541260.74	1569417.4		
Total	18	66397490.63			

	Coefficients	*Standard Error*	*t Stat*	*P-value*	*Lower 95%*	*Upper 95%*	*Lower 95.0%*	*Upper 95.0%*
Intercept	35102.90045	1837.226911	19.106459	6.11E-12	31186.94158	39018.8593	31186.94158	39018.85932
A Made	2.065953296	1.664981779	1.2408264	0.233727	-1.482873542	5.61478013	-1.48287354	5.614780134
B Made	4.176355531	1.681252566	2.4840738	0.025288	0.592848311	7.75986275	0.592848311	7.759862751
C Made	4.790641037	1.789316107	2.6773587	0.017223	0.97680169	8.60448038	0.97680169	8.604480385

- *Process Simulation and Modeling* – advanced techniques like Monte Carlo simulations or process modeling can be used to quantify process variability by simulating the behavior of a process under different conditions and input parameters. An example of a Monte Carlo run of 1,000 iterations is provided:

Process Simulation and Modeling

	B	C	D	E	F
1					
2	Trial			mean	0.495952
3	1	0.813262			
4	2	0.288988		Fraction	
5	3	0.939361		0-.25	0.2575
6	4	0.786287		.25-.50	0.2425
7	5	0.91443		.50-.75	0.2475
8	6	0.26157		.75-1	0.2525
9	7	0.336107			
10	8	0.503733			
11	9	0.105186			
12	10	0.956549			
13	11	0.857657			
14	12	0.126325			
15	13	0.558723			
16	14	0.351238			
17	15	0.856488			
18	16	0.77694			
19	17	0.626955			
20	18	0.552412			
21	19	0.718024			
22	20	0.548031			

THE IMPORTANCE OF THE NORMAL DISTRIBUTION

The normal distribution, also known as the Gaussian distribution or bell curve, is a fundamental concept in statistics and probability theory. It has significant importance in various fields and especially Lean Six Sigma, due to several key reasons. Figure 8.1 illustrates a normal distribution and eight of those key reasons.

Reason One, Commonality in Nature and Data – the normal distribution is often found in real-world phenomena, such as the heights of individuals, IQ scores, errors in measurements, threads of composite wrap that are flawed, and many other natural processes. This makes it a useful model for approximating and understanding a wide range of data.

Reason Two, Central Limit Theorem – the central limit theorem is a fundamental statistical concept that states that the sampling distribution of the sample mean of a sufficiently large number of independent, identically distributed random variables will be approximately normally distributed, regardless of the distribution of the original variables. This theorem is crucial for statistical inference, as it allows us to make inferences about parameters using the normal distribution even when the population itself is not normally distributed.

Reason Three, Statistical Inference – many statistical methods, such as hypothesis testing, confidence intervals, and regression analysis, rely on assumptions of normality. When data approximate a normal distribution, these methods tend to be more robust and reliable.

Reason Four, Parametric Statistics – Normality simplifies statistical analysis. Many parametric statistical tests and models, like t-test and linear regression, assume that the data comes from a normal distribution. When data conforms to this assumption, these tests are more valid and powerful.

Reason Five, Predictive Modeling – in fields like machine learning, the normal distribution assumption is often made for error terms or residuals. Linear regression models, for example, assume normally distributed residuals. Violation of this assumption can affect the model's predictive accuracy.

Reason Six, Quality Control – in manufacturing and quality control, the normal distribution is often used to model variations in product characteristics. Control charts,

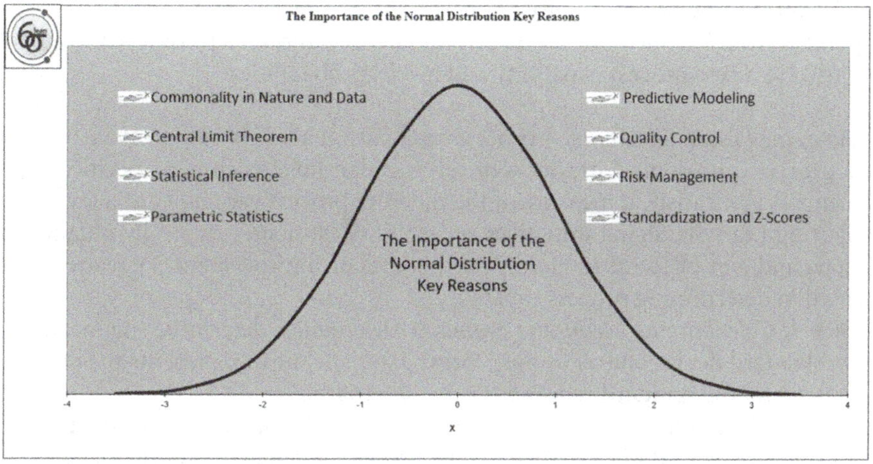

Figure 8.1 The Importance of the Normal Distribution: Key Reasons

process capability analysis, and quality control procedures often rely on the normal distribution to determine process stability and conformance to specifications.

Reason Seven, Risk Management – in finance and risk analysis, the normal distribution is used to model returns on investments and the distribution of asset prices. In Lean Six Sigma and general project management it is used to assess probability of success based on DMAIC methodology execution. Tools like Value at Risk (VaR), a way to quantify the risk of potential losses for a firm or an investment, can be used. The VaR metric can be computed in three ways: the historical, variance-covariance, and Monte Carlo methods. Another tool that is often used is the Black-Scholes option pricing model. The Black-Scholes model, a.k.a. the Black-Scholes-Merton (BSM) model, is a differential equation widely used to price options contracts. The Black-Scholes model requires five input variables: the strike price of an option, the current stock price, the time to expiration, the risk-free rate, and the volatility.

Reason Eight, Standardization and Z-Scores – the normal distribution allows for standardization of data Z-scores, which are calculated via the following equation:

$$\frac{Z = X - \mu}{\sigma}$$

This facilitates comparison and assessments across different datasets and variables.

While the normal distribution is a powerful and widely used tool, it is important to note not all data follow a perfectly normal distribution. In practice, many datasets exhibit deviations from normality. In such cases, the Lean Six Sigma practitioner often employs techniques such as Box-Cox or the standard T-test to transform the dataset.

USING THE NORMAL DISTRIBUTION CONCEPTS TO ASSESS CAPABILITY AND Z-SCORES TO MODEL PROBABILITIES

Applying normal distribution concepts, including Z-scores, to assess "capability" is a common practice in Lean Six Sigma projects that are DMAIC driven and in statistical process control and quality management. While the Gaussian distribution is widely used to model the variation in processes and measurements, the Z-score is used to quantify how far a data point is from the mean in terms of standard deviation. Here is how these concepts can be used to assess process capability and model probabilities:

- *Assessing Process Capability* – process capability analysis is used to evaluate how well a process can produce products or services that meet customer specifications. It is defined as a statistical measure of the inherent process variability of a given process. During Lean Six Sigma initiatives, a capability estimate is typically obtained at the start and end of the study to reflect the level of improvement. Here are four steps used in determining process capability:

  Step 1. Calculate the Mean and Standard Deviation – determine the mean (μ) and standard deviation (σ) of the process data. The mean represents the process center, and the standard represents process variation.

  Step 2. Define the Specification Limits – identify the upper and lower specification limits (USL and LSL) that define the acceptable range of product or service characteristics according to customer requirements.

  Step 3. Calculate Capability Indices:
  - C_p (Process Capability Index) $C_p = \frac{ULS - LSL}{6\sigma}$
  - C_{pk} (Process Capability Index – Centered) $Cpk = \min(\frac{\mu - LSL}{3\sigma}, \frac{USL - \mu}{3\sigma})$
  - P_p (Process Potential Index) $Pp = \frac{USL - LSL}{6\sigma}$
  - P_{pk} (Process Performance Index – Centered) $Ppk = \min(\frac{\mu - LSL}{3\sigma}, \frac{USL - \mu}{3\sigma})$

  Step 4. Interpret the Capability Indices:
  - A C_p or P_p value close to 1 indicates that the process is small relative to the specification width, which is desirable.
  - A C_{pk} or P_{pk} value close to 1 suggests that the process is centered within the specification limits.
  - When C_{pk} or P_{pk} is significantly lower than 1, it indicates that the process is not capable of consistently producing products within the specifications.

An example of how this is used is presented Table 8.1.

Capability

Machine	Standard Deviation	Machine Capability	Specification Width	C_p
A	0.1	0.6	0.8	1.333333333
B	0.08	0.48	0.8	1.666666667
C	0.16	0.96	0.8	0.833333333

Non centered

Machine	Process Mean	Standard Deviation	Lower Specification	Ratio	Upper Specification	Ratio	C_{pk}
A	9.2	0.3	7.5	1.888888889	10.5	1.444444444	1.444444444

With a C_p and C_{pk} above 1, both machines A and B would be acceptable. An index of 1 would mean the process is *capable*, but machine A, with a C_p of 1.33, would be widely viewed as being *optimal.*

- *Modeling Probabilities with Z-Scores* – Z-scores are used to calculate probabilities associated with the normal distribution. They indicate how many standard deviations a data point is from the mean. You can use Z-scores to model the probability of specific events occurring within the normal distribution. There are three steps that are used to model probabilities with Z-scores. The following is an example situation that I have encountered using these three steps.

Example situation: A sample of 100 composite threaded rods has been taken to assess process capability stability. The samples are normally distributed with a mean (μ) of 75 and a standard deviation (σ) of 10. There was a need to find the probability that a randomly selected sample would have a mean above 85.

Step 1. The Z-score was calculated:

$Z = x - \mu / \sigma$
$Z = (85-75)/10$
$Z = 1.0$

Step 2. The Z-score was looked up using a Z-table – using a Z-table, the probability associated with the Z-score of 1.0 was found. The table then told us that approximately 0.8413 of the data fell below $Z = 1.0$. We then found the probability of scoring above 85 by subtracting cumulative probability from 1: Probability $(X > 85) = 1 - 0.08413 \approx 0.1587$.

So, the probability that a random selected composite threaded rod would have a mean above 85 is approximately 0.1587 or 15.87%.

By using Z-scores and the normal distribution, you can calculate probabilities, confidence intervals, and tolerance intervals, which allows you to make informed decisions about process capability and product specifications. Both concepts are fundamental in all DMAIC-driven Lean Six Sigma initiatives, quality control, risk assessment, and statistical analysis.

PROBLEM SOLVING USING CAUSE AND EFFECT ANALYSIS

In a DMAIC-driven Lean Six Sigma project, when "cause and effect" analysis is referred to, thought automatically turns to the *Ishikawa or fishbone diagramming* process. At one level of process assessment, when using the DMAIC methodology, this process methodology is particularly useful when dealing with basic issues or when there is a need to understand the relationships between various factors contributing to a problem.

There is, however, another statistical cause and effect analysis process that allows the Lean Six Sigma practitioner to systematically identify the process inputs that could significantly affect the output of interest in identifying those cause and effect attributes that are causing the problem. This process is often referred to as "input variable section" or "factor identification." The overall goal is to determine which input variables have the most substantial impact on the output variable so that resources can be focused on optimizing and controlling those factors.

Ishikawa or Fishbone Cause-and-Effect Diagramming

The Ishikawa or fishbone cause-and-effect diagram offers a structural approach to search for probable causes of a process problem. It is known as a fishbone diagram because of its shape, or an Ishikawa diagram after the Japanese professor who developed the approach to aid workers overwhelmed by the number of possible sources of problems when solving problems. The tool is often used for brainstorming sessions to organize the ideas generated. Figure 8.2 illustrates one form of a cause-and-effect diagram.

Here is how to use cause-and-effect analysis for problem solving:

Step 1 – Define the Problem – clearly articulate the problem requiring action. Make sure the problem statement is specific and well defined before leaving this step.

Step 2 – Create the Fishbone Diagram – Figure 8.2 illustrates one of many types of formats the fishbone diagram can take. However, each type has a common characteristic, which is that a horizontal arrow pointing to the right constitutes the problem. A problem statement is included at the end of the arrow.

Step 3 – Identify Major Categories – on the horizontal arrow, draw diagonal lines (like fishbones). These lines represent major categories of potential causes related to the problem. Common categories are like those included in Figure 8.2, management, person, method, measurement, machine, and material.

Step 4 – Identify Sub-Causes – along each category line, identify and write down the specific factors or sub-causes that might contribute to the problem. Brainstorming or basic data analysis is recommended to generate ideas about potential causes.

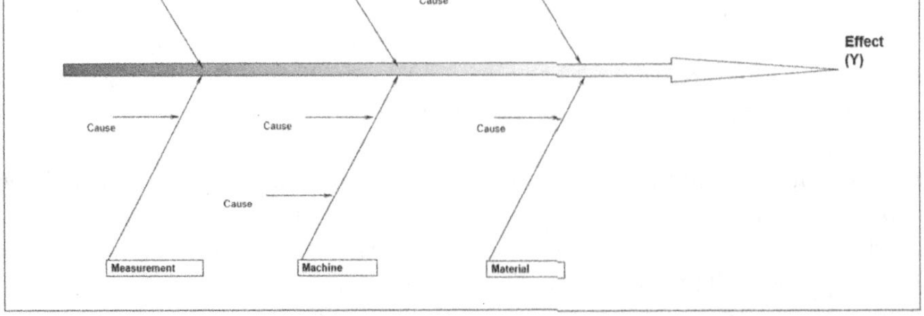

Figure 8.2 One Format of a Cause-and-Effect Diagram

Step 5 – Analyze and Explore Causes – examine the cause-and-effect relationships among the sub-causes and how they might be interconnected. Recommend using the 5-Why process where you ask "Why" repeatedly to dig deeper into the root causes and how they might be interconnected.

Step 6 – Prioritize Causes – not all causes are equally important. Use tools like Pareto analysis to identify the most significant causes that, if addressed, are likely to have the most impact on solving the problem.

Step 7 – Develop Solution – Once you have identified the root causes or significant contributing factors, brainstorm potential solutions for each cause. Ensure that your solutions are actionable, specific, and targeted at addressing the identified causes.

Step 8 – Implement and Monitor – put your solution into action and monitor the results. Track the changes and improvements in the problem over time. Adjust your approach if necessary and continue to monitor to ensure the problem remains solved.

Step 9 – Reflect and Learn – after implementing the solutions, conduct a post-implementation review to assess the effectiveness of actions taken. Learn from the process and apply any insights gained to future problem-solving efforts.

Step 10 – Documentation – keep a record of the cause-and-effect analysis, including the identified cause, potential solutions, and outcomes. This documentation can be valuable for future reference and sharing insights with your team.

Cause-and-effect analysis is a structured approach to problem solving that encourages a systematic exploration of potential causes and helps prevent simply addressing symptoms of problems. It promotes a deeper understanding of the issues, leading to a more effective and potentially sustainable solution.

INPUT VARIABLE SELECTION OR FACTOR IDENTIFICATION

Systematically identifying process cause-and-effect inputs that could significantly affect the output of interest is a crucial step in DMAIC-driven Lean Six Sigma process improvement and quality control projects.

Statistical-based feature selection methods involve evaluating the relationship between an input variable and the target variable using statistics and selecting those input variables that have the strongest relationship with the target variable. The overarching goal is to determine and select those variables having the most impact on the target variable. Here is a tried and proven step-by-step approach to identifying those critical input variables, along with some recommended statistical tools that can help with the selection process.

Step 1 – Define the Output of Interest – clearly define the output or response variable that needs to be improved or controlled. This could be product quality, process yield, customer satisfaction score, and so on.

Step 2 – Collect Historical Data – gather any historical data available from past process runs or operations, including both input variables and corresponding output variables.

Step 3 – Data Processing – ensure the data collected is "clear" (free from errors), and preprocess (transform it into a format that can be understood and analyzed) the data to ensure its accuracy and consistency. Address missing values, outliers, or any data issues that may affect the analysis.

Step 4 – Select an Analysis Technique – choose an appropriate statistical or data analysis technique based on the nature of the data under study. Common techniques include:

- Regression analysis – a powerful statistical method that allows the examination of the relationship between two or more variables of interest. While there are many types of regression analysis, at their core they all examine the influence of one or more independent variables on a dependent variable.
- Design of experiments (DoE) – also known as experiment design or experimental design, it is the design of any task that aims to describe and explain the variation of information under conditions that are hypothesized to reflect the variation. Through the use of a designed experiment, a prediction is made on the outcome by introducing a change of the preconditions, which is represented by one or more independent variables, also referred to as "input variables" or "predictor variables." The change in one or more independent variables is hypothesized to result in a change in one or more dependent variables, also referred to as "output variables" or "response variables."
- Correlation analysis – a statistical method used to measure the strength of the linear relationship between two variables then compute their association. Simply put – correlation analysis calculates the level of change in one variable due to the change in the other.
- Data mining – the process of sorting through large data sets to identify patterns and relationships that can help solve business problems through data analysis. Data mining techniques and tools enable the prediction of future trends, thus promoting more informed business decisions.

Step 5 – Perform Initial Analysis – start by conducting an initial analysis to explore the relationship between input variables and the output variables of interest. Here is a recommended order of next steps to consider:

- *First, start with descriptive statistics* – calculate summary statistics for input variables and the output to understand their distributions.
- *Second, perform correlation analysis* – calculate correlation coefficients using as an example Pearson correlation (a correlation coefficient that measures linear correlation between two sets of data) or Spearman (the Spearman correlation between two variables is equal to the Pearson correlation between the rank values of those two variables) to identify variables that are linearly or non-linearly related to the output.
- *Third, create scatter plots* – create scatterplots or other visualization techniques to visualize the relationship between input variables and output variables.
- *Fourth, perform hypothesis testing, including the T-test (a statistical test used to compare the means of two groups).* It is often used in hypothesis testing to determine whether a process or treatment influences the population of interest or whether two groups are different from one another) and ANOVA (a statistical formula used to compare variances across the means (or average) of different groups. A range of scenarios use it to determine if there is any difference between the means of different groups) to determine if input variables significantly impact the output.

Step 6 – Feature Selection – if there is a large number of variables, consider using "feature selection" techniques like the following to identify a subset of the most relevant variables:

- *Stepwise regression* – a step-by-step iterative construction of a regression model that involves the selection of independent variables to be used in a final model. It involves adding or removing potential explanatory variables in succession and testing for statistical significance after each iteration.
- *Forward selection* – in forward selection, the first variable selected for an entry into the constructed model is the one with the largest correlation with the dependent variable. Once the variable is selected, it is evaluated based on certain criteria. The most common ones are Mallows' C_p or Akaike's information criterion (a mathematical method for evaluating how well a model fits the data it was generated from. In statistics, AIC is used to compare different possible models and determine which one is the best fit for the data).
- *Backward elimination* – backward elimination is a statistical method used to find the simplest model that explains the data. It can be used to find the best model by iteratively removing variables that are not statistically significant.

Step 7 – Modeling and Regression Analysis – develop statistical models like linear regression, multiple regression to quantify the relationship between input variables and the output variable. Assess the model's coefficients and significance levels to identify the most influential factors.

Step 8 – Prioritize Input Variables – based on the analysis results and the significance levels of input variables, prioritize them according to their impact on the output. Variables with the highest influence should be given the most attention.

Step 9 – Validation and Testing – validate the identified input variables and their impact on the output through additional data collection or experimentation. Verify that the relationships hold true under different conditions.

Step 10 – Continuous Monitoring – implement a system for continuous monitoring of the prioritized input variables to ensure they remain within acceptable limits and that their impact on the output variable is controlled over time.

Step 11n – Iterate and Refine – as the process evolves or new data becomes available, periodically revisit the input variable selection process to refine understanding of their impact and adjust as needed.

By systematically identifying and focusing on the most significant input variables, more targeted improvements can be made to the process under study, quality control efforts can be enhanced, and overall performance can be experienced.

ASSESSING VARIATION THROUGH MEASUREMENT SYSTEM ANALYSIS

Measurement systems analysis (MSA) is a critical process in quality management and statistical process control and is central to the successful execution of any DMAIC-driven Lean Six Sigma project. MSA is defined as

> an experimental and mathematical method of determining the amount of variation that exists within a measurement process. Variation in the measurement process can directly contribute to our overall process variability. MSA is used to certify the measurement system for use by evaluating the system's accuracy, precision, and stability.

The following are steps that can be taken when assessing variation through MSA.

Step 1 – Define the Purpose and the Scope – before beginning an MSA analysis, you must clearly define the purpose of the measurement system and the specific components, characteristics, or processes you want to measure. Sources of variation in the measurement process can include the following:

- Process – test method, specification.
- Personnel – the operators, their skill level, training, and so on.
- Tools/equipment – gauges, fixtures, test equipment used, and their associated calibration systems.
- Items to be measured – the part or material samples measured, the sampling plan, and so on.
- Environmental factors – temperature, humidity, and so on.

Most MSA activities examine two primary sources of variation: the parts and the measurement of those parts. The sum of these values represents the total variation in the measurement system. All sources of variation should be considered during the MSA analysis.

Step 2 – Select a Measurement Method – choose the appropriate measurement method, equipment, and tools for the specific measurements you need to make. Common tools and techniques of measurement systems analysis include:

- calibration studies,
- fixed-effect ANOVA,
- components of variance,
- attribute gauge study,
- gauge R&R,
- ANOVA gauge R&R, and
- destructive testing analysis.

The tool selected is usually determined by the characteristics of the measurement system itself

Step 3 – Gather Data – to perform an MSA analysis, you should first obtain a sample of data and establish the reference value compared to a traceable standard. The data could be attribute data or variable data. Attribute data is classified into specific values where variable or continuous data can have an infinite number of values. Some processes will already have "master samples" established for the high and low end of the expected measurement specification. This collected sample of measurement data must then be repeatedly measured using the same items or samples. Ensure that the samples represent the full range of variation expected in the process under evaluation.

Step 4 – Conduct a Gauge R&R Study – a gauge R&R study is a standard technique for assessing the level of uncertainty with a measurement system for both discrete and continuous datasets. This process will be addressed in depth in a separate section of the chapter.

Step 5 – Calculate and Analyze the Components of Variation – after conducting the gauge R&R study, calculate the following components of variation:

- Total variation (TV) – the total variation in the measurement data.
- Repeatability (R/T) – the variation due to equipment repeatability.
- Reproducibility (R&R/T) – the variation due to differences between operators.
- Measurement error (ME) – the sum of repeatability and reproducibility, which represents the measurement system's overall variation.

Step 6 – Determine the Percent of Variation – calculate the percent of variation due to repeatability (R/T) and reproducibility (R&R/T) to understand their contribution to the total variation.

Step 7 – Evaluate the Measurement System – use a statistical tool like analysis of variance to assess the significance of the components of variation. Then, compare the variation introduced by the measurement system (R&R) to the acceptable limits or tolerances for the specific application. Note that a common rule of thumb is that the measure system variation should be much smaller than the process variation you are trying to measure and control.

Step 8 – Make Improvements – if the measurement system's variation is too high, identify and address the scores of errors. This involves the calibration of equipment, providing training to operators, or using a more reliable measurement method.

Step 9. Repeat as Necessary – conduct periodic MSA studies to ensure that the measurement system remains stable and reliable over time.

Measure systems analysis is fundamental and crucial in ensuring that the data collected accurately reflects the true characteristics of the process or product being measured. It helps identify and eliminate sources of measurement error that could negatively affect your DMAIC-driven Lean Six Sigma project, leading to better decision-making and improved quality control.

PRECISION AND ACCURACY

Precision and accuracy are two fundamental concepts in measurement systems analysis used to assess the quality and reliability of a measurement system. Each represents various aspects of how well a measurement system performs. The following are characteristics of each:

- Precision
  - Refers to the degree of consistent or repeatability in measurements obtained from the same measurement system when applied to the same object or characteristic repeatedly.
  - Assesses the variation in measurements that occurs when the measurement system is used under the same conditions and with the same operators and equipment.
  - It is typically quantified using statistics such as standard deviation, variance, or the range of measurements.
  - Precise measurements have low variation. Data points are clustered closely together.
- Accuracy
  - Is the degree to which measurements obtained from a measurement system are close to the true or target value of the characteristic being measured.
  - Assesses the bias or systematic error in measurements, the difference between the measured value and the true value.
  - Is typically quantified by comparing measurements to a known reference or standard or by analyzing measurement error.
  - Accurate measurements have a low bias and are centered around the true value.

Figure 8.3 illustrates graphically the fundamental concepts of precision and accuracy.

Interpretation of Figure 8.3 is as follows:

- *Low Precision–Low Accuracy* – measurements are inconsistent and illustrate systematic error. The measurement system is neither reliable nor accurate, and significant improvements are required.
- *High Precision–Low Accuracy* – this situation occurs when measurements are consistent and repeatable by consistently deviating from the true value. It represents a systematic error that requires correction.
- *High Precision–High Accuracy* – this is the ideal scenario, where measurements are both consistent and close to the true value. It indicates a reliable and trustworthy measurement system.
- *Low Precision–High Accuracy* – measurements consistently deviate from the true value, but they are not consistent among themselves. While the measurements are biased, they are still predictable.

In measurement system analysis, the goal is to achieve both high precision and high accuracy. When assessing the acceptability of either precision or accuracy measurements, here are some rule-of-thumb statistics to keep in mind.

- When measuring precision, use the average precision (AP) value. The higher the value (between 1 and 0), the better.
- When measuring accuracy, an average reading greater than 70% is acceptable, and the kappa value (compares the probability of agreement to that expected if the ratings are independent. The values of range lie between −1 and +1, with +1 presenting complete agreement and −1 meaning no agreement or independence). A negative statistic implies that the agreement is worse than random. A positive statistic ranging from 0.40 to 0.85 represents good correspondence.

By understanding and improving precision and accuracy, you can have confidence that the measurement system being used is providing reliable data for decision-making and quality control conditions.

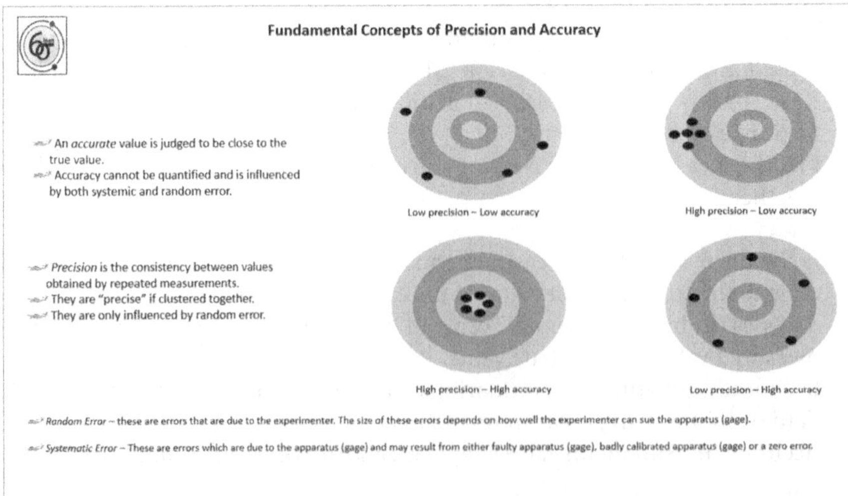

Figure 8.3 Fundamental Concepts of Precision and Accuracy

BIAS, LINEARITY, AND STABILITY

In measurement systems analysis, bias, linearity, and stability are three important factors assessed to ensure a measurement system's reliability and accuracy. These factors evaluate the performance of the measurement system over time and under varying conditions. Figure 8.4 shows a graphical representations of these three factors.

Bias

Bias, also known as systematic error or accuracy, refers to the consistent deviation of measurement results from the true or target value. It indicates whether the measurement system tends to consistently overestimate or underestimate the true value. Bias can be caused by various factors, such as instrument calibration errors, environmental conditions, or operator bias. To assess bias, you typically compare measurements from the measurement system to a known reference or standard. The difference between the measured values and the true values is a measure of bias.

To assess bias, the following steps should be followed:

1. Compare measurements from a measurement system to reference standards or known values.
2. Calculate and analyze the bias, which is the difference between measured values and true values.
3. Correct bias by adjusting the measurement system if necessary.

Linearity

Linearity assesses how well the measurement system produces measurements that are proportional to the true values across the entire measurement range. Non-linearity can result from sensor non-linearities, instrument limitations, or calibration issues. To evaluate linearity, measurements are taken at multiple points across the measurement range. A linear relationship between the measured values and true values is expected. Deviations from linearity indicate non-linearity.

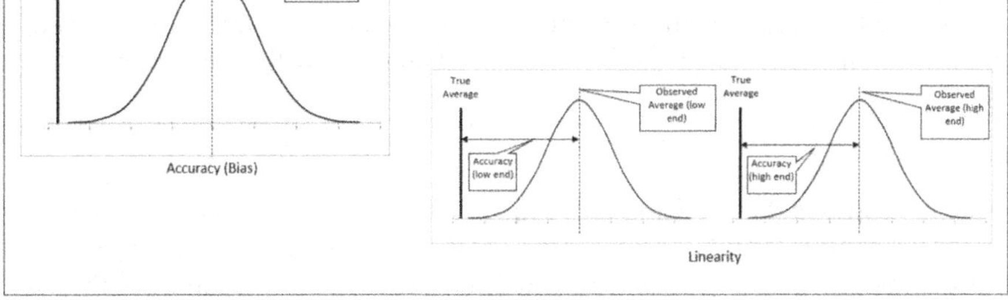

Figure 8.4 Graphical Representation of Bias, Stability, and Linearity

To assess linearity, the following steps should be followed:

1 Collect measurements at multiple points across the measurement range.
2 Create a plot or use regression analysis to assess how closely the measurements follow a linear relationship with the true values.
3 Identify and address non-linearities, which may involve re-calibration or correcting for non-linear errors.

Stability

Stability assesses the consistency of a measurement system's performance over time and under varying conditions. It checks whether the measurement system exhibits significant drift or variation that could affect measurement accuracy. Factors that can affect stability include changes in environmental conditions like temperature or humidity, wear and tear of measurement equipment, or degradation of sensors. Stability is often assessed through calibration and performance checks over time. Monitoring trends or shifts in measurement results helps identify stability issues.

To assess stability, the following steps should be followed:

1 Conduct regular calibration checks and performance monitoring to ensure that the measurement system remains stable.
2 Track measurement results over time and look for trends or shifts that may indicate instability.
3 Address stability issues through maintenance, calibration, or environmental control measures.

Bias, linearity, and stability are critical aspects of MSA that help ensure the accuracy and reliability of measurement systems. Regular monitoring, calibration, and addressing any issues that arise are essential for maintaining the quality of measurement data.

GAUGE, REPEATABILITY, AND REPRODUCIBILITY

In measurement systems analysis, the terms "gauge", "repeatability", and "reproducibility" are closely related and often used to evaluate the performance and reliability of measurement systems. They are commonly assessed using a gauge R&R study. Figure 8.5 is a graphical representation of a gauge R&R.

Gauge

In MSA, a "gauge" refers to the measuring instrument or device used to obtain measurements. It can be any tool or equipment that qualifies a characteristic or dimension of an object, product, or process. The term "gauge" is also used interchangeably with "measurement system".

Repeatability

Repeatability assesses the precision and consistency of measurements obtained using the same measurement system, under the same conditions, by the same operator or with the same instrument, when measuring the same item repeatedly. It quantifies the variation

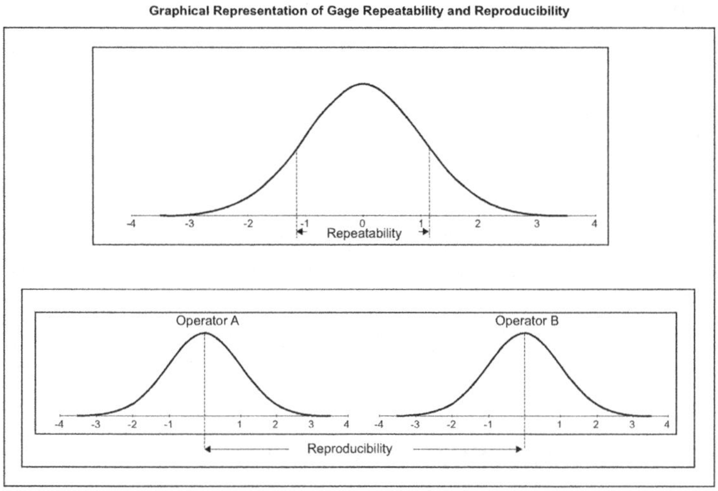

Figure 8.5 Graphical Representation of Gauge Repeatability and Reproducibility

introduced by the measurement system itself when measurements are taken by the same person, using the same equipment, on the same object. Repeatability is typically expressed as a standard deviation or a percentage of the total variation and is a measure of how well the measurement system consistently reproduces results.

Reproducibility

Reproducibility assesses the variation in measurements introduced when different operators or different instruments use the same measurement system to measure the same artifact. It evaluates the measurement systems' ability to produce consistent results when operated by different individuals or using different equipment. Reproducibility is also typically expressed as a standard deviation or a percentage of the total variation and is a measure of the variation introduced when multiple operators are involved.

A gauge R&R study is a structured approach to quantifying the contributions of repeatability and reproducibility to the overall measurement system variation. It helps distinguish between variation caused by the measurement system itself and other sources of variation such as the item being measured or environmental factors. The following is an example of how a gauge R&R is conducted:

1 Select a representative sample of items/parts to be measured. Rule of thumb is a random sample of at least 10.
2 Choose a group of operators, typically 2 or 3, who will perform the measurements.
3 Each operator measures each item/part multiple times using the same measurement system *(repeatability)* and records the results.
4 Repeat the measurements with different operators *(reproducibility)*.
5 Analyze the data to calculate the contributions of repeatability and reproducibility to the total variation in the measurements.

6 Express the results as percentages or standard deviations and assess whether the measurement system can provide reliable and consistent measurements.

Guidelines for making a "rule-of-thumb" determination on the effectiveness of the measurement systems are:

- The measurement system is acceptable if the GR&R score falls below 10%.
- The measurement system may be deemed acceptable depending upon the relative importance of the application or other factors if the GR&R falls between 10% and 20%.
- Any measurement system with R&R/T greater than 30% requires action to improve.

ATTRIBUTE MEASUREMENT SYSTEMS ANALYSIS

Attribute measurement systems analysis (attribute MSA), also known as attribute agreement analysis (AAA), is a technique used to assess the reliability and accuracy of measurement systems when dealing with categorical or attribute data. In contrast to continuous or variable data, attribute data involves discrete categories or classifications, such as pass/fail, yes/no, good/bad, or other qualitative data.

Here is a step-by-step process that I have found effective in performing an attribute MSA:

1 *Select appropriate attributes* – identify the specific attributes or categories that require assessment. These could be product characteristics, defects, visual inspections, or other qualitative assessments.
2 *Collect data* – create a representative sample of items, products, or situations that require attribute measurements. Select a group of operators or inspectors who will perform the assessments or classifications.
3 *Create a master evaluation reference* – establish a reference or master set of evaluations for each item or situation in your sample. This represents the "true" or reference assessment that you aim to compare with the assessments by operators.
4 *Operator evaluations* – have each operator independently assess or classify each item in the sample according to the chosen attributes.
5 *Perform Attribute MSA analysis* – use statistical analysis methods to analyze the data and determine the measurement system's reliability and accuracy. The specific analysis can vary but typically involves the following steps:
   a Calculate the overall agreement rate between operators and the master reference.
   b Assess the agreement for each attribute category or classification.
   c Calculate kappa (k) or another appropriate statistics metric to quantify the level of agreement beyond chance.
6 *Take action* – based on the results, take appropriate actions to improve the measurement system if necessary. This may involve additional training for operators, clarifying evaluation criteria, or revising attribute categories to enhance agreement.

7 *Document and monitor* – document the results of the attribute MSA study and any actions taken to improve the measurement system. Periodically monitor the measurement system's performance to ensure ongoing reliability.

An attribute gauge R&R is crucial in a DMAIC-driven Lean Six Sigma project because of its power to aid decision making in such areas as quality control via the evaluation of qualitative data. It helps ensure that attribute measurements are consistent, reliable, and accurate, enabling the team and the organization in general to make informed judgements and assessments with confidence.

CALIBRATION OF A MEASUREMENT SYSTEM

Calculation of a measurement system is a critical component of MSA. It is the process of adjusting or verifying a measurement system to ensure that it provides accurate and reliable measurements. Calibration is necessary to establish and maintain the traceability of measurements to a known standard and to reduce measurement errors. Figure 8.6 illustrates a 12-step guide on how to calibrate a measurement system.

- *Step 1. Establish a Calibration Program* – begin by developing a comprehensive calibration program or policy that outlines the procedures, frequency, and responsibilities for calibration activities. Ensure that it complies with relevant industry standards and regulations.
- *Step 2. Identify Measurement Standards* – identify appropriate measurement standards or reference standards traceable to national or international standards. These standards should have a known and documented level of accuracy.
- *Step 3. Select Calibration Equipment* – choose calibration equipment or instruments capable of measuring and verifying the performance of the measurement system under calibration. These instruments should have a higher level of accuracy than the measurement system being calibrated.

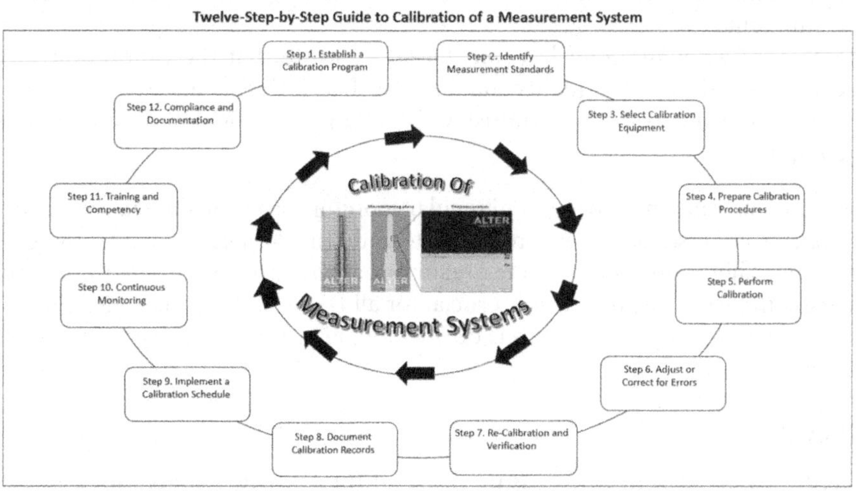

Figure 8.6 Step-by-Step Guide to Calibration of a Measurement System

- *Step 4. Prepare Calibration Procedures* – develop detailed calibration procedures that specify how the calibration process will be cried out, including equipment and standards to be used, measurement points, and acceptance criteria.
- *Step 5. Perform Calibration* – conduct the calibration by comparing the measurements obtained from the measurement system under calibration to the measurements obtained from the reference standard. Record all measurements and ensure that the calibration process is well documented.
- *Step 6. Adjust or Correct for Errors* – if the measurements obtained from the measurement system differ from the reference standard, take corrective action to adjust or correct the measurement system. This may involve making physical adjustments or applying correction factors.
- *Step 7. Re-Calibration and Verification* – after adjustments are made, re-calibrate the measurement system to ensure that it now meets the desired level of accuracy. Verify that the adjustments have been successful in reducing measurement errors.
- *Step 8. Document Calibration Records* – maintain detailed records of all calibration activities, including the date of calibration, the standard used, the results of the calibration, adjustments made, and the individuals responsible for the calibration.
- *Step 9. Implement a Calibration Schedule* – develop and implement a regular calibration schedule to ensure that measurement systems are routinely checked and adjusted. The frequency of calibration may vary depending on the criticality of the measurement system and industry standards.
- *Step 10. Continuous Monitoring* – continuously monitor the measurement system's performance in between calibration intervals. This includes assessing measurement system variation, stability, and other factors that may affect measurement accuracy.
- *Step 11. Training and Competency* – ensure that personnel responsible for calibration activities are adequately trained and competent in performing calibration tasks. This includes training on calibration procedures and the use of calibration equipment.
- *Step 12. Compliance and Documentation* – ensure that the calibration program complies with relevant quality standards such as ISO 9001 and regulatory requirements in your respective industry. Maintain documentation to demonstrate compliance.

Calibration is an ongoing process, and regular monitoring and maintenance of measurement systems are essential to ensure accurate and reliable measurements. By following a systematic calibration process, your organization can have confidence in the accuracy of the measurement system, which is crucial for all DMAIC-driven Lean Six Sigma projects and related quality control, decision making, and compliance with standards and regulations.

SUMMARY

Chapter 8 continued with the Measure phase of the DMAIC methodology and started with a discussion of importance of central tendency measurements. It then proceeded into quantifying process variability. From there, a discussion on the importance of normal distribution was conducted. A section was then presented on assessing variation through measurement systems analysis where precision and accuracy, bias, linearity and stability, gauge repeatability, and reproducibility along with attribute MSA was addressed. Calibration of the measurement system was then addressed.

LEAN SIX SIGMA AT WORK!

Lean Six Sigma Tools at Work

Understanding Variation

A plating operation within a large aircraft heavy metal fabrication factory is seeking to reduce the amount of time to perform a plating operation. An analysis of the methods used by the operators performing the plating has revealed that one of the operators completes the plating in 75 percent of the time it takes another operator performing the same plating operation. Further investigation determines that the two operators use solutions mixed on different mixers.

The histograms in Figures A&B below are based on depth measurements of the part plating from the different processes. In Figure B, the spread of the process is considerably smaller, enabling the faster operator to pass the part more quickly and with less effort. The slower operator must measure the depth of plating on each part to ensure it meets specifications. If it does not, the part receives a re-plate or is rejected, which results in a delay in production. Repeating the operations when the part is flawed has made the operation much less efficient.

However, the operator's lack of speed was actually caused by the process and is not the fault of the operator. Mixing machine #2 had missed a calibration cycle of its measurement system, which caused the mixture to be inaccurate and caused an inaccurate amount of plating to be applied to the part during treatment. Had managers not investigated variation in the process, they might have made an incorrect judgement about the operator's performance. Instead, they now realize that management intervention will be necessary to improve production and produce plated parts that meet specifications with first pass quality inspection.

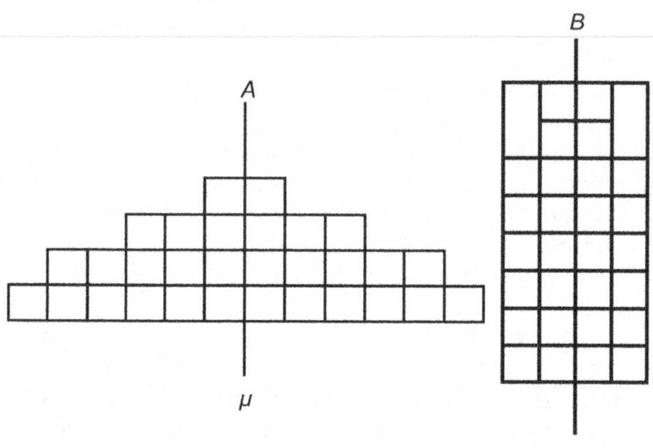

Histograms from two mixer machines

Figure 8.7

CHAPTER 8 DISCUSSION QUESTIONS

1 Why are measures of central tendency a fundamental aspect of descriptive statistics? Describe/discuss several common measures of central tendency used by LSS practitioners.
2 Explain why quantifying process variability is an essential step in LSS projects. Describe some of the more common methods and techniques used to do so.
3 Explain why the normal distribution is a fundamental concept in statistics and probability theory. Cite in your response several of the key reasons for its importance.
4 Explain how process capability indices affect an organization's ability to meet customer satisfaction.
5 Compare and contrast regression analysis and design of experiments.
6 Describe measurement system analysis.
7 Define and explain the "accuracy and precision" concept.
8 Define and explain bias, linearity, and stability in the context of assessing reliability and accuracy of a measurement system.
9 Define and explain gauge, repeatability, and reproducibility in the context of evaluating the performance and reliability of measurement systems.

BIBLIOGRAPHY

Abdelhamid, Tariq S. "Six sigma in lean construction systems: Opportunities and challenges." In *Proceedings of the 11th Annual Conference for Lean Construction*, 2003. https://www.academia.edu/125814384/Six_Sigma_in_Lean_Construction_Systems_Opportunities_and_Challenges

Altman, Douglas G., and J. Martin Bland. "Statistics notes: The normal distribution." *BMJ* 310.6975 (1995): 298.

Anderson-Cook, Christine M., et al. "Quantifying reliability uncertainty from catastrophic and margin defects: A proof of concept." *Reliability Engineering & System Safety* 96.9 (2011): 1063–1075.

Arumugam, V., Jiju Antony, and Alex Douglas. "Observation: A lean tool for improving the effectiveness of lean six sigma." *The TQM Journal* 24.3 (2012): 275–287.

Borror, Connie M. "Measurement systems analysis, attribute." In *Wiley StatsRef: Statistics Reference Online*. Wiley, 2014. https://onlinelibrary.wiley.com/doi/abs/10.1002/9781118445112.stat04139

Bryc, Wlodzimierz. *The Normal Distribution: Characterizations with Applications*. Vol. 100. Springer Science & Business Media, 2012.

Cepova, Lenka, et al. "Measurement system analyses–gauge repeatability and reproducibility methods." *Measurement Science Review* 18.1 (2018): 20–27.

Chakrabarty, Dhritikesh. "Computational methods of analysis of data: More measures of central tendency." In *National Seminar on Advances in Electronics and Allied Science & Technology (RW-NaSAEAST-2020), Electronic Scientists and Engineers Society (ESES)*, 2020. https://doi.org/10.13140/RG.2.2.12533.55525

Chakrabarty, Dhritikesh. "Measuremental data: Seven measures of central tendency." *International Journal of Electronics* 8.1 (2021).

Chakrabarty, Dhritikesh. "Model describing central tendency of data." *International Journal of Advanced Research in Science, Engineering and Technology* 8.9 (2021): 18193–18201.

Chatterjee, Samprit, and Ali S. Hadi. *Regression Analysis by Example*. John Wiley & Sons, 2013.

Chaudhary, Alok Kumar, Pramod Bahadur Shrestha, and Subodh Kumar Ghimire. "Application of lean six sigma in manufacturing of precision tools and die: A case study." In *Proceedings of IOE Graduate Conference*, 2019. https://conference.ioe.edu.np/ioegc2019-summer/papers/IOEGC-2019-Summer-021.pdf

Chen, MingNan, and Jung Lyu. "A lean six-sigma approach to touch panel quality improvement." *Production Planning and Control* 20.5 (2009): 445–454.

Cloete, Bronwyn C., and André Bester. "A lean six sigma approach to the improvement of the selenium analysis method." *Onderstepoort Journal of Veterinary Research* 79.1 (2012): 1–13.

Colan, Steven D. "The why and how of Z scores." *Journal of the American Society of Echocardiography* 26.1 (2013): 38–40.

Conklin, Joseph D. "Measurement system analysis for attribute measuring processes." *Quality Progress* 39.3 (2006): 50.

Costa, Federica, et al. "Readiness level assessment for lean six sigma implementation in the healthcare sector." *International Journal of Lean Six Sigma* 15.1 (2023): 131–152.

Deshpande, Amol A., et al. "Applications of gauge reproducibility & repeatability (GRR): Understanding and quantifying the effect of variations from different sources on a robust process development." *Organic Process Research & Development* 18.12 (2014): 1614–1621.

Díaz-Ruiz, Gonzalo, and Mariana Trujillo-Gallego. "A six sigma and system dynamic integration for process variability reduction in industrial processes." *International Journal for Quality Research* 16.4 (2022).

Draper, Norman R., and Harry Smith. *Applied Regression Analysis*. Vol. 326. John Wiley & Sons, 1998.

Durakovic, Benjamin. "Design of experiments application, concepts, examples: State of the art." *Periodicals of Engineering and Natural Sciences* 5.3 (2017).

Durivage, Mark Allen. *Practical Attribute and Variable Measurement Systems Analysis (MSA): A Guide for Conducting Gauge R&R Studies and Test Method Validations*. Quality Press, 2015.

Ershadi, Mohammad Javad, Roozbeh Aiasi, and Shirin Kazemi. "Root cause analysis in quality problem solving of research information systems: A case study." *International Journal of Productivity and Quality Management* 24.2 (2018): 284–299.

Etienne, Eisenhower C. "Empirical verification of a mathematical model for measuring the required reduction in process variation to achieve six-sigma quality benchmarks." *International Journal of Six Sigma and Competitive Advantage* 5.4 (2009): 359–379.

Fisher, Ronald Aylmer. "The design of experiments." In *The Design of Experiments*. Oliver & Boyd, 1960 xiv, 7th ed., p. 245.

Franzese, Robert, and Cindy Kam. *Modeling and Interpreting Interactive Hypotheses in Regression Analysis*. University of Michigan Press, 2009.

Galelli, Stefano, et al. "An evaluation framework for input variable selection algorithms for environmental data-driven models." *Environmental Modelling & Software* 62 (2014): 33–51.

Giechaskiel, Barouch, et al. "Calibration and accuracy of a particle number measurement system." *Measurement Science and Technology* 21.4 (2010): 045102.

Haleel, Aseel Jameel, Rosul Hussein, and Farah Abd Alkareem. "Gauge repeatability and reproducibility study." *Association of Arab Universities Journal of Engineering Sciences* 25.1 (2018): 213–225.

Hu, Qingying, et al. "Calibration of a three-dimensional shape measurement system." *Optical Engineering* 42.2 (2003): 487–493.

Ismail, Abdullah, et al. "Application of lean six sigma tools for cycle time reduction in manufacturing: Case study in biopharmaceutical industry." *Arabian Journal for Science and Engineering* 39 (2014): 1449–1463.

Jacobs, J. H., et al. "Quantifying variability of batching equipment using effective process times." *IEEE Transactions on Semiconductor Manufacturing* 19.2 (2006): 269–275.

Jiang, Tao, Haihua Cui, and Xiaosheng Cheng. "Accurate calibration for large-scale tracking-based visual measurement system." *IEEE Transactions on Instrumentation and Measurement* 70 (2020): 1–11.

Kumar, Sameer, Marietsa L. McCreary, and Daniel A. Nottestad. "Quantifying supply chain tradeoffs using six sigma, simulation, and designed experiments to develop a flexible distribution network." *Quality Engineering* 23.2 (2011): 180–203.

Li, Wenjing, et al. "Concentration estimation of dissolved oxygen in Pearl River Basin using input variable selection and machine learning techniques." *Science of the Total Environment* 731 (2020): 139099.

Liang, Kung-Yee, and Scott L. Zeger. "Regression analysis for correlated data." *Annual Review of Public Health* 14.1 (1993): 43–68.

Limpert, Eckhard, and Werner A. Stahel. "Problems with using the normal distribution–and ways to improve quality and efficiency of data analysis." *PLoS ONE* 6.7 (2011): e21403.

Ma, Junwei, et al. "A comparative study of mutual information-based input variable selection strategies for the displacement prediction of seepage-driven landslides using optimized support vector regression." *Stochastic Environmental Research and Risk Assessment* 36.10 (2022): 3109–3129.

Marsaglia, George. “Evaluating the normal distribution.” *Journal of Statistical Software* 11 (2004): 1–11.

Matloff, Norman S. *From Algorithms to Z-Scores: Probabilistic and Statistical Modeling in Computer Science*. Gainesville: University Press of Florida, 2009.

May, Robert, Graeme Dandy, and Holger Maier. “Review of input variable selection methods for artificial neural networks.” *Artificial Neural Networks-Methodological Advances and Biomedical Applications* 10.1 (2011): 19–45.

Mayne, John. “Contribution analysis: Addressing cause and effect.” *Evaluating the Complex* (2011): 53–96.

Montgomery, Douglas C., Elizabeth A. Peck, and G. Geoffrey Vining. *Introduction to Linear Regression Analysis*. John Wiley & Sons, 2021.

Okes, Duke. *Root Cause Analysis: The Core of Problem Solving and Corrective Action*. Quality Press, 2019.

Pai, Fan-Yun, Tsu-Ming Yeh, and Yung-Hsien Hung. “Analysis on accuracy of bias, linearity and stability of measurement system in ball screw processes by simulation.” *Sustainability* 7.11 (2015): 15464–15486.

Pukelsheim, Friedrich. “On Hsu’s model in regression analysis.” *Statistics: A Journal of Theoretical and Applied Statistics* 8.3 (1977): 323–331.

Roland-Holst, David W. “Bias and stability of multiplier estimates.” *The Review of Economics and Statistics* (1989): 718–721.

Sagnak, Muhittin, and Yigit Kazancoglu. “Integration of green lean approach with six sigma: An application for flue gas emissions.” *Journal of Cleaner Production* 127 (2016): 112–118.

Sarkar, Ashok, Arup Ranjan Mukhopadhyay, and Sadhan Kumar Ghosh. “Measurement system analysis for implementing design for six sigma.” *International Journal of Productivity and Quality Management* 14.3 (2014): 373–386.

Schliserman, Matan, and Tomer Koren. “Stability vs implicit bias of gradient methods on separable data and beyond.” In *Conference on Learning Theory*. PMLR, 2022.

Shagluf, Abubaker, Andrew P. Longstaff, and Simon Fletcher. “A preliminary study of applying lean six sigma methods to machine tool measurement.” University of Huddersfield, 2015. https://eprints.hud.ac.uk/id/eprint/24342/

Shah, Punit P., and R. L. Shrivastava. “Identification of performance measures of lean six sigma in small-and medium-sized enterprises: A pilot study.” *International Journal of Six Sigma and Competitive Advantage* 8.1 (2013): 1–21.

Simion, Carmen. “Assessing bias and linearity of a measurement system.” *Applied Mechanics and Materials* 760 (2015): 621–626.

Sweet, Arnold L., Shinta Tjokrodjojo, and Phoerny Wijaya. “An investigation of the measurements systems analysis ‘Analytic method’ for attribute gages.” *Quality Engineering* 17.2 (2005): 219–226.

Telford, Jacqueline K. “A brief introduction to design of experiments.” *Johns Hopkins APL Technical Digest* 27.3 (2007): 224–232.

Templeton, Gary F. “A two-step approach for transforming continuous variables to normal: Implications and recommendations for IS research.” *Communications of the Association for Information Systems* 28.1 (2011): 4.

Verspecht, Jan. *Calibration of a Measurement System for High Frequency Nonlinear Devices*. Ph. D. Thesis. Brussels: Belgium Vrije Univeriteit Brussels, 1995.

White, Andrew A., et al. “Cause-and-effect analysis of risk management files to assess patient care in the emergency department.” *Academic Emergency Medicine* 11.10 (2004): 1035–1041.

Xu, Zhaoguang, and Yanzhong Dang. “Automated digital cause-and-effect diagrams to assist causal analysis in problem-solving: A data-driven approach.” *International Journal of Production Research* 58.17 (2020): 5359–5379.

Zanobini, Andrea, et al. “Repeatability and reproducibility techniques for the analysis of measurement systems.” *Measurement* 86 (2016): 125–132.

Zou, Yuxin, et al. “Fine-mapping from summary data with the ‘Sum of Single Effects’ model.” *PLoS Genetics* 18.7 (2022): e1010299.

9
Developing a Data Collection Plan

LEARNING OBJECTIVES

1. Describe the primary objectives and development steps of a sampling plan and differentiate between probability and non-probability sampling methods.
2. Explain the concepts of throughput yield and rolled throughput yield and analyze the importance of the process sigma level.
3. Identify the different types of trend charts and explain their purposes in data analysis.
4. Describe how control charts assess process stability, including the purpose of X-bar and R charts.
5. Explain the significance of rational sub-grouping and discuss methods for assessing normality and transforming non-normal data.

DEVELOPING A SAMPLING PLAN

Sampling plans are an essential part of many research efforts, quality control, or data collection, especially for DMAIC-driven Lean Six Sigma initiatives. As initially addressed in Chapter 6, a sampling plan outlines how you will select a subset (sample) from a larger population for analysis (the sampling frame). The primary objectives of a sampling plan include:

- *Representativeness* – one of the primary goals of a sampling plan is to select a sample that accurately represents the larger population from which it is drawn. This helps in making inferences about the larger population based on the characteristics of the sample.
- *Reduce Cost* – sampling plans are more practical and cost effective than collecting data from an entire population. By selecting a smaller sample, your team and organizations save time and resources.
- *Efficiency* – sampling plans call for efficient data collection and analysis. It is generally impossible to gather data from an entire population, so selecting a representative sample streamlines the process.

DOI: 10.4324/9781032650531-12

- *Statistical Significance* – a well-designed sampling plan ensures that the selected sample size is statistically significant. This means that the results obtained from the sample can be generalized to the entire population with a certain level of confidence.
- *Accuracy* – sampling plans aim to minimize errors and biases in the data collection process. This involves random sampling techniques to reduce the risk of bias and improve the accuracy of the results.
- *Timeliness* – sampling plan allows for quicker data collection, enabling organizations to make more timely and informed decisions on next steps in project or program execution.
- *Risk Management* – sampling plans help manage the risks associated with data collection. They allow for the assessment of the risk of making incorrect inferences about the population under study.
- *Resource Allocation* – by using a sampling plan, your team and organization at large can allocate resources more efficiently. For example, for Lean Six Sigma quality control, sampling helps determine which products or processes require more attention and resources for improvement.
- *Comparison* – a sampling plan enables your team to compare different sub-groups within a population or compare populations across different time periods. This is valuable for identifying trends and making timely and informed decisions.
- *Compliance* – in many cases during project execution, sampling plans are used for compliance purposes with regulations and standards; for example, in assessing product quality of plating artifacts produced, the contract required a sampling plan be developed for types configured item.
- *Continuous Monitoring* – in Lean Six Sigma and various other quality-oriented projects, sampling plans are used for continuous monitoring of processes and product quality production. In DMAIC-driven projects, it is a standard part of the Control phase to ensure that changes made during the project are consistently maintained over time.

The key objective of a sampling plan is to balance the need for accuracy with resource constraints and time considerations, ensuring that the sample selected is representative of the population and provides reliable information for decision making and inference.

Once the sampling plan objectives are clearly defined and established, the plan can be developed. Presented in Figure 9.1 is a step-by-step sampling plan development guide that I have found effective.

Step 1: Define the Population – start by clearly defining the population requiring study or data collection. The population is the entire group of individuals, items, or events to be studied or analyzed. Make sure your definition is specific and unambiguous.

Step 2: Determine the Sampling Method – there are various sampling methods to choose from depending upon your research objectives, available resources, and nature of the population. Figure 9.2 presents examples of both probability and non-probability sampling.

Step 3: Determine the Sample Size – the sample size is the number of items or individuals you include in the sample. The number will depend on several factors, including desired level of confidence, the margin of error, and the variability within the population. Statistical tools such as sample size calculators can help determine the appropriate sample size.

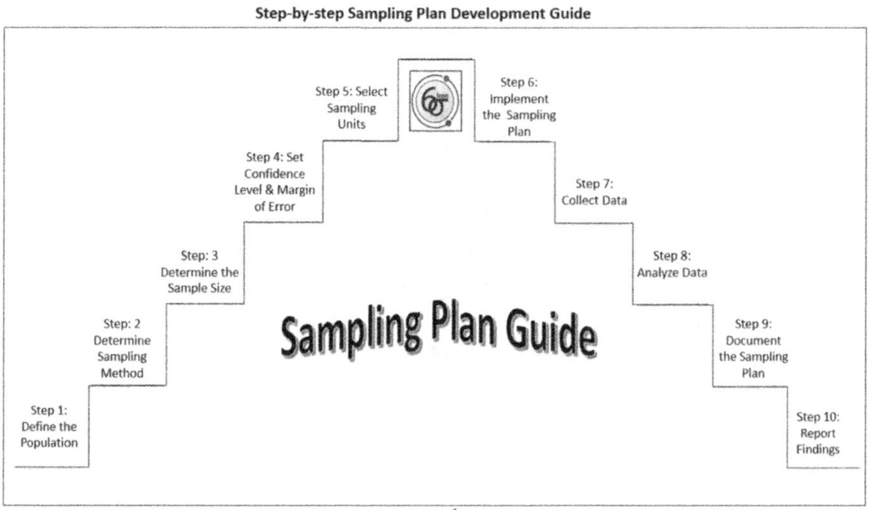

Figure 9.1 Step-by-Step Sampling Plan Development Guide

Step 4: Set Confidence Level and Margin of Error – a confidence level (normally 95% confidence level) and margin of error (normally +/–5%) need to be decided upon. These parameters affect the precision and reliability of the sample.

Step 5: Select Sampling Units – identify the units or elements that will make up the sample based on the chosen sampling method.

Step 6: Implement the Sampling Plan – execute the sampling plan by selecting the required number of samples according to the defined sampling methodology chosen. Be careful to avoid bias during the selection process.

Step 7: Collect Data – once you have selected the samples, gather the necessary data or information from each unit within the sample.

Step 8: Analyze the Data – perform the analysis, using appropriate statistical methods, to draw conclusions and make inferences about the entire population.

Step 9: Document the Sampling Plan – keep a detailed record of the sampling plan, including the population definition, sampling method, sample size, confidence level, margin of error, and all steps taken during the sampling process. This documentation is crucial for the transparency and replicability of the research conducted.

Step 10: Report the Findings – finally, present the findings from the research, including the sampling methodology employed, the results, and any limitations or potential sources of bias in the research.

Remember that the quality of the sampling plan is essential for the validity and reliability of the DMAIC-driven Lean Six Sigma team project it is engaged in. Be mindful of the potential sources of bias and errors in the sampling process and take steps to minimize them.

As previously mentioned in sampling plan development discussion, Step #2 requires that a sampling methodology be chosen. Figure 9.2 illustrates some of the more common methods to choose from depending upon the type of research engaged in.

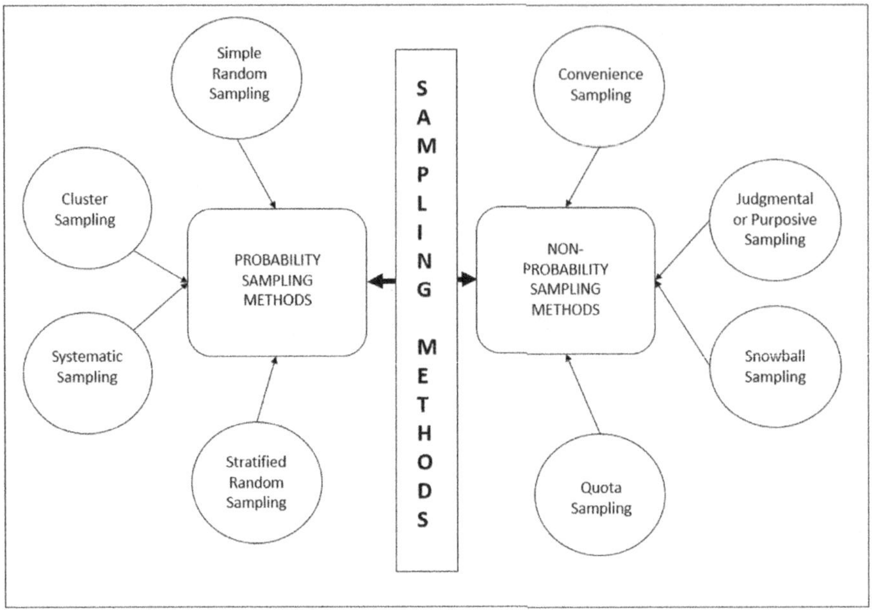

Figure 9.2 Common Types of Sampling Methodologies

First, probability sampling. In probability sampling, every population member has a known and non-zero chance of being elected in the sample. This means that the selection process is based on random chance, and each member of the population has an equal or known probability of being included in the sample.

Simple Random Sampling – in this method, every individual or item in the population has an equal chance of being selected. This is typically done using random number generators or drawing lots.

Cluster Sampling – in this method, the population is divided into clusters or groups, and then a random sample of clusters is selected. All individuals within the chosen clusters are included in the sample. Cluster sampling is often used when it is difficult to sample individuals directly.

Systematic Sampling – in systematic sampling, you select every *n*th individual from the population after a random start. For example, if there is a population of 1,000 and a sample of 100, you could select every 10th individual or item after starting with a random sample.

Stratified Sampling – the population is divided into subgroups or strata based on certain characteristics, such as age, gender, or location, and then random samples are taken from each stratum. This ensures each subgroup is adequately represented.

Now, non-probability sampling. This type of sampling does not rely on random selection. It involves the researcher's judgment or convenience in selecting elements from the population. As a result, not all members of the population have a known or equal chance of being included in the sample.

Convenience Sampling – this method involves selecting individuals who are the most convenient to access. While it is easy and inexpensive, it can introduce bias because it may not be representative of the entire population.

Judgmental or Purposive Sampling – also known as selective sampling, this method involves deliberately selecting specific individuals or items based on the researcher's judgment and expertise. It is often used in qualitative research when the goal is to gather information from experts or individuals with specific characteristics.

Snowball Sampling – snowball sampling is used when the population is hard to reach or define. It starts with an initial participant, and then additional participants are recruited through referrals. This method is often used in social network studies and for rare populations.

Quota Sampling – quota sampling is similar to stratified sampling, but it does not involve random selection. Instead, the researcher selects individuals non-randomly but ensures that the sample has predefined proportions of certain characteristics.

Probability sampling methods aim to provide a more unbiased and representative sample, making it suitable for research where generalizability to the entire population is important. Non-probability sampling methods, on the other hand, are useful in situations where it is difficult or impractical to use random selection, but they may yield less generalized results and can be more susceptible to bias. Of course, the choice of sampling method depends on the research question, nature of the population, available resources, and desired level of precision sought. The goal is to obtain a sample representative of the population to make valid inferences and generalizations.

ESTABLISHING BASELINE PERFORMANCE

Establishing baseline performance is a fundamental step in various fields, including project management, quality control, performance assessment, and especially DMAIC-driven Lean Six Sigma projects. It involves measuring and documenting the current state or performance of a system, process, or project before any changes or improvements are made. This baseline serves as a reference point against which future progress can be compared.

Selecting the appropriate measurement and interpreting the results of baselined system involves a systematic approach to ensure that the data collected aligns with the research objective and that valid conclusions can be drawn from the analysis. Here is a step-by-step guide on how this can be accomplished:

- Clearly define the research objective – define what you want to measure and the specific research questions or hypotheses you aim to address. This is the foundation for selecting the appropriate measurement.
- Choose the measurement method that aligns with the research objectives and the data's nature. Some common methods are listed in Table 9.1.
- Select data collection instruments – choose the specific tools or instruments for data collection (see Table 9.1). Ensure these instruments are reliable and valid for the type of research and system under observation.
- Design and pilot test the measurement instruments – if required, develop, or adapt measurement instruments based on the chosen method. Pilot test the instruments to identify and address any issues, such as unclear questions, ambiguities, or technical problems.
- Consider measurement scales – if necessary, decide on a measurement scale(s). Common scales include nominal, ordinal, interval, and ration scales. The choice of scale depends on the nature of the data and the research objectives.

Table 9.1 Common Measurement Methods

Measurement Method	Distinguishing Characteristic
Surveys and Questionnaires	Used for collecting self-reported data from individuals.
Observations	Involves direct or indirect observations of behaviors or events.
Experiments	Allows a manipulation of variables to assess cause and effect relationship.
Interviews	Useful for in-depth exploration of topics with structured or unstructured interviews.
Secondary Data Analysis	Involves using existing data sources for the research objective.
Sensor Data	Collecting data automatically from sensors or other devices.
Document Analysis	Analyzing written or electronic documents for content or patterns.

- Collect data – implement the data collection plan according to the selected measurement method and instruments. Ensure that data collection is conducted systematically and consistently.
- Quality control – implement quality control measures during the data collection to ensure accuracy and reliability. This includes double-checking data entry and validation.
- Analyze data – after data collection, conduct the appropriate data analysis based on the research objectives. Use statistical, qualitative, or mixed methods (using both qualitative and quantitative methods) as needed.
- Interpret the results – interpret the results by comparing the data analysis finding with the research objectives and hypotheses. Determine of the data supports or contradicts the research question.
- Validate and generalize – assess the validity of your measurements by considering factors such as internal, external, and construct validity. Ensure the results can be generalized to the broader population or context under study.
- Draw conclusions and provide recommendations – based on the interpretation of the results, draw conclusions and offer practical recommendation.

Selecting the appropriate measurement and effectively interpreting results is a fundamental aspect of any DMAIC-driven Lean Six Sigma project. It requires careful planning, a clear understanding of the research objectives, and a systematic approach to collecting, analyzing, and drawing meaningful conclusions from the data analyzed.

UNDERSTANDING THROUGHPUT YIELD

Throughput yield and rolled throughput yield are critical performance metrics used in various fields, including manufacturing, process improvement, and quality control and is central to any DMAIC-driven Lean Six Sigma initiative. They measure the proportion of units or items that successfully pass through a process or system without defects or errors. Both are key indicators of process efficiency and quality and are expressed as a percentage. Let us discuss, calculate, and interpret each of these metrics:

First, throughput yield (TY) – throughput yield, also known as first pass yield (FPY), measures the proportion of units or items that pass through a process without defects. Throughput yield is calculated using the following formula:

*Throughput yield percentage (%) = (Number of defect-free units/items produced)/ (Total number of units/items) * 100)*

Key components are:

1. Number of defect-free units/items: this is the count of units/items that meet all quality and specification requirements without any defects, rejections, or rework.
2. Total number of units/items input: this represents the total number of units or items that enter the process. It includes both defect-free and defective units/items as well.

Here is an example that illustrates throughput yield:

A heavy aircraft electronics manufacturing plant produces components for 787 glass cockpit displays. The production line has 1,000 components in process at any one time. After going through various stages of production and quality control, you find that 950 components meet the quality standards. Using the previously described formula, throughput yield is calculated:

Throughput yield % = 950 (number of good components)/1,000 (total number of components produced); throughput yield % = 0.95 or 95%.

The throughput yield is 95%, which means that 95% of the components that entered the production process successfully passed through all the stages of production without defects and met the quality standards. The remaining 5% were either rejected or had defects during the process.

Interpreting TY:

- A high TY indicates that most units/items pass through the process without defects, which is a sign of efficiency and quality.
- A low TY suggests that there are many defects or issues within the process. This can be a key indicator of where process improvements are needed.

  Second, rolled throughput yield – rolled throughput yield measures the overall yield of a multi-step process, accounting for the fact that some units may pass through multiple steps without defects, while others may be rejected at various stages. Rolled throughput yield is calculated using the following formula:

  *Rolled throughput yield (RTY) percentage % = TY at Step 1 * TY at Step 2 * TY at Step 3 . . . TY at Step n.*

RTY is calculated by multiplying the TYs of each step in the process.

Here is an example that illustrates rolled throughput yield:

Recall the same heavy aircraft electronics manufacturing plant that produces components for the 787-glass cockpit had a TY of 95%, which means that the overall process is deemed efficient, with only a 5% rejection percentage. However, because the manufacturing process is complex, a rolled throughput yield assessment was conducted at each stage of development. Each stage (A, B, C) had its own yield rate calculated. The following are the yields derived:

- Stage A = 90%
- Stage B = 85%
- Stage C = 95%

Using the previous RTY equation:

RTY % = yield at stage A (90%) * yield at stage B (85%) * yield at stage C (95%)
RTY = 0.90 * 0.85 * 0.95
RTY = 0.72225 or 72.225%

The RTY is approximately 72.225%. This means that after passing through all three stages of the manufacturing process, about 72.225% of the units or items are defect free and meet quality standards. The remaining 27.775% of the units or items have defects or are rejected at some point during the process.

An RTY of 72.225% suggests that the overall process is not as highly efficient as the TY of 95% suggests. With nearly 28% of the units or items having defects at some point during the production process, there is room for improvement. A suggestion here would be to increase the TY at each step, reducing the likelihood of defects or rework and thus increasing the overall RTY.

Throughput yield and rolled throughput yield are valuable metrics assessing the quality and efficiency of multi-step processes. Both are unique statistical tools that are standards in any DMAIC-driven Lean Six Sigma initiative. Higher TY and RTY values indicate better performance, while lower values suggest the need for process improvement.

THE IMPORTANCE OF THE PROCESS SIGMA LEVEL

The process sigma level, denoted as σ (sigma), is a critical metric used in process improvement, particularly in the context of DMAIC-driven Lean Six Sigma projects. It measures the capability of a process to perform within specified tolerance limits and reflects process performance.

Table 9.2 lists ten compelling reasons the process sigma level is essential.

The process sigma level quantifies the number of standard deviations between the process mean and the nearest specification limit. A higher process sigma level indicates a more capable and controlled process. To calculate and interpret the results of the process sigma level, the following steps should be performed:

- *Define the Parameters* – determine the specifications or tolerance limits for the process. These are typically the upper specification level (USL) and the lower specification level (LSL).
- *Calculate the Process Variation* – collect data and calculate the process variation. Common measures of variation include the standard deviation (σ) or the (R) within a subgroup. The standard deviation is preferred when the data is normally distributed.

Table 9.2 Ten Compelling Reasons the Process Sigma Level Is Essential

Process Sigma Level Essential Reason	*Process Sigma Level Impact*
Quality Control and Assurance	The sigma level provides a clear and standardized way to measure the quality of a process. It helps organizations assess their ability to consistently produce products or deliver services that meet customer requirements. Higher sigma levels indicate better quality control.
Defect Reduction	A higher sigma level is associated with a lower defect rate. As the sigma level increases, the number of defects per unit of output decreases. This is crucial for reducing rework, scrap, customer complaints, and warranty claims, leading to cost savings and increased customer satisfaction.
Customer Satisfaction	Consistently meeting or exceeding customer expectations is a key driver of customer satisfaction. High sigma levels ensure that products or services are delivered with minimal variations, which enhances customer trust and loyalty.
Process Improvement	The sigma level serves as a diagnostic tool to identify areas of a process that need improvement. A low sigma level indicates that a process is not performing well, while a high sigma level suggests that the process is stable and capable. This information helps organizations target areas for improvement effectively.
Data-Driven Decision Making	The sigma level is a quantifiable and data-driven metric. It provides a common language for discussing process performance and enables informed decision-making. Teams can set specific sigma level goals and measure progress toward those goals.
Competitive Advantage	Higher sigma levels can give an organization a competitive advantage. Superior quality and performance can set a company apart in the market, allowing it to charge premium prices and win customer loyalty.
Cost Reduction	Improved process performance, as indicated by a higher sigma level, leads to cost reduction. This is achieved by reducing waste, rework, and the need for inspection and by increasing process efficiency.
Risk Mitigation	Low sigma levels represent a higher risk of defects and deviations from specifications. These deviations can lead to safety concerns, product recalls, regulatory non-compliance, and financial losses. A high sigma level mitigates these risks.
Continuous Improvement Culture	The concept of striving for higher sigma levels is integral to the philosophy of continuous improvement. Organizations that adopt Six Sigma and similar methodologies emphasize an ongoing commitment to enhancing processes and maintaining high sigma levels.
Standardization	The sigma level provides a standardized and universally understood measure of process capability. This consistency facilitates communication across departments, industries, and even different organizations.

- *Calculate the Process Capability Indices* – these indices, addressed in Chapter 8, are Cp and CpK. Recall that Cp (process capability) measures the potential capability of the process to product within specifications., Whereas CpK (process capability index) takes into account the centering of the process mean relative to the specification limits and measures the actual capability of the process.
- *Calculate the Process Sigma Level (σ)* – once the Cp and CpK have been derived, calculate the process sigma level. It is determined by the lower of the two values (Cp and CpK) with the formula (σ) = min(Cp, CpK).

Interpreting the process sigma level is based on two criteria:

1. A higher process sigma level indicates a more capable and controlled process.
2. The sigma level relates to the proportion of defects in the process. The higher the sigma level, the lower the defect rate. The scale of interpreting sigma levels is illustrated in Figure 9.3.

An example of how the sigma level can be determined is as follows:

Using the same example of heavy aircraft electronics manufacturing as when we determined RTY, we want to assess Stage #2 of the process, which had an 85% defect-free production rate. Using a sample from the stage #2 process, we derived the following:

- USL = 105 units
- LSL = 95 units
- Process mean (μ) = 100 units
- Process standard deviation (σ) = 3 units
- Calculated the C_p: $C_p = (105 - 95)/(6 * 3) = 0.33$
- Calculated the C_pK: $C_pK = \min[(105 - 100/(3 * 3)] = 0.56$
- Determined the process sigma level: $\sigma = \min(C_p, C_pK) = \min(0.33, 0.56) = 0.33$

The process sigma level is 0.33, which is below 1σ. This indicates a poor-quality process and a high defect rate.

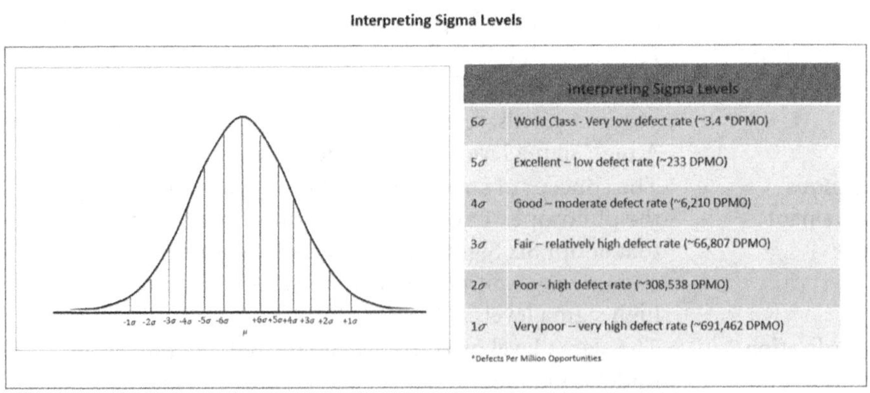

Figure 9.3 Interpreting Sigma Levels

Organizations strive to achieve higher sigma levels by reducing process variability, centering the process mean, and aligning the process with customer specifications to minimize defects and improve product quality.

CHARTING PROCESS BEHAVIOR

Charting process behavior using trend charts is a common quality control and process improvement technique often used on quality control and is a fundamental tool used in a DMAIC-driven Lean Six Sigma initiative. Trend charts help monitor how a specific process or system changes over time, making it easier to identify trends, shifts, or abnormal variations.

Trend Charts (Run Charts)

There are several types of trend charts, but the choice of which to use really depends upon the data. Typical types of trend charts are:

- *A time series chart is a graphical representation of data points collected over time.* These charts are used to visualize and analyze trends, patterns, and changes in data, making them valuable tools for understanding historical and future data trends. Trend charts or times series charts are commonly used in various fields including finance, economics, marketing and sales, environmental sciences, and general business planning and are especially valuable in all DMAIC-driven Lean Six Sigma initiatives. Figure 9.4 shows a times series graph where the trend and forecast of a plating solution were assessed over a set period.
- *Run charts are like a time series chart but can include additional analysis reference lines.* The cadmium plating examples of batch process analysis presented in Chapter 8 could be classified as a type of run chart; see Figure 9.5.

Time Series Graph Showing Trend and Forecast Over Time

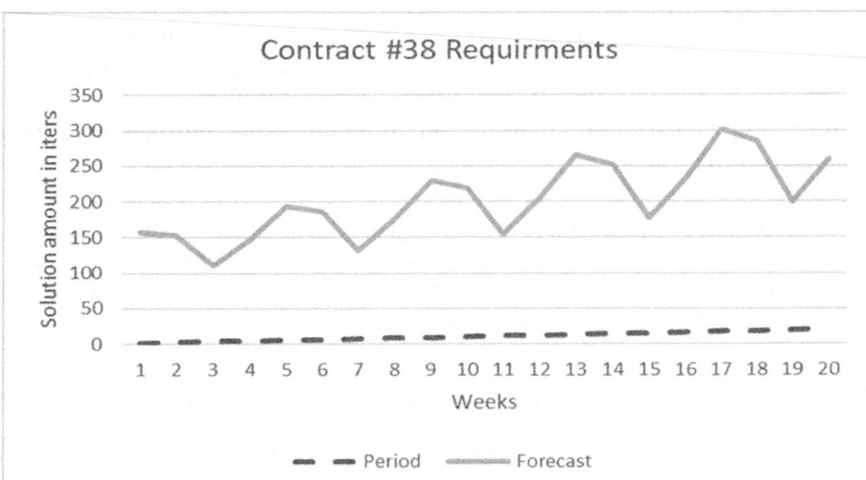

Figure 9.4 Time Series Graph Showing Trend and Forecast Over Time

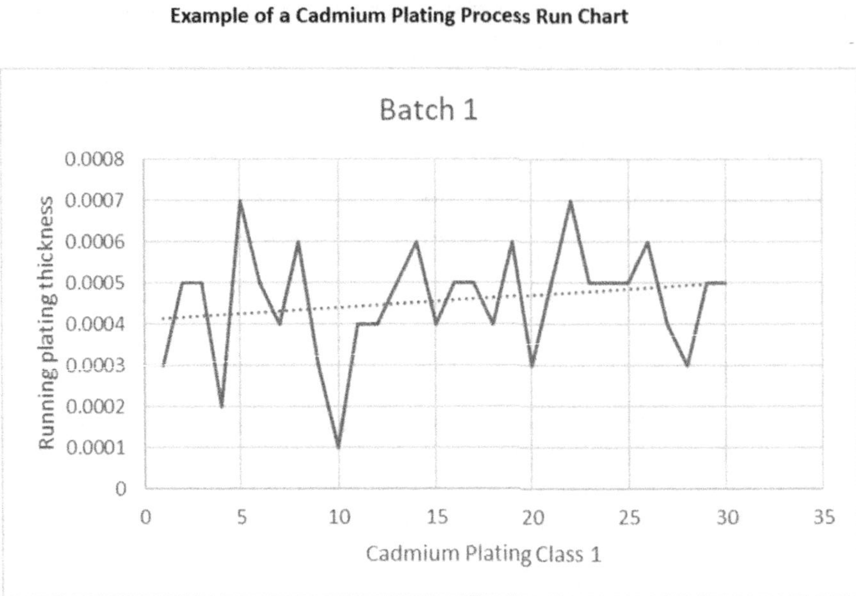

Figure 9.5 Example of a Cadmium Platting Process Run Chart

- *Control* charts are typically used in statistical process control (SPC). This type of chart includes upper and lower control limits to identify statistically significant variations. SPC and control charts will be addressed in depth in the next section.

Regardless of the type of trend chart selected, when analyzing it, you should look for the following patterns and signs:

1 Trends – is the data consistently increasing, decreasing, or remaining stable over time?
2 Seasonal Patterns – are there recurring patterns that occur at regular intervals?
3 Outliers – are there data points significantly different from the general trend?
4 Control Limits – in control charts, data points outside the control limits indicate an out-of-control process.

Trend charts should be updated regularly to track ongoing behavior of the process. New data should continuously be analyzed and adjustments made as necessary. Because they are such a valuable tool for quality control and process improvement, they are considered fundamental for all DMAIC-driven Lean Six Sigma initiative.

STATISTICAL PROCESS CONTROL AND CONTROL LIMITS

Statistical process control is a methodology used in overall quality management and is a cornerstone of all DMAIC-driven Lean Six Sigma initiatives. SPC relies on statistical techniques to assess stability and consistency of a process to ensure it operates within specified control limits. The following are some key concepts and of SPC and control limits:

- *Process Variation* – SPC recognizes that every process has inherent variation, which can be classified into two main types:
  a Common cause variation (or random variation) – this is the natural variability that occurs due to multiple factors inherent in the process itself. Common cause variation is expected and predictable, and it is present even when a process is in control.
  b Special cause variation (or assignable cause variation) – this variation arises from specific, identifiable factors or events not part of the normal process operation. Special cause variation indicates a problem or abnormal condition in the process.
- *Control Charts* – control charts, also known as Shewhart charts (after their designer), or process behavior charts, are the primary and tool of choice in SPC. They graphically represent process data over time and help distinguish between common and special cause variation.
  Control charts typically consist of a central line (representing the process mean) and upper and lower control limits. These limits are derived from statistical calculations (which will be described in the following section) and serve as reference lines for identifying variation in the process.
- *Central Line* – the central line on a control chart represents the average or mean value of the process. It is typically calculated based on historical data.
- *Control Limits (UCL and LCL)* – control limits are lines on the control chart that help assess the stability of the process. There are two types of control limits:
  a Upper control limits – this line is set at a certain number of standard deviations (generally +2 or 3) above the process mean (CL) and represents the upper boundary which common cause variation is not expected.
  b Lower control limit (LCL) – the lower control limit is set at a certain number of standard deviations (generally –2 or 3) below the process mean and serves as the lower boundary.

Figure 9.6 illustrates the basic components of a control chart, initially built for a Stage #1 sampling frame process of new production for structural joining flanges.

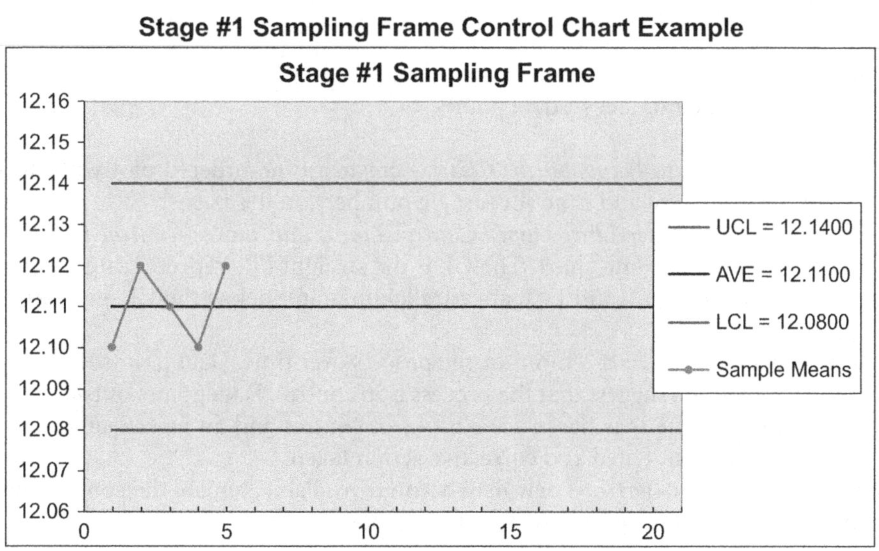

Figure 9.6 Stage #1 Sampling Frame Control Chart Example

- *In Control vs. Out of Control* – a process is considered "in control" when all data points fall within the control limits, and the variation is primarily due to common causes. In contrast, a process is considered "out of control" when data points exceed the control limits or exhibit unusual patterns, indicating the presence of special causes.

Building a Control Chart

To build a control chart, you will require data directly from the process under study. This data normally is collected at regular intervals from the process. Dat points can be measurements, counts, or any other relevant metrics. Once this is done, perform the following steps:

Step 1. Calculate the Center Line (CL) – the center line represents the process mean or average. Calculate it by finding the average of your data points:

CL = (sum of data points)/number of data points

Step #2. Calculate the Control Limits (Upper Control Limits and Lower Control Limits) – control limits determine if the process is in or out of control. The control limits are typically set at a certain number of standard deviations from the mean. These are +/−3 sigma (σ) for a 3-sigma control chart or +/−2 (σ) for a 2-sigma control chart. These are calculated as follows:

Upper control limit = CL + (kσ) Lower control limit = (k*σ)*

Where: * k is constant, typically 3 for a 3-sigma chart or 2 for a 2-sigma chart.
*σ is the standard deviation of the data points.

Step #3. Calculate the standard deviation (σ) of the data points. This qualifies the spread or variability in the process.

$\sigma = \sqrt{}\ (\Sigma\ (xi\text{-}cl^2)/(n\text{-}1))$

Where: * xi represents individual data points.
* n is the number of data points

Step #4. Plot the Data Points on the Chart – create a time-ordered plot with the data points on the *y-axis* and time (or sample number) on the *x-axis.*

Step #5. Plot the Center Line, Upper Control Limit, and Lower Control Limit – plot these lines on the same chart. The CL is the straight line representing the process mean, while the UCL and LCL are parallel lines and below the CL, indicating the control limits.

Step #6. Interpret the Chart – monitor the process over time. Data points that fall with the control limits suggest that the process is in control. Data points outside the control limits indicate that the process is out of control and an investigation into the cause should be initiated and corrective action taken.

Step #7. Update the Chart – as new data becomes available, update the control chart to monitor the ongoing performance of the process.

Selecting the Appropriate Statistical Process Control Chart

Statistical process control uses several types of control charts to monitor and analyze the variation in processes. Selecting the appropriate SPC chart for a specific situation is essential for effective monitoring and improving a process. The choice, of course, depends upon the type of data being collected, the nature of the process, and the specific quality characteristics requiring control. Table 9.3 provides some of the more commonly used SPC charts used in any DMAIC-driven Lean Six Sigma initiative.

The choice of appropriate SPC chart depends upon the specific characteristics of the process and data type. It is essential to understand the nature of the data being analyzed, the objectives of the SPC efforts, and the type of variation requiring control.

Table 9.3 Commonly Used SPC Charts

SPC Chart Type	*Data Type*	*When to Use*
X-bar and R ($\bar{X}$-R) chart	Continuous or variable data	Monitoring the central tendency (mean) and variation of a process when you have continuous data. It is useful for detecting shifts or trends in the process mean or variability.
Individual/moving range (I-MR) chart	Continuous or variable	You have individual measurements, not sub-grouped data. It is helpful when dealing with small sample sizes, such as measurement per unit or time point. It monitors both the process mean and variation.
p-chart (proportion chart)	Attribute data	Monitoring the proportion of defective items in a sample. Appropriate when you have a categorical response variable such as pass/fail.
np-chart (number of defects chart)	Attribute data	You want to monitor the number of defects in a sample, especially when the sample size varies from sub-group to sub-group.
c-chart (count of defects chart)	Attribute data	Monitoring the number of defects in a constant-sized sample such as "scratches on a surface".
u-chart (defects per unit chart)	Attribute data	You want to monitor the average number of defects per unit, especially when the sample size varies.

(*Continued*)

Table 9.3 (Continued)

SPC Chart Type	*Data Type*	*When to Use*
Gauge range and reproducibility (R&R) chart	Measurement system analysis	Evaluating the measurement system's accuracy and repeatability. It is not for process control but for assessing the measurement process itself.
Exponentially weighted moving average (EWMA) chart	Continuous or variable data	You want to give more weight to recent data and smooth out noise in the process. It is effective for detecting shifts in the process.
Cumulative sum (CUSUM) chart	Continuous or variable data	You need to quickly detect small or gradual shifts in the process by cumulatively summing deviations from the target.
Multivariate control chart	Multiple correlated variables	Monitoring the joint behavior of multiple variables in a process. Useful for complex processes with interdependences.
Time series control chart	Time-ordered data	You are dealing with data collected over time and want to monitor temporal patterns, trends, and seasonality.
G-chart (geometric chart)	Continuous or variable	Used when dealing with rare or infrequent events, such as equipment breakdowns or accidents. It helps track the time between rare events or the number of events in a given time period.

RATIONAL SUB-GROUPING

Rational sub-grouping is a key concept in statistical process control and is used to group data points into sub-groups based on logical and meaning criteria. The primary purpose of rational sub-grouping is to reduce variation within sub-groups while enhancing the ability to detect and understand variation between sub-groups. It is used extensively in the aviation and aerospace industries, especially in heavy structural manufacturing, where there are significant composite and plating activities. Figure 9.7 illustrates some of the key aspects of rational sub-grouping and its significant factors.

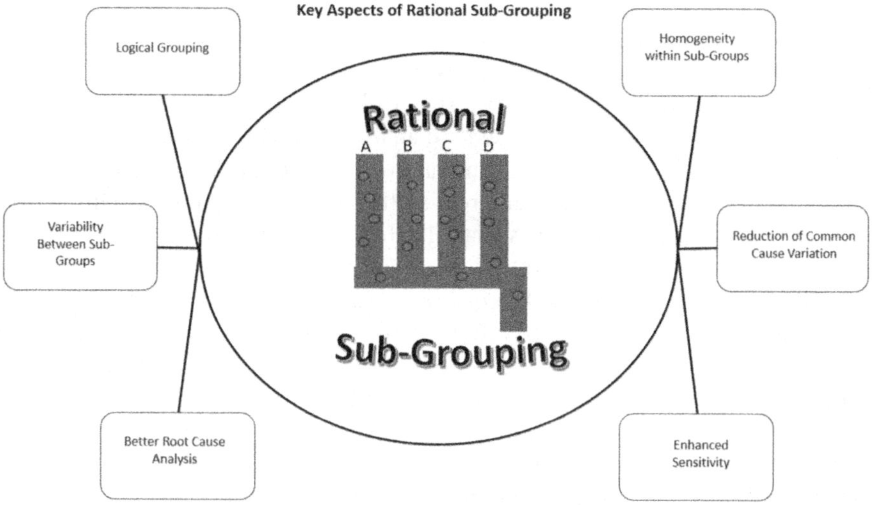

Figure 9.7 Key Aspects of Rational Sub-Grouping

- *Logical Grouping* – rational sub-grouping involves grouping data points in a way that makes logical sense for the process being monitored. These groupings are based on factors that can influence process variability or behavior.
- *Homogeneity Within Sub-Groups* – the idea is to make the sub-groups as homogeneous as possible in terms of process conditions, materials, equipment, operators, or other relevant factors. When sub-groups are homogenous, the variability within each sub-group is primarily due to common cause variation.
- *Reduction of Common Cause Variation* – by creating homogeneous sub-groups, common cause variation can be minimized within each sub-group, making it easier to detect special cause variation or abnormal behavior.
- *Enhanced Sensitivity* – rational sub-grouping increases the sensitivity of control charts in detecting shifts or trends in the process. It allows you to distinguish between common and specific cause variation more effectively.
- *Better Root Cause Analysis* – when special cause variation is detected, it is easier to pinpoint the root cause of the variation because the sub-groups are more consistent in terms of input or conditions.
- *Variability Between Sub-Groups* – rational sub-grouping enables the identification and understanding of variations that occur between sub-groups, which can be due to different conditions, changes, or factors affecting the process.

The goal of rational sub-grouping is to create sub-groups that make it easier to understand the sources of variation within a process. This helps the Lean Six Sigma team and organization implement effective process control and continuous improvement efforts by identifying and addressing both common and special cause variations. Table 9.4 provides some examples of how rational sub-grouping is used.

Table 9.4 Examples of Rational Sub-Grouping

Time-based sub-grouping	Data collected at different times can be grouped into sub-groups. For instance, daily, weekly, or monthly sub-groups can be created to analyze behavior over time.
Shift-based sub-grouping	In aviation and aerospace manufacturing, data collected during different shifts is grouped separately. This helps identify variations that are specific to certain shifts or workers.
Batch- or lot-based sub-grouping	In batch processes, data from different batches or lots are grouped into sub-groups based on contractual requirements and to analyze variations between those sub-groups.
Machine- or equipment-based sub-grouping	If a process involves multiple machines or equipment, data collected from each machine is placed in sub-groups so wear and adjustment can be better analyzed.
Operator-based sub-grouping	If different operators are involved in a process, data from each operator is grouped separately to assess variations associated with that individual operator.
Location-based sub-grouping	In cases where geographical locations are relevant, such as the building of a large system such as an aircraft, data from those different locations is grouped separately into sub-groups so that specification alignment can be ensured.
Product- or product line–based sub-grouping	In quality control, products from different product lines or types are grouped separately into sub-groups for sales and forecasting purposes.

NORMALITY ASSESSMENT AND TRANSFORMATION OF NON-NORMAL DATA

Normality assessment and transformation of non-normal data are critical steps in the analysis of data, especially when dealing with statistical methods that assume data to be normally distributed. If not appropriately handled, non-normal data can lead to inaccurate conclusions, which causes significant issues if not immediately remedied. Here are some keyways to determine if the data being analyzed is non-normal.

Normality Assessment

Perform a visual inspection – inspect the data visually using graphical methods. Common tools are histograms, probability plots (such as quantile-quantile or Q-Q plots), and box plots. A normal distribution will show a bell-shaped curve, symmetrical histogram, and points closely following a diagonal line on the Q-Q plot.

Use descriptive statistics – calculate summary statistics such as skewness and kurtosis. Skewness measures the asymmetry of the data distribution, and kurtosis assesses the shape of the tails. A normal distribution has a skewness of 0 and kurtosis of 3.

Perform a Shapiro-Wilk test – this is a formal hypothesis test for normality. It assesses whether the data significantly deviates from a normal distribution. The Shapiro-Wilk test statistics is calculated using the following formula:

$$W = \frac{(\sum_{i-1}^{n} a_i x_{(i)})^2}{\sum_{i=1}^{n} (xi - \overline{x})^2}$$

Where:

W is the test statistic.

n is the sample size.

$X_{(i)}$ is the i-th ordered value (the smallest value) in the sample.

X_i is the i-th value in the sample.

$\overline{X}$is the sample mean.

The a_i values are constantly calculated based on the sample size n and used to give the test its specific properties.

Once the test statistic W is computed, it can be compared to the critical values from a Shapiro-Wilk test table or through software such as Python SciPy library to obtain the test's p-value. The p-value is used to determine whether the null hypothesis should be rejected (whether the data follows a normal distribution). If the p-value is less than the selected significance level (alpha), the null hypothesis should be rejected, indicating the data does not follow a normal distribution.

Perform a Kolmogorov-Smirnov (KS) test – it is used to determine whether a dataset follows a specific theoretical (normal) distribution. The formula for the Kolmogorov-Smirnov test statistic for a one-sample test is as follows:

$$D = maxi \, | \, F(xi) - \frac{i}{n} \, |$$

Where:

D is the Kolmogorov-Smirnov test statistic.

$F(x_{(i)})$ is the cumulative distribution function (CDF) of the theoretical distribution evaluated at the *i-th* ordered value in the sample, $x_{(i)}$.

i is the index of the ordered value.

n is the sample size.

The KS test statistic D measures the largest vertical distance between the empirical cumulative distribution function (ECDF) of the data and the CDF of the theoretical distribution. A larger value of D suggests a great discrepancy between the data and the theoretical distribution.

Once calculated, the test statistic D should be compared to the critical values from the Kolmogorov-Smirnov table, or Python's SciPy library can be used to obtain the p-value. If the p-value is less than the chosen significance level (alpha), the null hypothesis would be rejected, suggesting that the data does not follow the specified distribution.

Perform an Anderson-Darling test – it is a statistical test used to determine whether a given sample of data follows a specific normal distribution. The test statistic is based on the square differences between the observed cumulative distribution function and the expected CDF from the distribution under test. The formula for the Anderson-Darling test statistics is as follows:

$$A^2 = -n - \frac{1}{n}\sum\nolimits_{i-1}^{n}[2i-1)(1n(F(X_{(i)})) + 1n(1 - F(X_{(n+1-i)})))]$$

Where:

A^2 is the Anderson-Darling test statistic.

n is the sample size.

$X_{(i)}$ is the *i-th* ordered value in the sample (the *i-th* smallest value).

$F(X_{(i)})$ is the empirical cumulative distribution function of the data at the *i-th* observed data distribution (normal distribution). Larger values of A^2 indicate a greater deviation from the expected distribution.

When performing the Anderson-Darling test, the test statistic A^2 is compared to the critical values from the Anderson-Darling test table or from software that provides the p-value for the test. If the p-value is less than the chosen significance level (alpha), the null hypothesis would be rejected, suggesting the data does not follow a normal distribution.

Transformation of Non-Normal Data

Transforming non-normally distributed data is a common practice in statistics and especially so in DMAIC-driven Lean Six Sigma initiatives. It makes the data more amenable to parametric statistical tests and satisfies the assumptions of statistical models that assume normality. The normal distribution (a bell shaped curve) has some properties that make many statistical methods more valid and powerful. When the data is not normally distributed, it often can lead to issues like biased parameter estimates and inaccurate p-values. Figure 9.8 illustrates some of the more common types of statistical transformation processes that can be used to transform non-normal data.

- *Logarithmic Transformation* – this is often used when dealing with positively skewed data, which means the data is skewed to the right (skewed positively). A log transformation can help make the data more symmetrical. The formula for the logarithmic transformation is:

  transformed data = log (original data)

- *Square Root Transformation* – like the logarithmic transformation, this is suitable for positively skewed data. The formula for the square root transformation is:

  transformed data = sqrt (original data)

- *Box-Cox Transformation* – the Box-Cox transformation is a family of power transformations that includes the logarithmic and square root transformations as special cases. It is parameterized by a lambda (λ) value that is chosen to

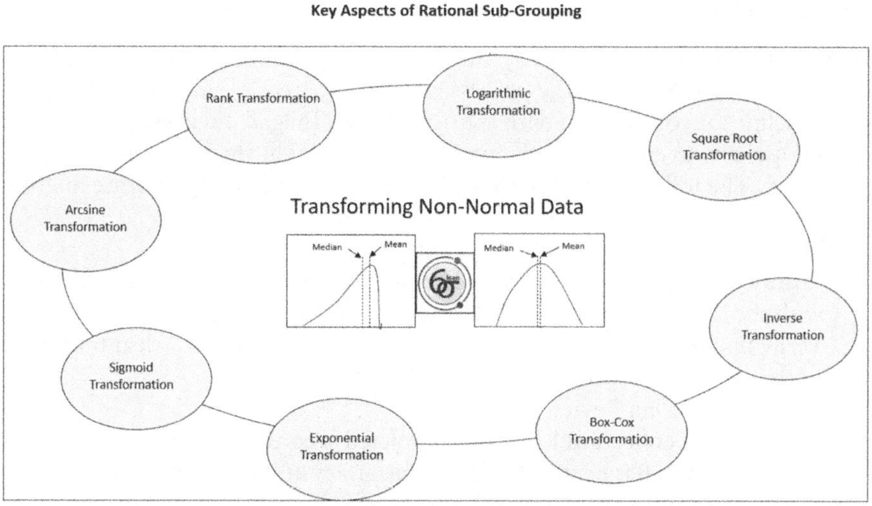

Figure 9.8 Common Types of Statistical Transformation Processes

maximize the normality of the transformed data. The formula of the box-cox transformation is:

transformed data $= (\textit{original data}^{\lambda} - 1)/\lambda$ *(for* $\lambda \neq$*) or log (original data) (for* $\lambda = 0$*)*

- *Exponential Transformation* – this is used for data that is exponentially distributed. An exponential transformation can help make the data more symmetrical. The formula for exponential transformation is:

  transformed data = exp (original data)

- *Sigmoid Transformation* – this transformation process is useful for data that is bounded between 0 and 1, such as proportions or percentages. The formula for sigmoid transformations is:

  transform data = 1/(1 + exp (-original data))

- *Arcsine Transformation* – arcsine transformation is another option for data bounded between 0 and 1, often used in proportions. The formula for arcsine transformation is:

  Transformed data = arcsine (sqrt (original data))

- *Rank Transformation* = if the data is severely non-normally distributed, the data can be ranked, turning it into a uniform distribution. This transformation is non-parametric and may be useful when other transformations do not work well.

It is important to note that selecting the appropriate transformation depends on the data's characteristics and the analysis goals. It may require some experimentation and visual inspection, using histograms and Q-Q plots, to determine which transformation works best. Additionally, after applying a transformation, you should check the normality of the transformed data to ensure that the transformation was successful.

TOLLGATE REVIEW

In the Measure phase of the DMAIC methodology, the focus is on gathering data to understand the current state of the process, identifying areas of improvement, and establishing a baseline for comparison with the future state. Tollgate reviews are checkpoints in the DMAIC process to ensure that the project is on the right track and should proceed to the next phase. The following is a checklist of what a Measure phase tollgate might entail:

- Project Charter Review (from the Define Phase):
  - Ensure that the project's goals, scope, and objectives are well defined and aligned with the strategic objectives presented in the Define stage.
  - Verify that the project team is adequately resourced and has a clear understanding of the project's purpose.
- Data Collection Plan Review:
  - Check if data collection has been completed according to the plan.
  - Verify that data has been validated for accuracy and completeness. Data integrity is crucial for making reliable measurements.
- Measurement Systems Analysis:
  - Confirm that MSA has been performed on critical measurements to assess the reliability and repeatability of the measurement system.
  - Address any issues identified during the MSA and ensure data accuracy.
- Process Performance Metrics:
  - Review the key performance metrics and indicators gathered during the Measure phase.
  - Ensure that there is a clear understanding of the current process performance and its variability.
- Data Analysis and Baseline Establishment:
  - Assess the results of the data analysis, including graphical representations and statistical summaries.
  - Verify that a stable baseline has been established for process performance.
- Process Capability Analysis:
  - Evaluate the process capability analysis, which may include calculating process capability indices (Cp, CpK) to determine how well the process meets customer requirements.
- Identify Root Causes for Process Variation:
  - Check if any preliminary analysis of the data has been conducted to identify potential root causes for process variation.
- Risk Assessment:
  - Evaluate any identified risks or challenges that might affect the project as it progresses into the Analyze phase.
- Documentation and Reporting:
  - Ensure that all data, analyses, and findings have been documented thoroughly.
  - Review the format of the report that will be presented to the project stakeholders.
- Project Status and Next Steps:
  - Provide a summary of the project's status in the Measure phase.
  - Determine if the project should proceed to the Analyze phase or if any corrective actions are required before progressing.
- Approval and Decision:

- Obtain approval from the project sponsor or relevant stakeholders to proceed to the Analyze phase.
- Ensure that everyone is aligned with the project's direction and understands their roles and responsibilities in the next phase.

A successful tollgate review in the Measure phase ensures that the project has gathered reliable data, established a clear baseline, and is ready to move on to the Analyze phase, where further in-depth analysis and problem identification will occur.

SUMMARY

Chapter 9 began with a discussion on the development of a sampling plan and the process by which effective guidelines can be developed. It then provided a section on understanding throughput and rolled yield. This discussion was followed by a section on the importance of process sigma level, which, by example, required the reader to calculate and interrupt the results. Charting process behavior through control charting was then covered. The reader was then required to form trend charts and interpret results. This was followed by a section on statistical process control concepts and control limits. The reader was then introduced to differing types of control charts, rational sub-groupings, $\bar{X}$ and moving average charting, and various types of attribute charting techniques. Normality assessment and the transformation of non-normal data were then addressed, followed by a Measure phase tollgate review.

CHAPTER 9 DISCUSSION QUESTIONS

1. What are the key objectives of the sampling plan? Briefly discuss each objective.
2. Compare and contrast probability sampling methods and non-probability sampling methods.
3. Briefly define and discuss measurement methods and their distinguishing characteristics.
4. Define and describe throughput yield and rolled throughput yield. Why are they considered critical performance metrics?
5. Briefly discuss the importance of process sigma level.
6. Define and briefly discuss statistical process control and its importance in DMAIC-driven Lean Six Sigma projects.
7. Why is selecting the appropriate SPC chart important when monitoring and analyzing variation in processes?
8. What is rational sub-grouping? Why is it used extensively in the aviation and aerospace industries?
9. Why is normality assessment and transformation of non-normal data considered a critical step in the analysis of data?
10. Briefly describe the common types of statistical transformation processes.

BIBLIOGRAPHY

Alvi, Mohsin. "A manual for selecting sampling techniques in research." University of Karachi, Iqra University, 2016. https://mpra.ub.uni-muenchen.de/70218/1/

Avram, Călin, and Marius Măruşteri. "Normality assessment, few paradigms and use cases." *Revista Romana de Medicina de Laborator* 30.3 (2022): 251–260.

Baldo, Crhistian R., Gabriel M. Probst, and Wim Dewulf. "Process behavior charts used to check the consistency of CT instruments." *Procedia CIRP* 96 (2021): 330–335.

Breyfogle, F. "Non-normal data: To transform or not to transform." *Quality Digest* (2009). https://www.qualitydigest.com/inside/six-sigma-column/non-normal-data-transform-or-not-transform-082409.html

Chakravorty, Satya S. "Six sigma programs: An implementation model." *International Journal of Production Economics* 119.1 (2009): 1–16.

Chou, Youn-Min, Alan M. Polansky, and Robert L. Mason. "Transforming non-normal data to normality in statistical process control." *Journal of Quality Technology* 30.2 (1998): 133–141.

Colosimo, Bianca M., and Massimo Pacella. "A comparison study of control charts for statistical monitoring of functional data." *International Journal of Production Research* 48.6 (2010): 1575–1601.

Czabak-Górska, Izabela Dagmara. "The classification and characteristics of control charts." *CBU International Conference Proceedings* 5 (2017).

Dudek-Burlikowska, M. "Using control charts XR in monitoring a chosen production process." *Journal of Achievements in Materials and Manufacturing Engineering* 49.2 (2011): 487–498.

Evans, Bill. "Statistical process control: Operating within limits." *Mechanical Engineering* 111.3 (1989): 78.

Flores, Miguel, et al. "Constructing a control chart using functional data." *Mathematics* 8.1 (2020): 58.

Games, Paul A., and Patrick A. Lucas. "Power of the analysis of variance of independent groups on non-normal and normally transformed data." *Educational and Psychological Measurement* 26.2 (1966): 311–327.

Garland, Michael, and David B. Kirk. "Understanding throughput-oriented architectures." *Communications of the ACM* 53.11 (2010): 58–66.

Gijo, E. V., et al. "An application of six sigma methodology for improving the first pass yield of a grinding process." *Journal of Manufacturing Technology Management* 25.1 (2014): 125–135.

Godfrey, A. Blanton, and August B. Mundel. "Guide for selection of an acceptance sampling plan." *Journal of Quality Technology* 16.1 (1984): 50–55.

Goh, T. N., and M. Xie. "Improving on the six sigma paradigm." *The TQM Magazine* 16.4 (2004): 235–240.

Graham, Ben B. *Detail Process Charting: Speaking the Language of Process*. John Wiley & Sons, 2004.

Graves, Spencer. "Six sigma rolled throughput yield." *Quality Engineering* 14.2 (2002): 257–266.

Gupta, Anshu, et al. "Productivity improvement in the chassis preparation stage of the amplifier production process: A DMAIC six sigma methodology." *International Journal of Reliability, Quality and Safety Engineering* 23.6 (2016): 1640012.

Haridy, Salah, and Zhang Wu. "Univariate and multivariate control charts for monitoring dynamic-behavior processes: A case study." *Journal of Industrial Engineering and Management* 2.3 (2009).

Hosseinifard, S. Z., et al. "A transformation technique to estimate the process capability index for non-normal processes." *The International Journal of Advanced Manufacturing Technology* 40 (2009): 512–517.

Ipek, H. A. L. İ. L., H. Ü. S. E. Y. İ. N. Ankara, and H. Ozdag. "The application of statistical process control." *Minerals Engineering* 12.7 (1999): 827–835.

Itay, Negrin, Parmet Yisrael, and Schechtman Edna. "Developing a sampling plan based on Cpk." *Quality Engineering* 21.3 (2009): 306–318.

Jones-Farmer, L. Allison, Jeremy D. Ezell, and Benjamin T. Hazen. "Applying control chart methods to enhance data quality." *Technometrics* 56.1 (2014): 29–41.

Jyothi, Sangeetha Abdu, et al. "Measuring and understanding throughput of network topologies." In *SC'16: Proceedings of the International Conference for High Performance Computing, Networking, Storage and Analysis*. IEEE, 2016.

Kanakana, Mukondeleli Grace, Jan-Harm C. Pretorius, and B. Van Wyk. "Lean six sigma framework to improve throughput rate." In *2010 IEEE 17Th International Conference on Industrial Engineering and Engineering Management*. IEEE, 2010.

Korzenowski, André L., et al. "Control charts for flexible and multi-variety production systems." *Computers & Industrial Engineering* 88 (2015): 284–292.

Kumar, Sameer, and Michael Sosnoski. "Using DMAIC six sigma to systematically improve shop-floor production quality and costs." *International Journal of Productivity and Performance Management* 58.3 (2009): 254–273.

Kuwaiti, Ahmed Al, and Arun Vijay Subbarayalu. "Reducing patients' falls rate in an academic medical center (AMC) using six sigma 'DMAIC' approach." *International Journal of Health Care Quality Assurance* 30.4 (2017): 373–384.

Levy, Paul S., and Stanley Lemeshow. *Sampling of Populations: Methods and Applications.* John Wiley & Sons, 2013.

Li, Ying, Yi-min Shi, and Liang Wang. "Application of maximum likelihood estimation model in X-MR control charts." *Journal of Physical Sciences* 11 (2007): 1–9.

MacCarthy, B. L., and Thananya Wasusri. "A review of non-standard applications of statistical process control (SPC) charts." *International Journal of Quality & Reliability Management* 19.3 (2002): 295–320.

Makrymichalos, Miltiadis, et al. "Statistical thinking and its role for industrial engineers and managers in the 21st century." *Managerial Auditing Journal* 20.4 (2005): 354–363.

Marino, Stefano. "A successive sub-grouping method for multiple sequence alignments analysis." *arXiv preprint arXiv:0705.4429* (2007).

Matzke, Brett D., et al. *Visual Sample Plan Version 7.0 User's Guide.* No. PNNL–23211. Pacific Northwest National Lab. (PNNL). Richland, WA, 2014.

Miot, Hélio Amante. "Assessing normality of data in clinical and experimental trials." *Jornal Vascular Brasileiro* 16 (2017): 88–91.

Nahl, Diane. "A discourse analysis technique for charting the flow of micro-information behavior." *Journal of Documentation* 63.3 (2007): 323–339.

Noel, Dago Dougba, et al. "Normality assessment of several quantitative data transformation procedures." *Biostatistics and Biometrics Open Access Journal* 10.3 (2021): 51–65.

Oberoi, Er Harpreet Singh, et al. "SPC (statistical process control): A quality control technique for confirmation to ability of process." *International Research Journal of Engineering and Technology (IRJET)* 3.6 (2016): 666–672.

Park, Changsoon, Moonsup Song, and Jaeheon Lee. "A generalization of the discrete feedback adjustment by rational subgrouping." *Journal of the Korean Statistical Society* 27.2 (1998): 237–249.

Phillips, Patricia Pulliam, and Cathy A. Stawarski. *Data Collection: Planning for and Collecting All Types of Data.* John Wiley & Sons, 2008.

Rao, P. S. R. S. *Sampling methodologies.* Boca Raton, FL: Chapman & Hall/CRC, 2000.

Ravichandran, J. "Six-sigma milestone: An overall sigma level of an organization." *Total Quality Management* 17.8 (2006): 973–980.

Rochon, Justine, Matthias Gondan, and Meinhard Kieser. "To test or not to test: Preliminary assessment of normality when comparing two independent samples." *BMC Medical Research Methodology* 12.1 (2012): 1–11.

Sainani, Kristin L. "Dealing with non-normal data." *Pm&r* 4.12 (2012): 1001–1005.

Şengöz, Nefise Gönül. "Control charts to enhance quality." *Quality Management Systems – a Selective Presentation of Case-Studies Showcasing Its Evolution* (2018): 153–194.

Shahimi, Nur Syafiqah, Azmarini Ahmad Nazri, and Muhammad Hafizan Yosri. "Control chart in developing standard operating procedure (SOP)." *International Journal of Research and Innovation Management* 8.1 (2022): 1–10.

Shmueli, Galit. *Practical Acceptance Sampling: A Hands-on Guide.* Axelrod Schnall Publishers, 2016.

Valles, Adan, et al. "Implementation of six sigma in a manufacturing process: A case study." *International Journal of Industrial Engineering* 16.3 (2009): 171–181.

Waddell, Gordon, et al. "Normality and reliability in the clinical assessment of backache." *British Medical Journal (Clinical Research Ed.)* 284.6328 (1982): 1519.

Wu, Chien-Wei, and Shih-Wen Liu. "Developing a sampling plan by variables inspection for controlling lot fraction of defectives." *Applied Mathematical Modelling* 38.9–10 (2014): 2303–2310.

Wu, Chien-Wei, and Zih-Huei Wang. "Developing a variables multiple dependent state sampling plan with simultaneous consideration of process yield and quality loss." *International Journal of Production Research* 55.8 (2017): 2351–2364.

Yang, Zhilin, Xuehua Wang, and Chenting Su. "A review of research methodologies in international business." *International Business Review* 15.6 (2006): 601–617.

Part IV

The Measure Phase of DMAIC

10
Root Cause Identification and Validation

LEARNING OBJECTIVES

1. Describe the purpose and process of the "5 Whys" methodology and the overall goal of root cause analyses (RCA).
2. Explain how box plots and scatter diagrams, as well as correlation and regression analyses, aid in conducting RCA.
3. Differentiate between the Pearson and Spearman correlation coefficients and discuss their applications in analysis.
4. Explain the purpose of hypothesis testing, including the differences between the null and alternative hypotheses, and describe Type I and Type II errors.
5. Discuss the purpose of power analysis and the importance of selecting appropriate confidence intervals in statistical analysis.

ROOT CAUSE IDENTIFICATION AND VALIDATION

Finding the root cause of a problem is a fundamental concept in problem solving and troubleshooting across various fields, including science, engineering, medicine, business, and especially DMAIC-driven Lean Six Sigma initiatives. The process typically involves identifying the underlying reason or source of an issue rather than just addressing its symptoms.

The process starts by clearly identifying the problem or issue that requires addressing. The symptoms must be understood and an assessment of how the problem or issue could affect the overall system be conducted. A methodology that has proven effective in doing this is the "5 Whys" technique. Figure 10.1 shows some reasons for using this methodology.

The 5 Whys technique involves asking "why" five times to drill down to the root cause. For each answer, one would ask why it occurred until the fundamental cause could be identified. This method helps in uncovering multiple contributing factors.

This is followed by a systematic approach of root cause analysis. A structured RCA process will be addressed in depth in the following section, but it is used to identify the primary causes of the problem uncovered via techniques like the "5 Whys", then visualized and analyzed with techniques like Ishikawa diagrams and fault tree analysis.

DOI: 10.4324/9781032650531-14

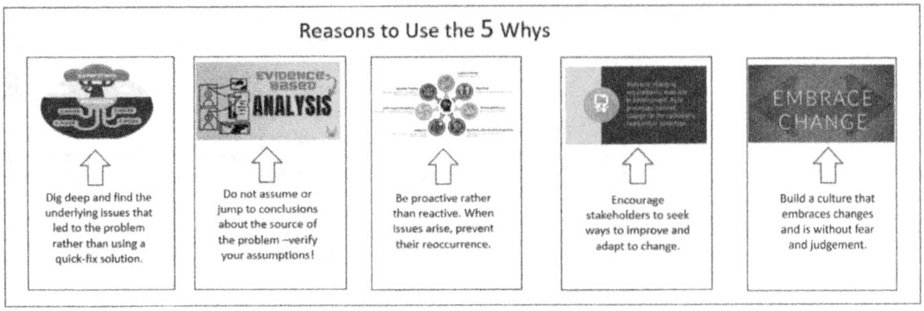

Figure 10.1 Reasons to Use the 5 Whys

Once this is performed, then data and information related to the potential root cause will be collected. This process normally takes many forms, like reviewing records, talking to those involved, or using data analysis tools.

Often, at this stage, the Pareto principle (the 80/20 rule) is used to prioritize the factors that have the most impact on the problem. The focus would now be on the one(s) that are the most critical; these will be addressed first. With the root cause now clearly identified, hypotheses are then proposed and tested to either confirm or refute. This is normally performed through either experiments or controlled trials (more on this in Chapter 11).

When the root cause(s) is "validated", corrective action is then taken. This situation is monitored to ensure that the problem does not recur. If it does, be prepared to revise your analysis and make further improvements.

Last, keep a record of the process, including the identified root cause(s), actions taken, and outcomes. Also, ensure all stakeholders are aware of the findings and actions.

Finding the root cause of a problem can be a complex and iterative process that involves collaboration and careful analysis. The goal is to not just address the immediate issue but to prevent its recurrence by dealing with the underlying causes.

Systematically Applying Root Cause Analysis

Root cause identification and validation, as previously addressed, are critical steps in the problem-solving and quality improvement processes and are defining steps in any DMAIC-driven Lean Six Sigma initiative. The overall goal is to identify the underlying causes of a problem or issue and then validate that those identified root causes are indeed the true sources of the problem.

Regardless of whether it is a service-related project or one related directly to producing a product such as an aircraft system, a structured approach is fundamental to root cause analyses. The following is a structured approach to root cause identification I have found to be highly effective that can be easily integrated into any LSS project initiative:

- *Step 1.* Define the problem – clearly define the problem or issue to be addressed. Ensure that the problem statement is clear, specific, measurable, and actionable.
- *Step 2.* Gather information – collect data and information related to the problem. This may include historical data, process documentation, incident reports, and input from individuals involved.
- *Step 3.* Brainstorm the potential causes with your team – conduct a brainstorming session with your cross-functional team to generate a list of potential causes for the problem. Encourage open and creative thinking.

- *Step 4.* Categorize causes – organize the potential causes into categories, such as human factors, or environmental factors.
- *Step 5.* Prioritize causes – use techniques like Pareto analysis to visually prioritize the potential causes. Focus on the impactful causes.
- *Step 6.* Data analysis – analyze data and conduct statistical tests, if applicable, to identify correlations and trends associated with the potential causes.
- *Step 7.* Root cause analysis – apply root cause analysis techniques, such as the 5 Whys, where you repeatedly ask why a series of times, to ensure you are drilling down on the root cause, to drive deeper into each potential cause. Ask why the problem occurred at each level until you reach the fundamental cause.
- *Step 8.* Validate the root cause – to validate the identified root causes, consider using the following approaches:
  - Factual evidence – look for factual data that links the identified cause to the problem.
  - Observation – conduct direct observations and interviews to verify that the identified causes are indeed contributing to the problem.
  - Experimental learning – implement changes based on the identified causes and assess the impact on the problem.
  - Expert opinions – seek the opinions of subject matter experts (SMEs) who can validate the identified root causes.
  - Benchmarking – compare your findings with industry benchmarks or best practices to validate the root causes.
- *Step 9.* Document the root causes – clearly document the validated root causes. Ensure that the documentation includes a description of the cause, the evidence supporting it, and its impact on the problem.
- *Step 10.* Develop corrective actions – once the root causes are validated, develop corrective actions or solutions to address them. Ensure that these actions are targeted at eliminating or mitigating the root causes.
- *Step 11.* Implement corrective actions – put the corrective actions into practice. Assign responsibility for the implementation and set a timeline for completion.
- *Step 12.* Monitor and review – continuously monitor the results of the corrective actions to ensure effective in addressing the problem. Adjust the actions as needed.
- *Step 13.* Prevent recurrence – develop strategies to prevent the problem from recurring by implementing preventive measures based on lessons learned.

Root cause analysis is an iterative process. If the first set of corrective actions does not resolve the issue, revisit the process, and continue making improvements. It is important to involve your cross-functional team and SMEs in the validation procedures to enhance the accuracy of the root cause analysis.

ASSESSING DATA BOX PLOTS AND SCATTER PLOTS

As described in the previous section, the analysis of the data when performing RCA is a critical step to clearly identifying the actual cause of the problem vice the symptoms. Two methods that have proven highly effective in identifying root causes are box plots and scatter diagramming. Both provide visual summaries of the data. First, box plots!

- *Box Plots* – a box plot, also known as a box-and-whisker plot, is a graphical presentation of the distribution of a dataset. It provides a visual summary of the key

Example of a Box Plot Using Batch Testing Data

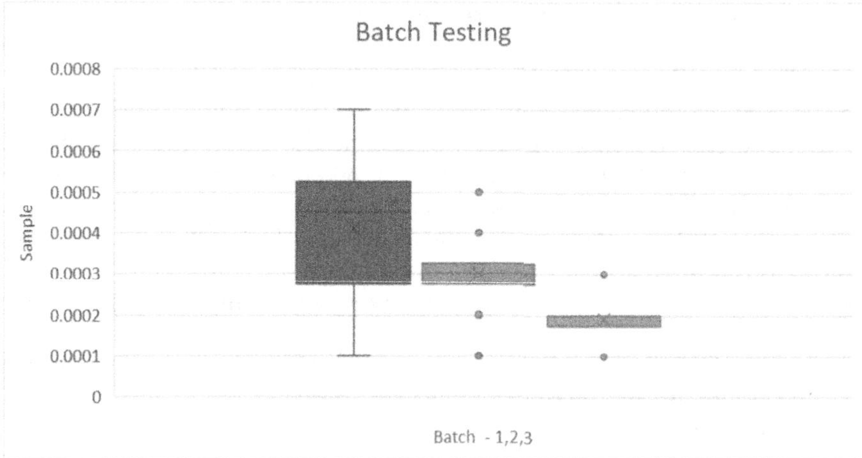

Figure 10.2 Example of a Box Plot Using Batch Testing Data

statistical characteristics of the data, including the median, quartiles, and potential outliers. Box plots are commonly used in statistical and data analysis and are a cornerstone technique used in all DMAIC-driven Lean Six Sigma initiatives to compare and summarize the distribution of different datasets. Figure 10.2 is an example of a box plot using data from the batch testing data initially introduced in Chapter 8.

Key components of a box plot are:

- *Median* – also referred to as the (Q2), this is the line inside the box that represents the median of the dataset, which is the middle value when the data is sorted in ascending order.
- *Box* – also known as the (IQR), represents the interquartile range (IQR), which is the range of the data.
- *Whiskers* – the lines extending from the box, called whiskers, represent the range of the data. These lines extend to the minimum and maximum within a specified range.
- *Outliers* – data points that fall outside the whiskers are considered potential outliers (data points that are significantly differ from the rest of the dataset) and are usually plotted as individual points.

Interpreting a box plot:

- The box provides information about the middle 50% of the data.
- The length of the box shows the spread of the data in the middle 50%.
- The whiskers show the range of the data, excluding potential outliers.
- The median (the line inside the box) represents the central value.
- Potential outliers, if present, are plotted individually outside the whiskers.

Box plots are valuable for comparing the distribution of multiple datasets, identifying central tendencies, and recognizing the presence of outliers. They are especially helpful when there are varying data distributions or when a quick overview of the data's spread and central values is needed.

- *Scatter Plots* – a scatter plot is a graphical representation of data points in a two-dimensional coordinate system. It is used to visualize the relationship between variables and to identify patterns or trends in the data. Scatter plots are commonly used in all types of data analysis and statistics and should be considered a cornerstone technique in all DMAIC-driven Lean Six Sigma initiatives. Figure 10.3 is an example of a scatter plot for units produced and monthly cost for a large aircraft component manufacturing organization.

Key components of scatter plots:

- *X-Axis* – the horizontal axis represents one variable (the independent variable) of the dataset.
- *Y-Axis* – the vertical axis represents the other variable (dependent variable) of the dataset.
- *Data Points* – each data point on the plot represents a pair of values from the two variables. These data points are often marked with dots, circles, or other symbols.

Interpreting a scatter plot depends on the relationship observed:

- *Positive linear relationship* – if the data points tend to form a straight line that slopes upward from left to right, it indicates a positive linear relationship between the two variables. As one variable increases, the other tends to increase.
- *Negative linear relationship* – if the data points form a straight line that slopes downward from left to right, it indicates a negative relationship. As one variable increases, the other tends to decrease.

Figure 10.3 Scatter Plot Chart of Monthly Cost and Units Produced

- *No relationship (random)* – if the data points do not show any clear pattern or trend and appear scattered randomly across the plot, it suggests that there is no apparent relationship between the variables.
- *Curvilinear relationship* – at times, the data may follow a curved or non-linear pattern, indicating a curvilinear relationship. This means that the relationship between the variables is not strictly linear.
- *Clusters or groups* – data points may form clusters or groups, suggesting that subpopulations within the dataset with different relationships exist. This is often found when testing different vendor plating solutions during receiving.

Scatter plots are valuable tools used for understanding and visualizing the relationships between variables. They aid in identifying correlation, outliers, and patterns that may not be evident through other methods.

CORRELATION AND REGRESSION ANALYSIS

Correlation and regression analysis are two fundamental statistical techniques used to understand the relationships between variables and make predictions. They are employed in various fields, including science, social sciences, and extensively in any DMAIC-driven Lean Six Sigma initiative. First, let us look at correlation analysis.

- *Correlation analysis* – correlation analysis assesses the degree and direction of the relationship between two or more variables. It quantifies how variables are related without implying causation. There are different measures of correlation, with the most common one being Pearson's correlation coefficient (r);
  - *Pearson's correlation coefficient (r)* – it measures the strength and direction of a linear relationship between two continuous variables. It ranges from −1 (perfect negative correlation) to 1 (perfect positive correlation), with 0 indicating no linear correlation. Figure 10.4 presents an example of a Pearson correlation between units produced without a production facility and monthly production cost.

Example of Pearson Correlation and Units Produced and Monthly Production Cost

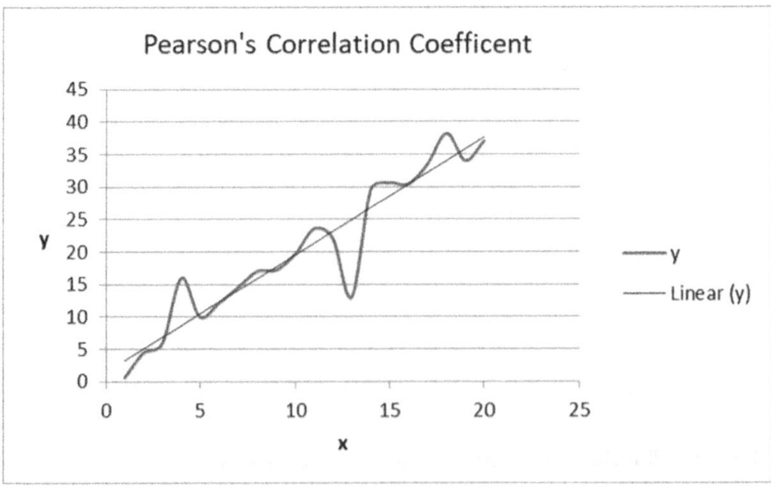

Figure 10.4 Example of Pearson Correlation and Units Produced and Monthly Production Cost

    - Positive (r) values indicate a positive correlation (as one variable increases, the other increases as well).
    - Negative (r) values indicate a negative correlation (as one variable increases, the variable decreases).
    - An (r) value of 0 suggests no linear correlation.
- *Spearman's rank order correlation (rho)* – the Spearman rank order correlation (rho) evaluates the monotonic relationship (in a monotonic relationship, the variables tend to change together, but not necessarily at a constant rate) between ranked values. Figure 10.5 presents an example of a Spearman correlation with data from the cure time of two batches of composite bonding resin.

Example of Spearman Correlation and Cure Time of Composite Bonding Resin

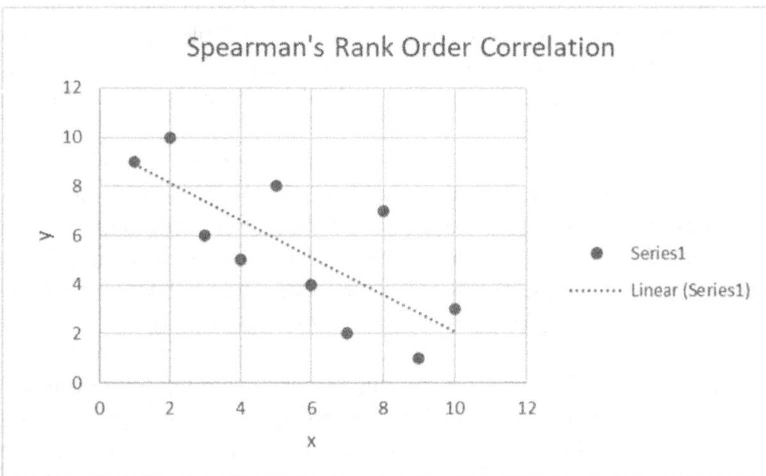

Figure 10.5 Example of Spearman Correlation and Cure Time of Composite Bonding Resin

Use a Spearman correlation:

1. If the data exhibits a non-linear relationship or is not normally distributed.
2. If at least one variable is ordinal.
3. If there are significant outliers.

The Pearson and Spearman correlation coefficients measure the strength and direction of the relationship between variables. The Pearson correlation assesses linear relationships, while the Spearman correlation evaluates monotonic relationships. Table 10.1 illustrates when to use each based on data type.

Table 10.1 Pearson and Spearman Correlation Coefficients: When to Use

Correlation Type	*Pearson Correlation Coefficient*	*Spearman Correlation Coefficient*
Data Types	Appropriate for interval and ratio data	Appropriate for ordinal and non-normally distributed data
Usage	Assessing linear associations and parametric tests	Assessing monotonic associations and non-parametric tests

Correlation analysis is primarily concerned with finding out whether a relationship exists between variables and then determining the magnitude and action of that relationship. When using any method of correlation analysis, key things to remember are:

1. Correlation does not equal causation. Correlation analysis identifies and evaluates a relationship between two variables, but a positive correlation does not automatically mean one variable affects the other.
2. The main benefits of correlation analysis are that it helps determine which variables require further investigation and allows for rapid hypothesis testing.
3. The main type of correlation analysis is performed using the Pearson (r) method to identify the degree of the linear relationship between two variables.

- *Regression analysis* – regression analysis goes a step further than correlation by modeling and quantifying the relationship between variables, allowing for predictive capabilities. In simple regression, there is one independent variable (predictor) and one dependent variable (outcome). In multiple regression, there are multiple independent variables.
  - *Simple linear regression* – this method models the relationship between two variables using a straight line (linear equation). The goal is to predict or explain the variation in the dependent variable (Y) using the independent variable (X). The equation takes the form: $Y = a + bX$, where "a" is the intercept and "b" is the slope. An example of a simple regression model that assesses the impact of one product on monthly operating project is illustrated in Figure 10.6.
- *Multiple regression* – using this regression approach, more than one independent variable is used to predict the dependent variable. The equation becomes $Y = a + b1X1 + b2X2 + \ldots + bnXn$. An example of a multiple regression equation that assesses which product(s) contribute to more revenue is illustrated in Figure 10.7.

Simple Regression Model of One Product's Impact on Monthly Operating Cost

Regression Statistics	
Multiple R	0.600693
R Square	0.360832
Adjusted R Square	0.323234
Standard Error	1580.007
Observations	19

ANOVA

	df	*SS*	*MS*	*F*	*Significance F*
Regression	1	23958339	23958339	9.597076	0.006533666
Residual	17	42439151	2496421		
Total	18	66397491			

	Coefficients	*Standard Error*	*t Stat*	*P-value*	*Lower 95%*	*Upper 95%*	*Lower 95.0%*	*Upper 95.0%*
Intercept	39720.08	1539.557	25.79967	4.5E-15	36471.89846	42968.26	36471.9	42968.26
A Made	5.239542	1.691313	3.097915	0.006534	1.671184658	8.8079	1.671185	8.8079

Figure 10.6 Simple Regression Model of One Product impact on Monthly Operating Cost

Multiple Regression Model Assessing Which Product(s) Contribute to Higher Revenue

Regression Statistics	
Multiple R	0.803398744
R Square	0.645449542
Adjusted R Square	0.57453945
Standard Error	1252.763898
Observations	19

ANOVA

	df	*SS*	*MS*	*F*	*Significance F*
Regression	3	42856229.89	14285410	9.10237	0.001126532
Residual	15	23541260.74	1569417.4		
Total	18	66397490.63			

	Coefficients	*Standard Error*	*t Stat*	*P-value*	*Lower 95%*	*Upper 95%*	*Lower 95.0%*	*Upper 95.0%*
Intercept	35102.90045	1837.226911	19.106459	6.1E-12	31186.94158	39018.8593	31186.94158	39018.8593
A Made	2.065953296	1.664981779	1.2408264	0.23373	-1.482873542	5.61478013	-1.48287354	5.61478013
B Made	4.176355531	1.681252566	2.4840738	0.02529	0.592848311	7.75986275	0.592848311	7.75986275
C Made	4.790641037	1.789316107	2.6773587	0.01722	0.97680169	8.60448038	0.97680169	8.60448038

Figure 10.7 Multiple Regression Model Assessing Which Product(s) Contribute to Higher Revenue

Both the simple and multiple regression models illustrated provide detailed information on the effects of independent variables on dependent variables. Each can be used to make strategic decisions by the organization as to product mix and logistically to when and what to procure to ensure customer demand is constantly met. They are valuable as well to any DMAIC-driven Lean Six Sigma initiative in that they can provide immediate visibility on cycle time issues and production leveling.

ESTIMATING POPULATION PROPORTION AND MEAN

Estimating a population involves using sample data to make an inference about the proportion or percentage of a specific attribute or characteristic within a larger population. This process is commonly used in surveys, research, quality control, and especially in any DMAIC-driven Lean Six Sigma initiative. It helps in drawing conclusions about a population based on a sample. There are two primary methods for estimating a population proportion: point estimation and interval estimation.

Point and interval estimates are the two forms of population parameter estimation based on sample data.

1. *Point estimation* – a point estimation involves calculating a single value (point estimate) that is believed to be the bast estimate of the population mean (X) based on sample data. The most common point estimates for a population mean is the sample mean ($\overline{x}$), which is the arithmetic average of the values in the sample. The point estimate ($\overline{x}$) is an unbiased estimate of the population (X), but it may not be exact and comes with uncertainty.
2. *Interval estimation* – interval estimation provides a range of values within which the true population (X) is likely to fall with a certain level of confidence. This range is called a confidence interval. The construction of a confidence interval involves the use of the point estimate ($\overline{x}$), a measure of uncertainty, and a critical value based on the desired level of confidence, (e.g., 95% confidence, the critical value typically around 1.96).

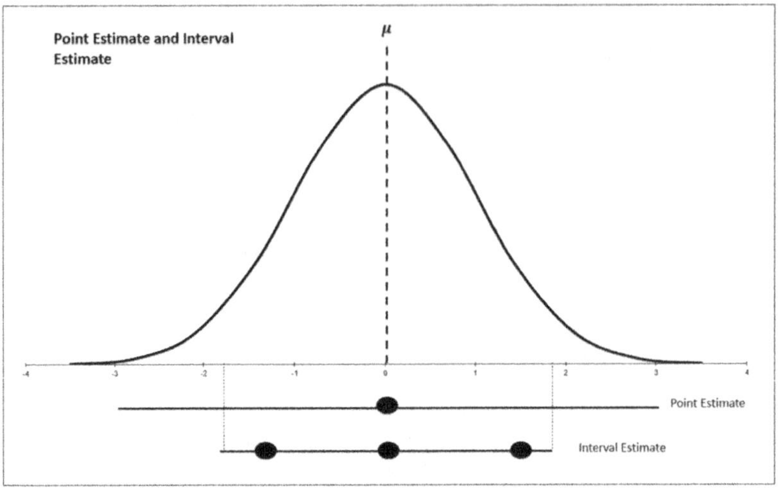

Figure 10.8 Illustration of a Point Estimate and Interval Estimate

An illustration of point estimation and interval estimation is given in Figure 10.8.

Estimation is a process in which the values of unknown population parameters can be obtained with the help of a sample. Estimation is a data analysis framework that combines effect sizes and confidence intervals to plan experiments and aid in the analysis of data and interpreting the results. The basic purpose of estimating methods is to estimate the size of an effect and report the effect size along with its confidence interval.

The estimator is a method, formula, or function that specifically tells how to compute an estimate which can then estimate the value of the population parameter from a sample. We use sample measures to estimate the population measures; these statistics are the estimators. There are three properties that good estimators exhibit:

1 An estimator should be consistent. For instance, if an estimator is consistent, its value approaches the parameter value estimated as the sample size increases.
2 The estimator should be unbiased. The expected value obtained from the sample should be equal to the parameter being estimated.
3 The estimator should be efficient. It should have minimal variance from the actual variance of the estimator.

As illustrated in Figure 10.8, a point estimate is a simple calculated statistic using the sample data to estimate the value of the corresponding unknown population parameter. The point estimate is derived from a single value in the sample to estimate the population value. The basic formula for this would be:

$$\bar{x} = \sum x / n$$

An example of this would be a sampling of plating components where you measured the depth of coating. Thirteen (13) cm is the average $\bar{x}$ depth of a coating sample of 15 randomly collected components from a total run of 250, which is considered the mean mark of the entire class. Because this is in a single numeric form, it is a point estimator. The drawback of point estimates is that no information is available regarding their reliability.

In fact, the probability that a single sample statistic is equal to the population parameters is very unlikely.

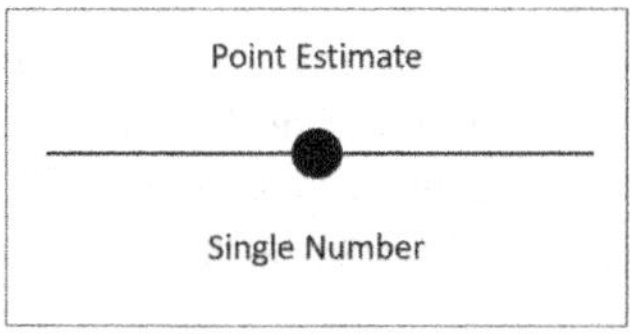

Because we would like a stronger confidence in the estimate range, there is a requirement to do a *confidence interval.* A confidence interval estimate is a range of values constructed from sample data so that the population parameters will occur within a range at a specified probability, which is the level of confidence. Compared to the point estimate, the interval estimate offers the following advantages:

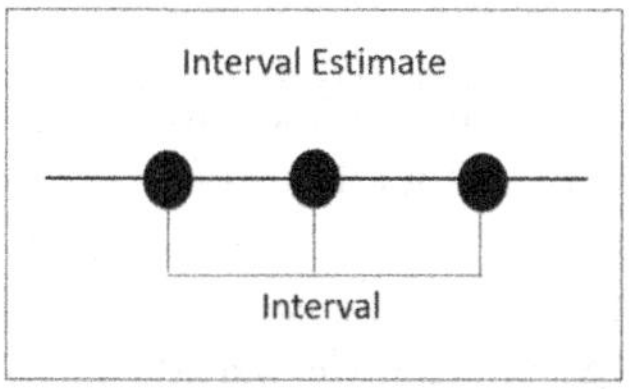

1 Broader and more accurate than the point estimate.
2 It is used with inferential statistics to develop a confidence level interval where we can, with a level of confidence, plan that the population lies.
3 Any parameter estimate that is based on a sample statistic has some amount of sampling error, which will affect the level of confidence statistic chosen.

The width of the confidence interval is determined by the sample size, population variability, and desired level of confidence.

An example of confidence interval estimation would be something like the following:

> A plastic injection molding process is using a new bonding chemical. Based on a sample of 25 trails, the average cycle time is 7.49 seconds with a standard deviation of .022 seconds. The machine's known process variance is 0.00576.

We want to find the confidence limits of μ and test at a confidence level of 99%. The following formula applies:

$\bar{x}$ 7.49 $t = \frac{\bar{x} - \mu}{s / \sqrt{n}}$

s 0.22

n 25

α 1%

$t(\alpha/2, df)$ t (.5, 24) 2.797 $<$ found by looking at T-table

$\bar{x} - t(\alpha/2, df) * (s/Squrt(n))$ $<\mu>$ $\bar{x} + t(\alpha/2, df) * (s/Squrt(n))$

7.366932 $<\mu>$ 7.613068

The use of a confidence interval provides a more informative estimate of the population mean because it accounts for the inherent uncertainty in the point estimate. It tells not only what the point estimate is but also how confident it is that the true mean falls within a certain range. In practice, when estimating a population mean, you collect a random sample, calculate the sample mean, determine the standard error, and conduct a confidence level. This interval estimation helps make informed decision/conclusions about the population without relying solely on a point estimate.

HYPOTHESIS TESTING: PURPOSE, CONCEPTS, AND LANGUAGE

Hypothesis testing is a fundamental statistical method used to make inferences about a population based on a sample of data. It is a systematic process for assessing and evaluating research questions, hypotheses, and claims and is a core analysis tool used in DMAIC-driven Lean Six Sigma initiatives.

The purpose of hypothesis testing is to:

1. *Assess claims* – hypothesis testing is used to evaluate claims or hypotheses made about a population, a process, or a relationship between variables.
2. *Making inferences* – it provides a framework for drawing inferences about a population based on sample data.
3. *Decision-making* – it helps make informed decisions by determining whether the evidence in the sample supports or contradicts a specific hypothesis.

There are eight key concepts in hypothesis testing that should be considered when planning it use. Figure 10.9 illustrates these eight concepts:

- *The null hypothesis (Ho)* – the null hypothesis is a statement that there is no significant effect, relationship, or difference in the population. It represents the status quo or a default assumption to be tested.

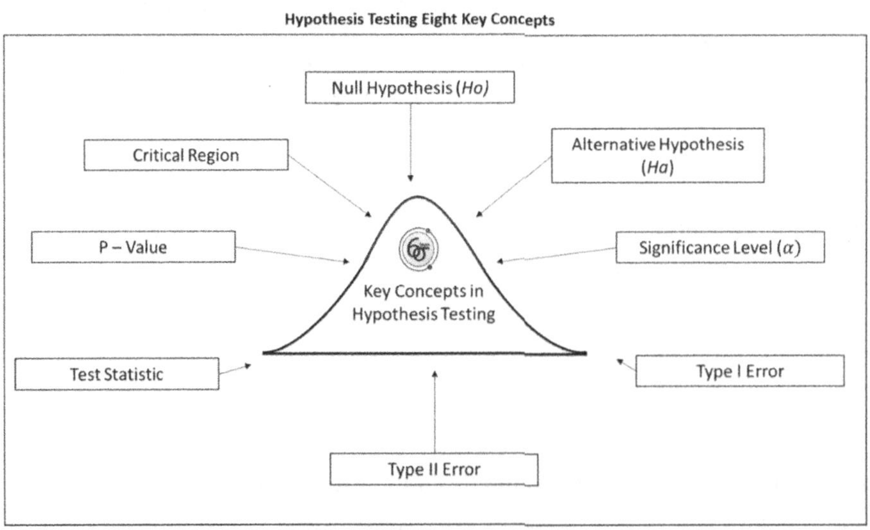

Figure 10.9 Hypothesis Testing: Eight Key Concepts

- *The alternative hypothesis (Ha) contradicts the null hypothesis.* It suggests the presence of a significant effect, relationship, or difference.
- *The significance level* (α) – the significance level, often denoted as α (alpha), represents the probability of making a Type I error. Common values for α include 0.05 (5%) or 0.01 (1%).
- *Type I error* – a Type I error occurs when the null hypothesis is rejected when it is true. It represents a false positive.
- *Type II error* – a Type II error occurs when the null hypothesis is not rejected when it is false. It represents a failure to detect a true effect or relationship.
- *Test statistic* – the test statistic is a value calculated from the sample data, which is used to assess the evidence against the null hypothesis. A test statistic is a number calculated by a statistical test, normally via a T-Z statistic. It describes how far your observed data is from the null hypothesis of no relationship between variables or no difference among sample groups.
- *The p-value* – the p-value is a probability that measures the strength of evidence against the null hypothesis. A smaller p-value indicates stronger evidence against the null hypothesis.
- *The critical region* – the critical region is a set of values of the test statistic for which the null hypothesis is rejected. It is determined based on the significance level (α). For example, the critical region for a 5 % significance test is: for a one-tailed test, the critical value is 1.645. So, the critical region is $Z < -1.645$ for a left-tailed test and $Z > 1.645$ for a right-tailed test. For a two-tailed test, the critical value is 1.96.

When performing the actual hypothesis testing, the following process procedures illustrated in Figure 10.10 aids in ensuring all elements required to test the hypothesis are effectively executed.

- *Formulate the hypothesis* – start by formulating the null hypothesis (*Ho*) and the alternative hypothesis (*Ha*).
- *Collect the data* – gather a sample of data relevant to the research question being explored.

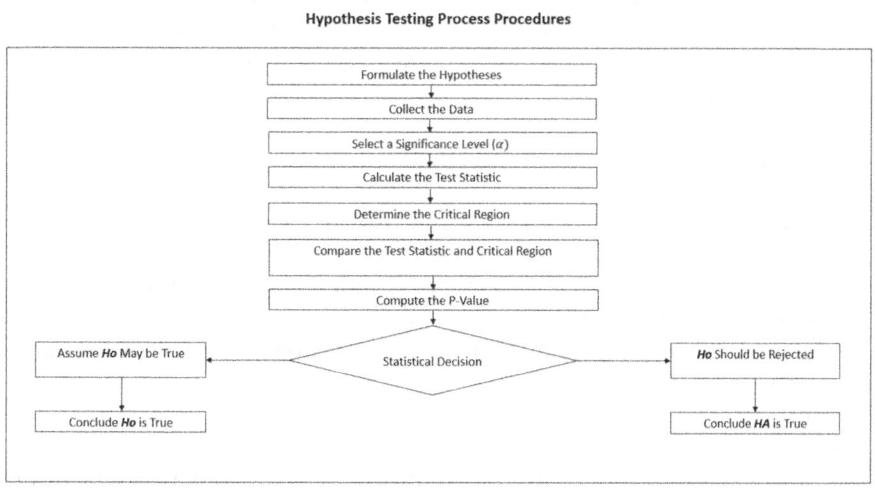

Figure 10.10 Hypothesis Testing Process Procedures

- *Select a significance level* (α) – determine the significance level, which represents the acceptable risk of a Type I error.
- *Calculate the test statistic* – compute the test statistic based on the sample data and the chosen statistical test (this will be covered in the next section).
- *Determine the critical region* – find the critical values or range of values for the test statistic that would lead to rejection of the null hypothesis.
- *Compare the test statistic and critical region* – compare the calculated test statistic to the critical region. If the test statistic falls within the critical region, reject the null hypothesis; otherwise, fail to reject it.
- *Compute the p-value* – calculate the p-value, which quantifies the strength of evidence against the null hypothesis.
- *Make the statistical decision* – based on the p-value and significance level, decide whether to reject or fail to reject the null hypothesis.
- *Draw conclusions* – based on the decision, draw conclusions, and interpret the results in the context of the research question.

When conducting hypothesis testing, it is important to properly format the hypothesis to ensure clarity and precision. The format of hypotheses typically follows a specific structure that includes the null hypothesis (*Ho*) and the alternative hypothesis (*Ha*). The format differs for various types of statistical tests. The following are some of the more common hypothesis testing statistical tests that are used in any DMAIC-driven Lean Six Sigma initiative:

1 *A one sample test* – used for testing the population parameter against a specific value:
   - Null hypothesis *(Ho)*: $\mu = \mu 0$
   - Alternative hypothesis (*Ha*): $\mu \neq \mu 0$ (two-tailed test) or $\mu < \mu 0$ (left-tailed test or $\mu > \mu 0$ (right-tailed test)

   Example.
   Ho: the mean cure time for a strut plating cure time 135 minutes, +/−.15 seconds
   Ha: the mean cure time for a struct plating cure time is not 135 minutes, +/−.15 seconds
2 A two-sample test – used for comparing two population parameters:
   - Null hypothesis (*Ho*): $\mu 1 = \mu 2$ (for a two-sample mean comparison)
   - Alternative hypothesis (*Ha*) $\mu 1 \neq \mu 2$ two-tailed test or $\mu 1 < \mu 2$ (left-tailed test or $\pi 1 > \mu 2$ (right-tailed test)

   Example:
   Ho: there is no difference in the plating thickness measurement between lot A and lot B.
   Ha: there is a difference in the plating thickness measurement between lot A and lot B (two-tailed test).
3 *A chi-square test* – used for testing the independence of categorical data:
   - Null hypothesis (*Ho*): there is no association between variable A and variable B.
   - Alternative hypothesis (*Ha*): there is an association between variable A and variable B.

   Example:
   Ho: there is no association between the mixed plating solution in vat A and vat B.
   Ha: there is an association between the mixed plating solution in vat A and vat B.

4 The goodness-of-fit test: used for testing the distribution of categorical data:
- Null hypothesis (Ho): the observed data follows and expected distribution.
- Alternative hypothesis (Ha): the observed data does not follow the expected distribution.

Example:
Ho: the observed curing time for zinc-coated articles in the test batch matches the expected distribution.
Ha: the observed curing time for zinc-coated articles in the test batch does not match the expected distribution.

5 The paired t-test – used for paired or matched observations.
- Null hypothesis (*Ho*): $\mu d = 0$ (where μd is the population mean of the differences)
- Alternative hypothesis (*Ha*): $\mu d \neq 0$ (two-tailed test) or $\mu d > 0$ (right-tailed test)

Example:
Ho: there is no significant difference between grip strength of the national course thread bolt when coated with a loc-tight solution.
Ha: there is a significant difference between the grip strength of the national course threaded bolt when coated with a loc-tight solution.
It is essential to be clear about what is being tested and which direction the effect will occur when formatting hypotheses. The null hypothesis represents a statement of no effect or no difference, while the alternative hypothesis represents the statement of an effect or a difference. The choice between one-tailed and two-tailed tests often depends on the specific research question and the nature of the hypothesis being tested. One-tailed tests are more sensitive to detecting a change in a particular direction, whereas two-tailed tests are more inclusive and can detect any significant difference, regardless of the direction.

Types of Error

In hypothesis testing, as mentioned in the previous section, there are two types of errors that can occur when making decisions about the null hypothesis *Ho* and the alternative hypothesis *Ha*. These errors are known as a Type I error (alpha, α) and Type II error (beta, β). They represent the potential mistakes or incorrect conclusions that can be made in the hypothesis testing process.

A Type I error (alpha, α) occurs when you reject the null hypothesis (*Ho*) when it is true. In other words, it is concluded that there is an effect, difference, or relationship when there is none. This error is often called a false positive. The probability of making a Type I error (the alpha α) is the significance level of the test. Common values for α include 0.05 (5%) and 0.01 (1%).

An example of a Type I error is:

A test of a composite resin product that has just been received is tested to ensure the resin meets mixture specification requirements. The test indicates the resin has an imbalance of chemicals. This is a "false positive" result.

A Type II error (beta, β) occurs when you reject the null hypothesis *(Ha)* when it is false. In other words, it is concluded that there is no effect or relationship when there is one. This error is often called a "false negative". The probability of making a Type II error is denoted by β (beta). The complement of β ($1 - \beta$) is referred to as the "power" of a statistical test, representing the probability of correctly rejecting a false null hypothesis.

An example of a Type II error is:

A test of a composite resin product that has just been received is tested to ensure the resin meets mixture specification requirements. The test failed to detect an imbalance (a "false negative") of chemicals and, when used, caused irregular bonding.

The relationship between Type I and Type II errors is inversely related: as you decrease the risk of making one type of error, you increase the risk of making the other type of error. It is common practice to set the significance level (α) and design statistical tests to control the probability of a Type I error while keeping the Type II error to a reasonable level.

Balancing these two types of errors is essential in hypothesis testing because the choice of α and the sample size can significantly impact the overall quality and reliability of the conclusions drawn from the analysis. The goal is to minimize both types of errors while considering the context and specific requirements of the research or application.

POWER ANALYSIS

Power analysis is a statistical technique used to determine the sample size needed for a research study to achieve a certain level of statistical power and is an essential statistical tool in any DMAIC-driven Lean Six Sigma initiative. Statistical power is the probability of correctly rejecting the null hypothesis when it is false, and it is a complement of Type II error (β) in hypothesis. Power analysis helps the researcher determine how likely they are to detect an effect, difference, or relationship when it exists in the population. The following are key concepts of statistical power analysis:

- *Statistical power* $(1 - \beta)$ – statistical power represents the probability of correctly rejecting a null hypothesis when it is false. It is the ability to detect a true effect or relationship. A higher power is desirable because it means a lower risk of making a Type II error.
- *Type II error* (β) – a Type II error is the probability of failing to reject the null hypothesis when it is false. It represents the risk of not detecting a real effect or relationship. Power analysis helps minimize β.
- Effect size (ES) – the effect size is a measure of the magnitude of the true effect or difference the researcher is trying to detect. In power analysis, the researcher needs to specify the expected effect size based on theoretical or practical knowledge.
- Significance level (α) – the significance level is the probability of making a Type I error (α often set at 0.05 or 0.01). Power analysis typically assumes a specific value for α.
- Sample size (n) – the sample size is the number of observations or participants in the study. Power analysis's aim is to determine the required sample size to achieve a desired level of statistical power.

There are five steps in performing a power analysis. Figure 10.11 illustrates the steps.

Step 1. Specify the effect size – define the expected effect size based on prior research, theory, or practical significance. Effect sizes are typically measured using standardized metrics like *Cohen's d* (for means), *odds ratio* (for proportions, or *Pearson's r* (for correlations).

Step 2. Set the significance level (α) – specify the significance level (e.g., $\alpha = 0.05$), which is the acceptable risk of Type I error.

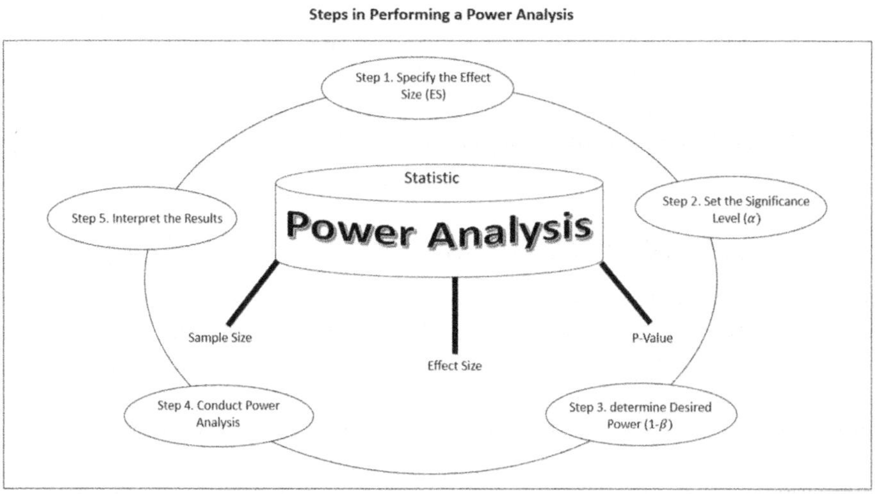

Figure 10.11 Steps in Performing a Power Analysis

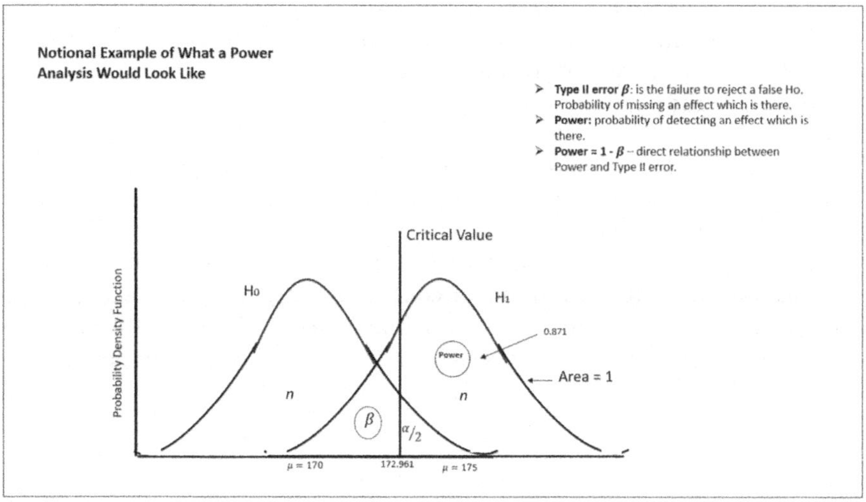

Figure 10.12 Example of What a Power Analysis Would Look Like

Step 3. Determine the desired power $(1 - \beta)$ – choose the desired level of statistical power (e.g., 0.80 or 0.90). The selection of power is often passed on conventions or research goals.

Step 4. Conduct power analysis – using statistical software or a calculator, perform a power analysis to calculate the required sample size (n) to achieve a specified power level given the effect size and significance level.

Step 5. Interpret the results – the power analysis provides the necessary size to achieve the desired power. If the required sample size is impractical, researchers may need to revisit the effect size assumption or consider a more feasible research interest.

Figure 11.12 provides an example of what a power analysis would look like when performed.

Power analysis helps researchers plan their studies effectively by determining the appropriate sample size needed to detect effects or relationships of interest. It ensures that research is conducted with sufficient statistical power, reducing the risk of missing important findings (Type II errors). Calculating the required sample size in advance allows for the efficient allocation of resources and reduces the likelihood of conducting underpowered studies.

CONFIDENCE INTERVAL SELECTION

A confidence interval is a range of values used to estimate an unknown population parameter with a certain level of confidence. It provides a way to quantify the uncertainty in estimating population parameters based on a sample of data. Confidence intervals are widely used in statistics and research and are central to a DMAIC-driven Lean Six Sigma initiative. The following are some key components of a confidence interval:

- *Point or interval estimate* – the point or interval estimate is the sample statistic(s) used to estimate the population parameter. For example, the sample mean ($\overline{x}$) is often used to estimate the population mean (μ).
- *Margin of error (MOE)* – the margin of error quantifies the degree of uncertainty in the estimation. It represents the range within which the population parameter is likely to fall. The margin of error is often expressed as a critical value times the standard error of the point.
  Example:
  The value of z^* for a confidence level of 95% is 1.96. After putting the value of z^*, the population standard deviation, and the sample size into the equation, a margin of error of 3.92 is found.
- *Level of confidence* ($1 - \alpha$) – the level of confidence is the probability that the true population parameter falls within the confidence interval. Common confidence levels include 90%, 95%, and 99%, corresponding to α values of 0.10, 0.05, and 0.01, respectively. Figure 10.13 presents an illustration of selecting a confidence level.

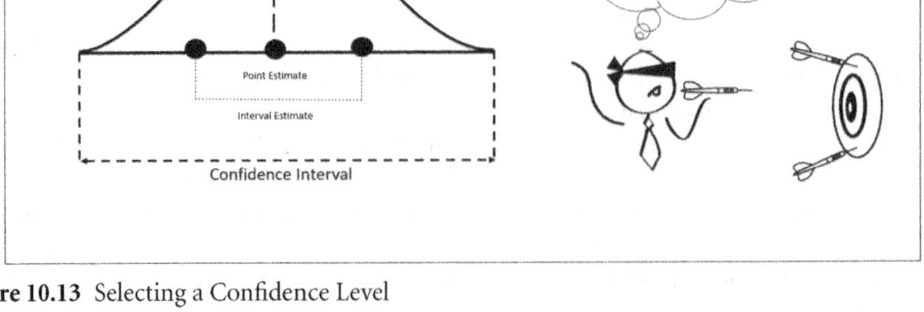

Figure 10.13 Selecting a Confidence Level

When constructing a confidence interval(s), the following seven steps should be followed:

Step 1. Collect the data – gather a random sample from the population you want to make inference(s) about.
Step 2. Choose a significance level (α) – decide on the level of confidence you want for your confidence level interval. As mentioned previously, common choices are 90%, 95%, and 99%. These correspond to theα values of 0.10, 0.05, and 0.01, respectively.
Step 3. Calculate the point or interval estimate – calculate the sample statistic(s), point, or interval, used to estimate the population parameter. For example, if you are estimating the population mean (X), calculate the sample mean ($\overline{x}$).
Step 4. Determine the critical value – determine the critical value from the standard *normal distribution* (for the population) or the *t-distribution* (for a sample) that corresponds to the chosen significance level (α) and the sample size.
Step 5. Calculate the standard error – calculate the standard error for the point or interval estimate(s). This involves using the standard deviation of the sample (σ), and the square root of the sample size.
Step 6. Compute the margin of error – multiply the critical value by the standard error to calculate the margin of error.
Step 7. Construct the confidence interval(s) – create the confidence interval by adding and/or subtracting the margin of error(s) from the point or interval estimate(s).

The confidence interval is typically stated as:

Confidence interval = point or interval estimate(s) +/−margin of error

Step 8. Interpret the confidence interval – normally it could be stated that "you are 95% confident that the true population parameter falls within the calculated confidence level(s)". This would mean that if you were to take many random samples and construct intervals, approximately 95% of those intervals would capture the true parameter.

Confidence intervals are essential in statistics and research because they provide a range of plausible values for population parameters. They allow the Lean Six Sigma team to make informed inferences about the population based on sample data while considering the inherent uncertainty in the estimation process.

SUMMARY

Chapter 10 began by showing the reader how they could systematically recognize and apply alternative methods of root cause identification and validation. It then provided them with examples of how the evaluation should be evaluated between variables, both discrete and continuous, should be evaluated statistically and graphically. Using regression analysis and the assessment of correlations, it guided the reader through the process of identifying relationships between multiple inputs and continuous output to build a model of those mathematical relationships that are critical to model validation. A discussion of estimating population proportion and mean was then conducted, followed by a hypothesis testing discussion emphasizing its purpose, concepts, and language. The chapter then went into detail on formatting hypotheses, setting confidence levels, measurements of error, and testing the null and alternative hypotheses. It concluded with a discussion on how to use power analysis as an aid to sample measurement and defining and setting confidence levels.

LEAN SIX SIGMA AT WORK!

Lean Six Sigma Tools at Work

Two machines have recently been installed at *C&L Metalworks Inc.* To determine whether additional noise dampening devices are needed, their safety engineer has taken several noise exposure measurements at a water jet cutting work center and a conventional grinding machine. The engineer would like to determine with 90% confidence that these samples represent the mean noise exposure expected to be experienced by workers throughout the plant. The values represent the percentage of allowable daily decibel (dB) dose. A value of 50% during a n8-hour shift represents 85 (dB).

For the water jet cutter work center, the ratios recorded were $X_1 = 0.45$, $X_2 = 0.47$, and $X_3 = 0.44$, resulting in an $\bar{X} = 0.45$ and $s = 0.015$; the water jet noise value is calculated as: $\frac{0.45 \pm 2.920(0.15)}{\sqrt{3}}$

where:
$\bar{X} = 0.45$
$N = 3$
$s = 0.015$
$\alpha = 0.10$
$1 - \alpha = 0.90$
$t(\alpha/2) = 2.920$
$df = 3-1 = 2$

The interval is (0.425, 0.475). The safety engineer can be 90% confident that the population mean is between these two values for the water jet cutting work center. Because these values are below the legal permissible decibel levels, no additional noise dampening is required.

For the conventional grinding machine, the rations recorded were $X_1 = 0.55$, $X_2 = 0.75$, and $X_3 = 0.57$, resulting in an $\bar{X} = 0.62$ and $s = 0.11$. The grinding machine noise value is calculated as: $\frac{0.62 \pm 2.920(0.11)}{\sqrt{3}}$

where:
$\bar{X} = 0.62$
$n = 3$
$s = 0.11$
$\alpha = 0.10$
$1 - \alpha = 0.90$
$t(\alpha/2) = 2.920$
$df = 2$

The interval is (0.43, 0.81). The safety engineer can be 90% confident that the population mean is between these two values.

Note that due to its large standard deviation, this is a much broader spread than the water jet interval. This broad interval includes values that are above the legal permissible decibel levels, and therefore additional dampening will be required.

Figure 10.14

CHAPTER 10 DISCUSSION QUESTIONS

1 Define and describe the "5 Whys" technique.
2 Define and describe root cause analysis and elaborate on the commonly used approach to executing it.
3 Define and describe correlation and regression analysis. Why are they considered fundamental during execution of Lean Six Sigma projects?
4 Compare and contrast a point estimation and interval estimation. How are they used in a Lean Six Sigma project?
5 Define and explain how hypothesis testing is used in executing Lean Six Sigma projects. Differentiate between the null hypothesis and alternative hypothesis.
6 Define and explain how power analysis is used in Lean Six Sigma projects.
7 Explain why a confidence interval is important when executing a Lean Six Sigma project.

BIBLIOGRAPHY

Aho, Ken, and R. Terry Bowyer. "Confidence intervals for ratios of proportions: Implications for selection ratios." *Methods in Ecology and Evolution* 6.2 (2015): 121–132.

Arumugam, V., Jiju Antony, and Alex Douglas. "Observation: A lean tool for improving the effectiveness of lean six sigma." *The TQM Journal* 24.3 (2012): 275–287.

Ashok Sarkar, Shri, Arup Ranjan Mukhopadhyay, and Sadhan Kumar Ghosh. "Root cause analysis, lean six sigma and test of hypothesis." *The TQM Journal* 25.2 (2013): 170–185.

Bhat, Shreeranga, E. V. Gijo, and N. A. Jnanesh. "Application of lean six sigma methodology in the registration process of a hospital." *International Journal of Productivity and Performance Management* 63.5 (2014): 613–643.

Dhallin, Arthur J. *The Identification, Validation, and Modeling of Critical Parameters in Lean Six Sigma Implementations.* Diss. University of Southern California, 2011.

Drohomeretski, Everton, et al. "Lean, six sigma and lean six sigma: An analysis based on operations strategy." *International Journal of Production Research* 52.3 (2014): 804–824.

Fuentes, Claudio, George Casella, and Martin T. Wells. "Confidence intervals for the means of the selected populations." *The Electronic Journal of Statistics* 12.1 (2018): 58–79. https://doi.org/10.1214/17-EJS1374

Games, Peter S., and Alark Joshi. "Visualization of off-screen data on tablets using context-providing bar graphs and scatter plots." In *Visualization and Data Analysis 2014.* Vol. 9017. SPIE, 2014.

Gastelum-Acosta, Carlos, et al. "Assessing the adoption of critical success factors for lean six sigma implementation." *Journal of Manufacturing Technology Management* 33.1 (2022): 124–145.

Harry, Mikel J., et al. *Practitioner's Guide to Statistics and Lean Six Sigma for Process Improvements.* John Wiley & Sons, 2010.

Howe, Christine, et al. "Hypothesis testing in science: Group consensus and the acquisition of conceptual and procedural knowledge." *Learning and Instruction* 10.4 (2000): 361–391.

Kabaila, Paul. "Valid confidence intervals in regression after variable selection." *Econometric Theory* 14.4 (1998): 463–482.

Kanjanabose, Rassadarie, Alfie Abdul-Rahman, and Min Chen. "A multi-task comparative study on scatter plots and parallel coordinates plots." *Computer Graphics Forum* 34.3 (2015).

Keller, Daniel, and Jesse Egbert. "Hypothesis testing ordinary meaning." *Brooklyn Law Review* 86 (2020): 489.

Kluxen, Felix M. "Scatter plotting as a simple tool to analyse relative organ to body weight in toxicological bioassays." *Archives of Toxicology* 93.8 (2019): 2409–2420.

Kruschke, John K., and Torrin M. Liddell. "The Bayesian new statistics: Hypothesis testing, estimation, meta-analysis, and power analysis from a Bayesian perspective." *Psychonomic Bulletin & Review* 25 (2018): 178–206.

Manfei, X. U., et al. "The differences and similarities between two-sample t-test and paired t-test." *Shanghai Archives of Psychiatry* 29.3 (2017): 184.

Myors, Brett, Kevin R. Murphy, and Allen Wolach. *Statistical Power Analysis: A Simple and General Model for Traditional and Modern Hypothesis Tests.* Routledge, 2010.

Newman, Michael C. "'What exactly are you inferring?' A closer look at hypothesis testing." *Environmental Toxicology and Chemistry: An International Journal* 27.5 (2008): 1013–1019.

Oppong, Felix Boakye, and Senyo Yao Agbedra. "Assessing univariate and multivariate normality. A guide for non-statisticians." *Mathematical Theory and Modeling* 6.2 (2016): 26–33.

Papaioannou, Agelos, et al. "Assessment and modelling of groundwater quality data by environmetric methods in the context of public health." *Water Resources Management* 24 (2010): 3257–3278.

Papic, Ljubisa, et al. "Significant factors of the successful lean six-sigma implementation." *International Journal of Mathematical, Engineering and Management Sciences* 2.2 (2017): 85–109.

Park, Hun Myoung. "Hypothesis testing and statistical power of a test." 2015. https://scispace.com/papers/hypothesis-testing-and-statistical-power-of-a-test-1g9op9sl3t

Rana, Rakesh, and Richa Singhal. "Chi-square test and its application in hypothesis testing." *Journal of Primary Care Specialties* 1.1 (2015): 69–71.

Rasch, Dieter. "Hypothesis testing and the error of the third kind." *Psychological Test and Assessment Modeling* 54.1 (2012): 90.

Seo, Jinwook, Heather Gordish-Dressman, and Eric P. Hoffman. "An interactive power analysis tool for microarray hypothesis testing and generation." *Bioinformatics* 22.7 (2006): 808–814.

Shokri, Alireza, David Oglethorpe, and Farhad Nabhani. "Evaluating six sigma methodology to improve logistical measures of food distribution SMEs." *Journal of Manufacturing Technology Management* 25.7 (2014): 998–1027.

Singh, Mahipal, et al. "A toolset for complex decision-making in analyze phase of lean six sigma project: A case validation." *International Journal of Lean Six Sigma* 14.1 (2023): 139–157.

Smith, William L. "Reading and understanding hypothesis testing research." In *Search and Re-search.* Routledge, 2002, pp. 75–102.

Stalvey, Harrison E., et al. "Students' understanding of the concepts involved in one-sample hypothesis testing." *The Journal of Mathematical Behavior* 53 (2019): 42–64.

Subudhi, Rabi N. "Testing of hypothesis: Concepts and applications." In *Methodological Issues in Management Research: Advances, Challenges, and the Way Ahead.* Emerald Insight, 2019, pp. 127–143. https://doi.org/10.1108/978-1-78973-973-220191009

Tang, Minh, et al. "A semiparametric two-sample hypothesis testing problem for random graphs." *Journal of Computational and Graphical Statistics* 26.2 (2017): 344–354.

Terek, Milan. "How to estimate the sigma level of the process." *Quality Innovation Prosperity* 27.3 (2023): 126–140.

Tuncel, Ertem. "On error exponents in hypothesis testing." *IEEE Transactions on Information Theory* 51.8 (2005): 2945–2950.

Uluskan, Meryem. "Analysis of lean six sigma tools from a multidimensional perspective." *Total Quality Management & Business Excellence* 30.9–10 (2019): 1167–1188.

Weinstein, Asaf, William Fithian, and Yoav Benjamini. "Selection adjusted confidence intervals with more power to determine the sign." *Journal of the American Statistical Association* 108.501 (2013): 165–176.

Zhao, Deyong, Weimin Ye, and Cuijuan Gao. "Research on process optimization for equipment maintenance based on lean six sigma management." In *2012 International Conference on Quality, Reliability, Risk, Maintenance, and Safety Engineering*. IEEE, 2012.

11

Selecting the Correct Test Structure and Modeling

LEARNING OBJECTIVES

1. Explain the basic hypothesis used in comparing one proportion to a standard and describe the importance of confidence intervals in estimating population parameters.
2. Apply the Z-test, chi-square test, and T-test during hypothesis testing of proportions.
3. Apply ANOVA (analysis of variance) and F-tests in hypothesis testing and differentiate when to use each test.
4. Describe various non-parametric tests suitable for non-normal data and explain the data-transformation process.
5. Describe the purpose of design of experiments (DoE) and identify methods for conducting DOE.

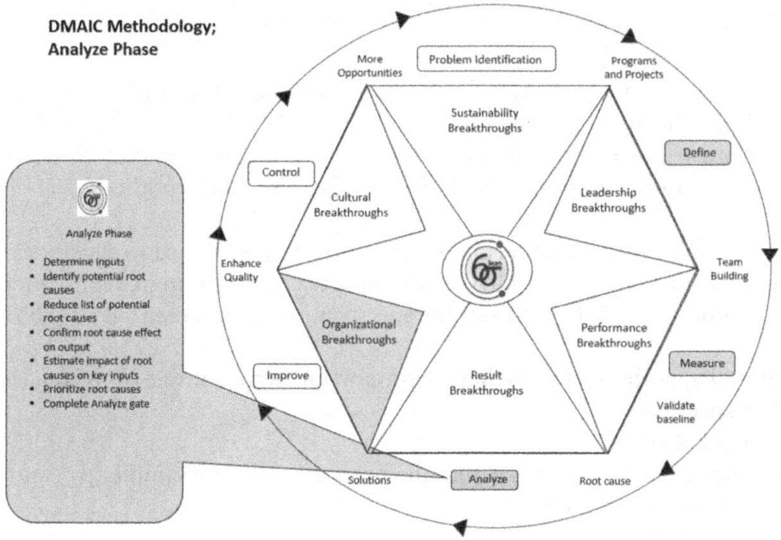

Figure 11.1 Analyze Phase Steps or Activities

DOI: 10.4324/9781032650531-15

COMPARING ONE PROPORTION TO A STANDARD

When comparing one proportion to a standard, there is interest in assessing whether the observed proportion is significantly different from the known or assumed value. This is normally done through hypothesis testing. The following is a general outline of the process used:

Step 1. Formulate hypotheses:

- *(Ho)* – this is a statement of no effect or no difference. It often includes the assumption that there is no change from a standard or known proportion. An example of this is ($p = p0$), where p is the observed proportion and p0 is the standard or assumed proportion.
- *(HA)* – this will be the assumption of no effect, difference or type of relationship. An example of this is *($p = p0$)* for a two-tailed test or *($p > po/p < po$)* for a one-tailed test.

Step 2. Choose a significance level (α) – Usual choices here are 0.05, 0.01, or 0.10. This is the probability of rejecting the null hypothesis when it is true.

Step 3. Collect the data – gather a sample and calculate the sample proportion (p).

Step 4. Calculate the test statistics – for proportions, the test statistic often follows a normal distribution. A Z-test and chi-square test are most often used for this purpose. Here are the formula structures for each:

Z-test for proportions: where (n) is the sample size, ($\dot{p}$) is the sample proportion, and (P_0) is the assumed or known population.

$$Z = \frac{\dfrac{(p - p_0)}{\sqrt{po(1 - po)}}}{n}$$

Chi-square test for proportions: where (o) is the observed frequency and (E) is the expected frequency.

$$x^2 = \frac{(0 - E)^2}{E}$$

Step 5. Decide – compare the calculated test statistics with the critical values(s) from the distribution or use a p-value.

Step 6. Draw a conclusion – if the p-value is less than or equal to α, reject the null hypothesis. Otherwise, you should fail to reject the null hypothesis.

Hers is an example of how comparing one proportion to standard would appear:

You are interested in testing whether the proportion of an ingredient contained in a solution is significantly different from the specification requirements 0.70 (70%).

- Your null hypothesis (Ho) is that the proportion in the sample (p) is equal to the 0.70 (70%) specified.
  - Ho: p = 0.70
- Your alternative hypothesis is that the proportion in the sample (p) is not equal to the 0.70 (70%) specified.
  - Ha: p = 0.70

A significance α level of 0.05 has been chosen. This is the probability of rejecting the null hypothesis when it is true.

Using the formula of the Z-test for a single proportion:

$$Z = \frac{(\dot{p} - p_0)}{\frac{\sqrt{po(1-po)}}{n}}$$

where:

$\dot{p}$ is the sample proportion.
p_0 is the assumed or known population proportion.
n is the sample size.

Assume you have taken over 200 samples from your supplying vendors over a one-month period and 140 test as meeting specification tolerance. We now calculate $\dot{p}$.

$$\dot{p} = \frac{140}{200} = 0.70$$

Substituting the values into the Z-test formula:

$$Z = \frac{(0.70 - 0.70)}{\frac{\sqrt{0.70(1-0.70)}}{200}}$$

Calculate the Z-value using the previous formula. If the Z-value is significantly different from zero, the null hypothesis can be rejected, and you can conclude that the proportion of specification differences between the vendors is in fact significantly different. The critical values or p-value will help you make this determination based on the chosen level of significance.

COMPARING TWO PROPORTIONS USING THE Z-TEST

When comparing two proportions using the Z-test, you are typically interested in determining whether the difference between two samples is statistically significant. The formula for the Z-test for comparing two proportions is as follows:

$$Z = \frac{(p_{1-} p_2)}{\sqrt{p(1-p)\left(\frac{1}{n_1} + \frac{1}{n_2}\right)}}$$

where:

p_1 and p_2 are the sample proportions of the two groups.
n_1 and n_2 are the sample sizes of the two groups.
p is the pooled sample proportion, calculated as $p = \frac{x_{1+x_2}}{n_{1+n_2}}$, where X_1 and X_2 are the total number of successes in each group.

Here is a step-by-step guide on how to conduct a Z-test for comparing two proportions:

Step 1. Formulate the hypothesis:

- H_0: $p_{1\,=}\,p_2$ (there is no difference in proportions).
- H_a: $p_1 = p_2, p_1 > p_2,$ *or* $p_1 < p_2$ (depending on the research question).

Step 2. Choose a significance level (α) – common choices are 0.05, 0.01, or 0.10.
Step 3. Collect the data – gather samples from the two groups and calculate sample proportions (*p1* and *p2*) and sample sizes for *n1* and *n2*.
Step 4. Calculate the pooled sample proportions (p) using the formula $P = \frac{x_{1+x_2}}{n_{1+n_2}}$.
Step 5. *Calculate the test statistics (Z).*

$$Z = \frac{(p_1 - p_2)}{\sqrt{p(1-p)\left(\frac{1}{n_1}+\frac{1}{n_2}\right)}}$$

Step 6. Decide – compare the calculated test statistic with the critical value(s) from the standard normal distribution or use a p-value.
Step 7. Draw a conclusion – if the p-value is less than or equal to α, reject the null hypothesis. Otherwise, fail to reject the null hypothesis.

Here is an example of how comparing two proportions using the Z-test is done:
Suppose you want to compare the proportions of chemical properties between two independent groups using the following information:

Group 1:
Sample size (n_1) – 200
Number of properties (X_1) – 30
Group 2:
Sample size (n_2) – 150
Number of properties (X_2) – 30

Use a significance level (α) of 0.05, follow the steps outlined previously to perform a Z-test, and then draw conclusions about whether there is a significant difference between the two proportions.

COMPARING MULTIPLE PROPORTIONS USING THE CHI-SQUARE TEST

When comparing multiple proportions, especially when dealing with categorical data involving more than two groups, the chi-square test for independence is often used. The chi-square test assesses whether there is a significant association between categorical variables. If you are comparing proportions across multiple groups, it can be used to determine if there is a significant difference in the distribution of the categorical variable among the groups.

The following is a step-by-step guide on how to conduct a chi-square test for comparing multiple proportions:

Step 1. Formulate the hypothesis:
- Null hypothesis (*H0*) – there is no association between the categorical variables (proportions are the same across groups).
- Alternative hypothesis *(Ha)* – there is an association between the categorical variables (proportions across groups).

Step 2. Choose a significance level (α) – common choices are 0.05, 0.01, or 0.10.

Step 3. Organize the data – create a contingency table that shows the counts and frequencies of each category for each group. The following example was taken from an analysis of composite thread by category.

	Category 1	*Category 2*	*Category 3*
Group 1	O11	O12	O1k
Group 2	O21	O22	O2k
–	–	–	–
Group M	Om1	Om2	Omk

where (*Oij*) represents the observed frequency for the (*i-th*) group and (*j-th*) category.

Step 4. Calculate the expected frequencies – calculate the expected frequency for each cell under the assumption of independence. The expected frequency (*Eij)* is obtained by the formula: $E_{ij} = \frac{R_{i+}C_j}{N}$

where R_i is the total count in the i-th row, C_j is the total count in the j-th column, and N is the total sample size.

Step 5. Calculate the test statistic (X^2):

$$X^2 = \Sigma_i^m \Sigma_{j=1}^k \frac{(O_{ij} - E_{ij})^2}{E_{ij}}$$

where:

X^2 = chi-square.
O = the observed value.
E = the expected value.

Step 5. Calculate the degrees of freedom – the degrees of freedom *(df)* is given by *(m – 1)* × *(k – 1).*

Step 6. Draw a conclusion – compare the calculated test statistic with the critical value from the chi-square distribution or use a p-value to draw a conclusion.

Suppose you have three different twisting methods for safety wiring (group1, group 2, and group 3) and you want to determine if there is a significant difference in the proportions of wiring that pass, fail, or pass, but loose. (not enough twist). You collect data from each group and organize it into a contingency table (like the one shown). You can then follow the steps outlined previously to perform the chi-square test on proportions and draw conclusions.

COMPARING ONE MEAN TO A STANDARD – USING THE T-TEST

When comparing the mean of a sample to a known standard, such as a population mean or a specified target value, you can use a one-sample t-test. The one-sample t-test is a statistical method that assesses whether the mean of a sample is significantly different from a specified population mean or target value. The following is a step-by-step guide on how to perform a one-sample t-test.

Step 1. Formulate the hypotheses:

- Null hypothesis (H_0): there is no significant difference between the sample mean ($\bar{X}$) and the population mean (μ) or the target value. H_0: $\bar{X} = \mu$.
- Alternative hypothesis (*Ha*): there is a significant difference between the sample mean ($\bar{X}$) and the population mean (μ) or the target value.
  - Ha: $\bar{X} > \mu$ or $\bar{X} < \mu$ (for a one-tailed test) or
  - Ha: $\bar{X} = \mu$ (for a two-tailed test)

Step 2. Collect the data – collect a sample of the data. Ensure the sample represents the population or context being studied.

Step 3. *Calculate the test statistic* – the formula for a one-sample t-test statistic is:

$$t = \frac{\bar{X} = \mu}{s / \sqrt{n}}$$

where:

$\bar{X}$ is the sample mean.
μ is the population mean or the target value.
S is the sample standard deviation.
n is the sample size.

Step 4. Determine the critical region – based on the chosen significance level (α), (normally 0.05, 0.01, or 0.10), degrees of freedom (*df*), (generally 90% or 95%), and whether it is a one-tailed or two-tailed test, you will find the critical value(s) from a t-distribution table or through the use of statistical software such as Minitab.

Step 5. Deciding if the calculated t-statistics falls into a critical region, reject the null hypothesis. If it does not, fail to reject the null hypothesis. If you reject the null hypothesis, it suggests that there is a significant difference between the sample mean and the population mean or target value.

Remember that the assumption of the t-test includes a normal distribution of the data and that the population standard deviation is unknown (replaced by the sample standard deviation). If the sample size is large enough (typically $n > 30$), the central limit theorem often ensures that the distribution of sample means is normal.

The following is an example of comparing one mean to a standard using the t-test:

- Suppose you are conducting an experiment to test a fiber wrapping process with a structural standard to ensure it is consistently in compliance with specification. The known standard is 75 fiber warps per artifact.
  - The hypotheses:
    - *Null hypothesis (H_0)* – the average fiber wrap ($\bar{X}$) is equal to the structural standard of 75 wraps. $H_0 = 75$.

- *Alternative hypothesis (H_a)* – the average fiber wrap is different from the structural standard of 75 wraps. $H_a = 75$.
- You have collected samples from 30 fiber-wrapped artifacts. The sample mean $\overline{X}$ is 78. The sample standard deviation (s) is 8. A significance level of 0.05 has been chosen.
- A t-test will be performed using the following formula:

$$t = \frac{X = \mu}{s / \sqrt{n}}$$

where:
$\overline{X}$ is the sample mean.
μ is the population mean or the target value.
S is the sample standard deviation.
n is the sample size.

- Substitute the values derived previously into the formula:
- Now calculate the t-value. Once you have it, you can compare it with the critical t-value from the t-distribution table or use statistical software such as Minitab to find the p-value. If the t-value is significant (falls in the rejection region), you would reject the null hypothesis and conclude that the average fiber wrap is significantly different from the structural standard. If it is not significant, you would fail to reject the null hypothesis.

COMPARING TWO MEANS USING THE T-TEST

If you have independent samples and there is a need to compare the means of each sample to a known standard, a two-sample t-test can be used. This test assesses whether the means of two samples are significantly different from each other. The following is a step-by-step guide on how to conduct a two-sample t-test comparing means to a standard:

Step 1. Formulate hypotheses:

- Null hypothesis (H_0) – there is no significant difference between the two-sample means ($\overline{X}_1$ and $\overline{X}_2$) or between the combined mean and the population mean (μ) or target value.

$$(H_0\text{: } \overline{X}_1 = \overline{X}_2 = \mu)$$

- Alternative hypothesis (H_a) – there is a significant difference between the two sample means or between the combined mean and the population mean or target value.

(H_a: at least one of $\overline{X}_1$ or $\overline{X}_2$ is different from μ)

Step 2. Collect the data – collect two independent samples of data. Ensure that the samples are representative of populations or contents you are investigating.

Step 3. Calculate the test statistic – the formula for the two-sample t-test statistic is:

$$(\bar{X}_1 - \bar{X}_2 - (\mu_1 - \mu_2)$$

$$t = \sqrt{S^2 \frac{1}{n_1} + S^2 \frac{2}{n_2}}$$

where:
$\bar{X}_1$ and $\bar{X}_2$ are the sample means, μ_1 and μ_2 are the population means or target values, s_1 and s_2 are the sample standard deviations, and n_1 and n_2 are the sample sizes.

Step 4. Determine the critical region – based on your chosen significance level (0.05, 0.01, or 0.10), degrees of freedom, (99%, 95%, or 90%), and whether it is a one-tailed or two tailed test, find the critical value(s) from the t-distribution table or use statistical software such as Minitab.
Step 5. Decide if the calculated t-statistic falls into the critical region; reject the null hypothesis. If it does not, fail to reject the null hypothesis.
Step 6. Interpret the results – ensure that the assumptions of the t-test are met, including normality of the data and equality of variances, or use a modified version of the test if variances are unequal. If the sample sizes are large enough, violations of normality are less of a concern due to the central limit theorem.

The following is an example of comparing two means using the t-test:

- Suppose you are interested in comparing the average cure time of two groups of composite bonding compound, groups A and B, to determine if there is a significant difference in their bonding cure strength.

The hypotheses are:

Null hypothesis (H_0): the average cure score for group A ($\bar{X}_1$) is equal to the average cure score for group B ($\bar{X}_2$).
Alternative hypothesis (H_0): the average cure score of group A is different from the average cure score of group B.

H_0: $\bar{X}_1 = \bar{X}_2$
H_a: $\bar{X}_1 = \bar{X}_2$

The sample information:

- Cure scores have been collected from a random sample of 25 artifacts in group A.
    - The sample mean ($\bar{X}_1$) is 82.
    - The sample standard deviation (s_1) is 7.
- Cure scores have been collected from a random sample of 30 artifacts in group B.
    - The sample mean ($\bar{X}_2$) is 78.
    - The sample deviation (s_2) is 6.
- A significance level of 0.05 has been selected.

The independent samples t-test can be performed now using the following formula:

$$t = \frac{(\bar{X}_1 - X_2)}{\sqrt{\frac{S^2{}_1}{n_1} + \frac{S^2{}_2}{n2}}}$$

where:

$\bar{X}_1$ and $\bar{X}_2$ are the sample means of group A and group B, respectively.
s_1 and s_2 are the sample standard deviations of group A and group B, respectively.
n_1 and n_2 are the sample sizes of group A and group B, respectively.

Substituting the values into the formula:

$$t = \frac{(82-78)}{\sqrt{\frac{7^2{}_1}{25_1} + \frac{6^2{}_2}{30_2}}}$$

Now, calculate the t-value. Once you have the t-value, you can compare it with the critical t-value from the t-distribution table or use statistical software such as Minitab to find the p-value. If the p-value is significant (falls in the rejection region), you would reject the null hypothesis and conclude that there is a significant difference in the average cure scores between group A and group B. if it is not significant, you would fail to reject to the null hypothesis.

COMPARING MULTIPLE PROPORTIONS USING ANOVA AND THE F-TEST

When comparing multiple means to a standard, ANOVA is a suitable statistical method. ANOVA assesses whether there are any statistically significant differences between the means of three or more independent groups. The F-test is used in ANOVA to determine whether the variances between the group means are significantly different. The following is a step-by-step method that can be used to compare the means of multiple groups:

Step 1. Formulate the hypotheses:

- Null hypothesis (H_0): there is no significant difference between the means of the groups or between the combined means and the population mean or target value.
  - H_0: $\mu_1 = \mu_2 = \mu_3 \ldots.. = \mu$
- Alternative hypothesis (H_a): there is a significant difference between at least one of the groups means or between the combined mean of the population mean or target.
  - H_a: *at least* μ_i *is different from the others.*

Step 2. Collect the data – collect data from multiple independent groups. Ensure that the groups are representative of the populations or contexts you are researching.

Step 3. Calculate the test statistic:

- The formula for the F-test in ANOVA is:

$$F = \frac{MSB}{MSW}$$

where:

MSB is the μ mean square *between* groups.
MSW is the μ mean square *within* groups.

$$MSB = \frac{\sum_{i=1}^{k} n_i (X_1 - X)^2}{k = 1}$$

$$MSW = \frac{\sum_{i=1}^{k} \sum_{j=1}^{n_i} (X_y - \bar{X}_i)^2}{N - k}$$

where:

k is the number of groups.
n_i is the sample size of group i.
$\bar{X}_1$ is the mean of group i.
X_{ij} is the j-th observation in group i.
$\bar{X}$ is the overall mean.
N is the total number of observations.

Step 4. Determine the critical region – based on your chosen significance level (0.05, 0.01, or 0.10) and degrees of freedom for the numerator (df_B) and denominator (df_W) for *MSB is k-1 MSW is N-k,* find the critical value from the F-distribution table or use statistical software such as Minitab.

Step 5. Draw a conclusion – if the calculated F-statistic is greater than the critical value, reject the null hypothesis. If it is not, fail to reject the null hypothesis.

Step 6. Interpret the results – if you reject the null hypothesis, it indicates that there is a significant difference between the means of at least one group or between the combined mean and the population mean or target value. Ensure that the assumptions of ANOVA are met, including the normality of the data, homogeneity of variances, and independence of observations. If these assumptions are violated, consider using non-parametric alternatives or transformations of the data.

The following is an example of comparing multiple proportions using ANOVA and the F-test.

Suppose you are conducting an experiment to compare the average repeatability and reproducibility (R&R) datasets across three different measurement systems, method A, method B, and method C.

Here are the hypotheses:

Null hypothesis (H_0) – the average R&R datasets are equal across all three measurement systems.

Alternative hypothesis (H_a) – at least one R&R has a different average score.

H_0: $\mu_a = \mu_b = \mu_c$

H_a: at least one μ_i is different.

Sample information:

R&R Dataset A	78	85	88	92	80	75	82	88	90	85
R&R Dataset B	70	75	68	72	65	78	80	74	72	76
R&R Dataset C	85	88	92	78	80	85	90	88	85	89

Ten measurement system R&R datasets have been randomly collected from all three methods (A, B, and C).

Significance level α *0.05*

Our F-test formula is:

$$F = \frac{MSB}{MSW}$$

where:

$MS_{between}$ is the mean square between groups.
MS_{within} is the mean square within groups.
The degrees of freedom for $MS_{between}$ is $k - 1$ (where k is the number of groups).
The degrees of freedom for MS_{within} is $N - k$ (where N is the total number of observations).

Calculate the group means:

$$\bar{X}_A = 85$$

$$\bar{X}_B = 73.4$$

$$\bar{X}_C = 86.7$$

Calculate the overall mean using the following formula:

$$\bar{X}_{total} = \frac{1}{30} \sum_{i=1}^{30} x_{i \approx 81}$$

Calculate the sum of squares using the following formula:

$$SS = \sum_{t-1}^{n} x_i^2$$

where:

Σ represents the summation symbol.
N is the number of elements in the set.
x_i represents each individual element of the set.

$SST_{total} \approx 583.4$
$SSB_{between} \approx 228.3$
$SSW_{within} \approx 355.1$

Calculate the degrees of freedom (*df*) using the following formula:

$$df_{between} = k - 1$$
$$df_{within} = N - k$$

where:

k is the number of groups.
N is the total number of observations.

$df_{between} = 2$ (3 groups – 1)
$df_{within} = 27$ (30 observations – 3 groups)

Calculate the mean square using the following formula:

$$MS = \sum_{i-1}^{n} (x_i - x)^2$$

where:
n is the number of data points.
X_i is each individual data point.
$\bar{X}$ is the mean (average) of the data set.

$MS_{between} \approx 114.2$
$MS_{within} \approx 13.15$

Calculate the F-statistic:

$$F \approx \frac{114.2}{13.15} \approx 8.69$$

Determine the critical value or p-value – the stated significance level α was 0.05. So, you would compare the calculated F-statistic value from an F-distribution table or use statistical software, such as Minitab, to find the p-value. If the p-value is less than 0.05, you would reject the null hypothesis, indicating that there is a significant difference in the mean score R&R datasets.

USING CONFIDENCE INTERVALS TO EVALUATE OBSERVED DIFFERENCES

Confidence intervals (CIs) are a statistical tool used to estimate a range within which the true value of a population parameter is likely to fall. CIs are commonly used to estimate the range in which a population parameter, such as mean or a difference between means, is likely to fall. Also, when comparing observed differences between groups or conditions, CIs can provide valuable information about the precision and uncertainty associated with those differences.

Here are some ways CIs are used to evaluate observed differences:

- *Understanding confidence intervals* – a confidence interval is typically expressed as a range around a point estimate, such as a mean or difference between means. For a 95% confidence interval, the mean difference between two groups might be from 2 to 8. This means that there is a 95% chance that the true mean difference lies within this interval.
- *Overlap or exclusion of zero* – if the confidence interval for a difference between two groups includes zero, it suggests that the observed difference is not statistically significant at the chosen confidence level. Zero within the interval indicates that the null hypothesis (no difference) is a plausible value for the true difference.
- *Width of the confidence interval* – the width of the confidence interval provides information about the precision of the estimate. A narrower interval indicates greater precision, while a wider interval suggests more uncertainty. Precision is influenced by factors such as sample size and variability within the data.

- *Comparing multiple intervals* – when comparing multiple groups or conditions, look at the overlap of confidence intervals. If the intervals for two groups do not overlap, it suggests a potential significant difference between them. However, be cautious, as statistical significance also depends on the chosen confidence level (e.g., 99%, 95% or 90%) and the correction for multiple comparisons.
- *Practical significance* – consider not only statistical significance but also practical significance. A difference may be statistically significant if it is too small to be meaningful in the real-world context.
- *Effect size* – alongside confidence intervals, consider calculating and reporting effect sizes. Effect sizes measure the magnitude of the observed difference, helping interpret the practical significance of the findings.
- *Interpretation* – if a confidence excludes zero, you can conclude that the observed difference is statistically significant at a chosen confidence level. If it includes zero, you cannot confidently reject the null hypothesis, and the observed differences may not be statistically significant.

Confidence intervals are a powerful tool for assessing the precision and significance of observed differences. They provide a more informative and nuanced perspective than p-values alone and can aid in the interpretation of research findings.

The following is an example of how CIs are used to estimate the range in which a population parameter falls:

Suppose you are conducting a study to compare the average tolerance hold precision of two machines, machine A and machine B. Both are identical in build architecture, and both are being used on a project that requires exact tolerance held by contract specification. You have collected random sample data from each machine, and you want to estimate the difference in their average tolerance hold along with a confidence interval.

Sample information:

Machine A: sample size $n_a = 50$	Sample mean $\bar{X}_A = 75$	Sample standard deviation $s_a = 10$
Machine B: sample size $n_b = 60$	Sample mean $\bar{X}_B = 78$	Sample standard deviation $s_a = 12$

Calculate the difference in means:

The difference in means $(\bar{X}_A - \bar{X}_B)$ is $75 - 78 = -3$

Calculate the standard error of the difference:

The standard error (*SE*) of the difference is given by the formula:

$$\sqrt{\frac{s_a^2}{n_a} + \frac{s_b^2}{n_b}}$$

$$SE = \frac{10^2}{50} + \frac{12^2}{60}$$

Choose a confidence level:

We have chosen a 95% confidence level.

Calculate the margin of error:

The margin of error (ME) is given by multiplying the standard error by the critical value from the t-distribution corresponding to the chosen confidence level and degrees of freedom with the formula:

$$ME = t_{\frac{a}{2}} \, x \, SE$$

Note that the t-distribution can be derived from the t-distribution table or from statistical software such as Minitab.

Calculate the confidence interval:

The confidence interval will be derived by using the following formula:

$$(\bar{X}_A - \bar{X}_B) \mp ME$$

Calculating these statistics, we can construct a confidence interval, starting with:

$t_{\frac{a}{2}}$ (for a 95% confidence interval with $n_a + n_b - 2$ degrees of freedom). Once the ME is derived, we can construct the confidence interval by using the following formula:

$$CI = (\bar{X}_A - \bar{X}_B) \mp ME$$

This interval will provide a range within which you can be reasonably confident that true tolerance holds different levels. If the interval includes zero, it suggests that there is not enough evidence to conclude there is a significant difference. If the interval does not include zero, it suggests a significant difference at the chosen confidence level.

COMPARING ONE VARIANCE TO A STANDARD USING THE F-TEST

Often the F-test is used to compare the variance of a sample to a known standard variance or to compare the variances of two independent samples. To compare one variance to a standard, you would conduct a one-sample F-test.

The following is a step-by-step method for how you can perform a one-sample F-test to compare a sample variance (S^2) to a known standard variance (σ^2):

Step 1. Formulate the hypotheses:

Null hypothesis (H_0): the sample variance is equal to the known standard variance.

$$H_0: S^2 = \sigma^2$$

Alternative hypothesis (H_a): the sample variance is not equal to the known standard variance.

$$H_a: S^2 = \sigma^2$$

Step 2. Collect the data – collect a sample of data for which you want to compare the variance to a known standard.

Step 3. Calculate the test statistic – the formula for the F-test for a one-sample variance is:

$$F = \frac{S^2}{\sigma^2}$$

Step 4. Determine the critical region – based on your chosen significance level (0.01, 0.05, or 0.10) and degrees of freedom for the numerator (df_1) and denominator (df_2), then find the critical value from the F-distribution table or use statistical software.

Step 5. Draw a conclusion – if the calculated F-statistic falls into the critical region, reject the null hypothesis. If it does not, fail to reject the null hypothesis.

Step 6. Interpret the results – if you reject the null hypothesis, it suggests that there is a significant difference between the sample variance and the known standard variance.

It is important to note the F-test assumes that the data is normally distributed. If the sample size is small or if the data does not follow a normal distribution, the assumption of normality becomes more critical. Additionally, the F-test is sensitive to departures from normality and can be influenced by outliers. If the deviation is significant, or if you have concerns about outliers, you should consider using a non-parametric test or transformation of the data.

If you have two independent samples and want to compare their variances, you can use a two sample F-test. The null hypothesis in this case would be that the variances are equal, and the alternative hypothesis would be that the variances are not equal. The test statistic in this case would be the ratio of the variances.

Let us now walk through an example of the F-test that can be used to test whether the variance of a sample is different from a hypothesized population variance.

You are conducting an experiment to test whether the variance of a certain test is significantly different from the assumed population variance of 25.

Your hypotheses are:

Null hypothesis (H_0): the population variance (σ^2) is equal to 25.
Alternative hypothesis (H_a): the population variance is different from 25.

H_0: $\sigma^2 = 25$
H_a: $\sigma^2 = 25$

Sample information – you have collected 30 artifact random samples. The sample variance is (s^2) is 30.

The chosen significance level is 0.05.

Now we perform the F-test using the formula:

$$F = \frac{s^2}{\sigma^2}$$

Substituting the values into the formula:

$$F = \frac{30}{25} = 1.2$$

Once you have calculated the critical value, it can be compared to the critical value from the F-distribution table or though statistical software such as Minitab to find the p-value. If the p-value is significant (falls in the rejection region), you would reject the null hypothesis and conclude that the population variance is significantly different from the assumed value of 25. If it is not significant, you would fail to reject the null hypothesis.

When performing this type of test (F-test), remember the interpretation is highly dependent on the context of the experiment or study and research question(s) you are addressing.

HYPOTHESIS TESTING WITH NON-NORMAL DATA

Hypothesis testing is often more robust when assumptions are met, and for many classical parametric tests, normality is one of the key assumptions. However, there are situations where the assumption of normality is not strictly met, and yet hypothesis tests can still provide meaningful results, especially with larger sample sizes. The following are some strategies and some alternative tests that can be employed when dealing with non-normal data.

- *Increase the Sample Size; Count on the Central Limit Theorem* – for large samples, the central limit theorem states that the sampling distribution of the sample mean will be approximately normally distributed, regardless of the shape of the original population distribution. This would allow the use of parametric tests even if the underlying data is not normal.
- *Transform the Data* – applying mathematical transformations to the data can make it more normal. Some common transformation types include the natural logarithm, square root, or reciprocal. It is, however, worth mentioning that the interpretation becomes more complex after using a transformation process.
- *Bootstrapping* – bootstrapping is a resampling method that can provide estimates of the sampling distribution of a statistic. It is particularly useful when the assumptions of classical statistical methods are violated.
- *Permutation Tests* – permutation tests involve randomly reallocating the observed data to create a null distribution of a test statistic. These tests are distribution free and can be used when assumptions about the shape of the distribution are uncertain.
- *Robust Statistics* – certain statistical models are designed to be robust against violations of normality assumptions. Robust regression, for example, can handle outliers and non-normality better than standard regression techniques.
- *Non-Parametric Tests* – non-parametric tests are distribution free and less sensitive to the assumption of normality and generally the method of choice when dealing with non-normal data. Table 11.1 provides some of the more common non-parametric tests grouped by their parametric counterparts and general characteristics.
- Let us work through some examples of several non-parametric tests, starting with the *one-sample sign test.*

You have a set of median test scores, and you want to test whether these medians are equal to the hypothesized median.

Randomly selected data:

80,78,72,76,79,81,75,77,74

Hypotheses are:

H_0: median = 75
H_a: median = 75

Table 11.1 Parametric and Non-Parametric Test Comparison

Parametric Tests	*Non-Parametric Tests*	*Characteristics of Non-Parametric Tests*
1-sample t or Z test	1-sample sign test	Test on the median for data from a non-symmetric distribution.
	1-sample Wilcoxon test	Test on the median for data from a no-symmetric distribution.
2-sample t-test	Mann-Whitney U test	Test on two medians using ranks of the sample data.
One-way ANOVA	Kruskal-Wallis test	Test on the equality of medians from two or more populations. More powerful than Mood's median test but less robust to outliers.
	Mood's median test	Test on the equality of medians from two or more populations. More robust to outliers than the Kruskal-Wallis test but less powerful.
Two-way randomized block ANOVA	Friedman test	Test on medians using randomized block experiments.

Sign test steps:

You have chosen a significance level σ of 0.05.
Hypothesized median: 75

Calculated differences are:

5,3,10,–3,1,4,6,0,2,–1

Count sign:

Positive differences: 7
Negative differences: 2

Test statistic:

Use the smaller count: min (7,2) = 2

Critical value or p-value:
Using a sign test table or statistical software such as Minitab, you can find the critical value or p-value.

Decide:

If the test statistic is greater than the critical value or p-value is less than 0.05, reject the null hypothesis. This would lead to the conclusion that the median of the population is not equal to 75 based on the data given.

Next, let us work through an example of the *Mann–Whitney U test* using two independent groups, Group A and Group B.

Randomly gathered data from two independent groups, A and B, has been obtained.

Group A: 25,30,35,40,45
Group B: 15,20,25,30,35

The hypotheses:

H_0: there is no difference in distributions between group A and group B.
H_a: there is a difference in distributions between group A and group B.

The chosen significance level $\sigma = 0.05$.

Steps:

Combine data and rank:

Combined data: 15,20,25,30,35,25,30,35,40,45
Rank the combined data: 2,4,6,8,9.5,3,6,8,10,11 (averaging ranks for tied values)

Calculate U statistic:

$$U_1 = n_1 x n_2 + \frac{n_{1x}(n_{1=1})}{2} - R_1$$

$$U_1 = n_1 x n_2 + \frac{n_{2x}(n_{2=1})}{2} - R_2$$

$$\text{For group A: } U_1 = 5x5 + \frac{5x(5+1)}{2} - 40 = 10$$

$$\text{For group A: } U_2 = 5x5 + \frac{5x(5+1)}{2} - 19.5 = 20.5$$

Calculate the critical U value:

Use the Mann-Whitney U distribution table or statistical software such as Minitab.

With $n_1 = 5$ *and* $n_2 = 5$ *at* $\alpha = 0.05$, *the critical U value is* 5

Compare the U statistics with the critical value:

$$U_{calculated} = \min(U_1, U_2) = 10$$

$$U_{critical} = 5$$

Draw conclusions:

Since $U_{calculated} > U_{critical,}$ you cannot reject the null hypothesis.

There is not enough evidence to suggest a significant difference in distribution between Group A and Group B based on the Mann-Whitney U test at $\alpha = 0.05$.

- Let us now go through an example of *Mood's median test* using two independent groups, Method A and Method B.

Randomly gathered data from two independent methods, Method A and Method B, has been obtained:

Method A: 78,80,82,75,77,79,81,76,79,83
Method B: 85,88,80,82,79,81,84,87,82,80,83

Hypotheses stated:

H_0: the medians of scores for Method A and Method B are equal.
H_a: at least one method has a different median score.

Significance level:

$\alpha = 0.05$

Combine data and rank:

Data combined: 75,76,77,78,79,79,80,80,81,82,82,83,83,84,85,87,88
Ranked combined data: 1,2,3,4,5,5,7,7,9,10,10,12,12,14,15,16,17

Calculate the test statistic (X^2):
Calculate the chi-square statistic using the following formula:

$$X^2 = \frac{12}{N(N+1)} \sum_{i-1}^{k} \frac{R_i^2}{n_i} - 3(N+1)$$

where:
N is the total number of observations.
k is the number of groups.
R_i is the sum of ranks for group i
n_i is the number of observations in group i.

$$X^2 = \frac{12}{17(18)} \frac{5^2}{10} + \frac{140^2}{11} - 3(18)$$

Determine the degrees of freedom:

$df = k - 1 = 2 - 1 = 1$

Now find the critical value or p-value:

For this, use a chi-square distribution table or statistical software such as Minitab.
Draw a conclusion:
Compare the calculated test statistic with the critical value or p-value. If X^2 > the critical value or the p-value < α, reject the hypothesis.

$$X^2 = \frac{12}{306}\frac{25}{10} + \frac{19600}{11} - 54$$

Critical value:

$$df = 1 \textit{ and } \alpha = 0.05, \textit{ the critical value is approximately } 3.841$$

Conclusion:

After comparing the calculated test statistic with the critical value, if $X^2 > 3.841$ *or the p – value is* <0.05, reject the null hypothesis; if not, you would fail to reject the null hypothesis.

- Now let us examine the *Friedman test* using three related methods: Method A, Method B, and Method C.

Random data has been collected from each method:

Method A: 78,80,82,75,77,79,81,76,79,83
Method B: 85,88,80,82,79,81,84,87,82,80,83
Method C: 70,75,72,68,74,71,73,70,72,75,71

Hypotheses stated:

H_0: there is no difference in the effects of Methods A, B, and C.
H_a: there is a difference in the effects of at least one method.

Significance level set:

$$\alpha = 0.05$$

Combine and rank the data:

70,71,72,73,74,75,76,77,78,79,79,80,80,81,82,82,83,83,84,85,87

Calculate the Friedman test statistic using the following formula:

$$F = \frac{12}{k\left(n\left(n+1\right)\right)} \sum_{i-1}^{k} R_i^2 - 3n\left(n+1\right)$$

where:

k is the number of treatments.
n is the number of articles.
R_i is the sum of ranks for treatment i.

$$F = \frac{12}{3(21(22))} \frac{39^1}{10} + \frac{146^2}{11} + \frac{65^2}{10} - 3(21(22))$$

Determine the degrees of freedom:

$$df = k - 1 = 3 = 1 = 2$$

Determine the critical value or p-value:
Use a chi-square distribution table or statistical software such as Minitab.
Compare the calculated test statistic with the critical value or p-value.
if $F >$ the critical value or $p -$ value is $< \alpha$, reject the null hypothesis.
Calculation:

$$F = \frac{12}{3(21(22))} \frac{1521}{10} + \frac{21316}{11} + \frac{4225}{10} - 3(21(22))$$

Critical value: for $df = 2$ and $\alpha = 0.05$, the critical value is approximately 5.991

Draw conclusion:
After comparing the calculated test statistic with the critical value, if F =5.991 or the *p*– value is < 0.05, reject the null hypothesis. If not, you would fail to reject the null hypothesis.

DATA TRANSFORMATION

Hypothesis testing with non-normal data would not be complete without a discussion of data transformation.

Data transformation is a common technique used to make data more suitable for statistical analysis or to meet the statistical assumptions of certain statistical methods. In any DMAIC-driven Lean Six Sigma initiative, it plays a crucial role when dealing with non-normal distributed data. Data transformation can help improve the distributional properties, stabilize variance, and make relationships between variables more linear.

Here are some ways in which data transformation is used in Lean and Six Sigma initiatives.

- *Data cleaning and preprocessing* – before conducting any analysis, it is essential to clean and preprocess the data to ensure accuracy. Data transformation is often used to handle missing values, outliers, and inconsistencies in the data. It is also used to normalize and standardize data by transforming it into a common scale (normalization) or adjusting it to have a mean of zero and a standard deviation of one (standardization).
- *Variable transformation and reduction* – when using statistical analysis in Lean Six Sigma while transforming variables, often methods such as log transformation (good for skewed datasets) may be applied to achieve a normal distribution. It can also be applied to data reduction. Transformation methods such as principal component analysis (PCA) or factor analysis may be used to reduce the dimensionality of data while retaining essential information.
- *Root cause analysis and simulation* – data transformation is employed to analyze root causes of defects or issues within a process. By transforming and aggregating data,

patterns and trends that contribute to problems are more easily identified. It is also employed to model different scenarios and predict the impact of process changes. In doing this, it has proven essential to ensure the simulated data represents the real-world process, not theoretical.

Table 11.2 contains some of the more commonly used transformation methods that have proven effective in Lean Six Sigma initiatives:

The following is an example of how data transformation is used in a Lean Six Sigma (LSS) actual project:

Consider a scenario where you are using LSS to reduce the defect rate in a structural manufacturing process. You have collected data on the time it takes to complete different manufacturing tasks, and you want to identify areas for improvement. You generate different visualizations aids, such as histograms and mean $\bar{X}$ and range R charts with the original data and note that the variation and distribution are not normally distributed. You meet with your team and recommend that data transformation be applied before proceeding further with the project.

In this situation you elect to use a Z-score transformation or standardization data transformation technique. This type of transformation scales the data to have a mean of 0 and a standard deviation of 1. The original dataset(s) are uploaded into a Python application called "standardscaler" and placed in a "sklearn.preprocessing" module. When executed, this will transform the data to have a mean of 0 and a standard deviation of 1. This is achieved by subtracting the mean form each data point and then dividing by the standard deviation, a "Z-transformation." A script of the data as it is represented in Python is presented in Figure 11.2.

Table 11.2 Commonly Used Data Transformation Methods

Transformation	*Formula*	*Application*
Log transformation	$y = (\acute{y})\, or\ \acute{y} = log(y + c)$	Particularly useful for right-skewed data.
Square root transformation	$\acute{y} = \sqrt{y}$ or $\acute{y}\,\sqrt{y+c}$	Effective for reducing the influence of extreme values.
Box-Cox transformation	$\acute{y} = \frac{y^{\lambda} - 1}{\lambda}$ for $y > 0\, and\, \lambda = 0$, or $= \log(y)$ when $\lambda = 0$	Generalizes the power transformation by allowing a range of transformations, including the logarithm.
Reciprocal transformation	$\acute{y} = \frac{1}{y}$ or $\acute{y} = \frac{1}{y+c}$	Useful for data that follows a reciprocal relationship.
Square transformation	$\acute{y} = y^2$ or $\acute{y} = (y+c)^2$	Can be used to emphasize differences between small values.
Exponential transformation	$\acute{y} = e^{y}$ or $\acute{y} = e^{(y+c)}$	Useful for data with exponential growth or decay.
Z-score transformation	$Z = \frac{x - \mu}{\sigma}$	Particularly useful in situations where the scale of the variables may affect the outcome of the analyses.

Python Script for Z-Transformation

```python
import numpy as np
import matplotlib.pyplot as plt
from sklearn.preprocessing import StandardScaler

# Generate synthetic data (representing time taken for tasks)
np.random.seed(42)
task_completion_times = np.random.normal(loc=15, scale=5, size=100)

# Original data analysis
plt.figure(figsize=(12, 6))

plt.subplot(1, 2, 1)
plt.hist(task_completion_times, bins=20, color='blue', alpha=0.7)
plt.title('Original Data - Task Completion Times')

# Apply Standardization (z-score transformation)
scaler = StandardScaler()
standardized_times = scaler.fit_transform(task_completion_times.reshape(-1, 1)).flatt

# Transformed data analysis
plt.subplot(1, 2, 2)
plt.hist(standardized_times, bins=20, color='green', alpha=0.7)
plt.title('Transformed Data - Standardized Task Completion Times')

plt.show()
```

Figure 11.2 Python Script for Z-Transformation

After transformation, the data was visualized again via histogram and submitted to both mean $\bar{X}$ and R charting. The histogram was much more symmetrical (bell shaped), and both $\bar{X}$ and R were stable. The now-standardized data has a mean of 0 and a standard deviation of 1.

DESIGN OF EXPERIMENTS: PURPOSE AND PRINCIPLES

The primary purpose of DoEis to systematically investigate and optimize process, products, and systems. DoE provides a structured approach for experimentation to efficiently explore the effects of multiple factors, interactions between factors, and identify the optimal conditions. It is widely used in various fields, including manufacturing, engineering, chemistry, biology, and social sciences, and is a powerful tool that is used in any DMAIC-driven Lean Six Sigma initiative.

Design of experiments is a method of experimenting with the complex interactions among parameters in a process or product with the objective of optimizing that process or product. To design an experiment means creating a situation in which an organized investigation into all the different factors that can affect process or product parameters occurs. The design gives a layout of the different factors and their values.

A complete study of designing experiments is beyond the scope of this text. Coverage in this text is designed to provide the reader with an introduction to the different components that constitute a DoE structure and to the most common types used in executing Lean Six Sigma initiatives. A case study is additionally included that will take the reader through a step-by-step methodology of designing an experiment and interpreting the results of that experiment.

Design of experiments are comprised of eight key components:

1. *Factors* – these are the independent variables that are intentionally varied during the experiment.
2. *Levels* – these are the specific values or settings of the factors chosen for experimentation.
3. *Response variables* – the dependent variables measured or observed to evaluate the effects of the factors.
4. *Experimental design* – the plan that outlines how the factors will be varied and the conditions under which observations will be made.
5. *Randomization* – the process of randomly assigning experimental units to different treatments to control unobserved variables.
6. *Replication* – repeating the experiment with the same factor settings to estimate experimental errors and enhance the reliability of results.
7. *Blocking* – grouping experimental units that are similar in some way to reduce variability and improve precision.
8. *Interaction effects* – effects that occur when the combined influence of two or more factors is different from what would be expected based on their individual effects.

In Lean Six Sigma, DoE is a powerful statistical tool used to systemically vary input factors and observe their effects on output to optimize processes and improve performance. Figure 11.3 illustrates the most common types of designs of experiments used in Lean Six Sigma initiatives.

- *Full Factorial Design* – in a full factorial design, all combinations of levels for each factor are tested.

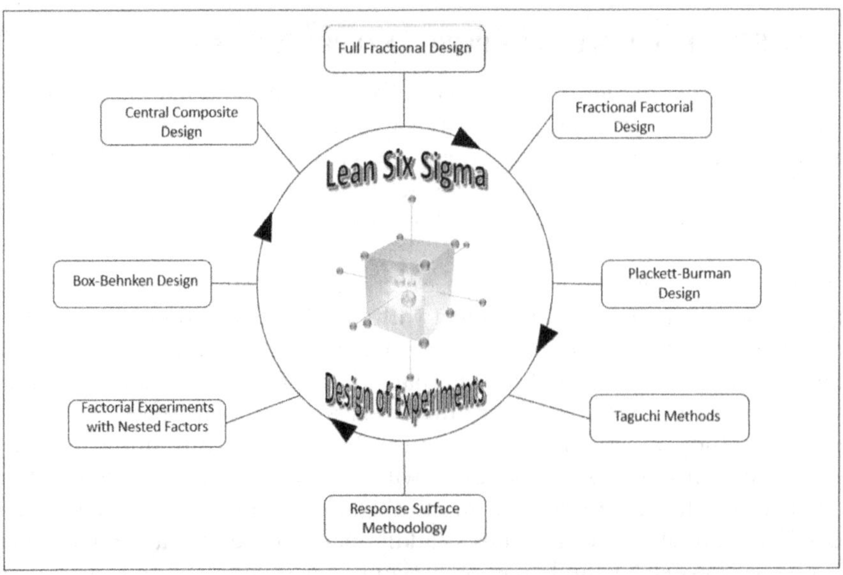

Figure 11.3 Common Types of DoE used in Lean Six Sigma

- *Fractional Factorial Design* – these types of designs are used when the number of factors is large and it is not feasible to test all combinations. Only a fraction of the full set of combinations are tested and the effects of the untested combinations are estimated.
- *Placket-Burman Design* – this is a type of fractional design specially used for screening purposes.
- *Taguchi Methods* – developed by statistician Genichi Taguchi, these methods aim to find the optimal settings for factors that minimize the variation in the output. Taguchi designs are robust to variations and are often used when the focus is on improving the reliability and performance of a process.
- *Response Surface Methodology (RSM)* – RSM involves mathematical models to represent the relationship between input factors and the output. This type of model helps in finding the optimal settings for factors to achieve a desired level of performance.
- *Central Composite Design (CCD)* – CCD is a type of response surface design that combines full factorial and fractional factional designs with axial points to model quadratic effects.
- *Box-Behnken Design* – this is another type of response surface design that uses a central composite design with fewer experimental points. It is useful for exploring the response surface with less experimentation.
- *Factorial Experiments with Nested Factors* – in some cases, factors may be nested within others, and factorial experiments with nested factors are designed to study such situations.

Choosing the appropriate design depends on factors such as the number of factors to be assessed, the resources available, and the experiment's objective. Each design has its strengths and limitations, and the selection should be based on the specific requirements of the Lean Six Sigma initiative being executed.

To illustrate how DoE is applied in a real-world scenario, a case study is provided that exhibits how DoE was used to optimize an ordering process in an aircraft manufacturing organization.

OPTIMIZING ORDER, PICK, PACK, AND SHIP USING DESIGN OF EXPERIMENTS

Order picking, packing, and shipping from a warehouse or distribution center is a complex task. Orders are submitted by customers that consist of multiple product types in various quantities. The products on these orders must be picked from the storage locations, packaged for safe shipment, and labeled with the appropriate destination. This would be simple if the organization carried only a few items in inventory to be shipped to a few customers. The complexity increases exponentially as the number of items and customers increases.

Doing the job right at every step is critical not only because the customer wants to receive the correct item but also because shipping costs are based on the cube of space the package uses up, whether in a truck or the cargo hold of an aircraft.

At JL Shipping (Figure 11.4), an automated distribution center, pickers, packers, and shippers handle orders that may contain as many as 50 unique products, numbering up to 5,000 of each unique product. JL shipping uses "wave" processing, also known as batch picking. This method consolidates orders from several customers into an optimal inventory picking cycle.

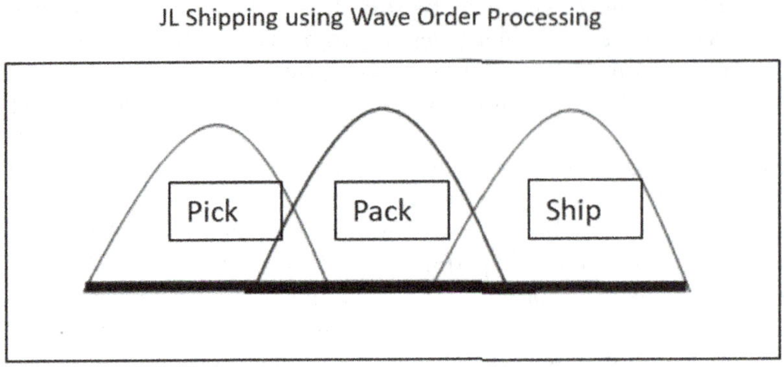

Figure 11.4 JL Shipping Using Wave Order Processing

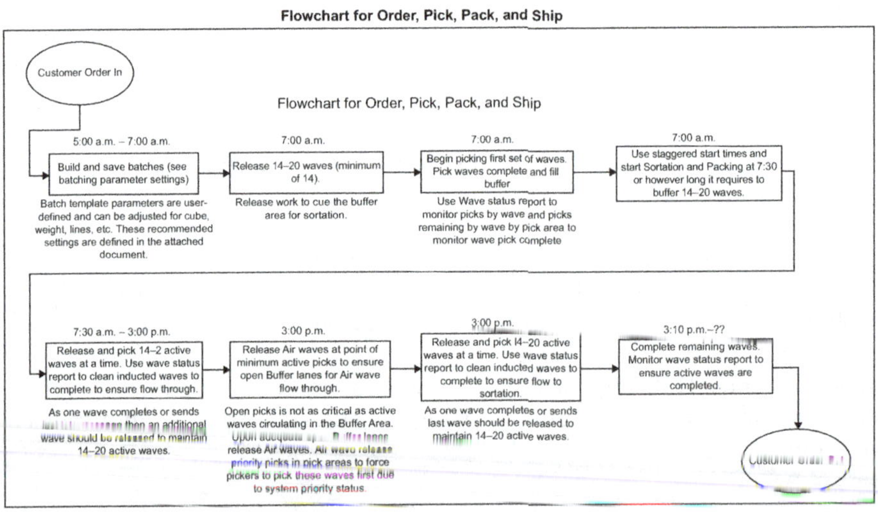

Figure 11.5 Flowchart for Order, Pick, Pack, and Ship

Optimal picking cycles consolidate what has been ordered, the amount ordered, and where items are stored in the warehouse. As shown in Figure 11.5, once the pick is complete, the wave continues to the packing department, where the orders are automatically sorted using barcodes by the individual customer order and packed. Once packed, the orders proceed to a shipping station to be labeled and staged for shipment via truck or plane. Buffer staging lanes exist between each area. Downtime in a particular area results if orders are not in the system or are held at an upstream area.

Wave processing is different from "discrete" processing. Discrete processing involves picking one order at a time, packing it, and then readying it for shipment. To manage the wave, order characteristics that optimize flow include how many times the picker visits a particular location in the warehouse, how many items are picked each time, and how much space is taken up by the items picked.

The key departments involved are Pick, Pack, and Ship. Members of the workforce in these departments receive what they need when they need it. To minimize costs, maximize flexibility, and enhance customer success, the express logistics center manager has asked the industrial Lean Six Sigma team to optimize order picking, packing, and shipping. In other words, they want to level the peaks and valleys in Table 11.3 through an LSS methodology. The LSS team proceeded using the standard DMAIC process until reaching the Analyze phase, where they then elected, because of the many intervening variables, to use a DoE methodology. The team proposed the following experimental design:

Factors:

Quantity	Total number of pieces picked within a given wave.
Lines	The different items (products) on the order needing to be picked
Cube	The space needed for the quantity of lines for a particular order (largest outbound parcel box cube or tote (box without a top).
Weight	The weight of the quantity of lines for a particular order.

Levels:

Max Quantity	Max Lines	Max Cube	Max Weight
5000 (+)	50 (+)	Parcel (+)	150 (+)
100 (-)	10 (-)	Tote (-)	25 (-)

Controllable Factors:
When a factor is controllable, it is possible to establish and maintain the particular level throughout the experiment. In this experiment, the team was able to set the levels for quantity, lines, cube and weight.

Response Variable:
These variables are used to describe the reaction of a process to variations in the chosen factors. The response variable for this experiment is *Order Per Hour.*

Effect:
the effect is the result or outcome of the experiment. The team is interested in determining the optimal wave parameters. A wave is a batch of customer orders consolidated to optimize warehouse picking activities. Instead of picking one order at a time, many orders are picked.

Treatment:
The number of treatments is based on the number of factors and the levels associated with each factor. Based on the number of waves processed per day and the ease of wave building, a full factorial design chosen. See Table 1.

Degrees of Freedom:
The degree of freedom is the total number of levels for all factors minus 1. Here there are two levels for each factor (4 x 2 = 8) so the degrees of freedom equals (8 – 7 = 7).

Interaction:
Because the four factors will work together to produce a result different from what would result if each were single, interactions exist between the four that must be considered in the experiment.

Noise Factor:
A noise factor is an uncontrollable source of variation. For this experiment the noise factors are buffer downtime, pick downtime, and shipping downtime.

Run:
A run is an experimental trial, the application of one treatment to one experiment unit. A quantity of 100, with 10 lines, using a tote, and weighing 25 pounds is one run.

Replicate:
When an experiment is replicated, it refers to a repeat of the treatment condition, a complete rerunning of the design.

Repetition:
Repetitions are multiple results of a treatment condition.

Significance:
The determination of whether the changes to the factor levels had a significant effect on the response variable. Did changing the quantity, lines, cube, or weight affect the result?
To conduct the experiment, the team set up controlled runs based on each of the 16 runs denoted in Table 1, These runs, from actual customer orders, took place on a Saturday, outside of the normal workweek.

Figure 11.6

Table 11.3 Experiment Design for Optimizing Order Pick, Pack, and Ship

Test Wave	*Max Quantity*	*Max Lines*	*Max Cube*	*Max Weight*
1	500	50	Parcel	150
2	100	50	Parcel	150
3	5000	10	Parcel	150
4	100	10	Parcel	150
5	5000	50	Total	150
6	100	50	Total	150
7	5000	10	Total	150
8	100	10	Total	150
9	5000	50	Parcel	25
10	100	50	Parcel	25
11	5000	10	Parcel	25
12	100	10	Parcel	25
13	5000	50	Total	25
14	100	50	Total	25
15	5000	10	Total	25
16	100	10	Total	25

Table 11.4 Experiment Design for Optimizing Order Pick, Pack, and Ship

Test Wave	*Max Quantity*	*Max Lines*	*Max Cube*	*Max Weight*	*Order/Hour*
1	500	50	Parcel	150	8.2
2	100	50	Parcel	150	8.1
3	5000	10	Parcel	150	6.1
4	100	10	Parcel	150	6.3
5	5000	50	Total	150	7.9
6	100	50	Total	150	8.2
7	5000	10	Total	150	4.5
8	100	10	Total	150	5.1
9	5000	50	Parcel	25	8.3
10	100	50	Parcel	25	8
11	5000	10	Parcel	25	5.9
12	100	10	Parcel	25	6.2
13	5000	50	Total	25	7.8
14	100	50	Total	25	8.1
15	5000	10	Total	25	5.1
16	100	10	Total	25	4.9

Following the experiment, the team analyzed the results, Table 11.4, to identify the optimum wave settings to maximize flow through, pick, pack and ship.

They begin their analysis with the simplest of methods: analysis of goods (ANOG). This simple but effective technique ranks the results of the experiment by the most desirable outcome: high orders per hour; see Table 11.5. Run 9, with a quantity of 5,000 and 50 lines, allows 8.3 orders to be picked per hour.

Further statistical analysis using ANOVA and ANOM revealed that the factor having the most significant impact on the number of orders per hour was lines per waves, the number of products with a unique part number and their quantity.

By comparison, the weight and cube size were insignificant. The experiment determined that the combination of unique part numbers that maximizes quantities results in the optimal picking sequence. Now, JL shipping batches its orders based on the combination of unique part numbers that provides the greatest quantity: as an example, 25 unique part numbers whose order quantity totals 4,925 or 3 unique part numbers whose order quantity totals 4,976 or 1 unique part number whose order quantity totals 5,000. The goal is to have a high number of items in the pick.

ANALYZE STAGE TOLLGATE REVIEW

In the context of the Lean Six Sigma methodology, the Analyze stage is the most critical phase within the DMAIC framework. The overarching goal of the Analyze stage is to identify the root causes of the problem defined in the earlier stages and to gain a deeper understanding of the process.

Table 11.5 Analysis of Goods for Optimizing Order, Pick, Pack, Ship

ANOG Test Wave	*Max Quantity*	*Max Lines*	*Max Cube*	*Max Weight*	*Order/Hour*
9	5000	50	Parcel	25	8.3
1	5000	50	Parcel	150	8.2
6	100	50	Total	150	8.2
2	100	50	Parcel	150	8.1
14	100	50	Total	25	8.1
10	100	50	Parcel	25	8
5	5000	50	Total	150	7.9
13	5000	50	Total	25	7.8
4	100	10	Parcel	150	6.3
12	100	10	Parcel	25	6.2
3	5000	10	Parcel	150	6.1
11	5000	10	Parcel	25	5.9
8	100	10	Total	150	5.1
15	5000	10	Total	25	5.1
16	100	10	Total	25	4.9
7	5000	10	Total	150	4.5

During the Analyze stage, as described in this chapter's context, various tools and techniques are used to analyze data and investigate potential causes of identified issues. Tollgate checkpoints or milestones in the Lean Six Sigma process are where project leaders and team members assess the progress and determine whether to proceed to the next phase. Common tollgate requirements for the Analyze stage in the DMAIC methodology are:

- *Data validation* – ensure that the data collected in the Measurement stage is accurate and reliable. The measurement system must be validated for accuracy and precision.
- *Root cause analysis* – demonstrate a thorough understanding of potential root causes.
- *Data analysis tools* – apply statistical tools and techniques to analyze the data effectively. This may include hypothesis testing, regression analysis, and statistical process control charting.
- *Visual representation* – present data visually to facilitate better understanding. This could involve creating charts, graphs, or other visual aids to highlight key findings.
- *Identify critical X factors* – determine the critical process variable Xs that have a significant impact on the problem. Prioritize factors based on their influence on the outcome.
- *Risk assessment* – identify potential risks associated with the selected solutions. Evaluate the impact and likelihood of each risk and develop mitigation strategies.
- *Verification of findings* – validate the findings with subject matter experts (SMEs) or other relevant stakeholders. Ensure that the analysis aligns with the problem definition and project goals.

- *Documentation* – document all findings, analyses, and conclusions. Clearly articulate the rationale behind the selected factors and potential root causes.
- *Interim results presentation* – present interim results to the project team and stakeholders. Seek feedback and input to refine the analysis further.
- *Confirmation of project goals* – confirm that the analysis aligns with the project goals and objectives. Ensure that the selected factors and root causes are consistent with the specific projects.

The requirements for the Analyze stage tollgate may vary depending on the project, organizational standards, and problem being addressed. It is essential to tailor the tollgate requirements to fit the unique characteristics of each Lean Six Sigma project.

SUMMARY

Chapter 11 began by illustrating to the reader how comparing one proportion to a standard is conducted using various types of tests. It then addressed the process of comparing one means to a standard using a T-type testing process and comparing multiple means using an ANOVA or F-test. It then showed by example how confidence intervals are evaluated using the F-test. Hypothesis testing with normal data was illustrated using a one- and two-sample T-test. This was followed by an examination of hypothesis testing with non-normal data using an array of means like the Mann-Whitney and Friedman tests. The subject of DoE was then covered, emphasizing its components and types of designs performed. This subject was concluded with a discussion of how selecting the right experimental design is critical in achieving a successful model. This discussion was followed by a detailed DoE case study of aircraft manufacturing organizations' ordering process to emphasize the practical application of DoE. The chapter concluded with an Analyze tollgate review.

CHAPTER 11 DISCUSSION QUESTIONS

1 Define and briefly describe the following:
   a Comparing one proportion to a standard
   b Comparing two proportions using the Z-test
   c Comparing multiple proportions using the chi-square test
2 Define and briefly describe the following:
   a Comparing one mean to a standard – using the T-test
   b Comparing two means – using the T-test
   c Comparing multiple proportions – using the ANOVA and the F-test
3 Define and briefly describe using confidence intervals to evaluate observed differences.
4 Briefly discuss the strategies and alternative tests by which non-normal data can be evaluated.
5 Briefly explain why an understanding of data transformation is essential for Lean Six Sigma practitioners.
6 Define and briefly discuss DoE.

BIBLIOGRAPHY

Antony, Jiju, et al. "An evaluation of lean and six sigma methodologies in the national health service." *International Journal of Quality & Reliability Management* 40.1 (2023): 25–52.

Arcidiacono, Gabriele, Nico Costantino, and Kai Yang. "The AMSE lean six sigma governance model." *International Journal of Lean Six Sigma* 7.3 (2016): 233–266.

Barad, Miryam. "Design of experiments (DOE) – A valuable multi-purpose methodology." *Applied Mathematics* 2014 (2014).

Barrentine, Larry B. *An Introduction to Design of Experiments*. Quality Press, 2001.

Beasley, T. Mark, and Randall E. Schumacker. "Multiple regression approach to analyzing contingency tables: Post hoc and planned comparison procedures." *The Journal of Experimental Education* 64.1 (1995): 79–93.

Bilgen, Bilge, and Mutlu Şen. "Project selection through fuzzy analytic hierarchy process and a case study on six sigma implementation in an automotive industry." *Production Planning & Control* 23.1 (2012): 2–25.

Blanca Mena, M. José, et al. "Non-normal data: Is ANOVA still a valid option?" *Psicothema* 29.4 (2017): 552–557.

Brahman, Leonard E. "Confidence intervals assess both clinical significance and statistical significance." *Annals of Internal Medicine* 114.6 (1991): 515–517.

Chan, Ivan S. F., and Zhongxin Zhang. "Test-based exact confidence intervals for the difference of two binomial proportions." *Biometrics* 55.4 (1999): 1202–1209.

Chang, Ching-Hui, et al. "Comparing several population means: A parametric bootstrap method, and its comparison with usual ANOVA F test as well as ANOM." *Computational Statistics* 25 (2010): 71–95.

Chou, Chih-Ping, Peter M. Bentler, and Albert Satorra. "Scaled test statistics and robust standard errors for non-normal data in covariance structure analysis: A Monte Carlo study." *British Journal of Mathematical and Statistical Psychology* 44.2 (1991): 347–357.

Crawford, John R., and David C. Howell. "Comparing an individual's test score against norms derived from small samples." *The Clinical Neuropsychologist* 12.4 (1998): 482–486.

Davies, Huw T. O., and Iain K. Crombie. *What Are Confidence Intervals and P-Values*. London: Hayward Medical Communications, 2009.

Delacre, Marie, et al. "Taking parametric assumptions seriously: Arguments for the use of Welch's F-test instead of the classical F-test in one-way ANOVA." *International Review of Social Psychology* 32.1 (2019): 13.

De Winter, Joost C. F. "Using the student's t-test with extremely small sample sizes." *Practical Assessment, Research, and Evaluation* 18.1 (2019): 10.

Drohomeretski, Everton, et al. "Lean, six sigma and lean six sigma: An analysis based on operations strategy." *International Journal of Production Research* 52.3 (2014): 804–824.

Durivage, Mark Allen. *Practical Design of Experiments (DOE)*. Quality Press, 2016.

Fink, Edward L. "The FAQs on data transformation." *Communication Monographs* 76.4 (2009): 379–397.

Franke, Todd Michael, Timothy Ho, and Christina A. Christie. "The chi-square test: Often used and more often misinterpreted." *American Journal of Evaluation* 33.3 (2012): 448–458.

Heer, Jeffrey, Joseph M. Hellerstein, and Sean Kandel. "Predictive interaction for data transformation." *CIDR*, 2015. http://creativecommons.org/licenses/by/3.0/

Hosken, D. J., D. L. Buss, and D. J. Hodgson. "Beware the F test (or, how to compare variances)." *Animal Behaviour* 136 (2018): 119–126.

Johnson, William D., et al. "Use of Pearson's Chi-square for testing equality of percentile profiles across multiple populations." *Open Journal of Statistics* 5.5 (2015): 412.

Kim, Tae Kyun. "T test as a parametric statistic." *Korean Journal of Anesthesiology* 68.6 (2015): 540–546.

Koehler, Kenneth J., and Jeffrey R. Wilson. "Chi–square tests for comparing vectors of proportions for several cluster samples." *Communications in Statistics-Theory and Methods* 15.10 (1986): 2977–2990.

Lachenbruch, Peter A. "Comparisons of two-part models with competitors." *Statistics in Medicine* 20.8 (2001): 1215–1234.

Lee, James. "Comparison of variance between correlated samples." *Bioinformatics* 8.4 (1992): 405–406.

Lord, Edith. "The use of range in place of standard deviation in the t-test." *Biometrika* 34.1/2 (1947): 41–67.

Manikandan, S. "Data transformation." *Journal of Pharmacology and Pharmacotherapeutics* 1.2 (2010): 126.

Mishra, Prabhaker, et al. "Application of student's t-test, analysis of variance, and covariance." *Annals of Cardiac Anaesthesia* 22.4 (2019): 407.

Oliveira, Stanley R. M., and Osmar R. Zaiane. "Privacy preserving clustering by data transformation." *Journal of Information and Data Management* 1.1 (2010): 37–37.

Padhy, Ramakrushna K., and S. Sahu. "A real option based six sigma project evaluation and selection model." *International Journal of Project Management* 29.8 (2011): 1091–1102.

Politis, Stavros N., et al. "Design of experiments (DoE) in pharmaceutical development." *Drug Development and Industrial Pharmacy* 43.6 (2017): 889–901.

Roman, Eve, et al. "A comparison of standardized and proportional mortality ratios." *Statistics in Medicine* 3.1 (1984): 7–14.

Ruxton, Graeme D. "The unequal variance t-test is an underused alternative to student's t-test and the Mann–Whitney U test." *Behavioral Ecology* 17.4 (2006): 688–690.

Ruxton, Graeme D., David M. Wilkinson, and Markus Neuhäuser. "Advice on testing the null hypothesis that a sample is drawn from a normal distribution." *Animal Behaviour* 107 (2015): 249–252.

Sainani, Kristin L. "Dealing with non-normal data." *Pm&r* 4.12 (2012): 1001–1005.

Schober, Patrick, Sebastiaan M. Bossers, and Lothar A. Schwarte. "Statistical significance versus clinical importance of observed effect sizes: What do P values and confidence intervals really represent?" *Anesthesia and Analgesia* 126.3 (2018): 1068.

Shah, Rachna, Aravind Chandrasekaran, and Kevin Linderman. "In pursuit of implementation patterns: The context of lean and six sigma." *International Journal of Production Research* 46.23 (2008): 6679–6699.

Sheps, Mindel C. "An examination of some methods of comparing several rates or proportions." *Biometrics* 15.1 (1959): 87–97.

Shokri, Alireza. "Quantitative analysis of six sigma, lean and lean six sigma research publications in last two decades." *International Journal of Quality & Reliability Management* 34.5 (2017): 598–625.

Soms, Andrew P. "Exact confidence intervals, based on the Z statistic, for the difference between two proportions." *Communications in Statistics-Simulation and Computation* 18.4 (1989): 1325–1341.

Steiger, James H. "Beyond the F test: Effect size confidence intervals and tests of close fit in the analysis of variance and contrast analysis." *Psychological Methods* 9.2 (2004): 164.

Sunder, M. Vijaya. "Synergies of lean six sigma." *IUP Journal of Operations Management* 12.1 (2013): 21.

Tian, C. H. E. N., et al. "Relationship between Omnibus and Post-hoc tests: An investigation of performance of the F test in ANOVA." *Shanghai Archives of Psychiatry* 30.1 (2018): 60.

Tukey, John W. "Comparing individual means in the analysis of variance." *Biometrics* (1949): 99–114.

Witt, Philip L., and Peter McGrain. "Comparing two sample means t tests." *Physical Therapy* 65.11 (1985): 1730–1733.

Wooditch, Alese, et al. "Comparing two-sample means or proportions." In *A Beginner's Guide to Statistics for Criminology and Criminal Justice Using R*. Cham: Springer International Publishing, 2021, pp. 169–182.

Zollanvari, Amin. "Supervised learning in practice: The first application using scikit-learn." In *Machine Learning with Python: Theory and Implementation*. Cham: Springer International Publishing, 2023, pp. 111–131.

Zou, Guang Yong. "Toward using confidence intervals to compare correlations." *Psychological Methods* 12.4 (2007): 399.

Part V

The Improve Phase of DMAIC

12

Gather the Best Ideas to Fix the Problem

LEARNING OBJECTIVES

1 Describe the eight core steps of the Improve phase of the DMAIC methodology and how error proofing is critical during its execution.
2 Explain how benchmarking and brainstorming complement the Improve phase, and differentiate between the nominal group technique, Delphi technique, and multi-voting.
3 Illustrate how the weighted criteria matrix and the impact and effort matrix are used to facilitate the selection and prioritization of improvement solutions.
4 Describe the basic steps of the theory of constraints (TOC) and explain the drum-buffer-rope concept for optimizing workflow.
5 Identify the key elements of an SMED (single minute exchange of die) event and discuss the importance of FMEA and the corrective action matrix in driving accountability within the Improve phase.

INTRODUCTION

The DMAIC methodology, Define, Measure, Analyze, Improve, and Control, is a structure approach used in Lean Six Sigma and other process improvement methodologies. The Improve phase is the fourth step in the DMAIC process and focuses on identifying and implementing solutions to address the root causes of the problem identified in the previous phases. Depending upon the Lean Six Sigma project you are executing, the type and number of steps or activities involved in executing the Improve phase may differ. However, I have found that eight core steps or activities need to be executed at a minimum when going through this phase. Figure 12.1 illustrates these graphically, and they are explained in the following paragraphs.

- *Generate solutions* – in this step, stakeholders and implementation team members brainstorm and generate solutions to the identified problem(s). Tools such as mind maps, affinity diagrams, or other brainstorming techniques are used to organize and evaluate ideas.
- *Evaluate and select the solution* – each potential solution(s) is assessed based on predefined criteria such as feasibility, impact, and alignment with project goals. They are then prioritized based on their ability to directly address root causes effectively.

DOI: 10.4324/9781032650531-17

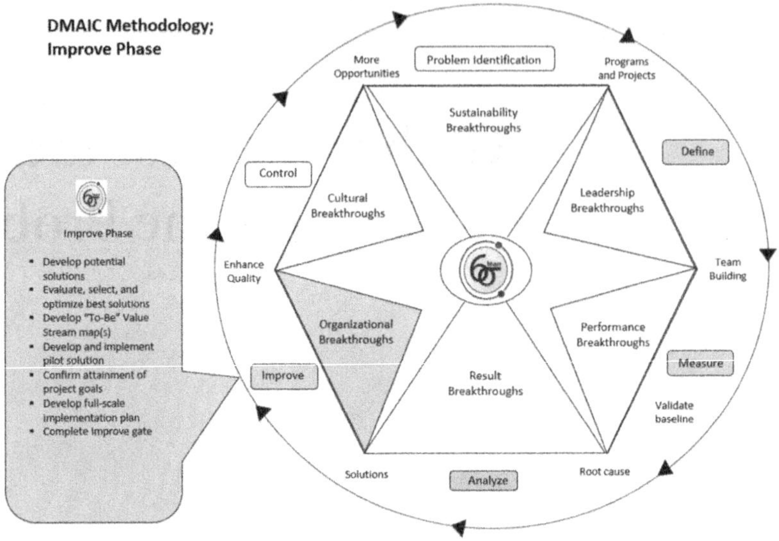

Figure 12.1 Improve Phase Steps or Activities

- *Perform pilot testing* – implementation of solution(s) will be done on a small scale initially in a controlled environment. Performance of each solution(s) will be monitored and evaluated for effectiveness. Data from pilot implementations will be collected, evaluated for potential issues, and readied for full-scale implantation.
- *Solution refinement* – based on the pilot testing evaluation, stakeholders and all team members will be presented with the potential solution results and their feedback solicited. This will be incorporated and any unforeseen issues addressed before full implementation.
- *Full-scale implementation* – once the solution(s) have been refined and proven effective, full-scale implementation can proceed. Ensure that relevant stakeholders are communicated with concerning any potential impact from the implementation plan and that adequate training has been conducted.
- *Monitor and measure* – implementation of the solution must be continuously monitored to ensure improvements are sustained over time. Data must be collected and analyzed and the impact of the implemented solution measured.
- *Document changes* – as a result of the previous step, all changes to the solution must be documented, including standard operating procedures and any other relevant documents. Ensure the organization has a clear record of the improvements made and the associated impact on process performance.
- *Feedback and learning* – feedback from team members, stakeholders, and process users must be performed continuously to ensure the solution is being internalized into use. Also, solicit lessons learned to identify what worked well and areas where improvements can be made. This will enhance future improvement projects and build organizational knowledge.

By following these core steps during the Improve phase of the DMAIC process, the implementation team, and the organization, can systematically identify, implement, and validate how improvements to their processes can lead to sustained positive change and increase efficiency through a Lean Six Sigma project.

CONDUCTING BENCHMARKING STUDIES

Benchmarking is a systematic process of comparing an organization's processes, products, services, and performance metrics against those of either internal partners or, more normally, external industry leaders. The goal of benchmarking is to identify best practices being executed in the competitive landscape and to look for opportunities for improvement.

Benchmarking can take many forms, such as, mentioned previously, internal benchmarking (comparing different units or departments within the same organization), competitive benchmarking (comparing with direct competitors), or functional benchmarking (comparing similar functions across industries). The choice depends on the specific goals and areas an organization wants to improve.

As used within Lean Six Sigma projects, benchmarking is a valuable tool and is used extensively during the Improve phase to ensure the solution being considered aligns with the organization's competitive strategy. It helps the organization ensure any process changes are aligned with best practices and industry standards.

Similar to the Improve phase steps or activities, each benchmarking activity (internal or external) will be composed of different types and number of steps during their execution. There are, however, some that are key to the success of the Lean Six Sigma effort. These are detailed in the following:

First, clearly define the objective – the objectives of the benchmarking study must be clearly defined. Determine what specific aspects of the Lean Six Sigma project will be benchmarked, such as cycle time, defect rates, cost efficiency, or customer satisfaction.

Second, identify metrics – select key performance indicators (KPIs) relevant to the Lean Six Sigma objective being addressed. These should be measurable and aligned with the goals of the overall Lean Six Sigma project. Some common metrics are cycle time, defect rates, throughput, and resource utilization.

Third, identify benchmarking partners – identify organizations or projects that are considered industry leaders or have achieved success in the areas or processes you are benchmarking. This may include competitors, industry peers, or organizations in unrelated industries with similar processes.

Fourth, collect the data – gather relevant data from your organization and benchmarking partners. Ensure consistency in data collection methods to enable accurate comparisons. Data may include process maps, performance metrics, and customer feedback.

Fifth, analyze data – analyze the collected data to identify gaps and areas for improvement. Use statistical tools and techniques coupled with the DMAIC methodology to compare your organization's processes performance against benchmarks. Identify root causes of any performance gaps.

Sixth, identify best practices – identify best practices from benchmarking partners that contribute to their success. These practices include specific process improvements, technologies, organizational structures, or cultural elements that contribute to superior performance.

Seventh, develop improvement strategies – based on the analysis and identification of best practices, develop improvement strategies for your Lean Six Sigma project. Consider how you can adapt and implement these best practices within your organization to achieve better results.

Eight, implement changes – implement the identified improvement strategies in your Lean Six Sigma project. Ensure that changes are well planned, communicated, and monitored. Use change management principles to facilitate a smooth transition.

Ninth, monitor and measure – continuously monitor and measure the impact of the implemented changes. Compare the update performance metrics against the benchmarks and track progress over time. This allows you to assess the effectiveness of the improvements.

Tenth, iterate and refine – because Lean Six Sigma is a continuous improvement process, iterate the benchmarking and improvement cycle regularly. Refine your strategies based on ongoing monitoring and feedback and be prepared to adapt to changing circumstances.

Some useful Lean Six Sigma benchmarking tips:

1 Ensure confidentiality agreements are in place when sharing sensitive information with benchmarking partners.
2 Involve stakeholders throughout the benchmarking process to gain valuable insights and, more importantly, their support.
3 Ensure both internal and external benchmarking is performed to gather a 360-degree view of your organization and Lean Six Sigma project.

By following these steps, you can effectively conduct benchmarking studies in Lean Six Sigma projects within your organization that drive continuous improvement and enhance overall performance.

FACILITATING EFFECTIVE BRAINSTORMING

Effective brainstorming is a collaborative and creative problem-solving technique aimed at generating a wide variety of ideas in a group setting. The goal of brainstorming is to encourage open communication and free thinking by all participants to explore different perspectives and possibilities to solve a problem or to develop a new process. Brainstorming is used extensively in all DMAIC-driven Lean Six Sigma activities.

Facilitating effective brainstorming in Lean Six Sigma involves creating an environment that encourages creative thinking and collaboration while aligning with the principles of Lean Six Sigma and the project objectives of processes improvement while eliminating waste. Each brainstorming session should be framed and facilitated in a manner that actively engages team members and stimulates idea generation. Figure 12.2 provides some tips that can facilitate this process.

- *First, define the problem* – clearly articulate the problem that needs to be addressed. A well-defined problem statement helps participants focus their brainstorming efforts on finding practical solutions.
- *Second, select diverse team members* – bring a diverse group of team members with different perspectives and expertise. This diversity will lead to a wider range of ideas and potential solutions.
- *Third, create a safe and inclusive environment* – establish an environment where team members feel comfortable sharing their ideas without fear of criticism. Encourage open communication and emphasize that all ideas are valued.
- *Fourth, set clear objectives* – clearly communicate the objectives of the brainstorming session. Whether the goal is to generate new ideas, identify potential root causes, or devise improvement strategies, everyone should be on the same page.

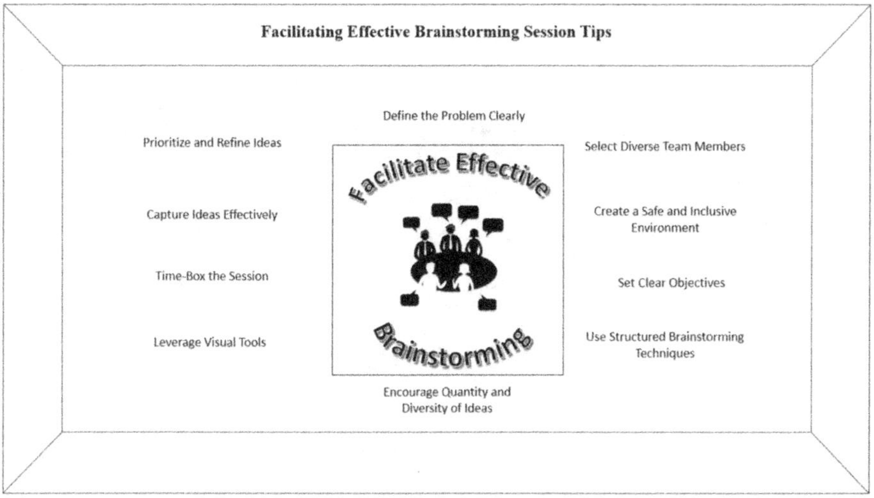

Figure 12.2 Facilitating Effective Brainstorming Session Tips

- *Fifth, use structured brainstorming techniques* – leverage structured brainstorming techniques such as mind mapping, the nominal group technique, or the Delphi method. These methods (as described subsequently) help organize thoughts and ideas, ensuring a more systematic approach.
  - *Mind Mapping* – mind mapping is a visual technique used to organize and represent information in a hierarchical and interconnected manner. It helps individuals brainstorm, plan, analyze, and visualize ideas and concepts. Mind maps are often used to facilitate creative thinking, problem-solving, decision-making, and learning. Figure 12.3 illustrates a notional mind map, with its key elements surrounded by the typical steps taken during its implementation.
  - *Central Topic or Idea* – placed at the center of the map, this represents the main theme or subject of the mind map.
  - *Branches* – radiating from the central topic, branches represent major categories or key concepts related to the central idea. These branches can further split into sub-branches.
  - *Nodes* – nodes are individual elements or ideas connected to the branches. They can contain keywords, short phases, or images to represent specific concepts.
  - *Connections* – arrows or lines connect branches and nodes to indicate relationships or dependencies between different elements. This helps show ideas are connected and how information flows.
  - *Color and Visual Elements* – mind maps often use color, icons, and other visual elements to enhance clarity and make the map more engaging. Assorted colors may be used to distinguish between categories or emphasize specific points.

  Mind maps can be created on paper or whiteboards; using various software tools designed for mind mapping; or, like Figure 12.3, via PowerPoint. Popular applications for creating digital mind maps include MindMeister, XMind, and MindNode. The non-linear and visually engaging nature of mind maps makes them a versatile tool for brainstorming, organizing thoughts, and presenting information in a more accessible format.
  - *The Nominal Group Technique* – the nominal group technique (NGT) is a structured group decision-making method that encourages active participation and

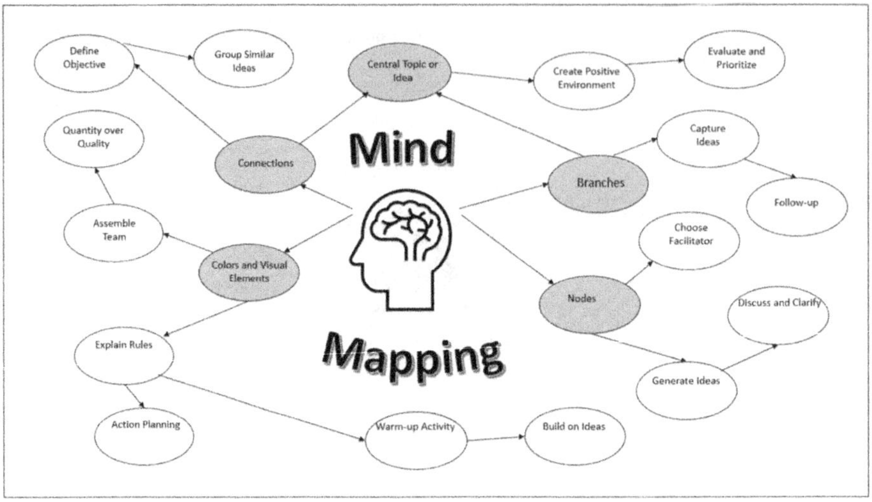

Figure 12.3 Notional Mind Map with Key Elements and Typical Steps

equal input from all members. It was developed to enhance the generation and prioritization of ideas within a group setting. NGT is particularly useful in situations where there is a need to gather input from a diverse group of individuals and to reach a consensus on a specific issue.

Figure 12.4 illustrates the steps involved in facilitating a NGT session:

- *Introduction and explanation* – the facilitator introduces the purpose of the session, explains the NGT process, and sets the agenda for the meeting.
- *Silent idea generation* – participants are given time (usually individually) to generate ideas or solutions to a specific problem or question in silence. Each participant writes down their ideas without discussing them with others.
- *Round-robin sharing* – in a round-robin fashion, participants share their ideas one at a time. The facilitator records all ideas on a flip chart or whiteboard visible to the entire group. There is no discussion or judgement of ideas during this phase.
- *Clarification and elaboration* – after all ideas are listed, the group discusses each idea. Participants can ask questions for clarification, but there is still no evaluation or judgement at this stage.
- *Voting and prioritization* – participants are provided with a specific number of votes (e.g. stickers or dots) and are asked to individually vote on the ideas they consider most important or valuable. This helps prioritize the ideas based on the collective preferences of the group.
- *Tally and discussion* – the facilitator tallies the votes and presents the prioritized list of ideas to the group. The group then discusses the results, and, if necessary, further prioritization or refinement may be done through additional rounds of voting or discussion.

The nominal group technique has several advantages, including the prevention of domination by a single individual, encouragement of equal participation, and the structured approach to idea generation and prioritization. It helps in harnessing the collective wisdom of the group while minimizing the potential groupthink.

- *The Delphi Technique* – is a structured communication method used to gather opinions and reach consensus on a particular topic or problem. It was

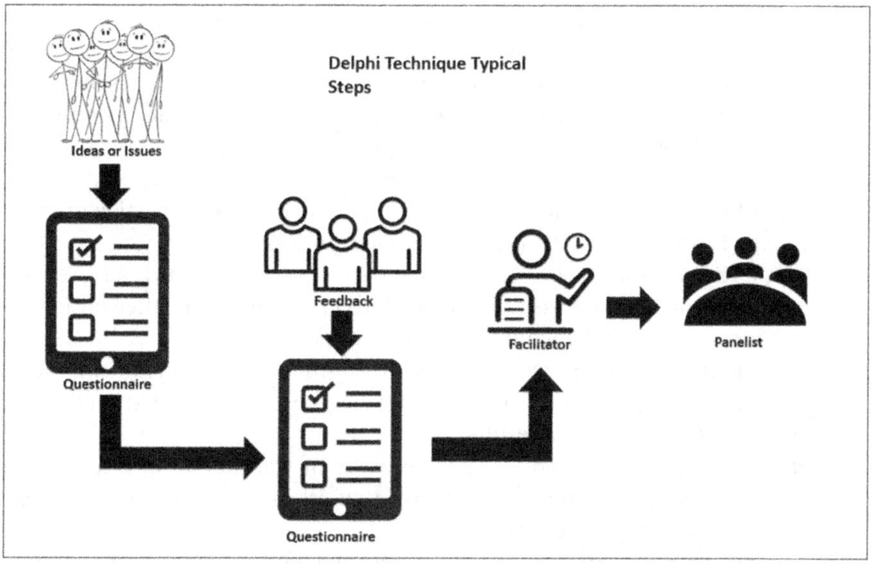

Figure 12.4 Delphi Technique Typical Steps

developed in the 1950s by the Rand Corporation as a forecasting tool, but it has since been widely adopted in various fields, including business, government, and academia. Figure 12.4 illustrates typical steps of the Delphi technique.

- *Ideas or issues* – as the first step, experts or individuals with relevant knowledge on the subject are selected to participate in the process. They provide ideas or issues that form the bases for building a questionnaire.
- *Questionnaire development* – based on the ideas or issues, a series of questionnaires are developed by the facilitator or a panel of experts. The questions are designed to gather opinions, insights, and predictions on ideas or issues.
- *Round 1* – the first round of the Delphi process involves distributing the initial questionnaire to the participants. Each participant responds independently to the questions, providing their opinions or estimates. The responses are usually anonymous to encourage honest and unbiased input.
- *Feedback and iteration* – after collecting the responses, the facilitator summarizes the findings and provides anonymous feedback to the participants. This feedback might include a summary of the group opinion areas of agreement and areas of disagreement. Participants are then given the opportunity to revise their responses after considering the group feedback.
- *Round 2 (and subsequent rounds)* – the process continues with multiple rounds of questionnaires and feedback until a consensus is reached or until the facilitator determines that further iterations are not necessary. The number of rounds can vary depending on the complexity of the issue or the willingness of participants to converge on a consensus.
- *Consensus building* – the goal of the Delphi technique is to achieve consensus or convergence of opinions among the participants. Consensus does not necessarily mean unanimous agreement; it may involve a general agreement or a defined level of convergence among the responses.

The Delphi technique is particularly useful in situations where face-to-face discussions are impractical, where there is a need to gather input from a geographically dispersed group of experts, or when dealing with complex or uncertain issues. It helps to minimize the influence of dominant personalities, reduce groupthink, and allow for the incorporation of diverse perspectives.

- *Sixth, encourage quantity and diversity of ideas* – emphasize the generation of a large quantity of ideas before evaluating or refining them. Encourage participants to think outside the box and consider unconventional solutions.
- *Seventh, leverage visual tools* – use visual aids such as whiteboards, charts, and diagrams to help participants visualize ideas. This can facilitate a better understanding of complex concepts and encourage more creativity.
- *Eighth, time-box the session* – set a specific time limit for the brainstorming session to keep it focused and prevent it from dragging on. Short, intense bursts of brainstorming often yield more creative results.
- *Ninth, capture ideas effectively* – use technology or traditional tools to capture and document ideas in real time. This ensures that all ideas are captured, and participants can see the progress being made.
- *Tenth, prioritize and refine ideas* – after generating a list of ideas, work with the team to prioritize them based on feasibility, impact, and alignment with project strategy and Lean Six Sigma principles. Refine the most promising ideas to develop actionable solutions.

By incorporating these tips, you can enhance the effectiveness of brainstorming sessions within any DMAIC-driven Lean Six Sigma framework, fostering innovation and driving continuous improvement in processes.

PRIORITIZING ACTIONS – EMPLOY MULTI-VOTING

Multi-voting, also known as multiple-voting or dot-voting, is a decision-making and prioritization technique used in group setting to narrow down a list of options or ideas. It helps identify the most important or critical items among a larger set of possibilities. This method is particularly useful in situations where a group needs to make choices or allocate resources based on a set of alternatives.

Here is how multi-voting typically works:

- *First, generate a list of options or ideas* – start with a list of options, ideas, or proposals that the group needs to prioritize or make decisions about. This list could come from a brainstorming session or other means of gathering input.
- *Distribute votes* – provide each participant with a set number of votes (usually represented by stickers, dots, or markers). The number of votes per participant depends on the total number of options and the desired level of granularity.
- *Vote allocation* – participants allocate their votes among the options. They can distribute their votes evenly across all options or concentrate them on the options they find most important or favorable. Participants can use all their votes on one option or spread them across multiple options.
- *Count the votes* – tally the votes for each option. The options with the highest number of votes are considered the most favored or prioritized by the group.

- *Discuss results* – discuss the results with the group. This may involve further exploration of the top-ranked options or consideration of why certain options received more votes.
- *Iterative process* – depending on the context, the group may decide to repeat the process, especially if there is a need to narrow down the options further or if new information emerges during the discussion.

Figure 12.5 provides an illustration of the steps involved in employing multi-voting for prioritization.

Step 1. Define the actions – clearly outline and list the actions or tasks that need to be prioritized. Ensure that all participants have a shared understanding of each action.
Step 2. Set the criteria – establish criteria for prioritization. This could include factors such as urgency, impact, feasibility, or strategic alignment. Ensure all participants understand the criteria they should consider when voting.
Step 3. Distribute voting tokens – provide each participant with a set of voting tokens. These tokens could be stickers, dots, or any other tangible markers. The number of tokens given to each participant depends on the total number of actions and the desired level of granularity desired.
Step 4. Explain the voting process – clearly explain how the voting process will work. Participants should understand how many votes they have, the criteria for voting, and whether they can allocate multiple votes to a single action.
Step 5. Participants vote – participants cast their votes by placing tokens on the actions they believe should be prioritized. They can distribute their votes evenly across multiple actions or concentrate them on a few actions.

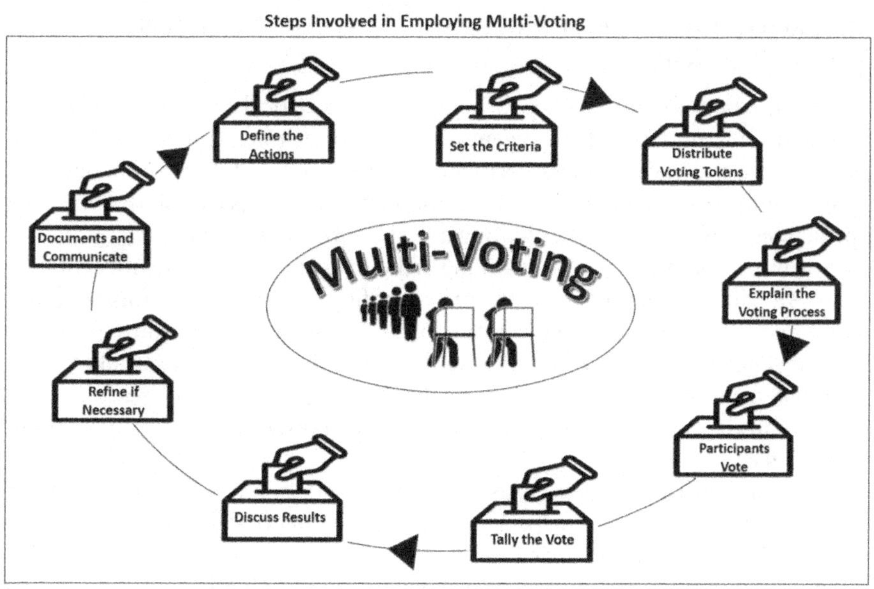

Figure 12.5 Steps Involved in Employing Multi-Voting

Step 6. Tally the votes – count the votes for each action. The actions with the highest number of votes are considered the top priorities.

Step 7. Discuss results – discuss the results with the team. Explore why certain actions received more votes and encourage participants to share their perspectives. This discussion can provide valuable insights and help refine priorities.

Step 8. Refine if necessary – based on the Step 7 discussion, the team may choose to refine or adjust priorities. This could involve additional rounds of voting or further discussion to reach a consensus.

Step 9. Document and communicate – document the prioritized actions and communicate the results to the team. This ensures that everyone is on the same page regarding the agreed-upon priorities.

Tips for successful multi-voting exercises:

Limit the number of votes – to prevent participants from spreading their votes too thin, consider limiting the number of votes each participant can cast on a single action. This encourages more focused decision-making.

Be transparent – ensure transparency throughout the process. Clearly communicate how the votes will be counted and how the prioritization results will be used.

Iterate as needed – depending on the complexity of the decisions and the nature of the actions, be open to iterating the process. You may need to repeat the prioritization exercise to fine-tune the results.

Multi-voting is effective for its simplicity and efficiency. It allows the team to quickly identify preferences and reach a consensus on which options are most important or deserving of attention. It is commonly used in various settings, including project planning, team decision-making, and prioritizing initiatives, and is central DMAIC-driven Lean Six Sigma projects.

ERROR PROOF: IMPLEMENT PROCESS CHANGES TO PREVENT ROOT CAUSE ERRORS

Error proofing, also known as *poka-yoke* in Japanese, is a critical concept in Lean Six Sigma. It is a proactive method aimed at preventing defects or errors in processes. The goal is to design processes in a way that makes errors principally impossible or immediately detectable. This reduces the likelihood of defects and hence improves overall quality. There are basic principles to observe when executing an error-proofing initiative.

First, you want to gain a deep understanding of the processes involved. Identify critical points where errors are likely to occur and where error-proofing measures can be most effective.

Second, simplify processes wherever possible. Complexity begets failure in most cases! Streamlining and simplification can inherently reduce the chances of mistakes.

Third, use frontline workers, those who touch the product or provide the services. Involve them in the error-proofing process, as they can provide valuable input on how to prevent mistakes.

Fourth, employ visual controls such as color-coding, labels, and visual cues to make it clear what steps need to be taken. This helps reduce the chances of errors due to misinterpretation.

Fifth, standardize work processes to ensure consistency and reduce variation. Well-documented and standardized procedures make it easier to identify and correct errors.

Along with ensuring basic principles are observed when implementing error-proofing processes, there are some strategies that can aid in implementation. Figure 12.6 illustrates several of these error-proofing strategies.

- *Checklists* – develop and use checklists at critical points in the process. This ensures that each step is completed correctly and that nothing is overlooked.
- *Automation* – implement automation where feasible. Automated systems can significantly reduce the risk of human error and increase efficiency.
- *Andon systems* – use Andon systems, which are visual or auditory signals that alert workers or management to problems. This allows for immediate intervention when an error is detected.
- *Autonomation (Jidoka)* – implement Jidoka, a principle that empowers machines and workers to stop the production process when a defect is detected. This prevents the production of defective products.
- *Mistake-proofing devices* – integrate mistake-proofing devices or mechanisms into the process. These devices are designed to prevent errors from occurring, such as sensors that detect missing components.
- *Zero-defect culture* – foster a culture of zero defects where every team member is committed to producing high-quality work consistently. Encourage a mindset of continuous improvements and learning from mistakes.
- *Failsafe design* – design processes and systems in a way that naturally prevents errors, for example, using asymmetrical connectors to ensure parts can only be assembled in the correct orientation.
- *Feedback systems* – implement feedback systems that provide immediate information on the process's status. This enables quick identification and correction of errors.
- *Training and education* – provide thorough training and education to employees to ensure they understand the importance of error prevention and are equipped with the necessary skills.

Remember, preventing root cause error and error-proofing processes is an ongoing activity and requires commitment to continuous improvement and learning from past experiences and mistakes. As the organizational environment evolves, new risks and challenges emerge, requiring the adoption of new error-proofing strategies. To deal with this, regular reviews, updates to error-proofing measures, and a sound culture that values quality and prevention over detection and correction must be present.

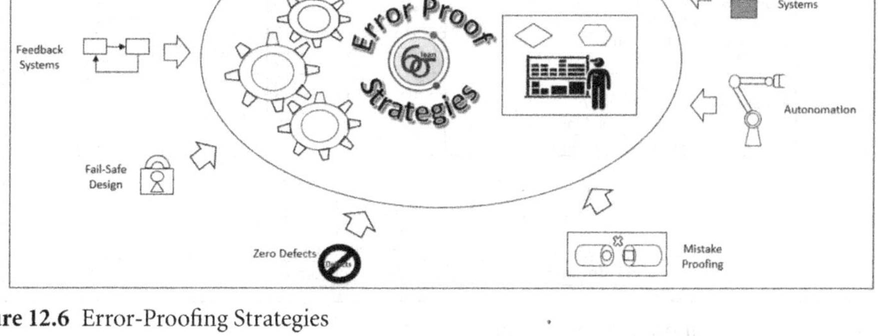

Figure 12.6 Error-Proofing Strategies

SYSTEMATICALLY SELECT IMPROVEMENT SOLUTION SETS

In Lean Six Sigma, selecting process improvement solution sets involves a systematic approach to identifying and implementing solutions that address the root causes of problems and lead to process improvement. While criteria for selecting improvement solution sets can vary based on the context and goals of the overall project and process selected, there are some common criteria that should be observed when considering types.

Solutions should be aligned with the overall strategic goals and objectives of the project and organizations in which they are to be employed. They should have a clear measurable and positive impact on the organization and process key performance indicators. Always assess the feasibility of implementing each solution set within the given resources, time, and budget. Solutions should be sustainable over the long term, meaning that the organization must have the ability to continue implementing the changes after the immediate need has been completed.

Potential risks associated with each solution set considered require evaluation. Implementation risk, resistance to change, and potential negative impacts of adjoining processes require evaluation, too. Solutions that involve and engage employees often are more successful, as are those that clearly enhance the customer's experience.

For each solution set considered, conduct a cost-benefit analysis. Directly compare the cost of implementation against the expected benefit, including both tangible and intangible benefits. Closely assess the time required for each solution set. If there are opportunities for quick wins that can demonstrate success early, they can be prioritized to occur sooner than others. Try to choose solution sets that are flexible and adaptable to changes in the business environment.

A key to improvement solution set selection is to ensure that the solution set is based on hard data and evidence from the Analyze phase of the DMAIC methodology. Also, just as with any other Lean Six Sigma initiative, cross-functional collaboration is critical, especially when multiple departments or teams are working together on complex problems. Figure 12.7 is a notional improvement solution set matrix used for initial screening of potential solution set selection. Its simplicity is what makes it effective for initial screening of solution sets, and because it is done as a team, participation and communications are jump-started. Generally, the top four or five candidates are taken to another level of evaluation, and the process continues until an improvement solution selection is made.

Notional Improvement Solution Set Matrix

Criterion		Feasibility	Cost	Impact	Score
Align with Business Goals		3	2	4	9
Impact on Critical Metrics		4	3	3	10
Feasibilty		1	2	4	7
Sustainability		2	2	5	9
Risk Assessment		3	3	4	10
Customer Impact		3	3	5	11
Employee Involvement		3	3	3	9
Cost-Benefit Analysis		4	2	3	9
Speed of Implmentation		3	3	3	9
Flexibility and Adaptability		3	3	3	9
Data-Driven Decision Making		1	2	5	8
Cross-Functional Collaboration		4	3	5	12

Item		1	5
Feasibility		Hardest	Easiest
Cost		Most Expensive	Most Cheap
Impact		Lowest	Highest

Figure 12.7 A Notional Improvement Solution Set Matrix

USING A WEIGHTED CRITERIA MATRIX

A weighted criteria matrix, also known as a decision matrix, is a tool used in Lean Six Sigma to systematically evaluate and prioritize different options based on multiple criteria. This matrix helps the team make informed decisions by assigning weights to criteria based on their importance.

Figure 12.8 is an example of a weighted criteria matrix that was developed to evaluate the use of a solution option.

Because a weighted criteria matrix is a systematic way to evaluate improvement solution sets, the criteria it is developed by should align with the organization's goals and objectives. The following are the steps in creating and implementing an effective weighted criteria matrix.

Step 1. Define the criteria – identify the criteria that are important for evaluating the improvement solution set. These criteria should align with the goals and objectives that are to be achieved.

Step 2. Assign weights – assign weights to each criterion based on its relative importance. Use a scale such 1 to 5 or 1 to 10, where a higher number indicates greater importance.

Step 3. List improvement solution sets – identify and list the potential improvement solution sets that require evaluation.

Step 4. Evaluate each solution set – assess each solution set against the defined criteria. Use a numerical scale to quantify the performance of each solution set for each criterion.

Step 5. Calculate weighted scores – multiple the scores for each criterion by their corresponding weights and calculate the weighted scores for each solution set.

Step 6. Rank solution sets – rank the solution sets based on their weighted scores, from highest to lowest. The higher the total weighted score, the better the solution set performs against the criteria.

Step 7. Review and adjust – review the results and assess whether they align with expectations and goals. If necessary, adjust the criteria weights or the evaluation process.

Step 8. Select the top solution sets – choose the solution sets with the highest total weighted scores. These are the ones that align best with the criteria and objectives.

Step 9. Implement and monitor – once a solution set has been chosen, implement it and establish a monitoring system to track its effectiveness over time. This ensures continuous improvement and allows for adjustments if necessary.

Weighted Criteria Matrix

	Cost To Implement	Time to Implement	Effort to Implement	Estimated savings after implementation	Importance to customer	
Importance	3	1	2	4	5	Total
	5 = $0.00 - $1,000	5 = 0 - 30 days	5 = No additional labor	5 = > than $50,000 annually	5 = Very important	
	3 = $1,000 - $5,000	3 = 31 - 60 days	3 = 1 to 5 additional labor	3 = Up to $50,000 annually	3 = Somewhat important	
Options	1 = > than $5,000	1 = > than 60 days	1 = > than 5 additional labor	1 = No savings	1 = Not important	
Solution Option 1	3	1	5	3	1	37
Solution Option 2	1	1	1	3	5	43
Solution Option 3	1	3	3	3	3	39
Solution Option 4	5	5	3	1	1	35
Solution Option 5	5	5	5	1	1	39
Solution Option 6	1	3	1	3	1	25
Solution Option 7	5	5	3	1	5	55
Solution Option 8	5	1	3	3	5	59

= (B6*B2)+(C6*C2)+(D6*D2)+(E6*E2)+(F6*F2)

Figure 12.8 Weighted Criteria Matrix

This approach provides a structured and objective way to assess and compare different improvement solution sets based on specific criteria. Adjustments to the process may be necessary based on the unique characteristics of the project or organization.

USING AN IMPACT AND EFFORT MATRIX

An impact and effort matrix is a tool used in Lean Six Sigma to prioritize improvement opportunities based on the potential impact of the improvement and the effort required to implement it. It helps teams focus on the initiatives that are likely to yield the most significant benefits with reasonable effort. Figure 12.9 is an example of an impact and effort matrix.

Here is a step-by-step guide on how to develop and use an impact and effort mat-rix.

Step 1. Define improvement opportunities – identify and define the improvement opportunities within your process. These could be areas for cost reduction, process efficiency enhancement(s), quality improvement, or any other aspect that aligns with the organization strategies and Lean Six Sigma initiative.

Step 2. Determine impact criteria – define the impact criteria that will be used to measure the impact of each opportunity. This could include factors such as customer satisfaction, cycle time reduction, defect reduction, or financial savings.

Step 3. Determine effort criteria – define the criteria used to measure the effort required to implement each improvement opportunity. Consider factors such as resource allocation, time, complexity, and organizational change.

Step 4. Create the impact and effort matrix – draw a matrix with the horizontal axis representing effort and the vertical axis representing impact.

Step 5. Rate the impact and effort – notionally rate each improvement opportunity based on the assigned impact and effort criteria. Use descriptive labels (like those used in Figure 12.9) to graphically position the opportunity in one of the grid quadrants.

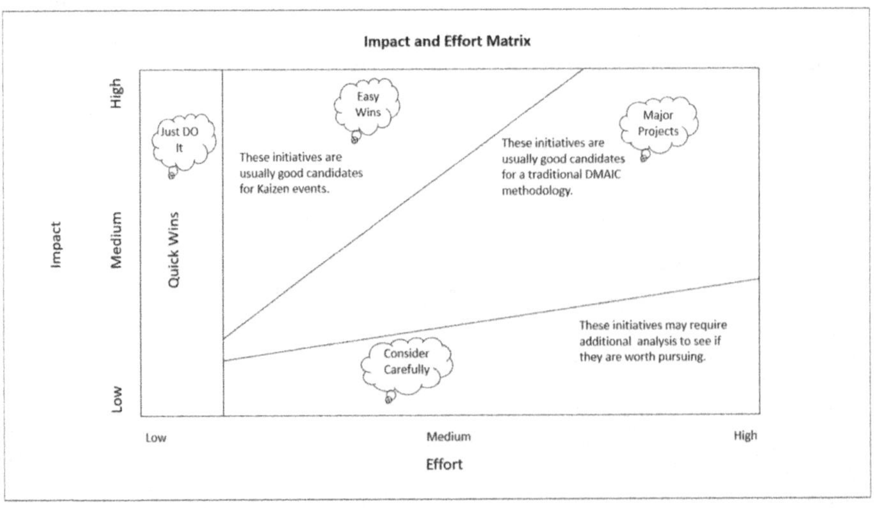

Figure 12.9 Impact and Effort Matrix

Quadrant analysis:

Low effort, high impact (quick wins) – prioritize opportunities in this quadrant for quick wins that can be implemented with relatively low effort but provide significant impact.

Low effort, low impact (easy wins) – these opportunities may not have an immediate impact, but they can be addressed quickly with minimal resource commitment.

High effort, high impact (major projects) – consider the opportunities for more significant projects that may require additional resources and planning.

High effort, low impact (consider carefully) – evaluate whether the effort required for these opportunities justifies the potential impact. Consider either de-prioritizing or bundling these opportunities.

Step 6. Validate the prioritization – discuss the prioritization with the team and relevant stakeholders. Ensure that the positioning of the opportunities reflects the potential effort and impact for each opportunity.

Step 7. Develop an action plan – based on prioritization, develop action plans for implementing the selected improvement opportunities. Define timelines, responsibilities, and key milestones for each initiative.

Here are some tips for getting the most from the impact and effort matrix.

1 Engage cross-functional teams – involve a diverse group of team members and stakeholders in the rating process to gather different perspectives.
2 Use consistent criteria – ensure that the criteria for impact and effort are well defined and consistently considered across all improvement opportunities.
3 Regularly review and update – periodically review and update the impact and effort matrix as new data becomes available or as project priorities evolve.
4 Consider risks – factor potential risks associated with each improvement opportunity when assessing impact and effort.
5 Align with organizational goals – ensure that the selected improvement opportunities align with the organization's goals and strategies and the Lean Six Sigma project in which they are employed.

An impact and effort matrix is a tool that systematically prioritizes improvement opportunities and aids in focusing team efforts on initiatives that provide the greatest impact with reasonable effort. It is also used as a comminutions tool to engage team members and drive self-ownership of the initiative.

ANALYZE AND RESOLVE CONSTRAINTS TO ACHIEVE CONTINUOUS FLOW

Achieving continuous flow in Lean Six Sigma projects is essential for maximizing efficiency and minimizing waste in processes. Continuous flow is a key element of the DMAIC methodology and is critical for both manufacturing and service industries. Its aim is clear: eliminate bottlenecks and interruptions. To analyze and resolve constraints and achieve continuous organization in a Lean project, you must balance the process and, more importantly, the overarching business strategy and the performance and commitment components. Next, a sequence of steps should be considered before embarking on the constraint improvement process. Figure 12.10 illustrates the organizational components that require balance and the recommended sequence of steps to follow when executing a constraint improvement process.

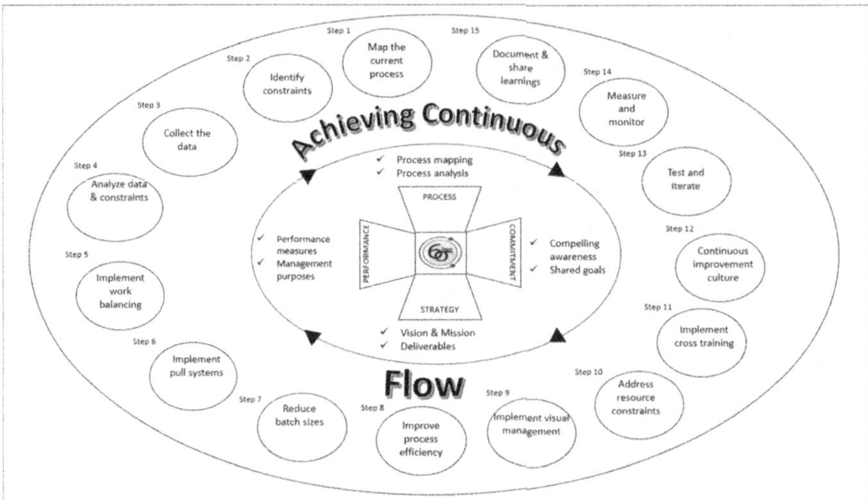

Figure 12.10 Achieving Continuous Flow Organizational Components and Steps

Step 1. Map the current process – create a value stream map or process map to visualize the current state of the process. Identify each step, including delays, handoffs, and bottlenecks. This map serves as a baseline for analysis.

Step 2. Identify constraints – analyze the value stream or process map to identify constraints or bottlenecks, those areas where work accumulates or slows down. Constraints are typically characterized by excessive work-in-progress (WIP) and longer cycle times.

Step 3. Collect data – gather data on key performance metrics such as cycle time, lead time, and WIP at each process step. This data provides quantitative insights into the performance of the process.

Step 4. Analyze the data and constraints – using statistical and Lean tools, analyze the data and identify the root causes of constraints. Some common tools include Pareto charts, control charts, and histograms.

Step 5. Implement work balancing – ensure that work is evenly distributed across all process steps. If certain steps are overloaded while others are underutilized, rebalance the workload to achieve a more uniform flow.

Step 6. Implement pull systems – introduce pull systems such as Kanban to regulate the flow throughout a process. Pull systems allow downstream processes to signal when they are ready for more work, preventing overproduction and reducing WIP.

Step 7. Reduce batch sizes – decrease batch sizes to reduce the amount of WIP at each step. Smaller batches improve flow and responsiveness, enabling a more continuous and predictable process.

Step 8. Improve process efficiency – identify opportunities to streamline and improve individual process maps. This may involve eliminating non-value-added activities, reducing setup times, or optimizing workflows.

Step 9. Implement visual management – use visual management techniques to make it easy to monitor the status of work and identify any issues at a glance. Visual cues such as Kanban boards help teams stay informed and take immediate action.

Step 10. Address resource constraints – ensure that resources, including equipment and personnel, are not bottlenecks. Address resource constraints by optimizing resource utilization and, if necessary, investing in additional capacity.

Step 11. Implement cross-training – cross-train employees, when possible, to perform multiple tasks. This flexibility allows teams to adapt to variations in demand and ensures that work can flow smoothly even when specific individuals are unavailable.

Step 12. Continuous improvement culture – foster a culture of continuous improvement where team members are encouraged to identify and address constraints regularly. Implement regular review meetings to assess process performance and adjust.

Step 13. Test and iterate – implement changes on a small scale at first, test their impact, and iterate as needed. This approach minimizes the risk of disrupting the entire process and allows for continuous refinement.

Step 14. Measure and monitor – establish key performance indicators (KPIs) to measure the success of the changes. Regularly monitor these metrics to ensure that the process continues to achieve continuous flow.

Step 15. Document and share learnings – document the changes made, the results achieved, and the lessons learned. Share this information with the team and stakeholders to promote knowledge sharing and continuous improvement.

By systematically analyzing constraints, implementing changes, and fostering a culture of continuous improvement, Lean Six Sigma projects can achieve and sustain continuous flow in their processes. Continuous monitoring and refinement are crucial to adapt to changing conditions and ensure ongoing improvements.

USING THEORY OF CONSTRAINTS TO RESOLVE BOTTLENECKS

The theory of constraints (TOC) is a management philosophy introduced by Eliyahu Goldratt in his book *The Goal* that focuses on identifying and improving the constraints or bottlenecks in a system to optimize overall process efficiency, enhance organizational operations, and the opportunity to achieve higher goals. In the context of Lean Six Sigma, TOC is a powerful tool that is used extensively to enhance throughput performance and drive buffer management strategies in both product or services settings. Figure 12.11 is a notional model that depicts the effects of a constrained system and the five TOC steps that are taken to deal with it.

Using an aviation organization experiencing aircraft maintenance delays, we will use the TOC steps illustrated in Figure 12.11 to improve aircraft maintenance processes.

Step 1. Identify the constraints – the maintenance processes for a particular type of aircraft are experiencing delays. The organization has identified that the maintenance hangar is a bottleneck in the process. The limited number of hanger bays and maintenance crews is causing delays in getting aircraft through maintenance checks.

Step 2. Exploit the constraint – prioritize the use of the limited hanger bays and maintenance crews for the aircraft that are closest to completion or have the highest priority. Ensure that the hanger is utilized efficiently by minimizing downtime between aircraft maintenance tasks.

Step 3. Subordinate other processes – adjust non-hanger activities to align with the pace of the maintenance hangar. For example, coordinate with supply chain management to ensure that required parts and materials are available when needed, reducing idle time for the maintenance crews.

Step 4. Elevate or eliminate the constraint – if possible, invest in additional space or maintenance crews to alleviate the bottleneck. This might involve hiring more skilled technicians or optimizing the existing workforce. Additionally, implement strategies to eliminate the constraints altogether. For instance, if the bottleneck is

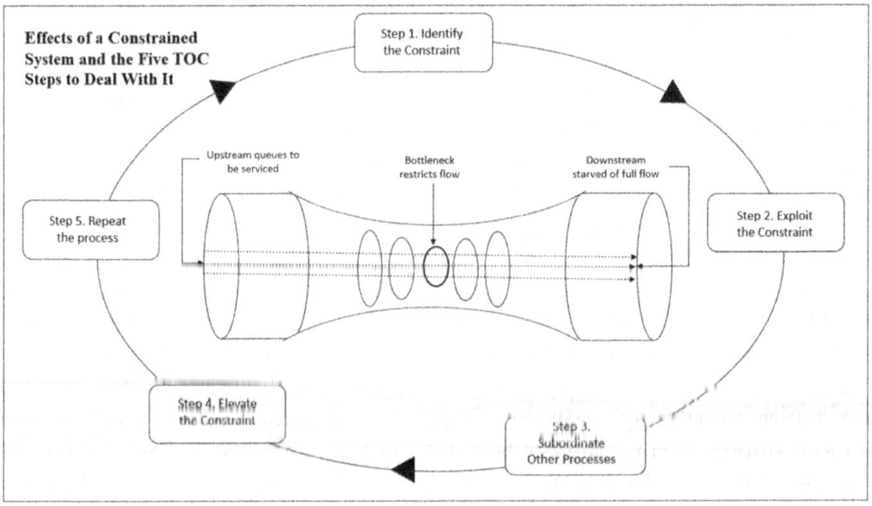

Figure 12.11 Effects of a Constrained System and the Five TOC Steps to Deal With It

due to a shortage of skilled technicians, invest in training programs or recruitment to build a larger pool of qualified technicians.

Step 5. Repeat the process – After addressing the initial constraint, reassess the entire system to identify new constraints that may have emerged. TOC is a continuous improvement process that seeks to identify and address constraints systematically.

When employing TOC, two important rules should always be observed.

1 *Avoid inertia* – TOC emphasizes the importance of avoiding inertia. Once a constraint is addressed, it does not mean the work is done. The team should keep looking for new constraints and opportunities for improvement.
2 *Measure performance by throughput* – in TOC, the primary measure of an organization's success is throughput, which is the rate at which the system generates money through production, which equates to sales. All efforts should be directed towards increasing throughput while reducing inventory and operating expenses.

BUFFER MANAGEMENT IN TOC

An additional aspect of TOC is that of buffer management. It is a key concept in TOC methodology. It involves strategically managing buffers to optimize the flow of work through a system and to protect against variability and uncertainty. The primary purpose of buffers is to ensure that the constraint is always utilized efficiently without causing disruptions to the overall process.

A key component in the execution TOC buffer management is the drum-buffer-rope (DBR) concept. Figure 12.12 is a notional illustration of how the DBR process works.

The DBR concept is particularly applicable in production and manufacturing environments. It is, however, used extensively in the service industries such as fast food, where the stocking of the "supermarket" is critical to building the customer's selection in an expeditious manner.

The "drum" depicted in Figure 12.12 refers to the constraint or bottleneck in the system. It is part of the process that limits the overall throughput of the entire system. The pace of production is set by the drum. In other words, the drum determines the rate at which products or services are produced to ensure that the constraints are not overburdened.

The "rope" represents the release mechanism for new work into the system. It ensures that work is released into the system at a rate that does not exceed the capacity of the constraint. The rope is used to synchronize the entire system. It communicates the pace set by the drum to the rest of the system, ensuring that work is released only when the constraint is ready to process it.

The "buffer" is a protective inventory placed in front of the constraint to ensure it always has a consistent flow of work. There are two main types of buffers recognized: time or queue buffers and material buffers.

- Time or queue buffers – it is a buffer that protects against disruptions and variations in the process, ensuring that the constraint is never starved.
- Materials buffers – it is a buffer of physical inventory that ensures the constraint is always supplied with the necessary materials.

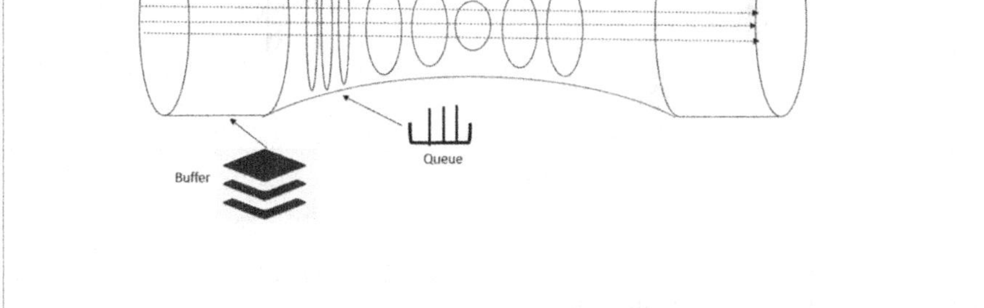

Figure 12.12 Notional Illustration of the Drum-Buffer-Rope Concept

The drum-buffer-rope concept aims to optimize the flow of work through a system by focusing on and managing the constraints. By doing so, the entire system's performance can be improved. It emphasizes the importance of maintaining a balance between demand and the constraint capacity to ensure efficient and effective operations. Implementing DBR involves continuous monitoring, adjustment, and improvement. The goal is to elevate the performance of the constraint and, consequently, enhance the overall performance of the entire system.

IMPROVING PROCESS FLOW; CELLULAR PROCESSING, REDUCING CHANGEOVER AND SETUP TIME

Improving process flow through cellular processing and reducing changeover and setup time are crucial aspects of Lean Six Sigma projects aimed at enhancing efficiency, minimizing waste, and optimizing overall performance.

Improving process flow through cellular processing in the context of Lean Six Sigma involves applying principles that eliminate waste, reduce variation, and optimize efficiency. Cellular processing, also known as cellular manufacturing, organizes the production process into cells where a dedicated team is responsible for a specific set of tasks. Figure 12.13 illustrates a typical U-shaped cellular process flow.

Figure 12.13 illustrates a typical cellular arrangement of a manufacturing process for a typical component. It is composed of a seven-step build process and a team of four technicians with shared responsibilities. It begins with raw material entering the cell where it goes into the "lathing" process. One team member monitors this process along with the final "packing" process. When the lathe process is completed, it is passed to the "drill" process. One team member monitors this process along with the preceding "mill" process. After the mill step, the component enters the 'testing" process where it has one technician whose job is to ensure the component is achieving the proper level of quality. From there, it enters the "de-burring" process where one technician monitors the process along with the "assembly" process step. After completing these two steps, the component goes to the "packing" process that is monitored by the same technician that monitored the initial lathe process.

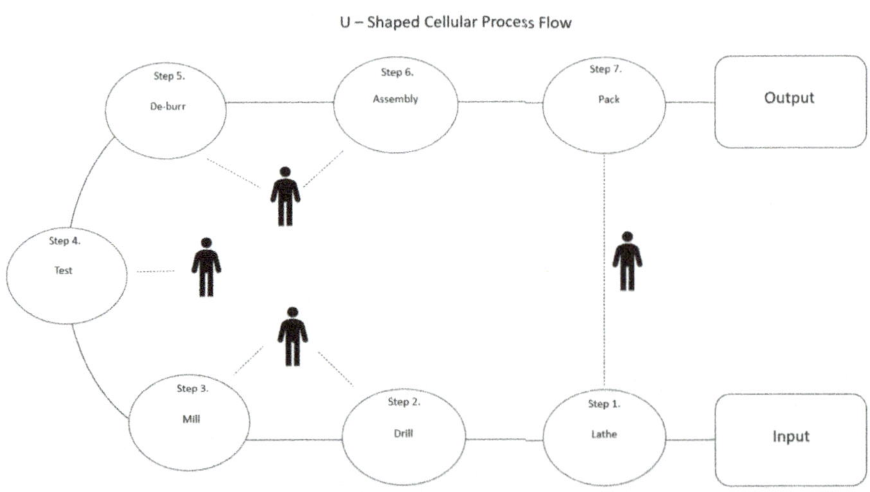

Figure 12.13 Typical U-Shaped Cellular Process Flow

The U-shaped cellular process optimizes the flow of material, helps manage throughput yield, and utilizes the multi-tasking of technicians "to do more with less" and offers job enlargement opportunities for increased employee challenge and compensation. Here are some strategies that can be used to enhance flow in cellular processing using the Lean Six Sigma methodology.

1 *Value stream mapping* (VSM) – begin by creating a VSM of the entire cellular processing workflow. Identify each step, material flow, and information flow. This visual representation helps to highlight areas of waste and efficiency.
2 *Cell design* – optimize the layout of cells to minimize material movement and streamline the flow of work. Ensure that workstations within the cell are arranged in a logical sequence to reduce unnecessary transportation and waiting times.
3 *Cross-training* – cross-train team members within the cell to perform multiple tasks. This flexibility allows for better resource utilization, enabling team members to support each other during peak workloads or absences.
4 *Workload balancing* – ensure that the workload is evenly distributed among team members in the cell. Balancing the workload helps to prevent bottlenecks and ensures that each team member is consistently engaged.
5 *Quality at the source* – emphasize the importance of producing quality products within the cell. Implement measures to ensure that defects are identified and corrected at the source rather than being passed downstream.

Reducing changeover and setup time is a critical aspect of the Lean Six Sigma methodology aiming to increase efficiency and minimize downtime of equipment between different production runs. To accomplish this, the Lean Six Sigma methodology has adopted the lean concept of single-minute exchange of die (SMED). SMED aims is to reduce the setup or changeover time of a process to as close to zero as possible. Its goal is to increase efficiency, reduce downtime, and improve overall process flow. Figure 12.14 illustrates the key elements for a SMED event, which are support, people, communication, equipment and supplies, and scope.

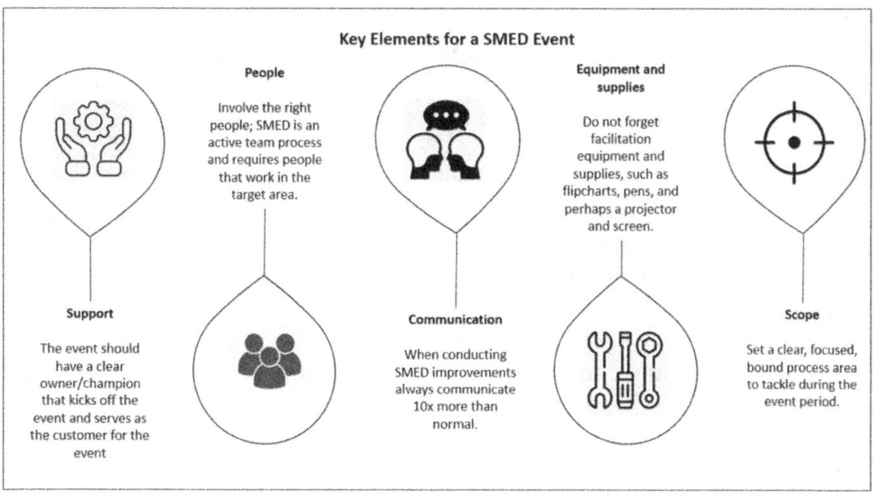

Figure 12.14 Key Elements for a SMED Event

Based on these key elements, here is a six-step guide on how to implement SMED to improve process flow within any organization.

Step 1. Understand the current process – analyze and document the current setup or changeover process. Identify and list all the steps involved in the changeover.
Step 2. Separate the internal from the external setup activities – identify opportunities to convert internal setup activities into external activities. Focus on tasks that can be done without stopping the equipment. This may involve redesigning equipment, changing tools, or modifying processes.
Step 3 – Parallelization of tasks – break down the setup process into smaller tasks and identify opportunities for parallelization. Determine which tasks can be performed simultaneously to reduce overall changeover time.
Step 4 – Quick-release mechanisms – integrate quick-release mechanisms, such as fasteners and clamps, to expedite the removal and installation of components. This reduces the time spent on physically changing parts.
Step 5 – Pilot implementation – choose a specific manufacturing line or process to pilot the SMED implementation. Apply the identified improvements and measure the impact on changeover times and overall efficiency.
Step 6 – Document and communicate – maintain comprehensive documentation of setup procedures and make it easily accessible to all relevant personnel. Establish clear communications channels to facilitate collaboration and coordination during changeovers.

Keep in mind when implementing SMED that it is an ongoing process of improvement. Because it is focused squarely on mechanical types of systems, calibration of that equipment is vital to continued operational gains.

MANAGING INVENTORY LEVELS TO ACHIEVE CONTINUOUS FLOW

Managing inventory levels in a Lean Six Sigma environment involves optimizing the balance between customer demand, production efficiency, and resource utilization. Because Lean Six Sigma is a methodology that combines Lean principles, which focus on eliminating waste and improving, combined with Six Sigma's focus on reducing variation and defects, the overall effect on inventory management can be substantial. Figure 12.15 illustrates some of the key considerations and strategies that have proven to be effective for managing inventory levels.

Strategy 1. Value stream mapping – begin by creating a value stream map to understand the current state of your processes. This visual representation will help identify areas of waste and opportunities for improvement.
Strategy 2, Demand forecasting – use accurate demand forecasting to align production with customer needs. This helps in avoiding overproduction and excessive inventory.
Strategy 3. Just-in-time manufacturing – implement just-in-time (JIT) manufacturing principles to produce items only as needed, reducing excess inventory and minimizing storage costs.
Strategy 4. Kanban system – utilize a Kanban system to control the flow of materials and information in the production process. Kanban helps prevent overproduction by signaling when it is time to replenish materials.

Strategy 5. Work-in-progress limits – set and enforce WIP limits to prevent excessive work from piling up at different stages of the production process. This helps maintain a smooth and efficient flow.

Strategy 6. Cycle time reduction – identify and reduce cycle times in the production process. Shorter cycle times enable quicker response to changes in demand and reduce the need for large inventory buffers.

Strategy 7. Standardized work – standardize work processes to minimize variation and ensure consistent quality. This reduces the likelihood of defects, which can contribute to excess inventory.

Strategy 8. Data analytics – use data analytics to monitor and analyze inventory levels, demand patterns, and other relevant metrics. Data-driven decision making can help in identifying opportunities for improvement.

Lean Six Sigma can be the cornerstone by which inventory management can be continuously optimized. Enhanced efficiency, reduced cost, and overperformance will be accomplished by regularly reviewing and adjusting strategies based on this continuous improvement process.

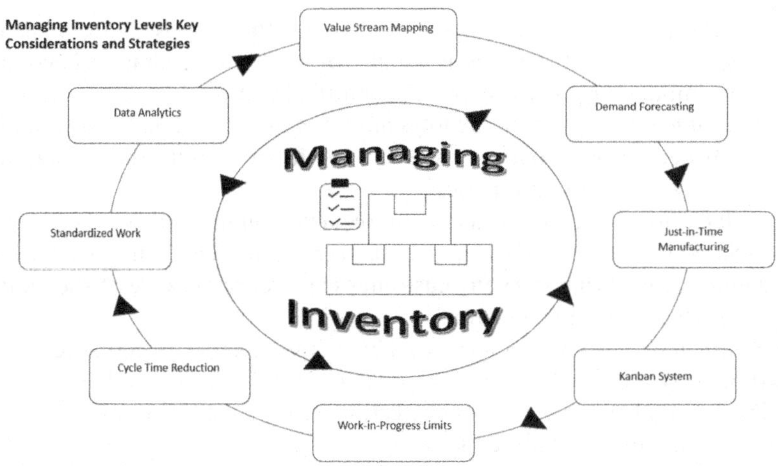

Figure 12.15 Managing Inventory Levels Key Considerations and Strategies

ASSESSING RISK: USING FAILURE MODES AND EFFECTS ANALYSIS

Failure modes and effects analysis is a step-by-step approach for identifying all possible failures in a design, a manufacturing or assembly process, or a product or service. "Failure modes" means the ways, or modes, in which something might fail. Failures are any errors or defects, especially ones that affect the customer, and can be potential or actual. "Effects analysis" refers to studying the consequences of those failures. It is a common analysis tool and is used extensively in DMAIC-driven Lean Six Sigma initiatives.

Failures are prioritized according to how serious their consequences are, how frequently they occur, and how easily they can be detected. The purpose of the FMEA is to take actions to eliminate or reduce failures, starting with the highest-priority ones.

FMEA additionally documents current knowledge and actions about the risks of failures, for use in continuous improvement. It is used extensively during the development of a system or process and becomes an integral part of its life cycle management tool set.

As a standard part of the DMAIC methodology, it is often applied:

- When a process, product, or service is being designed or redesigned.
- When an existing process, product, or service is being applied in a new way.
- Before developing control plans for a new or modified process.
- When improvement goals are planned for an existing process, product, or service.
- When analyzing failures of an existing process, product, or service.
- Periodically throughout the life of the process, product, or service.

Figure 12.16 is an example of FMEA that was constructed to assess the mixing ratio of the chemicals during a plating process.

The identifying information is located at the top of the FMEA form in Figure 12.16. The remaining steps ask for information that will go into the columns of the form and is described in the following.

- *Identify the function(s) of the scope.* Ask, "What is the purpose of this system, design, process, or service?" The scope is usually broken into separate subsystems, items, parts, assemblies, or process steps and identified by function.
- *For each function, identify all the ways failure could occur.* These are potential failure modes. If necessary, go back and rewrite the function with more detail to be sure modes show a loss of that function.
- *For each failure mode, identify all the consequences on the system, related systems, process, related processes, product, service, or regulations.* These are potential effects of the failure. Ask, "What does the customer experience because of the failure? What happens when the failure occurs?"
- *Determine how serious each effect is.* This is the severity rating. Severity is usually rated on a scale of 1–10, where 1 is considered insignificant and 10 catastrophic. If a failure mode has more than one effect, write on the FMEA table only the highest severity rating for that failure mode.
- *For each failure mode, determine all the potential root causes.* Use Lean Six Sigma cause analysis tools and the team's best knowledge and experience to assess each failure mode and list all possible causes on the form.
- *For each cause, determine the occurrence rating.* This rating estimates the probability of failure occurring for that reason during the lifetime of the scope. Occurrences are usually rated on a scale of 1–10, where 1 is extremely unlikely and 10 is inevitable.
- *For each cause, identify current process controls.* These are tests, procedures, or mechanisms that you now have in place to keep failures from reaching the customer. These controls might prevent the cause from happening, reduce the likelihood that it will happen, or detect failure after the cause has already happened but before the customer is affected.
- *For each control, determine the detection rating.* This rating estimates how well the controls can detect either the cause or its failure mode after they have happened but before the customer is affected. Detection is usually rated on a scale of 1–10, where 1 means the control is certain to detect the problem and 10 means it is certain not to detect it or no control exists.

FMEA Example

Function	Potential Failure Mode	Potential Effect(s) of Failure	Severity	Potential Cause(s) of Failure	Occurrence	Current Process Control	Detection	Risk Priority Number (RPN)	Critical Characteristic (CRIT)	Recommended Action(s)	Responsibility and Target Completion Date	Action Taken
Dispense the correct measured amount of chemical into the plating solution during each batch mixing sequence.	Does not dispense proper amount of chemical.	Plating thickness defective	8	Dispensing calibration off	7	Ensure calibration schedule is executed	6	336	N/A		Bill	
		Did not meet contract specification	6	Wrong composition of chemical base from supplier	8	Review inbound logistics testing practice	8	384	N/A		Mark	
		Deliverable late	6	Power interruption during mixing process	5	Check with facilities management prior to scheduling batch runs	5	150	N/A		Angela	
		Customer not happy	10	Sequence of mix incorrect	6	Ensure that SOP for mixing sequence is enforced	5	300	N/A		Jenn	

Figure 12.16 FMEA Example

- *Calculate the risk priority number (RPN).* The RPN is the sum of S (severity) × O (occurrence) × D (detection). These numbers provide guidance for ranking potential failures in the order that they should be addressed.
- *Critical characteristic(s) (operational).* Critical characteristics are measurements or indictors that reflect safety or compliance with government regulations and need special controls. If so, a column labeled "Classification" receives a "Y" or "N" to show whether special controls are needed. Usually, critical characteristics have a severity of 9 or 10 and occurrence and detection ratings above 3.
- *Identify recommended actions.* These actions may be design or process changes to lower severity of occurrence. They may recommend additional controls to improve detection.
- *Responsibility and target completion date.* Who is responsible for the actions and what the targeted completion date(s) is.

During the execution of a DMAIC-driven Lean Six Sigma initiative, there are several types of FMEAs that one might use, dependent upon the type of system, product, or service and situation under study. Here are some of the more common types:

- *Design FMEA* – focuses on identifying and mitigating potential failures in the design phase of a product or process. It assesses how design elements might fail and their potential effects on the overall systems.
- *Process FMEA* – concentrates on potential failures in the manufacturing or operational processes; it helps identify process-related failures and their effects on the product or service being produced
- *System FMEA* – examines the interactions between various subsystems or components within a larger system. It is particularly useful when analyzing complex systems with interconnected parts.
- *Functional FMEA* – focuses on the functions of a system or process and identifies potential failures in meeting those functional requirements. It helps ensure that the system or process functions as intended.
- *Maintenance FMEA* – concentrates on potential failures related to maintenance activities. It helps identify failure modes that may occur during maintenance and their impact on system reliability and supportability.
- *Service FMEA* – focuses on potential failures in service industries, such as healthcare, finance, or hospitality. It helps identify failure modes that may impact the delivery of services to customers.

By integrating FMEA into the Lean Six Sigma framework, you can enhance the effectiveness of your project process improvements efforts. With its structured framework and by using its proactive planning current and potential failures can be dealt with during process execution vice after-the-fact.

USING CORRECTIVE ACTION MATRICES TO DRIVE ACCOUNTABILITY

A corrective action matrix (CAM) is a valuable tool in driving planning and accountability within any DMAIC-driven Lean Six Sigma initiative. These matrices help identify and address issues, track corrective actions, and assign responsibilities. Figure 12.17 provides an example of a format that can be tailored to the situation, much like the FMEA format.

Here are some suggestions on how to use the corrective action matrix effectively to drive accountability.

1 Clearly identify the problem – Clearly define the problem or issue that needs corrective action. Ensure that the problem is well understood by all stakeholders.
2 Create the corrective action matrix – like the FMEA, the CAM is tailored to the situation. However, there are some essential elements that should be included regardless of area applied:
   a Problem statement – A brief description of the problem clearly stated.
   b Responsible party – Identify the person or team responsible for implementing the action.
   c Action steps – What is the plan to resolve the problem?
   d Status – What is the current status?

Heavy Lift LLC

John M. Longshore, D.B.A.
Professor of Management
David B. O'Maley College of Business
1 Aerospace Boulevard
Daytona Beach, Florida 32114
386-226-6696

Corrective Action Matrix

Prepared by: Dr. Angela Cheatham   **Date:**

PROBLEM STATEMENT	RESPONSIBLE PARTY	ACTION STEPS	STATUS	DUE DATES	DESIRED OUTCOMES
A shortage of Personnel Protective Equipment (PPE) for WC 105 Cadmium Plating shift 2.	Adolphus Parker and Schultz	• Schedule meeting with supplier. • Research alternative PPE brands and suppliers. • Create a tracking system for PPE inventory and usage.	☑ In progress ☐ Completed ☐ Not started ☐ Overdue ☐ Needs Review ☑ Approved	ASAP	PPE will be fully stocked and available for all employees every shift.

Figure 12.17 Example of a Corrective Action Matrix

   e Due date – if immediate action is required, then ensure the responsible party is alerted to the urgency.
   f Desired outcomes – what is ultimately required?
3 Regularly review progress – schedule regular reviews of the CAM and monitor the status of each action item, then address any delays or roadblocks promptly.
4 Communicate – maintain open communication channels among team members and stakeholders. Encourage transparency and the reporting of challenges.
5 Provide support and resources – ensure that individuals or teams have the necessary resources to complete assigned corrective actions.
6 Celebrate success – acknowledge and celebrate the successful completion of corrective actions. Reinforce a culture of accountability and continuous improvement.

By creating and consistently applying the corrective action matrix and following the previous steps, you, your team, and your organization can foster a culture of accountability, address issues proactively, and continually enhance operations. Like almost all instruments used in Lean Six Sigma, the CAM is a living document that requires regular review and continual updating to be optimally effective.

IMPROVE TOLLGATE REVIEW

The Improve phase in Lean Six Sigma is focused on identifying and implementing solutions to address the root causes of the issues identified during the Measure and Analyze phases. Tollgates are checkpoints or milestones that ensure the project is on track and progressing effectively. The following are typical requirements for the Improve phase tollgate.

- Completed failure mode and effects analysis – ensure that a comprehensive FMEA has been conducted to identify potential failure modes, their causes, and their effects on the process.
- Solution selection – clearly define criteria used to evaluate and select potential solutions. Document the selected solution and provide a rationale for why it was chosen.
- Pilot implementation plan – develop a detailed plan for piloting the selected solution in a controlled environment. Clearly outline the pilot objectives, scope, timeline, and success criteria.
- Data collection plan for pilot – establish a plan to collect relevant data during the pilot phase to assess the effectiveness of the solution.
- Risk mitigation plan – identify potential risks associated with the implementation of the solution. Develop a plan to mitigate these risks and address any potential obstacles.
- Implementation plan – provide a detailed plan for the full-scale implementation of the solution. Include a timeline, resource requirements, and key milestones.
- Verification of solution effectiveness – establish criteria and methods for verifying that the implemented solution effectively addresses the identified problem. Define key performance indicators to measure success.
- Statistical analysis – conduct statistical analyses to validate the impact of the implemented solution. Use statistical tools to compare data before and after implementation.
- Stakeholder communication plan – develop a communication plan to keep stakeholders informed about the progress of the improvement project. Clearly articulate the benefits achieved and any changes to existing processes.
- Lessons learned – document lessons learned during the Improve phase to inform future projects. Capture insights on what worked well and areas for improvement in the approach.

Remember that the specific requirements may vary depending on the organization and the nature of the improvement project. Customizing is appropriate based on the unique characteristics of the project and the organization. The overall goal is to ensure successful implementation of the solution.

SUMMARY

Chapter 12 began with a discussion on how to gather the best ideas to fix the problem observed. It addressed how to use benchmarking studies that measure and compare usability metrics against the baseline. It stressed that during the execution of a Lean Six Sigma project, these are performed regularly and that each iteration should be so designed in structured phases starting with an evaluation of the current state. Benchmarking was then addressed and a comparative analysis conducted, followed by a strategic prognosis. The chapter then presented to the reader a process for facilitating effective brainstorming. They were shown how to develop a plan, create an agenda, and define a shared space that was as clear and specific as possible. The chapter then showed the reader how to set ground rules so that all participants were comfortable and knew how to participate. They were then introduced to the topic of multi-voting. The reader learned that this process allows a team to quickly come to consensus on the relative importance of issues, problems, and solutions by accounting for individual importance rankings in a team's final priorities. The chapter then engaged the reader via a discussion of error-proofing, which was defined to implement process changes to prevent root cause errors. Two strategies were presented that the reader can use in this process: the first being a weighted criteria matrix and the second an impact effort matrix. The chapter then presented to the reader methods by which constraints could be analyzed and resolved by using the theory of constraints methodology. Cellular processing and the reduction of changeover time and setup time were then addressed. This discussion was followed by a review of process mapping, emphasizing value stream mapping. A discussion was then conducted on the impact of modeling where assessing risk using failures modes and effects analysis and corrective action matrices was discussed. The chapter concluded with an Improve phase tollgate review.

LEAN SIX SIGMA IN ACTION

Logo: Lean six sigma

Starbucks is known for its fresh coffee and baked goods. They are also advocates of Lean Six Sigma techniques. As reported in a recent article in the *Wall Street Journal*, they are running Kaizen events to help them optimize the movement of baked goods. In a recent Kaizen event, the team discovered that carrying newly delivered baked goods from the delivery receiving area to the pastry case took as many as 50 round trips. The total elapsed cycle time was one hour and 18 minutes. To speed up the process, rolling carts have been added. The carts allow them to move several trays at once, which has reduced the elapsed cycle time by 42%.

Other changes made through Kaizen team events have centered on "error proofing". Bins of coffee were being kept on top of the counter for easy access and aligned in trays by roast type. However, because each coffee package is almost identical packaging and size, when a barista selected a type and returned it to a tray, it was often returned to the wrong tray. This error often was not detected, and different roasts were often mixed, which often resulted in customer complaints. Now packages are color coded so that a barista can find a particular roast without having to read a label. In addition, to make it easy to select the right type of cream additive for the coffee and eliminate errors, pitchers of soy, nonfat, and low-fat milk are labeled with different-colored type.

CHAPTER 12 DISCUSSION QUESTIONS

1. Define and briefly describe the Improve phase of the DMAIC methodology.
2. Define and briefly discuss the importance of conducting benchmarking studies.
3. Why is effective brainstorming such an important part of the Improve phase of the DMAIC methodology?
4. Define and describe of the following brainstorming techniques:
   a. Mind-mapping technique
   b. Nominal group technique
   c. Delphi technique
5. Define and briefly discuss the importance of error proofing in the prevention of root cause errors.
6. Define and briefly describe the following
   a. The improvement solution set matrix
   b. Weighted criteria matrix
   c. Impact and effort matrix
7. Define and briefly discuss the theory of constraints.
8. Briefly explain how using cellular processing and reducing changeover and setup time can improve process flow.
9. Define FMEA. What is it used for Lean Six Sigma initiatives?

BIBLIOGRAPHY

Adebanjo, Dotun, Ahmed Abbas, and Robin Mann. "An investigation of the adoption and implementation of benchmarking." *International Journal of Operations & Production Management* 30.11 (2010): 1140–1169.

Anand, R. Vijay, and M. Dinakaran. "Multi-voting and binary search tree-based requirements prioritisation for e-service software project development." *Electronic Government, an International Journal* 13.2 (2017): 111–128.

Barber, Elizabeth, and Frances Miley. "Monitoring project progress: More than a series of feedback loops." In *Australasian Evaluation Society International Conference*, Vol. 30, 2002, pp. 1–9.

Barsalou, Matthew A. *Root Cause Analysis: A Step-by-Step Guide to Using the Right Tool at the Right Time*. CRC Press, 2014.

Bevilacqua, Maurizio, et al. "A changeover time reduction through an integration of lean practices: A case study from pharmaceutical sector." *Assembly Automation* 35.1 (2015): 22–34.

Bhattacharjee, Pushparenu, Vidyut Dey, and U. K. Mandal. "Risk assessment by failure mode and effects analysis (FMEA) using an interval number based logistic regression model." *Safety Science* 132 (2020): 104967.

Boland, Tony, and Alan Fowler. "A systems perspective of performance management in public sector organisations." *International Journal of Public Sector Management* 13.5 (2000): 417–446.

Byron, Kevin. "Creative reflections on brainstorming." *London Review of Education* 10.2 (2012): 201–213. https://doi.org/10.1080/14748460.2012.691284.

Cagliero, Roberto, et al. "Prioritising CAP intervention needs: An improved cumulative voting approach." *Sustainability* 13.7 (2021): 3997.

Cakmakci, Mehmet. "Process improvement: Performance analysis of the setup time reduction-SMED in the automobile industry." *The International Journal of Advanced Manufacturing Technology* 41 (2009): 168–179.

Chandel, Rohit, and Santosh Kumar. "Productivity enhancement using DMAIC approach: A case study." *International Journal of Enhanced Research in Science, Technology & Engineering* 5.1 (2016): 112–116.

Chao, Lawrence P., and Kosuke Ishii. "Design process error-proofing: Strategies for reducing quality loss in product development." *ASME International Mechanical Engineering Congress and Exposition* 42150 (2005).

Chua, David K. H., and Myriam Godinot. "Use of a WBS matrix to improve interface management in projects." *Journal of Construction Engineering and Management* 132.1 (2006): 67–79.

Chua, David K. H., L. J. Shen, and S. H. Bok. "Constraint-based planning with integrated production scheduler over internet." *Journal of Construction Engineering and Management* 129.3 (2003): 293–301.

Claunch, J. "SetupTime reduction to enhance cell performance and flexibility." In *Handbook of Cellular Manufacturing Systems*. John Wiley & Sons, Inc., 1999, p. 155. https://pdfcoffee.com/-handbook-of-cellular-manufacturing-systems-1999-pdf-free.html

Cooke, David L., and Thomas R. Rohleder. "Inventory evaluation and product slate management in large-scale continuous process industries." *Journal of Operations Management* 24.3 (2006): 235–249.

Danesh, Darius, Michael J. Ryan, and Alireza Abbasi. "A systematic comparison of multi-criteria decision making methods for the improvement of project portfolio management in complex organisations." *International Journal of Management and Decision Making* 16.3 (2017): 280–320.

Dwi, Dwi Susanti, Diah Puspaningrum, and Bakti Fatwa Anbiya. "Analysis of the utilization of mindmeister visual organizer application in building students' critical thinking in Islamic religious education learning." *JOTTER: Journal of Teacher Training and Educational Research* 1.2 (2023): 69–75.

Ehie, Ike, and Chwen Sheu. "Integrating six sigma and theory of constraints for continuous improvement: A case study." *Journal of Manufacturing Technology Management* 16.5 (2005): 542–553.

Fawcett, Stanley E., and John N. Pearson. "Understanding and applying constraint management in Today's." *Production and Inventory Management Journal* 32.3 (1991): 46.

Ferradás, Pablo Guzmán, and Konstantinos Salonitis. "Improving changeover time: A tailored SMED approach for welding cells." *Procedia CIRP* 7 (2013): 598–603.

Goldsby, Thomas J., and Sebastián J. García-Dastugue. "The manufacturing flow management process." *The International Journal of Logistics Management* 14.2 (2003): 33–52.

Gupta, Mahesh C., and Lynn H. Boyd. "Theory of constraints: A theory for operations management." *International Journal of Operations & Production Management* 28.10 (2008): 991–1012.

Hanafin, Sinéad. "Review of literature on the Delphi Technique." *Dublin: National Children's Office* (2004): 1–51.

Herrera, Marcos, Jesus Mur, and Manuel Ruiz. "A comparison study on criteria to select the most adequate weighting matrix." *Entropy* 21.2 (2019): 160.

Hinckley, C. Martin. *Make No Mistake!: An Outcome-Based Approach to Mistake-Proofing*. CRC Press, 2001.

Ilbahar, Esra, Cengiz Kahraman, and Selcuk Cebi. "Evaluation of sustainable energy planning scenarios with a new approach based on FCM, WASPAS and impact effort matrix." *Environment, Development and Sustainability* 25.10 (2023): 11931–11955.

Jan, Shu-Hui, and S. Ping Ho. "Construction project buffer management in scheduling planning and control." In *2006 Proceedings of the 23rd International Symposium on Robotics and Automation in Construction*, 2006, pp. 858–863. https://www.researchgate.net/profile/S-Ho-2/publication/268285930_Construction_Project_Buffer_Management_in_Scheduling_Planning_and_Control/links/54d79ce50cf2970e4e74957f/Construction-Project-Buffer-Management-in-Scheduling-Planning-and-Control.pdf

Kaid, Husam, et al. "Six sigma DMAIC phases application in Y company: A case study." *International Journal of Collaborative Enterprise* 5.3–4 (2016): 181–197.

Kangavari, Mehdi, et al. "An application of failure mode and effect analysis (FMEA) to assess risks in petrochemical industry in Iran." *Iranian Journal of Health, Safety and Environment* 2.2 (2015): 257–263.

Kaylani, Manal Qtishat Prof Anmar. "The Status Quo of crisis management implementation in Jordanian Public Secondary Schools in Amman, according to impact effort matrix, from the point of view of its school leaders." *Journal of Education and Practice* (2020). https://www.researchgate.net/publication/365605906_The_Status_Quo_of_Crisis_Management_Implementation_in_Jordanian_Public_Secondary_Schools_in_Amman_According_to_Impact_Effort_Matrix_from_the_Point_of_View_of_its_School_Leaders_Publication_date#full-text

Kramer, Thomas J., Gerard P. Fleming, and Scott M. Mannis. "Improving face-to-face brainstorming through modeling and facilitation." *Small Group Research* 32.5 (2001): 533–557.

Kyrö, Paula. "Revising the concept and forms of benchmarking." *Benchmarking: An International Journal* 10.3 (2003): 210–225.

Lee, Jun-Huei, et al. "Research on enhancement of TOC simplified drum-buffer-rope system using novel generic procedures." *Expert Systems with Applications* 37.5 (2010): 3747–3754.

Li, Miqing, and Xin Yao. "Quality evaluation of solution sets in multiobjective optimisation: A survey." *ACM Computing Surveys (CSUR)* 52.2 (2019): 1–38.

Li, Zheng, and Liam O'Brien. "Towards effort estimation for web service compositions using classification matrix." *Australian National University* 3.3/4 (2010): 1–16.

Liu, Hu-Chen, Long Liu, and Nan Liu. "Risk evaluation approaches in failure mode and effects analysis: A literature review." *Expert Systems with Applications* 40.2 (2013): 828–838.

Malcolm, H. A., et al. "Selecting zones in a marine park: Early systematic planning improves cost-efficiency; combining habitat and biotic data improves effectiveness." *Ocean & Coastal Management* 59 (2012): 1–12.

Maller, Patricio, et al. "New practices to structure and elicit improvement opportunities in scientific software development teams." In *2012 12th International Conference on Computational Science and Its Applications*. IEEE, 2012.

Mandal, Pathik. "Improving process improvement: Executing the analyze and improve phases of DMAIC better." *International Journal of Lean Six Sigma* 3.3 (2012): 231–250.

McMillan, Sara S., Michelle King, and Mary P. Tully. "How to use the nominal group and Delphi techniques." *International Journal of Clinical Pharmacy* 38 (2016): 655–662.

Mullen, Rosemary, et al. "A practical guide to the systematic application of nominal group technique." *Nurse Researcher* 29.1 (2021).

Nießl, Christina, et al. "Over-optimism in benchmark studies and the multiplicity of design and analysis options when interpreting their results." *Wiley Interdisciplinary Reviews: Data Mining and Knowledge Discovery* 12.2 (2022): e1441.

Odu, G. O. "Weighting methods for multi-criteria decision making technique." *Journal of Applied Sciences and Environmental Management* 23.8 (2019): 1449–1457.

Offner, Anne K., Thomas J. Kramer, and Joel P. Winter. "The effects of facilitation, recording, and pauses on group brainstorming." *Small Group Research* 27.2 (1996): 283–298.

Okes, Duke. *Root Cause Analysis: The Core of Problem Solving and Corrective Action*. Quality Press, 2019.

Rahman, Shams-ur. "Theory of constraints: A review of the philosophy and its applications." *International Journal of Operations & Production Management* 18.4 (1998): 336–355.

Ritter, Simone M., and Nel M. Mostert. "How to facilitate a brainstorming session: The effect of idea generation techniques and of group brainstorm after individual brainstorm." *Creative Industries Journal* 11.3 (2018): 263–277.

Roszkowska, Ewa. "Rank ordering criteria weighting methods–a comparative overview." *Optimum Studia Ekonomiczne* 5.65 (2013): 14–33.

Rother, Mike, and Rick Harris. *Creating Continuous Flow: An Action Guide for Managers, Engineers & Production Associates*. Lean Enterprise Institute, 2001.

Schragenheim, Eli. *Management Dilemmas: The Theory of Constraints Approach to Problem Identification and Solutions*. CRC Press, 1998.

Sehrawat, Rasna. "Exploring mindmeister as an effective mind mapping tool for online classes to enhance critical thinking skills in learners at K-12 level." *The 4th International Conference on Education 2021*. Prince of Songkla Universtiy, 2021. https://www.researchgate.net/profile/Abdullahi-Yunusa/publication/351478515_THE_MODERATING_EFFECTS_OF_GENDER_AND_AGE_ON_STUDENTS'_SATISFACTION_AND_LEARNING_WITHIN_AN_E-LEARNING_ENVIRONMENT_IN_NIGERIA/links/60bb472892851cb13d7aafa1/THE-MODERATING-EFFECTS-

Subriadi, Apol Pribadi, and Nina Fadilah Najwa. "The consistency analysis of failure mode and effect analysis (FMEA) in information technology risk assessment." *Heliyon* 6.1 (2020).

Sutia, Sabar, et al. "Benefit of benchmarking methods in several industries: A systematic literature review." *Systematic Reviews in Pharmacy* 11.8 (2020).

Terninko, John. "Reliability/mistake-proofing using failure mode and effect analysis (FMEA)." In *ASQ World Conference on Quality and Improvement Proceedings*. Vol. 57. American Society for Quality, 2003.

Thangaratinam, Shakila, and Charles W. E. Redman. "The delphi technique." *The Obstetrician & Gynaecologist* 7.2 (2005): 120–125.

Waller, Matthew A., and Terry L. Esper. *The Definitive Guide to Inventory Management: Principles and Strategies for the Efficient Flow of Inventory Across the Supply Chain*. Pearson Education, 2014.

Williams, Patricia L., and Christine Webb. "The Delphi technique: A methodological discussion." *Journal of Advanced Nursing* 19.1 (1994): 180–186.

Yuan, Kuo-Jung, Sheng-Hung Chang, and Rong-Kwei Li. "Enhancement of theory of constraints replenishment using a novel generic buffer management procedure." *International Journal of Production Research* 41.4 (2003): 725–740.

Zohrehvandi, S., and R. Soltani. "Project scheduling and buffer management: A comprehensive review and future directions." *Journal of Project Management* 7.2 (2022): 121–132.

Part VI

The Control Phase of DMAIC

13
Establishing a Process Management System

LEARNING OBJECTIVES

1 Describe the purpose of the DMAIC cycle's Control phase and the importance of a process management system.
2 Interpret control chart patterns and recommend actions based on that interpretation.
3 Identify different types of visual control techniques and explain how they improve process management.
4 Discuss how applying 5S techniques and total productive maintenance enhances process management.
5 Explain the components of standard work, the importance of documenting standard work, and the significance of transferring responsibility, including the three plans essential for successful completion.

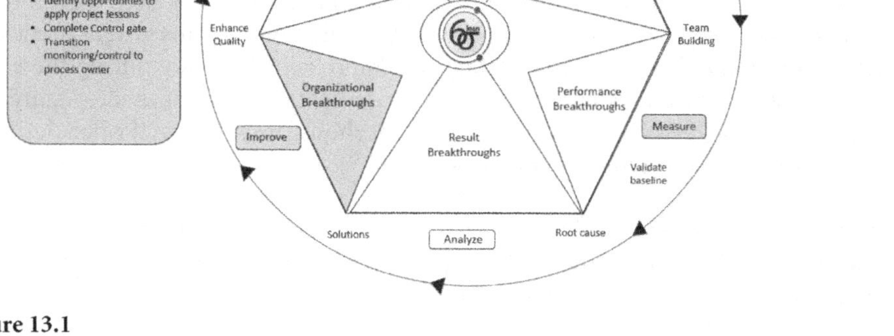

Figure 13.1

DOI: 10.4324/9781032650531-19

THE CONTROL PHASE OF DMAIC

In the DMAIC methodology, the Control phase is the final stage of the process improvement cycle. The primary goal of the Control phase is to sustain the improvements made during the previous phases and ensure that the process remains stable and within the desired performance parameters. Key activities and elements involved in the Control phase are:

- *Developing control plans* – this involves creating detailed plans that outline how the process will be monitored and controlled going forward. Control plans may include key metrics, process controls, and responsibilities for maintaining the improvements.
- *Implementing statistical process control (SPC)* – SPC tools are often used to monitor process performance. SPC involves the use statistical techniques to assess and control process variation, ensuring that the process stays within acceptable limits.
- *Establishing standard operating procedures (SOPs)* – documenting and implementing standard operating procedures helps to institutionalize the changes made during the Improve phase. SOPs provide clear guidelines for how the process should be executed to maintain the desired improvements.
- *Training and knowledge transfer* – ensure that the individuals responsible for the process are trained on the new procedures and are aware of their roles and responsibilities in maintaining the improvements. Knowledge transfer is crucial to sustain the gains achieved during the improvement initiative.
- *Monitoring and measurement* – regularly monitor key process metrics and performance indicators to verify that the process remains in control. This may involve using control charts, dashboards, and other monitoring tools to quickly identify any deviations from the desired performance.
- *Response planning* – develop plans for how to respond if the process starts to deviate from the desired performance. This may involve predefined actions to bring the process back into control or trigger a corrective action plan.
- *Continuous improvement* – while the DMAIC methodology cycle formally ends with the Control phase, the concept of continuous improvement is ingrained throughout the methodology. Teams should continue to assess the process and look for additional opportunities for improvement.

ESTABLISHING A PROCESS MANAGEMENT SYSTEM

The Control phase is centered around monitoring the ongoing process operation and executing a response. To accomplish this, the aforementioned key activities and elements are housed within a *process management system framework*. This system framework is designed to monitor, control, and sustain the improvements made during the earlier stages of a system operations after process improvements have been made. Figure 13.2 illustrates 12 proven key steps and components that should be considered when designing this process management system framework.

Step 1. Define key metrics and performance indicators – identify and define the critical metrics used to measure the process's performance. Ensure that these metrics align with the project goals and are relevant to customer requirements.

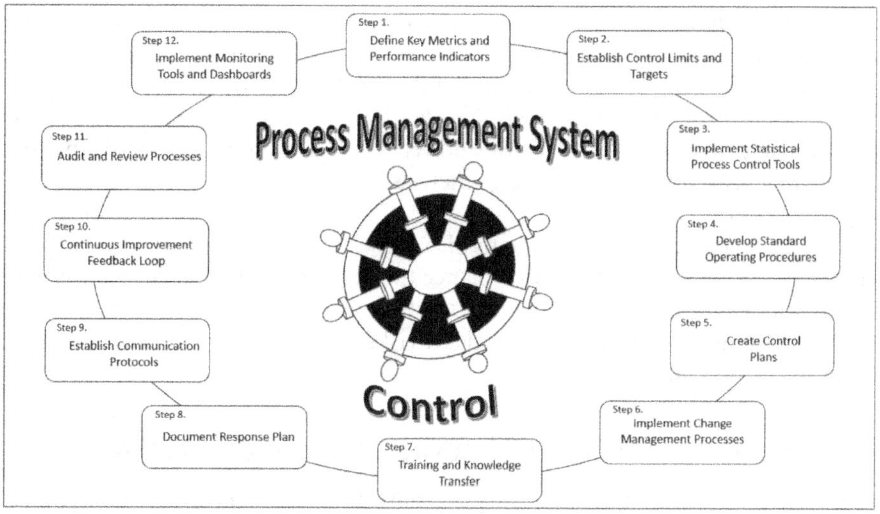

Figure 13.2 Control Phase Process Management System Framework

Step 2. Establish control limits and targets – set control limits for the key metrics based on historical data and acceptable variation. Define target values that represent the desired performance levels for each metric.

Step 3. Implement statistical process control tools – choose appropriate SPC tools, such as control charts, to monitor process stability and detect any unusual patterns or trends. Train team members on how to interpret and use SPC tools effectively.

Step 4. Develop standard operating procedures – document the improved process in detail, including step-by-step procedures, roles, and responsibilities, and any specific guidelines. Ensure that all team members are trained on the updated SOPs.

Step 5. Create control plans – develop comprehensive control plans that outline how the process will be managed. Ensure that details about monitoring frequency, data collection methods and responsibilities for each control activity are included.

Step 6. Implement change management processes – establish a formal change management process to handle any modifications to the process in the future. Ensure that changes are thoroughly assessed for potential impact on performance and that appropriate approvals are obtained.

Step 7. Training and knowledge transfer – conduct training sessions to transfer knowledge about the new processes and control measures to all relevant personnel. Develop training materials and resources to support ongoing education.

Step 8. Document response plans – define clear response plans for addressing deviations from the desired performance. Identify triggers that indicate when corrective actions or adjustments to the process are necessary.

Step 9. Establish communication protocols – define communication channels and protocols for disseminating information about the process performance. Establish a reporting cadence to keep stakeholders informed about key metrics and improvements.

Step 10. Continuous feedback loop – integrate a continuous improvement feedback loop into the process management system. Encourage team members to provide insight and suggestions for further enhancements.

Step 11. Audit and review processes – regularly audit processes to ensure they comply with established standards and procedures. Schedule periodic reviews to assess the effectiveness of the control measures and identify areas for refinement.

Step 12. Implement monitoring tools and dashboards – utilize technology and tools to automate data collection, analysis, and reporting. Develop dashboards that provide real-time visibility into key process metrics.

By incorporating Control phase key activities and elements into a robust 12-step process management system framework, you enhance the likelihood of sustaining improvements and maintaining a controlled, efficient, and effective process. This systematic approach helps organizations adapt to changes, mitigate risks, and continuously optimize their processes for better outcomes.

VERIFYING IMPROVEMENTS THROUGH CONTROL CHARTING

Control charting is a key tool used in the Control phase of the DMAIC methodology. Control charts help monitor and verify process stability over time by graphically displaying process data and identifying any trends or patterns that may indicate special cause variation. Here are some suggestions as to how control charting can be used to verify improvements during the Control phase:

- *Select relevant metrics – choose the key ones identified during the Measure and Analyze phases.* These metrics should be critical to the process and aligned with your project goals.
- *Gather data* – collect data points for the selected metrics. Ensure that the data is representative of the process performance.
- *Determine control limits* – calculate limits based on historical data or statistical methods. Control limits represent the range of variation expected in a stable process.
- *Create control charts* – plot the collected data on control charts. Common types of control charts include $\bar{X}$ charts for measuring the central tendency of a process and *R* charts for measuring process variability.
- *Analyze patterns and trends* – analyze the control charts for any patterns or trends. Look for points outside the control chart limits, runs, or shifts that may indicate special cause variation.

Figure 13.3 illustrates instructions on how to create a simple control chart using Excel and some common patterns that you would likely run into during Control phase monitoring.

- *Rule out common causes* – investigate any points outside the control limits to determine whether they are due to common causes (inherent in the process) or special causes (indicating a change in the process).
- *Document outcomes* – document the outcomes of the analysis. If there are points outside the control limits, determine whether they require corrective action or if they are within the expected variation.
- *Implement corrective actions if required* – if special cause variation is identified, implement corrective action to address the root cause(s) and bring the process back into control.

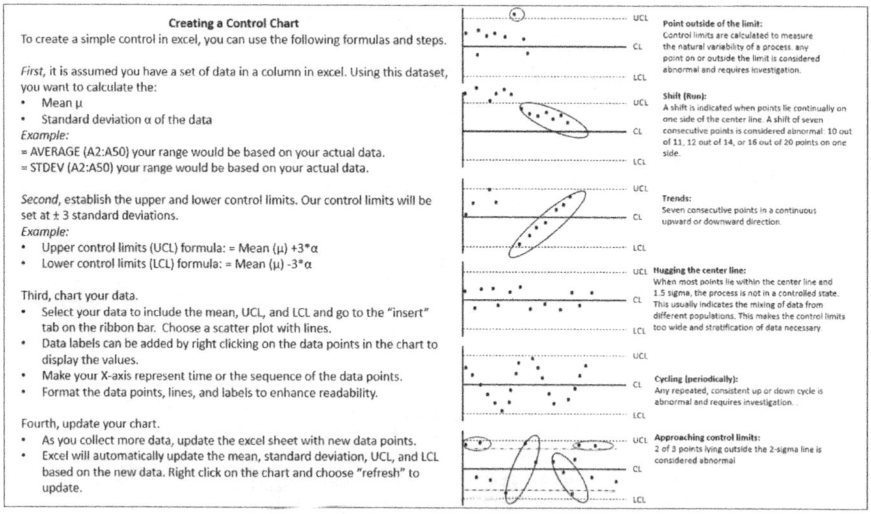

Figure 13.3 Simple Control Chart Using Excel and Reading Common Patterns

- *Continue to monitor* – continue to monitor the process using control charts over time. Regularly update the charts with new data to ensure ongoing control and stability.
- *Communicate results* – communicate the results of the control chart analysis to relevant stakeholders. Provide insights into the stability and performance of the improved process.
- *Adjust control limits if appropriate* – as the process stabilizes and performance improves, consider adjusting control limits based on the new level of variation.
- *Document any changes* – document all changes made to the process, control limits, or corrective actions taken. This documentation is essential for future reference and continuous improvement efforts.

By systemically applying control charting, you can ensure that the improvements achieved during the DMAIC methodology are not only implemented but sustained over the long term. Control charts provide a visual representation of process stability and help in making data-driven decisions to maintain a controlled and predictable process.

INSTITUTING VISUAL CONTROL TECHNIQUES TO IMPROVE PROCESS MANAGEMENT

Instituting visual control techniques during the Control phase of the DMAIC methodology involves implementing visual control tools and cues to enhance the understanding, monitoring, and management of the improved process. Visual controls make it easier for team members to comprehend complex information quickly and can aid in identifying deviations from the standard. Figure 13.4 illustrates some of the more common visual control techniques that can be used during the Control phase.

- *Process flowchart visuals* – develop and display process flowcharts that visually represent the steps of the improved process. This helps team members understand the overall workflow and the sequence of activities.

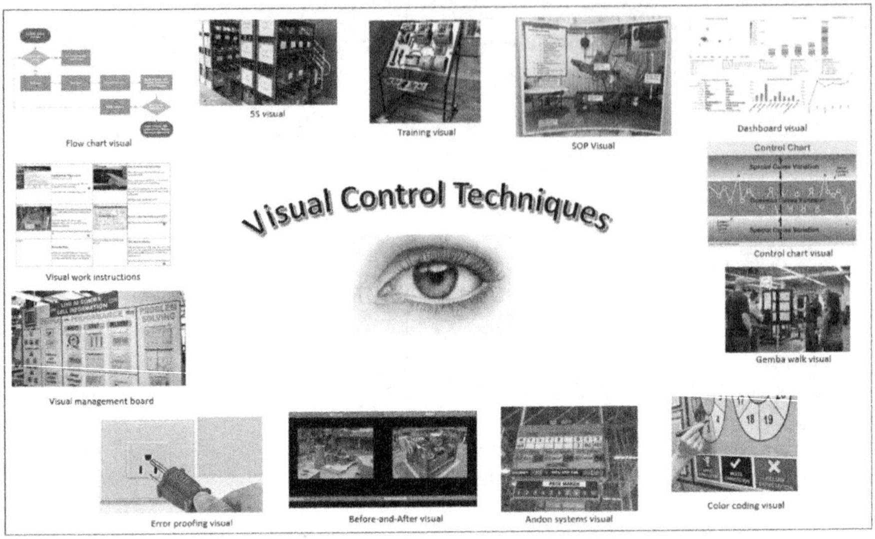

Figure 13.4 Visual Control Techniques

- *Standard operating procedure visuals* – create visual aids such as posters or infographics that summarize key points from the SOP. These visuals can serve as quick references for team members.
- *Visual work instruction* – use visual work instructions to guide employees through specific tasks. Include images, diagrams, or videos to illustrate the correct procedures visually.
- *Andon system visuals* – implement Andon systems to visually signal when there are issues or deviations from the standard. These can include lights, flags, or other visual indicators that immediately draw attention to a problem.
- *Control charts* – display control charts in easily accessible areas. This provides a visual representation of process performance over time, making it easier to identify trends, shifts, or outliers.
- *Dashboards* – create dashboards that consolidate key performance metrics. Dashboards provide a real-time snapshot of the process performance and highlight areas that may require attention.
- *Visual management boards* – establish visual management boards that communicate important information about the process, including goals, metrics, and performance against targets. Update these boards regularly to keep information current.
- *Color coding* – use color coding to quickly convey information about the status of a process or specific elements. As an example, green could indicate normal operations, while red may signal a problem.
- *5S visuals* – integrate visual cues into the workplace using the principles of 5S. Clearly mark locations for tools and materials and use visual indicators to show when items are in the correct place.
- *Error-proofing visuals* – implement visuals that help prevent errors. As an example, use color labels or shapes to ensure that the right components are used in a process.
- *Before-and-after visuals* – display visual comparisons of the process before and after improvement. This can serve as a motivating reminder of the positive changes achieved.

- *Training visuals* – develop visual training materials to support ongoing education. Visual aids can enhance the learning process and improve retention of information.
- *Gemba walk visuals* – conduct Gemba walks to visually inspect the workplace and verify that processes are being followed. Use this opportunity to engage with team members and identify areas for improvement.

By incorporating visual control techniques, you create a workplace that is more transparent, efficient, and responsive to changes. Visual controls simplify the monitoring and management of processes, making it easier for the team to maintain the improvements achieved during the Control phase of the DMAIC methodology.

APPLYING 5S TECHNIQUES IN THE WORKPLACE

Implementing 5S techniques during the Control Phase of the DMAIC methodology involves sustaining the improvements made in the workplace by focusing on organization, cleanliness, and standardization. The 5S methodology consists, as illustrated in Figure 13.5, of the following steps: Sort, Set in Order, Shine, Standardize, and Sustain.

1S Sort – the objective of Sort is to remove unnecessary items from the workplace to create a more organized and efficient environment. Activities that occur during this step include reviewing the current state of the workplace, identifying items that are not essential for daily operations, and removing unnecessary items and categorizing them appropriately as either "dispose of", "relocate", or "recycle".

2S Set in Order – the objective of Set in Order is to organize the remaining items after the "1S step" in a systematic way to improve accessibility and workflow. Activities that generally occur during this step are determining the optimal location for tools, equipment, and materials based on frequency of use and workflow. Also, labeling and the designation of specific storage areas for each item is done to facilitate easy retrieval.

3S Shine – the objective of Shine is to regularly clean and maintain the workplace to ensure a safe and efficient working environment. Activities that generally are

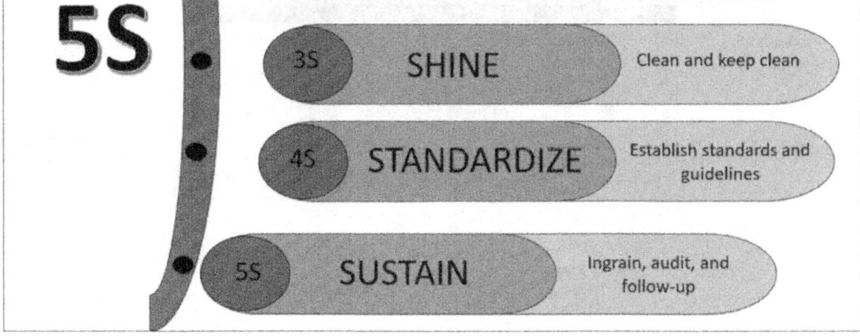

Figure 13.5 5S Methodology

completed during the step are: (1) the establishment of regular cleaning schedules for daily, weekly, and monthly tasks; (2) a plan and schedule for training and involving employees in maintaining cleanliness and order in the workplace; and (3) the implementation of visual controls to quickly identify and address cleanliness issues.

4S standardize – the objective of Standardize is to establish standardization processes and procedures to sustain the improvements made during the DMIAC cycle. Activities that generally occur during this step are (1) documentation capture and communications using a standardized process and procedure with visual aids, work instructions, or SOPs set in place; (2) employees are trained on standardized processes and procedures; and (3) regular reviews and updates of standards based on continuous improvement are set in place.

5S Sustain – the objective of Sustain is to instill a culture of continuous improvement and maintain the 5S practices over the long term. Activities during this step are the integration of 5S practices into the daily routine responsibilities. Conduct regular audits and inspections to ensure compliance with 5S standards. Recognize and reward employees for their contributions to maintaining a well-organized and efficient workplace.

By applying 5S techniques during the Control phase, you create a workplace culture that values organization, cleanliness, and efficiency. This contributes to the sustainability of process improvements and fosters a continuous improvement mindset among employees. Regular monitoring, training, and communication are key elements in ensuring the long-term success of 5S initiatives.

IMPLEMENTING TOTAL PRODUCTIVE MAINTENANCE

Implementing total productive maintenance (TPM) during the Control phase of the DMAIC methodology involves establishing a systematic approach to maintain and improve the effectiveness of equipment, machinery, and processes. TPM's objective is to maximize equipment efficiency, eliminate breakdowns, and involve all employees in the maintenance process. Figure 13.6 illustrates the eight pillars of TPM and a recommended 13-step process to aid you in implement TPM process.

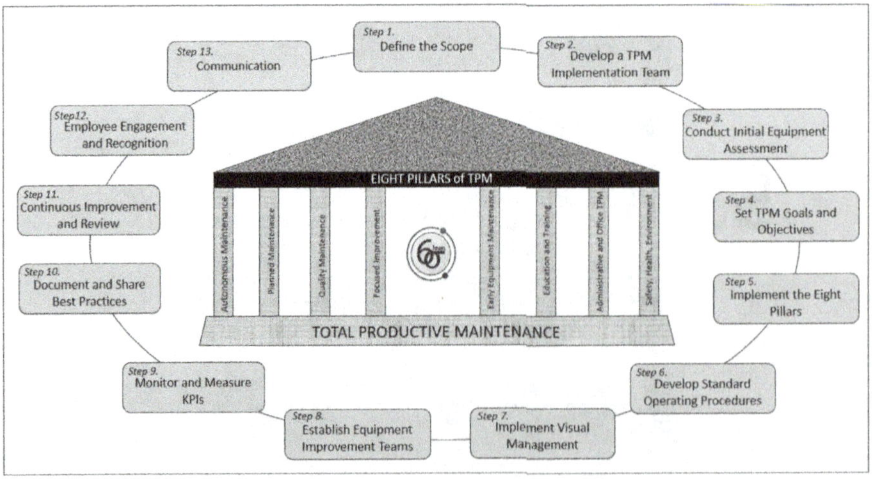

Figure 13.6 Eight Pillars of TPM with a 13-Step Implementation Process

Step 1. Define the scope – clearly define the scope of the TPM implementation. Identify the equipment and processes critical to the organization's overall operation and success.

Step 2. Develop a TPM implementation team – form a cross-functional team responsible for TPM implementation. Include representatives from maintenance, production, quality, and other relevant departments as required.

Step 3. Conduct initial equipment assessment – assess the current condition of equipment and machinery. Identify areas for improvement and prioritize actions based on criticality and impact on overall operations.

Step 4. Set TPM goals and objectives – define specific and measurable goals for TPM implementation. These goals may include reducing equipment downtime, increasing overall equipment effectiveness (OEE), and improving maintenance efficiency.

Step 5. *Implement the eight pillars of TPM* – adopt the pillars of TPM:

- *Autonomous maintenance* – empower operators to conduct routine maintenance tasks.
- *Planned maintenance* – schedule and perform maintenance activities based on a predetermined plan.
- *Quality maintenance* – focus on maintaining equipment to prevent quality defects.
- *Focused improvement* – encourage continuous improvement efforts to enhance equipment performance.
- *Early equipment management (EME)* – integrate maintenance considerations into the design and acquisition of new equipment.
- *Education and training* – train employees at all levels to ensure they have the skills and knowledge necessary for effective maintenance.
- *Administrative and office TPM* – extend TPM principles to administrative and office functions.
- *Safety, health, and environment (SHE)* – integrate safety and environmental considerations into maintenance activities.

Step 6. Develop standard operating procedures – document standard operating procedures for maintenance schedules. Ensure that these procedures are easily accessible and understandable.

Step 7. Implement visual management – use visual controls to communicate equipment status, maintenance schedules, and other relevant information. Visual management helps in quickly identifying issues and prompting accountability.

Step 8. Establish equipment improvement teams – create small teams focused on specific equipment or processes. These teams can work on continuous improvement initiatives and share best practices.

Step 9. *Monitor and measure key performance indicators* – define and track KPIs related to equipment reliability, OEE, maintenance costs, and other relevant metrics. Use these KPIs to assess the success of TPM implementation.

Step 10. Document and share best practices – encourage the documentation and sharing of best practices; create a knowledge-sharing culture where successful maintenance strategies and solutions are disseminated throughout the organization.

Step 11. Continuous improvement and review – establish a continuous improvement loop for TPM. Regularly review the effectiveness of TPM initiatives and adjust based on feedback and performance data.

Step 12. Employee engagement and recognition – recognize and celebrate the contributions of employees involved in TPM. Foster a culture of ownership and engagement in the maintenance process.

Step 13. Communication – maintain open communication channels to keep all stakeholders informed about TPM progress, challenges, and successes.

By incorporating TPM principles during the Control phase, organizations can enhance equipment reliability, reduce downtime, and optimize overall operational efficiency. TPM aligns with the DMAIC methodology's goal of sustaining improvements and ensures that maintenance practices are an integral part of the ongoing process management strategy.

ESTABLISH AND DOCUMENT STANDARD WORK

Establishing and documenting standard work during the Control phase of the DMAIC methodology is crucial for maintaining the improvements made in the process. Standard work refers to the documented, best-known way of performing a task or process to achieve consistent results. Figure 13.7 illustrates the components of standard work with the supporting elements. The following is a ten-step guide found effective in establishing a standard work system.

Step 1. Select key processes – identify the key processes that have been improved during the DMAIC cycle. Focus on those processes that have a significant impact on product quality, efficiency, or customer satisfaction.
Step 2. Define the scope of standard work – clearly define the scope of standard work. Specify the boundaries and objectives of the standard work documentation.
Step 3. Involve cross-functional teams – form a cross-functional team that includes representatives from different departments involved in the process. This would include operators, supervisors, quality assurance personnel, and other relevant stakeholders.
Step 4. Map the current process and identify best practices – document the current state of the process. Use process mapping techniques, such as flowcharts, to visualize the sequence of steps and activities involved. After assessing the current state, identify

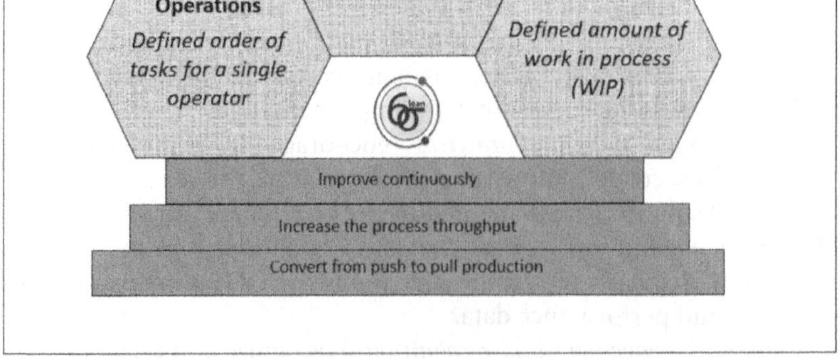

Figure 13.7 Components of Standard Work with Supporting Elements

and document the best-known way to perform the task within the process. Use input from experienced employees and subject matter experts (SMEs).

Step 5. Set standard work instructions and document key metrics – clearly define the steps, sequence, and methods for each task within the process. This includes equipment usage, cycle times, quality standards, and any other critical factors. Include key performance indicators and quality measures associated with the process.

Step 6. Include safety and compliance guidelines – integrate safety and compliance guidelines into the standard work documentation. Ensure all procedures adhere to safety standards and regulatory requirements.

Step 7. Review and validate and pilot implementation – conduct a thorough review of the standard work documentation with team members. Validate instructions by having team members perform the tasks and provide feedback. After assessing the feedback, implement the standard work on a small scale as a pilot. Monitor the process closely, and gather feedback from employees involved in the pilot.

Step 9. Incorporate change management and document version control – implement a change management plan to communicate any updates to the standard work. Establish a version control system to track changes and updates to the standard work. This helps maintain a clear record of the evolution of the process instruction.

Step 10. Measure and monitor performance – continuously measure and monitor performance against the defined KPIs. Use these metrics to assess the effectiveness of the standard work and identify opportunities for further improvement.

By following these steps, you can establish and document standard work that serves as a foundation for maintaining process improvement during the Control phase of the DMAIC methodology. Standard work provides a reference point for employees, supports consistent performance, and contributes to the overall stability of the improved process.

HANDOFF/TRANSFERRING RESPONSIBILITIES TO PROCESS OWNERS

Transferring responsibilities to the process owner is critical and often the most difficult aspect of the Control phase in the DMAIC methodology. A smooth transition of responsibilities helps ensure that the improvements achieved during the DMAIC cycle are institutionalized and sustained over the long term. Three types of planning processes are central to a seamless transitioning of process ownership: a transition(s) plan, a control(s) plan, and a response(s) plan. Figure 13.8 illustrates how each of these plans revolves around the transferring of responsibility to balance a smooth transfer of ownership.

Transition Planning

In the context of the DMAIC methodology, the *transition plan* is an integral part of the Control phase. It focuses on the smooth handover of the improved process from the project team to the process owners and operators. This ensures that the changes are sustained and integrated into the daily operations of the organization. Here are ten key elements to consider when developing a transition plan that have proved to aid in a smooth transferring of responsibility.

- *Document process changes* – clearly document all changes made to the process during the DMAIC phase, including modifications to procedures, workflows, and any new

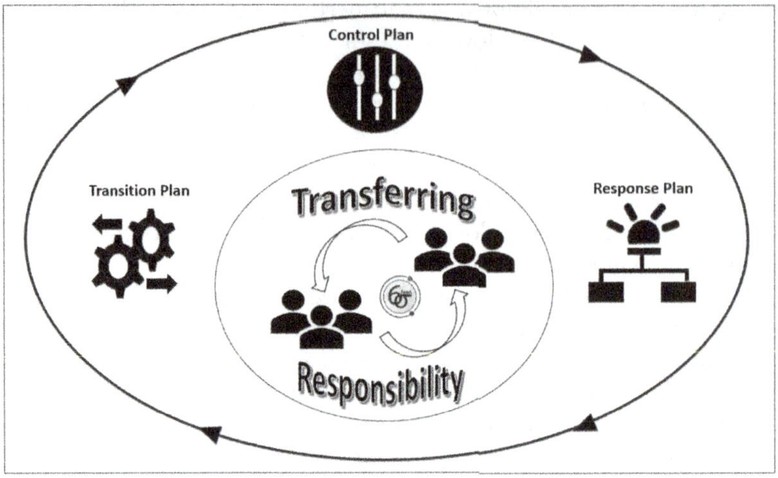

Figure 13.8 Transferring of Process Responsibility and Transitioning Plans

tools or technologies implemented. This documentation serves as a reference for process owners and operators.

- *Training and knowledge transfer* – develop a comprehensive training plan to ensure that process owners and operators are proficient in the updated process. This may involve conducting training sessions, creating training materials, and providing hands-on instruction. Knowledge transfer sessions between the project team and process owners is especially important.
- *Role and responsibility definition* – define roles and responsibilities of process owners, operators, and any other individuals involved in the ongoing execution of the process. This includes specifying who is responsible for monitoring key metrics, implementing the Control plan (covered in the next section), and responding to issues.
- *Communications plan* – develop a communication plan to keep all relevant stakeholders informed of the transfer process. This plan should include regular updates, milestones, and any changes to roles and responsibilities. Be transparent in your communications! It builds support for changes.
- *Pilot implementation* – consider a pilot implementation of the improved process in a controlled environment before full-scale deployment. This allows for the identification of any unforeseen issues and provides an opportunity to make adjustments before widespread implementation.
- *Performance monitoring* – establish a plan for ongoing performance monitoring to ensure that the process continues to meet its objectives. This generally involves using KPIs identified during the Measure and Analysis phases.
- *Feedback mechanism* – implement a feedback mechanism to capture input from process operators and other stakeholders. This feedback is used to identify areas for improvement, address any concerns, and ensure that the process remains effective and efficient.
- *Support and resources* – ensure that the necessary support and resources, including tools, technology, and personnel, are in place for the ongoing execution of the improved process. Additionally, address gaps or constraints that may impact a successful transition.

- *Contingency planning* – develop contingency plans for potential challenges or disruptions during the transition. This should include having backup procedures, alternative resources, and clear escalation paths when issues arise.
- *Post-implementation review* – schedule a post-implementation review to assess the success of the transition. Include an assessment of key metrics, feedback from stakeholders, and an analysis of the challenges encountered during the transition.

By incorporating these key elements into your transition plan, you increase the chances of a smoother handover of the improved process to owners and operators, promote sustainability, and maximize the long-term benefits of the DMAIC-driven project.

CONTROL PLANNING

Towards the conclusion of the Control phase of the DMAIC methodology, a *control plan* is developed as part of the transfer of responsibility to the process owner and/or operator. Its goal is to ensure that the improvements made during the DMAIC cycle are sustained over time and become a part of the regular business process. The control plan is a document that outlines the activities, responsibilities, and procedures to ensure the continued success of the improved process. The following are eight key elements that have proved effective in building a control plan that, if followed, can greatly aid in transferring responsibility.

- *Monitoring metrics* – define the key metrics that will be monitored to ensure the stability and performance of the improved process. These metrics are often the same as defined during the Measure phase, and they should defect rates, cycle time, customer satisfaction scores, and other relevant indicators.
- *Frequency of monitoring* – specify how often the identified metrics will be monitored. This should include daily, weekly, monthly, or as needed based on the nature of the process and the criticality of the metrics.
- *Control limits* – establish control limits for the monitored metrics. These are the statistical boundaries that indicate whether the process is in control or if there are signs of special cause variation that requires attention.
- *Response plan* – outlines specific actions to be taken if the monitored metrics go beyond the established control limits. This will involve investigating the cause of the variation, adjusting the process, or initiating corrective actions. (Note: this topic will be addressed in-depth in the following section.)
- *Documentation and reporting* – specify how data will be collected, documented, and reported. This ensures a systematic and standardized approach to tracking the process's performance.
- *Training and communication* – detail any ongoing training or communication plans to ensure all relevant personnel are aware of the changes made during the project and are equipped to maintain the improvements.
- *Clearly define roles and responsibilities* – clearly define the roles and responsibilities of individuals and teams responsible for the sustained success of the process.
- *Audit and review* – establish a schedule for regular reviews and audits of the control measures and processes to confirm they are effective and continue to meet the desired objectives.

By developing and implementing a comprehensive Control Plan, you and your team can institutionalize the improvements achieved through the DMAIC-driven project and ensure the long-term success and stability of the improved process.

RESPONSE PLANNING

A *response plan* is an essential component of the Control phase of the DMAIC cycle. It focuses on what actions should be taken if there are indications that the process is deviating from the desired performance. The response plan ensures that any issues are addressed promptly to prevent a return to the previous state. Here are ten proven key elements that should be considered when developing a response plan for your project.

- *Identification of signals* – define the signals or triggers that indicate a potential issue with the process. These signals should be based on the metrics identified during the Measure phase or any other KPIs.
- *Thresholds and control limits – establish clear thresholds and control limits for each signal.* These limits help differentiate between normal process variation and a situation requiring intervention.
- *Immediate actions* – specify the immediate actions to be taken when a signal surpasses the established control limits. These actions should include stopping the process, notifying relevant personnel, or implementing a temporary workaround.
- *Root cause analysis* – define a systematic approach for conducting a root cause analysis when a signal indicates a problem. This involves identifying the underlying cause(s) of the deviation from the desired performance.
- *Corrective actions* – outline a set of predefined corrective actions based on the identified root causes. These actions should be designed to address the specific issues causing the process deviation.
- *Communication plan* – develop a communication plan that outlines how and when information about process deviations and corrective actions will be communicated to relevant stakeholders.
- *Escalation procedures* – define an escalation procedure for situations where the predefined corrective actions are not effective or when the impact of the issue is significant. This ensures that higher-level management or additional resources can be involved when required.
- *Documentation and reporting* – establish a system for documenting all incidents, responses, and corrective actions. Regularly reporting on the effectiveness of the response plan helps continuous improvement and adjustment of the plan as needed.
- *Training and awareness* – ensure that personnel involved in the process are trained on the response plan and are aware of their roles and responsibilities. Training should include simulation exercises to practice the response to potential issues.
- *Continuous improvement* – build a mechanism for continuous improvement into the response plan. Regularly review the effectiveness of the plan and update it based on lessons learned and changes in the process or when new information is added.

By having a well-defined and documented response plan, you and your team can react swiftly to deviations in the controlled process and minimize the impact on overall performance. This type of proactive approach is crucial for maintaining the gains achieved during the DMAIC cycle.

CONTROL PHASE TOLLGATE REVIEW

The Control phase is the fifth and final phase of the DMAIC cycle, where the focus is on sustaining the improvements made during the DMAIC methodology execution. The tollgate review in the Control phase is designed to ensure the overall project has achieved its objectives and that the improvements are sustainable. Key elements and requirements for the Control phase tollgate review are:

1. *Project documentation review*:
   - Ensure that all project documentation is complete and up to date.
   - Review the project charter, scope, and objective to verify that they have been met.
   - Assess the accuracy and completeness of data collected during the earlier phases.
2. *Control plan implementation*:
   - Verify the control plan developed in the Improve phase has been fully implemented.
   - Check that the monitoring and control mechanisms are in place to sustain the improvements.
   - Ensure that the key process metrics are tracked and monitored regularly.
3. *Performance metrics:*
   - Evaluate the performance metrics to confirm that they meet the defined goals.
   - Compare current performance with baseline and target levels established during the Measurement and Analyze phases.
   - Assess whether there are any signs of deterioration in process performance.
4. *Statistical process control:*
   - Check if SPC charts are being utilized to monitor process stability.
   - Verify that the process is in control and that there are no special causes of variation.
   - Assess the effectiveness of control limits in identifying deviations.
5. *Training and skill development:*
   - Confirm that training programs have been conducted to process owners and operators.
   - Evaluate the effectiveness of training in ensuring the workforce can sustain the improvements.
6. *Standard operating procedures:*
   - Ensure that updated SOPs reflect the improved process that are in place.
   - Confirm that employees are following the new procedures and standards.
7. *Risk assessment and mitigation:*
   - Review the risk assessment conducted during the earlier phases.
   - Assess whether mitigation strategies have been effective in addressing identified risks.
8. *Communication plan:*
   - Evaluate the communication plan to ensure that key stakeholders are informed of the project outcomes and changes.
   - Confirm that a feedback mechanism is in place for continuous improvement.
9. *Customer and stakeholder satisfaction:*
   - Gather feedback from process stakeholders to assess their satisfaction with the improved process.
   - Address any concerns or issues during this feedback process.

10 *Lessons learned:*
- Document and review lessons learned from the project.
- Identify areas for improvement in future projects based on the current project's experience.

11 *Project closure:*
- Confirm that all project activities are completed and that the project can be officially closed.
- Transfer responsibility for the improved process to the process owner and/or operator.

SUMMARY

Chapter 13 started by defining what the DMAIC methodology Control phase is composed of and how it serves as a single reference point for understanding process characteristics, specifications, and standard operating procedures through a process management system. It then went into the procedures for verifying improvements through control charting and then, by illustration, how using visual control techniques can greatly improve process management. The reader was then walked through the process of using a 5S methodology to initiate a Lean Six Sigma project that can achieve optimal organization buy-in and then shown how using total productive maintenance and standard work methodologies can pay long-lasting dividends. Communications and instituting best practices were then addressed, followed by a discussion on how the finished Lean Six Sigma project can effectively be handed off, including the transfer of responsibilities to process owners. The chapter then concluded with a Control phase tollgate review.

LEAN SIX SIGMA IN ACTION!

The Importance of Training and Communication in Transferring Responsibility

John has just been hired as a color separator in a printing company that has just completed a DMAIC-driven process improvement program. John was familiar with the many types of separators within the shop, and each type had gone through the DMAIC process improvement cycle, meaning that each separator process needed to be relearned because of these improvement steps.

The Black Belt in charge of the transition team assured John that a process transition training program was in place. However, John's first day at work was a disaster. He was assigned to separator 3 and told to "run it". When he explained to the supervisor that he needed some training on the new process improvements on the machine, the supervisor grudgingly asked a fellow employee to spend 15 minutes with John. Wanting to get back to her machine, the other employee gave a quick five-minute run-through, and John was on his own.

John made many mistakes that first night, and production was lost. His supervisor now thinks John will not make it through his probationary period.

How has this affected John? What has been the effect of this transfer of responsibility for the separator process improvements on the shop? How has this affected the organization as a whole?

How has this affected John?

John stands a good chance of being let go permanently, affecting his future employment opportunities.

What has been the effect of this transfer of responsibility for the separator process improvements on the shop?

- Resistance to the process improvement of the separators.
- Employee confusion.
- Productivity loss.
- Cost impact to the shop.

How has this affected the organization as a whole?

- Has a direct impact of the organization's hiring practices based on the decision made to release John.
- Direct impact of the quality:
    - Internal failure costs (waste of time and effort)
    - Intangible costs (employee satisfaction)
    - External failure costs (job incorrectly done)

CHAPTER 13 DISCUSSION QUESTIONS

1 Define and briefly describe the key activities and elements involved in the Control phase of DMAIC.
2 Define and briefly describe a process management system.
3 How are control charting and the institution of visual control techniques alike and different?
4 Define and describe the following:
   a 5S technique
   b Total productive maintenance
   c Standard work
5 Define and describe transition planning and control planning in the context of transferring process responsibility.

BIBLIOGRAPHY

Benneyan, James C. "Design, use, and performance of statistical control charts for clinical process improvement." *Northeastern University, Boston MA* 12 (2001).

Benneyan, James C. "The design, selection, and performance of statistical control charts for healthcare process improvement." *International Journal of Six Sigma and Competitive Advantage* 4.3 (2008): 209–239.

Blanchard, Benjamin S. "An enhanced approach for implementing total productive maintenance in the manufacturing environment." *Journal of Quality in Maintenance Engineering* 3.2 (1997): 69–80.

Box, Simon, and Ken Platts. "Business process management: Establishing and maintaining project alignment." *Business Process Management Journal* 11.4 (2005): 370–387.

Brady, Denise Ann. *Using Visual Management to Improve Transparency in Planning and Control in Construction*. University of Salford (United Kingdom), 2014.

Carson, Monty L., and L. O. Levine. *Visual Operations Control in Administrative Environments*. No. PNL-SA-25156; CONF-950282-5. Pacific Northwest National Lab. (PNNL), Richland, WA, 1995.

Celik, Metin. "Establishing an integrated process management system (IPMS) in ship management companies." *Expert Systems with Applications* 36.4 (2009): 8152–8171.

Chapman, Stephen N. *The Fundamentals of Production Planning and Control*. Upper Saddle River, NJ: Pearson/Prentice Hall, 2006.

Choudri, Adi. "Design for six sigma for aerospace applications." In *Space 2004 Conference and Exhibit*, 2004. https://arc.aiaa.org/doi/pdf/10.2514/6.2004-6127

Fang, Chao, et al. "An integrated framework for risk response planning under resource constraints in large engineering projects." *IEEE Transactions on Engineering Management* 60.3 (2013): 627–639.

Gapp, Rod, Ron Fisher, and Kaoru Kobayashi. "Implementing 5S within a Japanese context: An integrated management system." *Management Decision* 46.4 (2008): 565–579.

Gauri, Susanta Kumar, and Shankar Chakraborty. "Recognition of control chart patterns using improved selection of features." *Computers & Industrial Engineering* 56.4 (2009): 1577–1588.

Georgakopoulos, Diimitrios, Mark Hornick, and Amit Sheth. "An overview of workflow management: From process modeling to workflow automation infrastructure." *Distributed and Parallel Databases* 3 (1995): 119–153.

Ghiani, Gianpaolo, Gilbert Laporte, and Roberto Musmanno. *Introduction to Logistics Systems Planning and Control*. John Wiley & Sons, 2004.

Girmanová, Lenka, et al. "Application of six sigma using DMAIC methodology in the process of product quality control in metallurgical operation." *Acta Technologica Agriculturae* 20.4 (2017): 104–109.

Gupta, Kapil. "A review on implementation of 5S for workplace management." *Journal of Applied Research on Industrial Engineering* 9.3 (2022).

Hammer, Michael. "What is business process management?" In *Handbook on Business Process Management 1: Introduction, Methods, and Information Systems*. Berlin and Heidelberg: Springer, 2014, pp. 3–16.

Hammer, Michael, and Steven Stanton. "How process enterprises really work." *Harvard Business Review* 77 (1999): 108–120.

Harsin, Paul. *Process Mastering: How to Establish and Document the Best Known Way to Do a Job*. Routledge, 2018.

Ireland, Frank, and Barrie G. Dale. "A study of total productive maintenance implementation." *Journal of Quality in Maintenance Engineering* 7.3 (2001): 183–192.

Islam, Syed Anwarul, et al. "Improving workplace by using 5'S tool-a typical application of sorting method." *International Journal of Services and Operations Management* 22.3 (2015): 323–335.

Kaid, Husam, et al. "Six sigma DMAIC phases application in Y company: A case study." *International Journal of Collaborative Enterprise* 5.3–4 (2016): 181–197.

Kioussi, Anastasia, et al. "Integrated documentation protocols enabling decision making in cultural heritage protection." *Journal of Cultural Heritage* 14.3 (2013): e141–e146.

Kobarne, Abhay R., et al. "Implementation of '5s' technique in a manufacturing organization: A case study." *Scholarly Research Journal For Interdisciplinary Studies* 3.23 (2016): 1851–1872.

Larsen, Michael Holm, and Ralf Klischewski. "Process ownership challenges in IT-enabled transformation of interorganizational business processes." In *37th Annual Hawaii International Conference on System Sciences, 2004. Proceedings of the*. IEEE, 2004.

Lee, David N. "A theory of visual control of braking based on information about time-to-collision." *Perception* 5.4 (1976): 437–459.

Ojutkangas, Anni. "Establishing process management: Case BillerudKorsnäs Finland Oy." Tampere University of Applied Sciences, 2016. https://www.theseus.fi/bitstream/handle/10024/115837/Ojutkangas_Anni.pdf?sequence=1

Prabu, K., et al. "Six sigma implementation through DMAIC: A case study." *International Journal of Process Management and Benchmarking* 3.3 (2013): 386–400.

Rennemo, Sigrid Johansen, et al. "A three-stage stochastic facility routing model for disaster response planning." *Transportation Research Part E: Logistics and Transportation Review* 62 (2014): 116–135.

Singh, Ranteshwar, et al. "Total productive maintenance (TPM) implementation in a machine shop: A case study." *Procedia Engineering* 51 (2013): 592–599.

Srinivasan, K., et al. "Six sigma through DMAIC phases: A literature review." *International Journal of Productivity and Quality Management* 17.2 (2016): 236–257.

Tabish, Muhammad. *Machine Vision Control Algorithm Design for Industrial Palletizing Robo Machines to Increase the Dynamic Stability by Real-Time Image Processing.* Diss. Victoria University, 2020.

Team, SCAMPI Upgrade. "Standard cmmi appraisal method for process improvement (scampi) a, version 1.3: Method definition document." In *Software Engineering Institute, Carnegie Mellon University, Tech. Rep. CMU/SEI-2011-HB-001*. Elsevier Science Direct, 2011. https://www.sciencedirect.com/science/article/pii/S2212017313002272

Vilminko-Heikkinen, Riikka, and Samuli Pekkola. "Changes in roles, responsibilities and ownership in organizing master data management." *International Journal of Information Management* 47 (2019): 76–87.

Westgard, James O. "Internal quality control: Planning and implementation strategies." *Annals of Clinical Biochemistry* 40.6 (2003): 593–611.

Woodall, William H., Benjamin M. Adams, and James C. Benneyan. "The use of control charts in healthcare." *Statistical Methods in Healthcare* (2012): 251–267.

Xiang, Zhang Tian, and Jeng Feng Chin. "Implementing total productive maintenance in a manufacturing small or medium-sized enterprise." *Journal of Industrial Engineering and Management (JIEM)* 14.2 (2021): 152–175.

Zairi, Mohamed. "Business process management: A boundaryless approach to modern competitiveness." *Business Process Management Journal* 3.1 (1997): 64–80.

Part VII

Technology Acceleration Through the Use of Lean Six Sigma in Aviation and Aerospace

14

The Case for Applying Lean Six Sigma to the Aviation and Aerospace Industry Design Process

LEARNING OBJECTIVES

1. Describe how the application of LSS in the aviation and aerospace industry drives technology acceleration.
2. Describe the difference between LSS, DFLSS, DMEDI, and DMADV.
3. Describe why the "assessment of current knowledge and skills" in the LSS step-by-step educational process is critical in educational process execution.
4. Describe the criteria for LSS certification progression.
5. Describe the significance of the building blocks of the Unified LSS BOK.
6. Describe the four structural cornerstones of the sustainability and collaborative management model.

INTRODUCTION

Lean Six Sigma is a methodology that combines the principles of Lean manufacturing and the Six Sigma DMAIC methodology to reduce waste, thereby accelerating the process and enhancing overall efficiency and effectiveness. In the context of the aviation and aerospace sectors, the application of LSS leads to technology acceleration through several key mechanisms. Figure 14.2 illustrates seven of these key mechanisms.

The first mechanism directly affected by LSS is *process optimization*. Here LSS focuses on identifying and eliminating waste in processes, thus reducing lead times by eliminating unnecessary steps in those processes and enhancing efficiency by streamlining workflows and non–value-added activities.

The second mechanism affected is *reduced defects and rework*. Through the application of the LSS DMAIC methodology, variation in processes is minimized. In aviation and aerospace, where safety and precision are paramount, minimizing error is crucial. By implementing LSS, these organizations can reduce defects in the design, manufacturing, and maintenance processes, leading to quicker development cycles and improving product quality.

Data-driven decision-making is the third mechanism affected through the implementation of LSS. Because LSS relies heavily on data analysis and statistical tools, it proves of

DOI: 10.4324/9781032650531-21

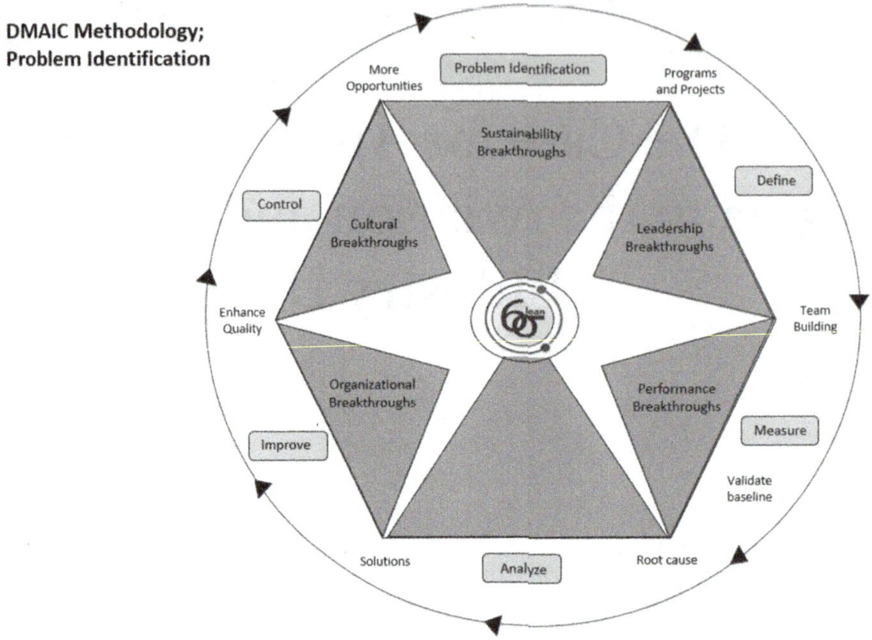

Figure 14.1 DMAIC Methodology: Problem Identification

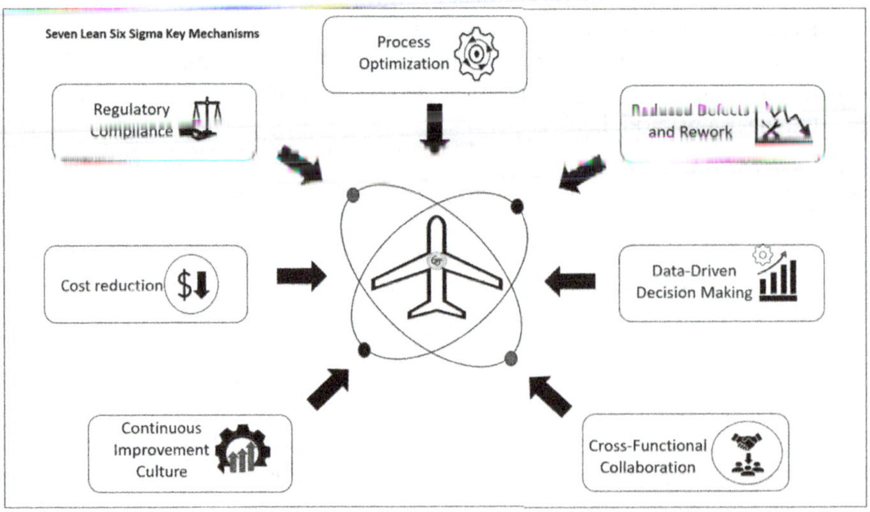

Figure 14.2 Seven Lean Six Sigma Key Mechanisms

immediate value within the aviation and aerospace environments where complex systems and components require rigorous analysis. Data-driven decision-making leads to more accurate predictions, improved risk management, and better resource allocation, all of which contribute to faster technology development.

The fourth mechanism affected is *cross-functional collaboration*. LSS encourages collaboration among different departments and functions within organizations. In aviation and aerospace, where interdisciplinary teams are common, this collaborative approach facilitates communication and knowledge sharing, faster problem-solving and innovation, and the breaking down of silos, thus ensuring teams work together seamlessly.

LSS instills a *culture of continuous improvement* as a fifth mechanism within the aviation and aerospace industries. In a rapidly evolving field like aviation and aerospace, the ability to adapt and improve continuously is crucial. Because the culture of LSS is one of continuous improvement, these organizations can better position themselves to stay ahead of technological advancements and respond quickly to market changes.

Cost reduction is the sixth mechanism affected by LSS implementation. LSS principles focus on eliminating unnecessary costs. By optimizing processes and reducing waste, aviation and aerospace organizations can allocate resources more efficiently, freeing up capital for research and development initiatives.

The seventh mechanism affected by the use of LSS within aviation and aerospace is *regulatory compliance.* In aviation and aerospace, adherence to stringent regulations is essential. LSS helps by establishing robust processes and documentation. It also aids by streamlining regulatory processes, thus accelerating the approval and certification of new technologies allowing them to be brought to market earlier.

The application of LSS principles in aviation and aerospace leads to more efficient processes, reduced time to market, improved product quality, and a culture of continuous improvement. All these factors contribute to technological acceleration in an industry where staying ahead is crucial for success.

APPLYING LEAN SIX SIGMA TO THE AVIATION AND AEROSPACE DESIGN PROCESS

The application of LSS to the design process in the aviation and aerospace industries offers a compelling case for improving efficiency, reducing costs, enhancing quality, and ensuring that products meet or exceed customer requirements.

Because LSS focuses on identifying and eliminating waste in processes, cost reduction can be achieved through streamlining the design process, reducing cost, which leads to cost-effective product development. Efficiency is improved via methods such as value stream mapping and continuous flow, where bottlenecks and inefficiencies are identified and corrected. Cycle time reduction and process optimization are also achieved, leading to faster time-to-market for aviation and aerospace products.

Through the DMAIC methodology, LSS is consistently applied throughout the design process, ensuring overall quality, and reliability is enhanced. By incorporating *customer feedback* into the design process, aviation and aerospace organizations enhance customer satisfaction, ensuring products align with expectations.

Because LSS is data driven, risk analysis and decision-making can be done early in the design stage. This helps identify potential issues and allows for proactive mitigation approaches to be exercised. Cross-functional collaboration is also optimized by bringing together teams from different departments to work collaboratively on design improvements. This interdisciplinary approach ensures a holistic view of product development and subsequently results in a reduction in design iterations.

Agility, flexibility, and adaptability are promoted through LSS. This enables aviation and aerospace organizations to better weather a constantly changing environment and meet unforeseen challenges. Supplier collaboration is also enhanced by this LSS-driven agility, flexibility, and adaptability. High-quality design practices ensure design planning is timely, and any changes are communicated timely and clearly, thus enabling the supplier to actively participate in the design process.

LSS additionally aids the aviation and aerospace industries in sustainability integration. This sector has historically faced challenges related to carbon emissions, noise pollution, and resource consumption. LSS, with its process improvement focus and waste reduction, is a prime enabler of sustainability integration.

IMPROVING DESIGN VELOCITY AND PRECISION WITHIN THE AVIATION AND AEROSPACE DOMAIN EMPLOYING DFLSS, DMEDI, AND DMADV

Improving system design velocity and precision within the aviation and aerospace industries involves integrating LSS principles into the early stages of the design process. This approach alone aims to enhance the speed, efficiency, and accuracy of the current system design while ensuring that the final product meets or exceeds customer requirements repeatedly.

There are, however, other LSS methodologies that warrant consideration when executing improvement initiatives that help aviation and aerospace organizations create new processes, products, or services. Figure 14.3 illustrates three of the more commonly employed ones.

Lean Six Sigma, of course, is a combination of Lean and Six Sigma methodologies, aiming to eliminate waste (Lean) and reduce variation (Six Sigma) in processes to improve efficiency and quality. It primarily follows the DMAIC framework, consisting of Define, Measure, Analyze, Improve, and Control phases. It is suitable for improving existing processes, products, or services.

Design for Lean Six Sigma is focused on designing new processes, products, or services that meet customer needs and are inherently efficient defect free. If follows the DMADV framework, emphasizing design aspects more than the DMAIC framework.

DMEDI is typically applied when an organization is looking to design and implement entirely new processes or products. It is commonly aligned with situations when radical

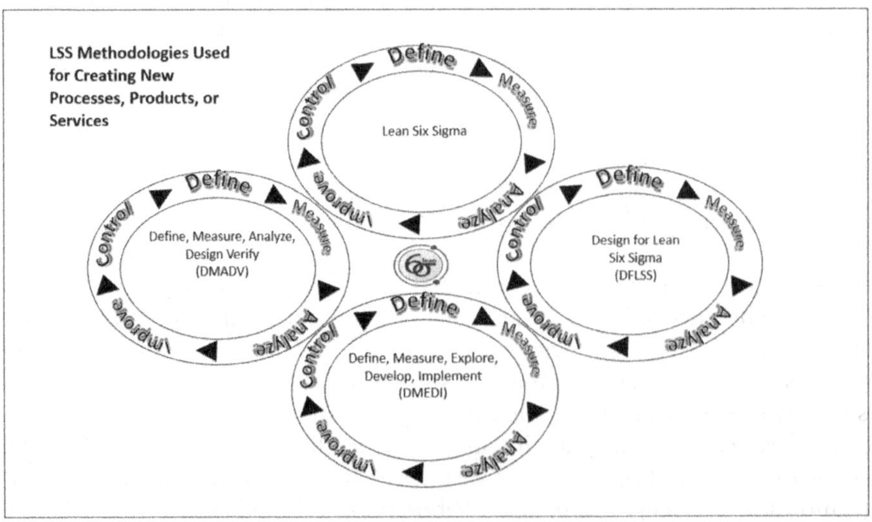

Figure 14.3 LSS Methodologies Used for Creating New Processes, Products, or Services

change and innovation are needed, such as introducing a new product, service, or process to the market.

DMADV is a set of steps used in the design phase of a project, with a focus on creating new processes, products, or services that meet customer requirements. Its phases are clearly defined:

Define – clearly define the project goals and customer requirements.
Measure – identify and measure critical-to-quality (CTQ) characteristics.
Analyze – analyze the data to develop design concepts.
Design – develop and optimize the detailed design of the process, product, or service.
Verify – validate the design through testing and pilot runs.

DMADV is commonly used when organizations embark on projects that involve significant change, such as introducing new products, services, or processes. It is a systematic approach to design and innovation within the LSS framework.

Establishing Lean Six Sigma as its core continuous improvement methodology and by combining the principles of DFLSS, DMEDI, and DMADV, aviation and aerospace organizations accelerate the development new processes, products, and services. These methodologies provide systematic and data-driven approaches, ensuring efficiency and precision in the rapidly evolving aviation and aerospace sector are firmly intrenched.

ENSURING THE AVIATION AND AEROSPACE PROFESSIONAL IS EDUCATED IN THE LEAN AND SIX SIGMA METHODOLOGY

Educating aviation and aerospace professionals in Lean Six Sigma involves a structured process to ensure effective learning and application of the principles and methodologies practiced in executing the LSS methodology. Figure 14.4 presents a step-by-step educational process that has been found effective in educating organizational members in the

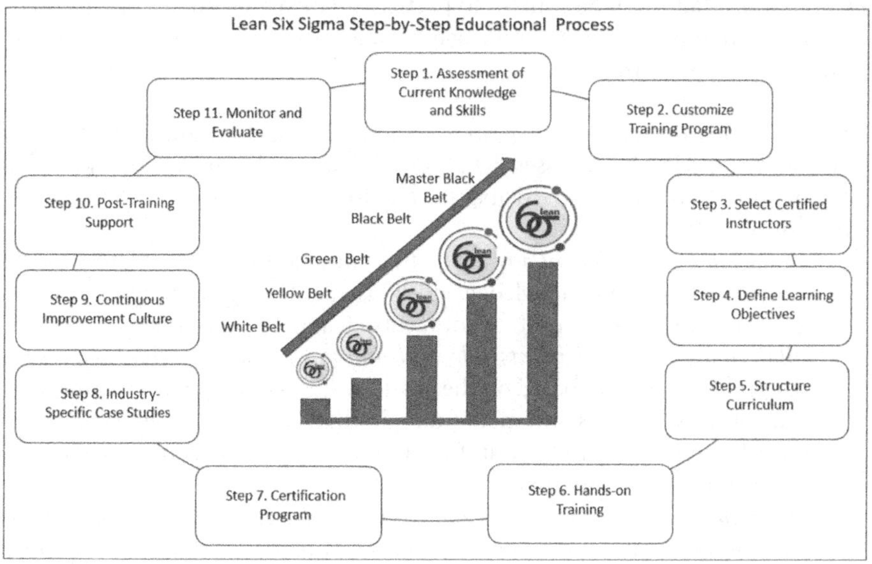

Figure 14.4 Lean Six Sigma Step-by-Step Educational Process

LSS methodology. This educational process is wrapped around a unifying Body of Knowledge that will be addressed in the following section.

- *Step 1. Assessment of current knowledge and skills* – assessing current knowledge and skills is an essential step in tailoring the LSS educational process. Some methods that have proved effective that can be used before initiating the LSS educational process:
  - *Self-assessment questionnaire and skills inventory* – provide participants with a questionnaire covering key LSS concepts and tools. Rate their familiarity and proficiency on a scale. Create a skills inventory of the participants to determine the appropriate projects.
  - *Pre-training test and interviews* – administer a pre-training test to assess the participant's understanding of LSS principles and methodologies. This could be multiple choice questions, case studies, or problem-solving exercises.
  - *Managerial input and observation of working* – seek input from the participant's manager or supervisor to understand their perspectives on the employee's current capabilities. If possible, observe the participants in their work environment to see how they approach problem-solving and process improvement.
  - *Portfolio review and group activities* – ask participants to submit a portfolio showcasing their past projects, highlighting their application of LSS principles and tools. Incorporate group activities or workshops at this assessment stage to observe how individuals collaborate and contribute to problem-solving.
  - *Feedback from peers and simulation exercises* – collect feedback from colleagues or team members who have worked with the participants on projects. Peer feedback can provide clear insight into teamwork, communication, and collaborative skills. Have participants engage in simulated LSS exercises to observe their problem-solving and analytical skills.

Once the assessment is complete, use the gathered information to customize the LSS educational program. Tailoring the content to participants' existing knowledge and skills will ensure that the training is relevant and engaging and meets the specific needs of the aviation and aerospace organization.

- *Step 2. Customize training program* – customizing an LSS educational program is crucial to ensuring it addresses the specific needs, goals, and existing knowledge of the organization and the participants. The following are customization steps that have proved effective.
  - *Conduct a need assessment and define training objectives* – review the results of the assessment of current knowledge and skills. Identify gaps, strengths, and areas for improvement based on participant feedback and self-assessment.
  - *Tailor content to participants role and adjust training duration and intensity* – customize the content based on the participants' role within the organization and focus of relevant tools and methodologies that align with their job responsibilities. Additionally, adjust the duration and intensity of the educational program to ensure it is realistic and manageable.
  - *Incorporate real-world examples and customize delivery methods* – use case studies and examples that resonate with the participants' area of responsibility, processes, and challenges. Customize the training delivery methods based on the learning preferences of the participants.

- *Provide advanced or refresher modules and integrate company-specific training processes* – when participants have varying levels of expertise, consider offering advanced modules for those with more experience and include refresher sessions for those who may need a review of fundamental LSS concepts.
- *Include collaborative opportunities and emphasize continuous improvement* – foster a collaborative learning environment by incorporating team projects or exercises. Stress the importance of continuous improvement and encourage participants to apply LSS principles in their everyday work. Provide resources for continuous learning beyond the formal educational program.
- *Offer post-educational support and evaluate and adjust* – provide resources, mentoring, or coaching after the training to support participants as they apply LSS concepts in their work. Create a forum for ongoing discussion and knowledge sharing. Continuously gather feedback during and after the educational program and use the feedback to evaluate the effectiveness of the program and adjust for future training initiatives.

By customizing the LSS educational program to the unique needs and context of the participants, aviation and aerospace organizations can maximize the impact of the training and enhance the application of LSS principles in their specific work environment.

- *Step 3. Select certified instructors* – selecting certified instructors for Lean Six Sigma educational courses is crucial to ensuring the delivery is high-quality and practical knowledge. The following are steps to consider when choosing certified instructors.
  - *Verify certification and assess industry experience* – ensure potential instructors hold recognized Lean Six Sigma certification. Common certifications include Green Belt, Black Belt, or Master Black Belt from reputable organizations such as the American Society for Quality (ASQ) or colleges and universities that are chartered as certificate awarding institutions such as Embry Riddle Aeronautical University (ERAU). After verifying the instructor's certification credentials, investigate the instructor's practical experience in applying LSS principles in real-world projects.
  - *Review teaching experience and check training experience* – evaluate the candidate's experience in delivering training and education content. Look for instructors who have a track record of effectively communicating complex concepts and engaging participants. Examine the instructor's background in instructional design, adult learning principles, or related fields. A strong foundation in education and training methodologies can contribute to the effectiveness of the training program.
  - *Seek recommendations and ensure alignment with learning objectives* – ask for recommendations or references from organizations or individuals who have previously engaged the instructor for LSS training. Confirm the instructor's expertise with the specific objectives of the Lean Six Sigma training program. Consider whether the instructor has experience in the industry or sector relevant to the participants.
  - *Evaluate communication skills and consider technology proficiency* – effective communication is critical for a successful training program. Assess the instructor's ability to convey complex clearly and engage participants. Additionally, assess the instructor's proficiency in using technology for virtual or blended learning environments. Ensure that the instructor can leverage online tools and platforms effectively if virtual training is part of the program.

- *Assess flexibility/adaptability and request a demo or sample session* – because LSS training involves changing the organization's culture and learning environments, look for instructors who are flexible, adaptable, and able to tailor their approach to meet the unique needs of the individuals who are going to drive the change effort.

By carefully evaluating these factors, organizations can select certified instructors who are well equipped to deliver impactful LSS educational training, contributing to the success of participants and the overall improvement initiatives within the organization.

- *Step 4. Define learning objectives* – defining clear and specific learning objectives is a crucial step in designing an effective LSS educational training program. Learning objectives serve as a roadmap, outlining the skills and knowledge participants are expected to gain by the end of the training period. The following are key components to consider when defining learning objectives for your LSS training.
  - *Aligning with organizational goals and be specific and measurable* – ensure that the learning objectives align with the overall strategic goals and objectives of the organization. Connect the training outcomes to the broader mission of implementing LSS for process improvement and operational excellence. Clearly articulate what participants should know or be able to do after completing the training. Use specific and measurable language to make the objectives tangible and assessable.
  - *Follow the SMART criteria* – ensure that learning objectives are Specific, Measurable, Achievable, Relevant, and Time-bound (SMART).
    - Specific: clearly define what participants should achieve.
    - Measurable: include criteria for assessing success.
    - Achievable: set realistic goals based on the participant's level and the training duration.
    - Relevant: ensure objectives are pertinent to the LSS principles and the participant's roles.
    - Time-bound – specify when participants are expected to achieve the objectives.
  - *Incorporate Bloom's Taxonomy* – apply Bloom's Taxonomy to create objectives that encompass various levels of cognitive skills.
    - Knowledge: remember LSS principles and terminology.
    - Comprehension: understand how LSSS tools and methodologies work.
    - Application: apply LSS concepts to real-world scenarios.
    - Analysis: analyze processes to identify improvement opportunities.
    - Synthesis: develop solutions using LSS methodologies.
    - Evaluation: assess the effectiveness of LSS interventions.
  - *Cover key LSS topics and promote practical application* – ensure that learning objectives cover key LSS topics, including DMAIC, statistical tools, process mapping, and problem-solving techniques. Emphasize objectives that encourage participants to apply LSS principles to real-world projects.
  - *Encourage collaboration and communication and include assessment criteria* – incorporate objectives that foster teamwork, effective communication, and collaboration among participants. Highlight the importance of sharing findings and insights with colleagues and stakeholders. Additionally, clearly define how the achievement of each learning objective will be assessed. Specify the criteria for success and the methods of evaluation, such as exams, project assessments, or other measurable indicators.

By thoughtfully defining objectives, aviation and aerospace organizations can create a focused and results-driven LSS educational training program that equips participants with the knowledge and skills needed to drive continuous improvement initiatives.

- *Step 5. Structure curriculum* – structuring curriculum for LSS educational training involves a systematic approach to cover key concepts and tools in a logical sequence. The following is a structure for a comprehensive LSS training program found effective in multiple applications.
  - *Module 1: Introduction to Lean Six Sigma*
    - *Overview*
      - Introduction to Lean and Six Sigma
      - Historical context and evolution
      - Integration of Lean and Six Sigma
    - *Key concepts:*
      - Define key terms and acronyms.
      - Understanding process improvement
    - *Importance in industry*
      - Case studies demonstrating successful LSS implementations.
      - Industry-specific examples
  - *Module 2: Fundamentals of Lean*
    - *Lean principles*
      - Explanation of core Lean principles
      - Identification waste and inefficiencies
      - Application of 5S methodology
    - *Value stream mapping*
      - Techniques for mapping and analyzing value streams
      - Identification of value-added and non–value-added activities
    - *Kaizen and continuous improvement*
      - Introduction to Kaizen events
      - Strategies for fostering a culture of continuous improvement
  - *Module 3: Fundamentals of Six Sigma*
    - *DMAIC methodology*
      - Overview of DMAIC framework
      - Explanation of each phase and its objective
    - *Understanding variation*
      - Concepts of common cause and special cause variation
      - Statistical overview
    - *Process capability*
      - Introduction to process capability and stability
      - Calculation and interpretation of capability indices
  - *Module 4: Define phase*
    - *Project selection and scoping*
      - Criteria for selecting LSS projects
      - Development of project charter and goals
    - *Stakeholder analysis*
      - Identification and analysis of stakeholders
      - Managing stakeholder expectations
    - *Voice of the customer (VOC)*

        - Techniques for capturing customer requirements.
        - Translation of VOC into project goals
- *Module 5. Measure phase*
    - *Process mapping*
        - Techniques for creating process maps
        - Flowcharting and SIPOC (suppliers, inputs, process, outputs, customer)
    - *Data collection*
        - Methods of effective data collection
        - Measurement systems analysis (MSA)
    - *Basic statistics for measurement*
        - Introduction to basic statistical tools (mean, standard deviation, etc.)
        - Use of statistical software
- *Module 6: Analyze phase*
    - *Root cause analysis*
        - Techniques for identifying root causes.
        - Ishikawa diagramming and 5 Whys analysis
    - *Hypothesis testing*
        - Overview of hypothesis testing
        - Practical application in process improvement
    - *Data-driven decision making*
        - Utilizing data to make informed decisions
        - Analytical techniques for process improvement
- *Module 7. Improve phase*
    - *Generating and selecting solutions*
        - Techniques for brainstorming and generating improvement ideas
        - Evaluation and selection of solutions
    - *Piloting and validating improvements*
        - Implementing changes on a small scale
        - Techniques for validation and assessing effectiveness
    - *Lean tools for improvement*
        - Introduction to lean tools like Kanban, poka-yoke, and VSM
- *Module 8. Control phase*
    - *Implementing and sustaining improvements*
        - Strategies for implementing changes on a larger scale
        - Building a sustainable process
    - *Control charts and monitoring*
        - Introduction to control charts
        - Monitoring and maintaining process stability
    - *Standardization and documentation*
        - Developing standard operating procedures
        - Documentation for continuous improvement
- *Module 9. Lean Six Sigma studies*
    - *Real-world examples*
        - Analysis of successful and unsuccessful LSS projects
        - Lessons learned and best practices
    - *Q&A and discussion*
        - Open forum for questions and discussions
        - Knowledge sharing among participants

- *Module 10. Examination and certification*
  - *Review key concepts*
    - Recap of essential LSS concepts
    - Preparation for the certification examination
  - *Assessment*
    - Certification examination covering key topics
    - Practical application or project assessment
  - *Certification process*
    - Issuance of LSS certificates

Remember to tailor the curriculum to the specific needs and context of the aviation and/or aerospace organization and the participants being trained. Adjust the duration of each module based on the depth of knowledge required and the participants' background.

- *Step 6. Hands-on training* – hands-on training is crucial for an LSS educational training programs, as it allows participants to apply theoretical concepts in real-world scenarios. The following are some tried and proved steps to structure hands-on training in the LSS educational program you design.
  - *Step 1. Select real projects and then define project charters* – identify real projects within the organization that align with LSS principles. Choose projects that have measurable outcomes and can make a significant impact on efficiency, quality, or cost reduction. For each selected project, guide participants in creating project charters. This involves clearly defining the problem, goals, and scope, stakeholders, and success criteria. This helps participants practice the Define phase of DMAIC.
  - *Step 2. Conduct process mapping and practice data collection and measurement* – facilitate process mapping sessions for the selected projects. Encourage participants to create current status maps and identify areas of waste and inefficiency. This corresponds to the Measure phase of DMAIC. Also, teach participants how to collect relevant data to measure the current performance of the processes being analyzed. This includes training on measurement system analysis (MSA) and the use of appropriate statistical tools.
  - *Step 3. Analyze data for root causes and conduct Kaizen event workshops* – guide participants through the analysis of collected data. Help them identify patterns, trends, and potential root causes of the identified issues. This corresponds to the Analyze phase of DMAIC. Organize Kaizen events where participants can implement quick and impactful changes in the process. This hands-on approach allows them to experience the Improve phase of DMAIC.
  - *Step 4. Implement changes and develop control plans* – support participants in implementing the changes identified during the Kaizen event workshops. This may involve creating an implementation plan, securing necessary resources, and executing the plan. Work with participants to develop control plans to ensure that the implemented changes are sustained over time. This includes defining key performance indicators (KPIs) and setting up monitoring systems.
  - *Step 5. Monitor and control, then document results and lessons learned* – train participants on the importance of ongoing monitoring and control. This involves using control charts, standard operating procedures, and regular audits to ensure the process stays on track. Guide participants in documenting the results of their projects, including quantifiable improvements and lessons learned.

- *Step 6. Share success stories and evaluate training impact* – provide a platform for participants to share their success stories and lessons learned. This fosters a culture of continuous improvement and allows for knowledge transfer among team members. Collect feedback from all participants to continuously improve their processes and share ongoing successes. This step reinforces the principles of LSS as an ongoing journey of improvement.
- *Step 7. Celebrate achievements* – acknowledge and celebrate the achievements of participants and the positive impact of their projects on the organization. This step is crucial because this recognition reinforces the value of LSS and motivates others to get involved.

Remember to customize the hands-on training based on the specific needs and context of your organization. Providing ongoing support, resources, and mentorship will further enhance the effectiveness of your LSS educational program.

- *Step 7. Certification program* – developing an LSS certification program involves structuring a comprehensive training curriculum and assessment process. The following is a guide that has proved effective in designing programs that have achieved certification status.
  - *Step 1. Define certification levels and establish prerequisites* – determine the different levels of LSS certification that align with the participants' roles and responsibilities. Common levels include White Belt (organizational orientation), Yellow Belt, Green Belt, and Black Belt, each representing different proficiency levels. Also, define the prerequisites for each certification level. For example, the Green belt certification would require completion of the Yellow belt certification, while a Black belt would require a Green Belt with extensive practical experience.
  - *Step 2. Design the curriculum and choose delivery modes* – develop a structured curriculum for each certification level. Outline the key topics, learning objectives, and duration of each module. Ensure the curriculum is based on the DMAIC methodology, Lean principle statistical tools, and practical application. Determine how the educational training will be delivered. Options include in-person workshops, virtual sessions, self-paced online modules, or a combination of these. Consider the needs of the target audience.
  - *Step 3.* Develop educational training materials and incorporate practical applications – create comprehensive training materials, including presentations, reference guides, and access to relevant software or tools. Ensure materials are clear, concise, and aligned with the certification objectives. Integrate hands-on exercises, simulations, and real-life projects into the curriculum. Practical application is essential for participants to demonstrate their understanding and skills in applying LSS principles.
  - *Step 4. Assessment, examination, and certification project* – design assessments and examinations to evaluate participants' understanding of the LSS methodologies. Consider an in-depth review with the participants during the training to gauge both their theoretical and practical understanding of the LSS methodology. A comprehensive examination would be administered to each participant at the conclusion of the training with a minimum established benchmark score, 70%. Additionally, participants would be required to complete an LSS project as part of their certification. This project should demonstrate their ability to apply the DMAIC methodology and produce measurable improvements in a real process.

- *Step 5. Final assessment/review and certification award* – conduct a final assessment to evaluate the participants' overall understanding and proficiency. Issue LSS certificates to participants who have successfully completed certification requirements.
- *Step 6. Post-certification support and monitor and evaluate program* – provide ongoing support and resources such as coaching and idea support during projects. There also could be additional training opportunities that could be offered as well as networking and knowledge sharing. Regularly monitor and evaluate the effectiveness of the certification program. Gather feedback from participants, mentors, and stakeholders to identify areas for improvement and refinement.

- *Step 8. Industry-specific case studies* – developing industry-specific case studies for LSS educational training is paramount to providing the participant with relevant aviation and aerospace examples that address specific challenges in this field. The following are sample LSS projects the author has performed over the years that warrant consideration when designing this educational training module.
- *Case study #1: Aircraft turnaround time reduction*
  - *Objective* – reduce the turnaround time for aircraft maintenance and ensure on-time departures.
    - *Challenges*
      - long wait times for maintenance tasks.
      - inefficient communication between ground crew and maintenance teams.
    - *LSS tools used*
      - Value stream mapping to identify bottlenecks.
      - 5S methodology for organizing workspaces.
      - DMAIC methodology to systematically improve processes.
    - *Results*
      - Reduced aircraft turnaround time by 20%.
      - 5S methodology for organizing workspace reduced material movement time by 12%.
      - On-time departure rate increased 22%.
- *Case study #2: Supply chain optimization*
  - *Objective* – streamline the supply chain process within Composite Fabrication Plant #2 that ensures timely availability of material flow to meet daily production requirements.
    - *Challenges*
      - Inconsistent lead times from Tier 1 and 2 suppliers.
      - Inventory management issues lead to stockouts.
    - *LSS tools used*
      - Just-in-time (JIT) principles.
      - Kanban system for inventory control.
      - Root cause analysis of supply chain disruptions.
    - *Results*
      - Reduced lead times by 30%.
      - Improved inventory accuracy by 22% and eliminated stockouts.
      - Improved Tier 1 and 2 response rates by 11%, with overall supply efficiency improvement of ~10%.
- *Case study #3: Aircraft engine overhaul*
  - *Objective* – enhance the efficiency of Marine Aircraft Group (MAG) 32 Intermediate Maintenance Activity (IMA) Aircraft engine overhaul processes.

    - *Challenges*
        - High turnaround time for engine overhauls.
        - Inconsistent quality in overhauled engines.
    - *LSS tools used*
        - DMAIC methodology for process improvement.
        - Failure mode and effects analysis (FMEA) for quality assurance.
        - Control charting for monitoring and maintaining process stability.
    - *Results*
        - Reduced overall engine overhaul time by 25%.
        - Improved first-pass engine quality by 31%.
        - Operational aircraft downtime due to engine rework reduced by 12%, resulting in 3% increase in system mission readiness.
- *Case study #4: Flight operations optimization*
    - *Objective* – to minimize fuel consumption and increase efficiency of Vertical Marine Attach Training (VMAT) squadron 203 AV8B aircraft and mission routing optimization.
        - *Challenges*
            - Inefficient flight route planning.
            - Sub-optimal fuel consumption rates.
        - *LSS tools used*
            - Value stream mapping for flight operations.
            - Statistical analysis for fuel consumption patterns.
            - Continuous improvement techniques for mission route optimization.
        - *Results*
            - Reduced fuel consumption by 15%.
            - Improved flight planning efficiency by 22% and increased flight training sort rate by 8%.
            - Overall cost savings and reduced environmental impact.
- *Case study #5: Aircraft washing process*
    - *Objective* – improve the efficiency of the Naval Aviation Rework Facility (NARF) aircraft washing process.
        - *Challenges*
            - Inconsistent cleaning times.
            - Issues with resource allocation.
        - *LSS tools used*
            - Time and motion studies for process analysis.
            - Value stream mapping for identifying waste and cycle time.
            - 5S methodology for work area organization.
        - *Results*
            - Standardization of cleaning processes improved individual washer efficiency by 12%.
            - Reduced overall cleaning time by 30%.
            - Improved resource allocation staff efficiency by ~7%.

These case studies can serve as practical examples for participants during Lean Six Sigma educational training sessions in the aviation and aerospace industry. They address specific challenges relevant to the sector while showcasing the application of the LSS methodology and tools that achieve measurable improvements.

- *Step 9. Continuous improvement culture* – creating a continuous improvement culture in aviation and aerospace organizations through LSS educational training involves fostering a mindset of ongoing enhancement, innovation, and efficiency. The following are some suggested steps that have proved successful in instilling this type of culture that you might want to try.
  - *Step 1. Leadership commitment and establish clear objectives* – commitment from top leadership that continuous improvement initiatives are prioritized and championed must be gained initially. To accomplish this, that same leadership should visibly support LSS principles and openly communicate the strategic importance of continuous improvement within the organization. Leaders should be encouraged to actively participate in improvement projects to reinforce the communication message. In conjunction with leadership commitment, objectives should be clearly communicated and the benefits of integrating LSS into the fabric of the organization. To do this, specific goals related to efficiency, quality, and cost reduction should be highlighted. Those same goals should also be connected to the overall strategic objectives and the expected outcomes of the LSS initiative communicated accordingly.
  - *Step 2. Develop a robust training program and create cross-functional teams* – all employees within the organization should be equipped with the knowledge and skills required to apply LSS methodologies. Educational training programs which reflect industry-specific content should be used as the foundation for the training. This content should be complemented with case studies and examples from the aviation aerospace sectors, and participants should be provided with ongoing training opportunities through cross-functional groups. This fosters a culture of open communication and idea generation.
  - *Step 3.* provide a supportive infrastructure with recognition and rewards – systems and tools that support a continuous improvement infrastructure should be firmly established. Visual management, Kanban boards, and Gemba walks should be routine occurrences without exceptions when establishing this infrastructure. Technology should also be leveraged for data collection, analysis, and project tracking. To complement this infrastructure initiative, a robust communication plan should be established to keep all employees informed about the infrastructure development and the continuous improvement path the organization has embarked on.
  - *Step 4. Iterative improvement and employee involvement* – encourage a mindset of continuous learning and iterative improvement among all organizational employees. Create forums for them to share ideas and suggestions. Empower them to identify and implement small-scale improvements in their daily work. Establish mechanisms for employees to directly participate in the decision-making process. All these initiatives foster a sense of ownership and involvement within the employee base that is crucial to making the cultural shift required for a successful LSS project implementation.
  - *Step 5. Sustain and reinforce* – ensure the LSS continuous improvement culture becomes ingrained in the organization's DNA. This requires a regular revisiting and updating of the educational training program, consistent reinforcement of the continuous improvement mindset through leadership messaging, and frequent celebrations of milestones and team accomplishments.

Organizations in the aviation and aerospace industries can create a culture of continuous improvement by following these steps, where Lean Six Sigma principles become integral to daily operations and decision-making processes.

- *Step 10. Post-training support* – post training support is crucial to ensure that employees in the aviation and aerospace industry can effectively apply LSS principles in their daily work. The following are some suggested steps that have proved effective in past projects for post-training support.
  - *Step 1.* Mentoring, coaching, and project guidance – assign experienced LSS practitioners as mentors during the Control phase of the DMAIC methodology. They can provide the ongoing coaching sessions needed for individuals and teams. Encourage training participants to apply LSS methodologies to their everyday work tasks. Offer guidance on project selection, charter development, and project execution.
  - *Step 2. Online resources and discussion forums* – establish an online repository of resources, templates, and reference materials. Provide access to e-modules if possible or webinars for continuous learning. Create online discussion forums as well. This will encourage participants to share challenges, ask questions, and seek advice.
  - *Step 3. Regular check-ins and refresher sessions* – conduct regular check-in sessions with participants post-training. Gather feedback on the application of LSS principles and identify challenges or roadblocks. Offer periodic refresher sessions to reinforce key concepts. Focus on specific tools or methodologies that participants may find challenging. This also helps address common misconceptions about the impact LSS has on the organization.
  - *Step 4. Recognition programs and integration with performance management* – implement recognition programs for outstanding LSS contributions. Acknowledge successful project completions or significant process improvements. Individually highlight those who consistently demonstrate a commitment to continuous improvement and align those LSS achievements with their performance evaluations. Use those performance metrics to assess the impact of organizational LSS initiatives.
- *Step 11. Monitor and evaluate* – monitoring and evaluating Lean Six Sigma education training in aviation and aerospace is essential to ensure that the program is effective, aligns with organizational goals, and delivers tangible improvements. Listed in the following are steps that have proved effective in monitoring and evaluating LSS educational training in multiple industries but are especially effective in the aviation and aerospace industries.
  - *Step 1. Define key performance indicators and baseline assessments* – identify specific KPIs related to the educational training effectiveness and impact. This may include project success rate, process improvement metrics, and participant satisfaction scores. Additionally, a baseline assessment before the educational training should be performed to understand the existing state. Measure current performance metrics, employee knowledge, and organizational processes.
  - *Step 2. Participant assessment and project impact metrics* – use pre- and post-educational training assessments to measure individual knowledge gain. Include practical assessments to evaluate the application of LSS tools. Also, track the impact of LSS projects initiated by trained participants. Measure improvement in key performance areas, such as cost reduction, cycle time reduction, and defect elimination.
  - *Step 3. Feedback mechanisms and post-training surveys* – implement feedback mechanisms for participants to share their experiences. Collect feedback on

educational training content, delivery, and most importantly value added. Use this feedback to adjust as needed to increase effectiveness.

- *Step 4. Time-to-value measurement and documentation of best practices* – measure the time it takes for LSS projects to deliver tangible value. Assess the efficiency of project execution and time-to-implementation for improvements. Document and share best practices identified during the educational training. Then establish a repository for successful project documentation and lessons learned.
- *Step 5. Strategic alignment assessment and sustainability of improvements* – evaluate the extent to which LSS initiatives align with the organization's strategic goals. Ensure that improvement efforts contribute directly to the organization's overall success. Assess the sustainability of improvements made through the LSS project. Monitor whether changes implemented during the project can be sustained over time.

By systematically monitoring and evaluating Lean Six Sigma educational training and its outcomes, organizations in the aviation and aerospace industry can continuously refine their approaches, ensure ongoing success, and maintain a commitment to continuous improvement.

ADAPTING A UNIFIED LEAN SIX SIGMA BODY OF KNOWLEDGE WITHIN AVIATION AND AEROSPACE INDUSTRIES

Adapting a unified Lean Six Sigma body of knowledge within the aviation and aerospace industries involves creating a standardized framework that integrates the principles, methodologies, and tools of LSS. This unified BOK ensures a consistent approach to process improvement, quality enhancement, and operational excellence across various functions within the industry. In the preceding section, the core of the step-by-step educational process was the progression ladder. Figure 14.5 illustrates the progression ladder resting upon the foundation of a unified BOK.

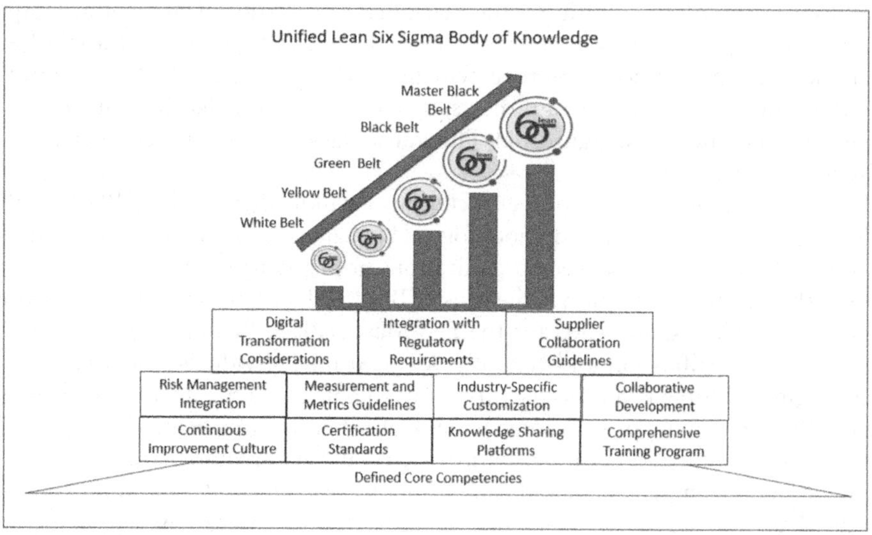

Figure 14.5 Unified Lean Six Sigma Body of Knowledge

The foundation of the unified Lean Six Sigma BOK is the defining of core criteria, competencies, and skills needed for professionals working within the aviation and aerospace sectors. The Lean Six Sigma BOK methodology utilizes a belt progression system to denote levels of expertise and responsibility.

The first level of qualification is the White Belt. The LSS White Belt certification is an introductory-level certification that provides a basic understanding of LSS principles and concepts. White Belts typically have a foundational knowledge of process improvement methodologies and may support improvement projects within their teams or organizations. Figure 14.6 illustrates White Belt criteria, competencies, and skill requirements.

These criteria, competencies and skill requirements represent common expectations for individuals seeking White-Level proficiency in the Lean Six Sigma methodology. However, these specific requirements for certification may vary between organizations and certification bodies.

The second level of qualification is the Yellow Belt certification. A Yellow Belt certification in LSS indicates a foundational understanding of the concepts and principles of the LSS methodology, with a focus on process improvement and problem solving. Yellow Belts generally are Kaizen team members who act in support of Green Belts and Black Belts. Figure 14.7 illustrates Yellow Belt criteria, competencies, and skill requirements.

Note that the requirements for Yellow Belt certification may vary between organizations and certifying bodies. Some may have additional criteria or variations in the certification process.

The third level of qualification is the Green Belt certification. The criteria, competencies, and skill requirements for the LSS Green Belt certification involve a deeper understanding of LSS concepts and methodologies compared to the Yellow Belt. Green Belts are expected to lead improvement projects within the organization and drive significant changes in processes to achieve measurable results. Figure 14.8 illustrates Green Belt criteria, competencies, and skill requirements.

The specific requirements for LSS Green Belt certification may vary between organizations or certifying bodies, but these criteria represent common expectations for individuals seeking Green Belt level proficiency in LSS methodology.

The fourth level of qualification is the Black Belt certification. The criteria, competencies, and skill requirements for the LSS Black Belt represent a significant level of expertise and leadership in process improvement methodologies. Black Belts are responsible for leading complex improvement projects, mentoring Green Belts and Yellow Belts, and driving strategic initiatives. Figure 14.9 illustrates Black Belt criteria, competencies, and skill requirements.

These criteria represent common expectations for individuals seeking Black Belt–level proficiency in Lean Six Sigma methodology. That said, specific requirements for Black Belt certification may vary between organizations or certifying bodies.

The fifth level of qualification is the Master Black Belt certification. The criteria, competencies, and skill requirements for the LSS Master Black Belt are the highest level of Lean Six Sigma certification and typically designed for individuals who will be leading and managing multiple LSS projects, providing guidance and mentoring Black Belts and Green Belts, and driving organization-wide deployment of LSS principles. Figure 14.10 illustrates Master Black Belt criteria, competencies, and skill requirements.

These criteria, competencies, and skill requirements represent common expectations for individuals seeking Master Black Belt–level proficiency in Lean Six Sigma methodology. Specific requirements, however, may vary by organization or certifying body.

White Belt Criteria, Competences, and Skill Requirements	
Training Requirements	Completion of a basic training program or workshop in LSS methodology. This training should cover introductory topics such as the fundamentals of LSS, the DMAIC methodology, basic problem-solving techniques, and an overview of key tools and concepts. White Belt training is shorter in duration compared to higher level certifications. It typically ranges from a few hours to a couple of days and can be offered as a self-paced online course of instruction virtual instructor-led training sessions.
Understanding of LSS concepts	Demonstration of basic knowledge and comprehension of LSS principles, including the concepts of waste reduction, process variation, customer focus, and continuous improvement. White Belts should understand the importance of data-driven decision-making and the role of teamwork in achieving process excellence.
Awareness of Improvement Projects	Awareness of ongoing LSS projects within their organization or team and a basic understanding of their objectives, scope, and impact. White Belts may be involved in supporting these projects by providing data, feedback, or assistance to project teams.
Participation in Improvement Activities	Involvement in basic improvement activities or initiatives within their areas of responsibility or influence. White Belts may participate in brainstorming sessions, process mapping exercises, or other activities aimed at identifying opportunities for improvement and implementing small-scale changes.
Examination or Assessment	Successful completion of a basic examination or assessment to evaluate understanding and retention of LSS concepts covered in the training program. The examination normally would cover fundamental principles, terminology, and basic problem-solving scenarios.
Application of Concepts	Application of LSS principles and tools to everyday work tasks or projects, demonstrating an understanding of how to apply continuous improvement concepts to improve processes, solve problems, and deliver value to customers.
Awearness of Roles and Responsibilities	Understanding of the roles and responsibilities of different stakeholders in LSS projects, including the roles of Green Belts, Black Belts, and Champions. White Belts should understand their role as contributors to the improvement process and how they can support the success improvement initiatives.
Certification Duration	White Belt certifications may have a validity period, after which re-certification or further training may be required to maintain certification status.

Figure 14.6 White Belt Criteria, Competencies, and Skill Requirements

Yellow Belt Criteria, Competences, and Skill Requirements	
Training Requirement	Completion of a formal training program in Lean Six Sigma which includes training in the use of the DMAIC (Define, Measure, Analyze, Improve, Control) methodology, process mapping with an emphasis on Value Stream Mapping (VSM), introduction to basic statistics and statistical tools, and root cause analaysis procedures. Yellow Belt training can occur in a workshop format over 3 to 4 days of intense training, often totaling 24-32 hours of instruction or, over an entire 16 week semesster as a stand-alone subject.
Understanding of Lean Six Sigma Concepts	Demonostrated understanding of fundamental LSS concepts, including identifying waste, defining customer requirments, measuring process performance, analyzing data, implementing improvements and sustaining results.
Participation in Improvement Projects	Participation in LSS proejects as a team member or supporting role, assiting in process improvement efforts, data collection, analysis, and implemtation of solutions under the guidance of a Green Belt or Black Belt.
Examination	Successful completion of an examination to evaluate knolwledge and comprehension of LSS principles and methodologies with a minimal score of 70%. The examinatinon should cover topics such as basic stattistics, process improvement tools, and problem solving.
Case Study or Project Report	Completion of a case study or a small-scale improvement project demonstrating or application of LS tools and methodologies to solve a specfici business problem or improve a process. This should be in the form of a writtent report or presentation.
Certification Duration	Yellow Belt certifications maay have a validty eriod, after which recertification or further trainnig may be required to maintain certification status.

Figure 14.7 Yellow Belt Criteria, Competencies, and Skill Requirements

Green Belt Criteria, Competences, and Skill Requirements	
Training Requirements	Completion of a formal training program in LSS, covering advanced topics in the DMAIC methodology, statistical analysis, hypotheis testing, process optimization techniques, proejct management, and Kaizen team leadership skills. The duration of Green Belt training can vary depending on the training provider and the depth of the curriculum, but generally ranges fron 2 to 4 weeks. Training generally will include a combination of classroom instruction, hands-on exerciese, case studies, and proejct work to provide particpants with a thorough understanding of LSS principles and tools.
Understanding of LSS Concepts	Demonstrated profinciency in LSS principles and methodologies, including the ability and prioritize improvement opportunities, collect and analyze data using statistical tools, and implement sustainable solutions to achieve measurable business outcomes.
Project Completion	Successful completion of one or more LSS improvement proejcts as a project leader or primary team member. Green Belts are eexpected to lead proejctd from inception to completion, applying LSS tools and techniques to drive process improvements, recude variation, and enhance efficiency and quality.
Project Dcoumentation and Results	Documentation of proejct work, including project charters, process maps, data collection plans, statistical analyses, improvement plans, and control mechsnisms. Green Belts must demonostrate the ability to driver tangible results, such as cost savings, cycle time reduction, or quality improvements, as a result of their project work.
Examination	Successful completion of a nexamination to evaluate comprehensive knowledge and profinciency in LSS concepts, methodologies, and tools with mimimum score of 70%. The examination should cover advanced statistical methods, process optimization techniques, project management ptinciples, and Kaizen team leadership skills.
Presentation and Defense	Presentation of project findings, recommendations, and outcomes to organizational leadership or stakeholders. Green Belts should effectively commmunicate project results, incldung the rationale behind improvement efforts, the methodology used, and the impact on Key Performance Indicators (KPIs).
Certification Duration	Gren Belt certifications can have a validatity period, after which recertification or ongoing professional development may be required to maintain certification status.

Figure 14.8 Green Belt Criteria, Competencies, and Skill Requirements

Black Belt Criteria, Competences, and Skill Requirements	
Training Requirements	Completion of an extensive and rigurous training program in Lean Six Sigma, typically spanning several weeks to several months. Intensive full-time course may last anywhere from 4-6 weeks, while part time course span several months, often with sessions held on weekends or evanings. Some programs are offered online or blended learning options, which may have flexibel duations. Black Belts training covers advanced topics in the DMAIC methodology statistical analysis, experimental design, proejct leadrship management, leadership, change management, and coaching skills.
Expertise in LSS Concepts	Mastery of LSS principles, methodologies, and tools, including advanced statistical analysis techniques, process optimization methods, root cause analysis, design of experiments (DOE), hypothesis testing, and advanced problem-solving methodologies.
Proejct Leadership snd Execution	Successful leadership and completion of multiple complex LSS projects, typically including proejcts with significant business impact, cross-functional scope, and strategic importance to the organization. Black Belts are expected to effectively manage proejct teams, stakeholders, resources, timelines, and budgets to achieve proejct objectives and deliver sustainable results.
Project Dcoumentation and Results	Thorough documentation of proeject work, including proejct charters, stakeholders analyses, process maps, data collection plans, statistical analyes, improvement plans, control mechanisms, and financial impact assessments. Black Belts must demonstrate the ability to drive measurable improvements in key performance metrics, such as cost savings, revenue enhancement, cycle time reduction, defect elimination, and costomer satisfaction improvement.
Examination	Successful completio of a comprehensive examination and assessment to evaluate indepth knowledge, expertise, and profinciency in LSS principles, methodologies, and tools. The examination should cover advanced statistical methods, project management principles, leadership skills, change management strategies, and organizational devleopment concepts.
Presentation and Defense	Presentation and Defense of proeject findings, recommendations, and outcomes to senior leadership, executives, or key stakeholders. Black Belts should effectively communicate the strategic importance of their porejcts, the methodology used, the impact on prganizational goals, and the sustainability of improvement achieved.
Mentoring and Coaching	Demomstrated ability to mentor and coash Green Belts and Yellow Belts in LSS methodologies, proejct manaegment techniques, and problem-solving skills. Black Belts play a crucial role in developing the next generation of LSS practioners within their organizations
Certification Duration	Black Belt certifcations may have a validity period, sfter which re-certification or onging professional devlopment may be required to maintain certification status.

Figure 14.9 Black Belt Criteria, Competencies, and Skill Requirements

Master Black Belt Criteria, Competences, and Skill Requirements	
Extensive Experience and Expertise	Signiffcent experience and expertise in LSS emthodologies, typically spanning many years of successful proejct leadership, mentoring, and coaching at the Black Beltlevel. Mater Black Belts are recognized as subject matter experts in LSS amd considered thought leaders in process improvemnt and organizational excellence.
Advanced Training and Certification	Completion of an advanced training and certifcation program specifically designed for Mater Black Belts, which typically includes advanced topics in LSS, statistics, project management, leadership development, change management, and organizational development. This training is more intense and its duration can vary significantly depending on the training provider and the depth of curricuoum. Training is often customers zed and tailored and involves a combination of classroom instrcution, practical application, mentoring, and proejct work. While there is not a standardized duration for Master Black Belt training, it generally spans several months to a year.
Strategic Leadership and Guidance	Demonostrated ability to provide strateguc leadership, guidance, and direction to organizational leaders, executives, and stakeholders in LSS methodology and deployment. Master Black Belts play a key role in shaping an organizations LSS strategy, setting pripoities, aligning improvment efforts with busines objective, and driving cultural transformation.
Mentorship and Coaching	Proven track record of mentoring, coaching, and developing Black Belts, Green Belt,s and other LSS practitioners. Master Black Belts are respnsibile for building and nutruinga pipeline of talent within the orgniazation, transferring knowledge, skills, and best practices, and fostering a culture of continuous learning and improvment.
Project Portfolio and Impact	Successful leadership and conpletion of a diverse portofolio of high impact LSS proejets that have delvered significant value. Master Black Belts are expected to lead complex, cross-functional initaitves, drive breakthrough improvements, and derived measurable results in terms of cost savings, revenue enhancement, customer satisfaction, and process efficiency.
Thought Leadership and Innovation	Contribution to the advancement of LSS methodology and best practices through research, onnoviation, and thought leadership. Master Black Belts are often involved in developing new tools, techniques, and appproaches tp address emeragingchallenges and drive continuous improvment in processes, systems, and organizational capabilitites
Executive Communication and Influence	Exceptional communication, interpersonal, and influencing skills, with the ability to effectvely engae and align senior leadership, executives, and key stakeholders. Master Black Belts must be able to articulate the strategic value of LSS, gainbuy-in for improvement initiatives, and drive organizational change at all levels.
Certification Duration	Mater Black Belt certification may have a validity period, after which recertification or ongoing development may be required to maint certification status.

Figure 14.10 Master Black Belt Criteria, Competencies, and Skill Requirements

CENTRAL BUILDING BLOCKS OF THE UNIFIED LSS BOK

Resting upon the core criteria, competencies, and skills of the LSS professionals that apply the methodology defined in the unified LSS BOK, there are 11 central building blocks, each of equal importance, that drive the standardization of the BOK educational content. The first of these building blocks is that of creating a culture of continuous improvement.

Building Block #1 – Creating a Culture of Continuous Improvement is of paramount importance in a unified Lean Six Sigma BOK for several reasons:

- *Sustained Efficiency* – Lean Six Sigma aims to eliminate waste and variation in processes to improve efficiency. A culture of continuous improvement ensures that efficiency gains are not temporary but sustained over time. It encourages employees to constantly seek out ways to optimize processes and make incremental improvements.
- *Adaptability* – In today's rapidly changing business environment, organizations need to be agile and adaptable to stay competitive. A continuous improvement culture fosters an environment where employees are encouraged to experiment, innovate, and adapt processes to changing circumstances, market demands, and customer needs.
- *Employee Engagement* – Employees are often the ones who are closest to the processes and can identify opportunities for improvement. A culture of continuous improvement empowers employees to take ownership of their work and contribute their ideas for making processes more efficient and effective. This, in turn, boosts employee engagement and morale.
- *Customer Focus* – Lean Six Sigma is about delivering value to the customer by providing high-quality products or services efficiently. A continuous improvement culture reinforces the importance of understanding customer requirements and feedback, driving organizations to continuously refine their processes to better meet customer needs and expectations.
- *Cost Reduction* – Continuous improvement leads to cost reductions by eliminating waste, streamlining processes, and improving productivity. This can have a significant impact on the bottom line of an organization, contributing to increased profitability and competitiveness.
- *Risk Mitigation* – By continuously improving processes, organizations can identify and address potential risks and vulnerabilities before they escalate into larger issues. This proactive approach to risk management helps organizations become more resilient and better prepared to navigate challenges.
- *Organizational Learning* – A culture of continuous improvement fosters a mindset of learning and growth within the organization. It encourages individuals and teams to reflect on their experiences, learn from both successes and failures, and apply these learnings to future projects and initiatives, driving ongoing improvement and innovation.

A culture of continuous improvement is essential for the successful implementation and sustainability of Lean Six Sigma BOK principles. It ensures that organizations remain agile, customer focused, and competitive in a constantly evolving business landscape.

Building Block #2 – Certification Standards play a significant role in a unified Lean Six Sigma BOK for several reasons:

- *Standardization of Knowledge and Skills* – Certification standards define the knowledge areas, methodologies, tools, and techniques that professionals need to master to become proficient in Lean Six Sigma. By establishing these standards, certification bodies ensure consistency in the knowledge and skills of certified practitioners, regardless of their background or industry.
- *Quality Assurance* – Certification standards serve as a benchmark for assessing the competency and expertise of Lean Six Sigma practitioners. By adhering to established standards, certification bodies ensure that certified professionals possess the necessary knowledge and skills to effectively apply Lean Six Sigma methodologies and deliver tangible results in process improvement projects.
- *Credibility and Recognition* – Certification from accredited bodies provides credibility and recognition to Lean Six Sigma professionals. Employers often prefer hiring certified practitioners, as they demonstrate a commitment to continuous learning and mastery of Lean Six Sigma principles. Similarly, clients and stakeholders may have more confidence in organizations that employ certified professionals to lead their process improvement initiatives.
- *Career Advancement* – Certification in Lean Six Sigma can open up new career opportunities and accelerate professional growth. Many organizations value employees who hold certifications, as it signifies their ability to drive performance improvements and contribute to achieving business objectives. Certified professionals may also command higher salaries and greater job prospects compared to their non-certified counterparts.
- *Global Alignment* – Certification standards help to align Lean Six Sigma practices across different industries and regions, facilitating collaboration and knowledge sharing among professionals worldwide. This global alignment ensures consistency in terminology, methodologies, and best practices, enabling organizations to leverage Lean Six Sigma principles effectively regardless of their geographical location or industry sector.

Certification standards provide a framework for ensuring the quality, consistency, and relevance of Lean Six Sigma education and practice, thereby enhancing the value proposition for both professionals and organizations invested in process improvement initiatives.

Building Block #3 – Having a Knowledge Sharing Platform within a unified Lean Six Sigma Body of Knowledge is crucial for several reasons:

- *Facilitates Continuous Learning* – A knowledge sharing platform provides a centralized space for Lean Six Sigma professionals to exchange ideas, experiences, best practices, and lessons learned. This fosters a culture of continuous learning where practitioners can stay updated on the latest developments, trends, and innovations in Lean Six Sigma methodologies.
- *Accelerates Skill Development* – By sharing knowledge and expertise, practitioners can accelerate their skill development and proficiency in Lean Six Sigma. Access to real-world case studies, success stories, and practical insights from peers and experts enables individuals to deepen their understanding of Lean Six Sigma principles and apply them effectively in their own projects and initiatives.

- *Promotes Collaboration and Networking* – A knowledge sharing platform facilitates collaboration and networking among Lean Six Sigma professionals both within and across organizations. Practitioners can connect with colleagues, mentors, and subject matter experts to seek advice, guidance, and support on challenging projects or issues. This collaboration not only enhances problem-solving capabilities but also builds a strong professional network within the Lean Six Sigma community.
- *Captures and Preserves Institutional Knowledge* – Organizations can leverage a knowledge sharing platform to capture and preserve institutional knowledge related to Lean Six Sigma initiatives. This includes documenting successful improvement projects, standard operating procedures, templates, tools, and methodologies used in process improvement efforts. By institutionalizing this knowledge, organizations can ensure continuity and sustainability in their Lean Six Sigma initiatives, even as personnel turnover occurs.
- *Drives Innovation* – Knowledge sharing fosters a culture of innovation within organizations. By exchanging ideas and exploring new approaches to problem-solving, practitioners can identify opportunities for innovation and experimentation in Lean Six Sigma projects. This can lead to the development of novel solutions, methodologies, and tools that enhance the effectiveness and efficiency of process improvement efforts.
- *Enhances Organizational Performance* – A knowledge sharing platform contributes to overall organizational performance by enabling employees to access relevant information, resources, and expertise needed to drive business results. By harnessing the collective intelligence of the workforce, organizations can make more informed decisions, mitigate risks, and achieve greater success in their Lean Six Sigma initiatives.

A knowledge sharing platform is crucial for promoting collaboration, accelerating learning, and fostering innovation within a Lean Six Sigma Body of Knowledge. It serves as a valuable resource for practitioners to access and contribute to a wealth of knowledge that enriches their understanding and application of Lean Six Sigma principles in practice.

Building Block #4 – A Comprehensive Training Program is essential in a unified Lean Six Sigma Body of Knowledge for several important reasons:

- *Standardized Knowledge Transfer* – A structured training program ensures that Lean Six Sigma practitioners receive consistent and standardized instruction in core methodologies, tools, and concepts. This helps establish a common foundation of knowledge across the organization or within a specific industry, enabling practitioners to speak the same language and approach improvement projects with a shared understanding.
- *Skill Development* – Training programs provide practitioners with the opportunity to develop and refine their skills in Lean Six Sigma methodologies such as DMAIC or DMADV. Through hands-on exercises, case studies, and simulations, participants can practice applying these methodologies to real-world scenarios, enhancing their ability to lead successful improvement projects.
- *Certification Preparation* – Many Lean Six Sigma training programs are designed to prepare participants for certification exams administered by accredited bodies such as the American Society for Quality or the International Association for Six

Sigma Certification (IASSC). A comprehensive training program covers the specific topics and competencies tested on these exams, equipping participants with the knowledge and skills needed to pass certification assessments.

- *Practical Application* – Effective Lean Six Sigma training goes beyond theoretical concepts and focuses on practical application in the workplace. Training programs often include case studies, group exercises, and project work that allow participants to apply Lean Six Sigma tools and methodologies to real-world problems within their own organizations. This hands-on experience is critical for building confidence and competence in applying Lean Six Sigma principles in practice.
- *Change Management* – Lean Six Sigma initiatives often involve driving organizational change and transforming processes to achieve improvement goals. Comprehensive training programs incorporate change management principles and techniques to help practitioners navigate resistance, overcome barriers, and effectively lead change within their organizations. This ensures that improvement efforts are sustainable and aligned with broader business objectives.
- *Employee Engagement and Retention* – Investing in comprehensive training programs demonstrates a commitment to employee development and professional growth. This can boost employee morale, engagement, and job satisfaction, leading to higher levels of retention and loyalty within the organization. Employees who feel supported in their development are more likely to invest their time and energy in driving improvement initiatives and contributing to organizational success.

A comprehensive training program is crucial for equipping Lean Six Sigma practitioners with the knowledge, skills, and mindset needed to drive successful improvement initiatives, foster a culture of continuous improvement, and achieve meaningful results within their organizations.

Building Block #5 – Risk Management Integration into a unified Lean Six Sigma Body of Knowledge is crucial for several reasons:

- *Identifying Potential Risks* – Lean Six Sigma focuses on improving processes to reduce variation and eliminate waste. However, during the process improvement journey, there are inherent risks associated with changes made to existing processes or the introduction of new methodologies. Integrating risk management into the BOK ensures that practitioners proactively identify potential risks that could impact the success of improvement initiatives.
- *Assessing Impact on Business Objectives* – By considering risk management principles, Lean Six Sigma practitioners can assess the potential impact of process changes on broader business objectives. This involves evaluating the likelihood and severity of risks occurring and their potential consequences on key performance indicators, customer satisfaction, financial performance, and organizational reputation.
- *Prioritizing Improvement Efforts* – Risk management integration helps prioritize improvement efforts by focusing on areas with the highest potential impact on business outcomes. By identifying and addressing high-risk areas early in the improvement process, organizations can mitigate potential negative consequences and ensure that resources are allocated effectively to initiatives that align with strategic objectives.

- *Enhancing Decision-Making* – Incorporating risk management principles into Lean Six Sigma methodologies enhances decision-making by providing a more holistic view of the potential benefits and drawbacks of proposed process changes. This allows stakeholders to make informed decisions based on a comprehensive understanding of the risks involved, rather than solely focusing on improvement opportunities.
- *Mitigating Unforeseen Consequences* – Despite careful planning and analysis, improvement initiatives may encounter unforeseen challenges or unintended consequences that could derail progress. Integrating risk management into the BOK helps practitioners anticipate and plan for potential risks, allowing them to implement mitigation strategies and contingency plans to address issues as they arise and maintain project momentum.
- *Ensuring Sustainability of Improvements* – Effective risk management is essential for ensuring the sustainability of process improvements over the long term. By systematically identifying and addressing risks throughout the improvement lifecycle, organizations can minimize the likelihood of regression to previous performance levels and ensure that gains achieved through Lean Six Sigma initiatives are maintained over time.
- *Building Stakeholder Confidence* – Demonstrating a proactive approach to risk management instills confidence in stakeholders, including senior leadership, employees, customers, and other key stakeholders. By transparently communicating risk assessment findings, mitigation strategies, and progress updates, organizations can build trust and credibility, garnering support for Lean Six Sigma initiatives and driving greater buy-in from all stakeholders.

Integrating risk management into a Lean Six Sigma BOK enhances the effectiveness and sustainability of improvement initiatives by ensuring that potential risks are proactively identified, assessed, and mitigated throughout the improvement lifecycle. By considering risk management principles alongside Lean Six Sigma methodologies, organizations can make more informed decisions, prioritize resources effectively, and achieve meaningful and lasting improvements in performance and outcomes.

Building Block #6 – Measurement and Metric Guidelines are considered essential components of a unified Lean Six Sigma Body of Knowledge for several reasons:

- *Performance Monitoring:* Measurement and metrics provide a means to monitor the performance of processes and projects. By defining key performance indicators and establishing measurement guidelines, organizations can track progress toward improvement goals, identify areas for intervention, and assess the effectiveness of Lean Six Sigma initiatives.
- *Data-Driven Decision Making:* Lean Six Sigma relies on data-driven decision making to identify root causes of problems, prioritize improvement opportunities, and validate the impact of process changes. Measurement and metric guidelines ensure that practitioners collect relevant data consistently, analyze it accurately, and draw meaningful insights to inform decision making throughout the improvement lifecycle.
- *Baseline Establishment:* Before embarking on process improvement initiatives, it is essential to establish a baseline performance level to understand current process capabilities and set improvement targets. Measurement guidelines help

define how performance will be measured, what data will be collected, and how baseline performance will be determined, providing a reference point for evaluating the impact of improvement efforts.

- *Goal Setting:* Metrics play a critical role in setting SMART goals for improvement projects. By defining clear and quantifiable objectives, organizations can align improvement efforts with strategic priorities, track progress over time, and hold teams accountable for achieving results.
- *Continuous Improvement:* Measurement and metric guidelines support a culture of continuous improvement by providing feedback on process performance and highlighting opportunities for further optimization. By regularly reviewing performance metrics, organizations can identify trends, patterns, and areas of variability that may indicate the need for additional improvement efforts or corrective actions.
- *Standardization and Consistency:* Consistency in measurement practices is essential for ensuring that data collected from different sources and across various projects is comparable and reliable. Metric guidelines help standardize measurement methods, units of measurement, data collection procedures, and reporting formats, enabling consistent interpretation and analysis of performance data across the organization.
- *Alignment with Business Objectives:* Effective measurement and metric guidelines ensure that performance metrics are aligned with broader business objectives and strategic priorities. By selecting metrics that are directly linked to customer requirements, organizational goals, and stakeholder expectations, organizations can focus improvement efforts on areas that will have the greatest impact on overall business performance and competitiveness.

Measurement and metric guidelines are critical components of a Lean Six Sigma BOK, as they provide a structured approach to monitoring performance, making data-driven decisions, setting goals, driving continuous improvement, ensuring consistency, and aligning improvement efforts with strategic objectives. By establishing clear guidelines for measurement and metrics, organizations can effectively track progress, drive accountability, and achieve meaningful results through their Lean Six Sigma initiatives.

Building Block #7 – Industry-Specific Customization in a Lean Six Sigma Body of Knowledge is important for several reasons:

- *Relevance to Industry Challenges* – Different industries face unique challenges and opportunities, ranging from regulatory requirements to customer expectations and market dynamics. Customizing Lean Six Sigma methodologies, tools, and techniques to address specific industry needs ensures that improvement efforts are aligned with industry-specific challenges and objectives, making them more relevant and impactful.
- *Optimized Process Improvement* – Industry-specific customization allows Lean Six Sigma practitioners to tailor improvement strategies to the intricacies of their industry's processes, workflows, and value streams. By understanding the nuances of industry-specific operations, practitioners can identify targeted improvement opportunities, streamline processes, and optimize performance in ways that are most beneficial to their industry sector.

- *Enhanced Stakeholder Engagement* – Customizing Lean Six Sigma approaches to fit the unique characteristics of an industry fosters greater engagement and buy-in from stakeholders, including executives, employees, customers, suppliers, and regulatory agencies. When improvement initiatives are tailored to address industry-specific challenges and priorities, stakeholders are more likely to perceive the value and relevance of Lean Six Sigma methodologies, leading to increased support and participation in improvement efforts.
- *Compliance and Regulatory Requirements* – Many industries operate within highly regulated environments with strict compliance requirements. Customizing Lean Six Sigma methodologies to address regulatory standards and industry-specific regulations ensures that improvement initiatives not only drive operational excellence but also help organizations maintain compliance with applicable laws and regulations. This alignment with regulatory requirements reduces the risk of non-compliance and associated penalties while fostering a culture of quality and accountability within the organization.
- *Industry Benchmarking and Best Practices* – Industry-specific customization allows organizations to benchmark their performance against industry peers and adopt best practices that have proved effective within their industry sector. By leveraging industry-specific data, benchmarks, and case studies, organizations can gain insights into leading practices, emerging trends, and innovative approaches to process improvement, enabling them to stay competitive and drive continuous improvement in their industry.
- *Alignment With Customer Expectations* – Every industry serves a unique customer base with distinct preferences, needs, and expectations. Customizing Lean Six Sigma methodologies to align with customer requirements ensures that improvement efforts focus on delivering value-added products and services that meet or exceed customer expectations. By incorporating customer feedback and insights into improvement initiatives, organizations can enhance customer satisfaction, loyalty, and retention, driving sustainable business growth and success.

Industry-specific customization in a Lean Six Sigma BOK is essential for ensuring that improvement efforts are relevant, targeted, and effective within the context of a specific industry sector. By tailoring Lean Six Sigma methodologies to address industry-specific challenges, opportunities, and priorities, organizations can optimize their process improvement efforts, engage stakeholders, maintain compliance, benchmark performance, and deliver greater value to customers, driving sustainable business success.

Building Block #8 – Collaborative Development is crucial in a unified Lean Six Sigma Body of Knowledge for several significant reasons:

- *Cross-Functional Expertise* – Lean Six Sigma initiatives often involve teams composed of individuals from diverse functional areas within an organization. Collaborative development facilitates the integration of cross-functional expertise, bringing together individuals with different perspectives, backgrounds, and skills to tackle complex problems and drive process improvement efforts.
- *Holistic Problem-Solving* – Collaborative development encourages a holistic approach to problem-solving by leveraging the collective knowledge, experience, and creativity of team members. By fostering collaboration and open communication, teams can identify root causes of issues, explore alternative solutions,

and implement comprehensive improvement strategies that address underlying systemic challenges rather than just symptoms.

- *Shared Ownership and Accountability* – When team members are actively involved in the development of improvement initiatives, they develop a sense of ownership and accountability for the outcomes. Collaborative development empowers individuals to contribute their ideas, insights, and expertise to the process, fostering a culture of shared responsibility and commitment to achieving success.
- *Alignment with Stakeholder Needs* – Collaboration with stakeholders, including customers, suppliers, employees, and other key stakeholders, ensures that improvement efforts are aligned with their needs, expectations, and priorities. By involving stakeholders in the development process, organizations can gain valuable insights into customer requirements, market trends, and industry best practices, enabling them to deliver solutions that meet or exceed stakeholder expectations.
- *Knowledge Sharing and Transfer* – Collaborative development facilitates knowledge sharing and transfer within the organization, enabling individuals to learn from each other, share best practices, and build upon existing expertise. By harnessing the collective intelligence of the team, organizations can accelerate learning, foster innovation, and drive continuous improvement across the organization.
- *Enhanced Decision-Making* – Collaboration enables teams to make more informed decisions by drawing upon the diverse perspectives, opinions, and insights of team members. By engaging in collaborative discussions, teams can weigh the pros and cons of different options, evaluate risks, and reach consensus on the best course of action, leading to more effective and sustainable outcomes.
- *Adaptability and Flexibility* – In a rapidly changing business environment, organizations must be agile and adaptable to respond to evolving market conditions, customer needs, and competitive pressures. Collaborative development enables organizations to quickly mobilize teams, leverage collective expertise, and adapt to changing circumstances, enabling them to stay ahead of the curve and drive continuous improvement in a dynamic marketplace.

Collaborative development is essential in a Lean Six Sigma BOK, as it fosters cross-functional collaboration, holistic problem-solving, shared ownership, alignment with stakeholder needs, knowledge sharing, enhanced decision-making, and adaptability. By embracing collaboration as a core principle, organizations can harness the collective intelligence and creativity of their teams to drive meaningful and sustainable improvement in processes, products, and services.

Building Block #9 – Digital Transformation Considerations integrated into a unified Lean Six Sigma Body of Knowledge is essential for several reasons:

- *Alignment with Industry Trends* – Digital transformation is reshaping industries across the globe, leveraging technologies such as big data, artificial intelligence, IoT, automation, and cloud computing to drive efficiency, innovation, and competitiveness. Integrating digital transformation considerations into the Lean Six Sigma BOK ensures that practitioners are equipped to address emerging trends and leverage digital tools and technologies to enhance process improvement efforts.

- *Enhanced Data Analytics* – Digital transformation enables organizations to collect, analyze, and leverage vast amounts of data from various sources to gain insights into process performance, customer behavior, market trends, and other key metrics. By incorporating digital analytics tools and techniques into Lean Six Sigma methodologies, practitioners can enhance their ability to identify patterns, detect anomalies, and derive actionable insights from data, leading to more informed decision-making and targeted improvement efforts.
- *Automation and Efficiency* – Automation plays a significant role in digital transformation initiatives, enabling organizations to streamline repetitive tasks, eliminate manual interventions, and improve process efficiency. By integrating automation principles into Lean Six Sigma methodologies, practitioners can identify opportunities for automation, design more efficient workflows, and optimize processes to minimize waste, reduce cycle times, and enhance productivity.
- *Process Digitization and Optimization* – Digital transformation involves digitizing manual processes and workflows to improve accuracy, speed, and scalability. Lean Six Sigma practitioners can leverage digital tools and technologies to map out existing processes, identify bottlenecks, and redesign workflows to optimize performance. By integrating digital transformation considerations into process improvement efforts, organizations can accelerate their journey towards digital maturity and unlock new levels of efficiency and effectiveness.
- *Customer-Centric Innovation* – Digital transformation enables organizations to deliver personalized, seamless, and convenient experiences to customers through digital channels. Lean Six Sigma practitioners can leverage digital technologies to understand customer preferences, analyze customer feedback, and identify opportunities for innovation and enhancement. By incorporating customer-centric digital solutions into process improvement initiatives, organizations can drive customer satisfaction, loyalty, and competitive differentiation in the digital age.
- *Agility and Adaptability* – Digital transformation requires organizations to be agile and adaptable to respond to rapidly changing market dynamics and technological advancements. By integrating digital transformation considerations into Lean Six Sigma BOK, practitioners can foster a culture of innovation, agility, and adaptability within their organizations, enabling them to thrive in a rapidly evolving digital landscape.

Integrating digital transformation considerations into a Lean Six Sigma BOK is essential for equipping practitioners with the knowledge, skills, and tools needed to drive process improvement efforts in the digital age. By leveraging digital technologies, data analytics, automation, and customer-centric innovation, organizations can unlock new opportunities for efficiency, innovation, and growth, positioning themselves for success in an increasingly digital world.

Building Block #10 – Integration of Regulatory Requirements into a Lean Six Sigma Body of Knowledge is of the utmost importance due to several critical reasons:

- *Compliance Assurance* – Regulatory requirements are often mandatory standards set by governing bodies to ensure safety, quality, and legality in products, services, and processes. By integrating regulatory requirements into Lean Six Sigma methodologies, organizations can ensure compliance with applicable regulations, standards, and industry guidelines, mitigating the risk of non-compliance penalties, lawsuits, and reputational damage.

- *Process Optimization* – Regulatory requirements often mandate specific processes, controls, and documentation practices to ensure quality, consistency, and traceability in operations. By integrating regulatory considerations into Lean Six Sigma methodologies, organizations can optimize processes to meet regulatory standards while also driving efficiency, reducing waste, and improving overall performance. This integration ensures that compliance efforts are aligned with broader process improvement goals, maximizing the value of Lean Six Sigma initiatives.
- *Customer Trust and Confidence* – Compliance with regulatory requirements enhances customer trust and confidence in products and services, as it demonstrates an organization's commitment to quality, safety, and integrity. By integrating regulatory considerations into a Lean Six Sigma BOK, organizations can strengthen their reputation, differentiate themselves in the marketplace, and build long-term relationships with customers based on transparency, accountability, and compliance assurance.
- *Global Market Access* – In today's interconnected world, organizations often operate in multiple jurisdictions with different regulatory frameworks and requirements. Integrating regulatory considerations into Lean Six Sigma methodologies ensures that organizations can navigate the complexities of global compliance seamlessly, enabling them to access new markets, expand their customer base, and drive international growth while maintaining compliance with local regulations and standards.

The integration of regulatory requirements into Lean Six Sigma BOK is essential for ensuring compliance, managing risks, optimizing processes, enhancing customer trust, accessing global markets, and driving continuous improvement. By incorporating regulatory considerations into Lean Six Sigma methodologies, organizations can achieve compliance excellence while also realizing the full benefits of process improvement initiatives, driving sustainable business success.

Building Block #11 – Supplier Collaboration Guidelines play a significant role in a Lean Six Sigma Body of Knowledge for several reasons:

- *End-to-End Process Improvement* – Lean Six Sigma extends beyond organizational boundaries to include suppliers and partners in the value chain. Supplier collaboration guidelines ensure that improvement efforts encompass the entire supply chain, from raw material sourcing to product delivery. By collaborating with suppliers, organizations can identify opportunities for process optimization, waste reduction, and cost savings across the entire value stream, leading to greater efficiency and competitiveness.
- *Quality Assurance* – Suppliers play a critical role in delivering quality inputs and components that meet the specifications and requirements of the organization's processes. Collaboration with suppliers allows organizations to establish clear quality standards, performance metrics, and expectations for product and service delivery. By aligning with suppliers on quality goals and objectives, organizations can minimize defects, reduce variation, and enhance overall product quality, improving customer satisfaction and loyalty.

- *Cost Reduction* – Collaborating with suppliers can lead to cost savings through various means, such as joint process improvement initiatives, value engineering, and negotiation of favorable terms and pricing. Supplier collaboration guidelines provide a framework for identifying cost-saving opportunities, optimizing procurement processes, and fostering long-term partnerships based on mutual trust and benefit. By leveraging the expertise and resources of suppliers, organizations can achieve greater efficiency and cost-effectiveness in their supply chain operations.
- *Sustainability and Corporate Social Responsibility* – Supplier collaboration guidelines can incorporate principles of sustainability and corporate social responsibility (CSR) to ensure ethical sourcing practices, environmental stewardship, and social accountability throughout the supply chain. By working with suppliers who share similar values and commitments to sustainability, organizations can mitigate reputational risks, enhance brand equity, and contribute to positive social and environmental outcomes.

Supplier collaboration guidelines are essential for organizations practicing Lean Six Sigma, as they enable end-to-end process improvement, ensure quality assurance, mitigate risks, reduce costs, drive innovation, and promote sustainability throughout the supply chain. By fostering collaboration and partnership with suppliers, organizations can achieve greater efficiency, resilience, and competitiveness in today's dynamic business environment.

DESIGNING A SUSTAINABILITY AND COLLABORATIVE MANAGEMENT MODEL INTO THE UNIFIED LEAN SIX SIGMA BOK FOR AVIATION AND AEROSPACE

Designing a sustainability and collaborative management model into the unified Lean Six Sigma BOK involves integrating sustainability principles and collaborative management practices into the existing framework of Lean Six Sigma through a structured approach. Figure 14.11 depicts the illustrates a sustainability and collaborative model that has been effectively used in an aviation and aerospace industry environment.

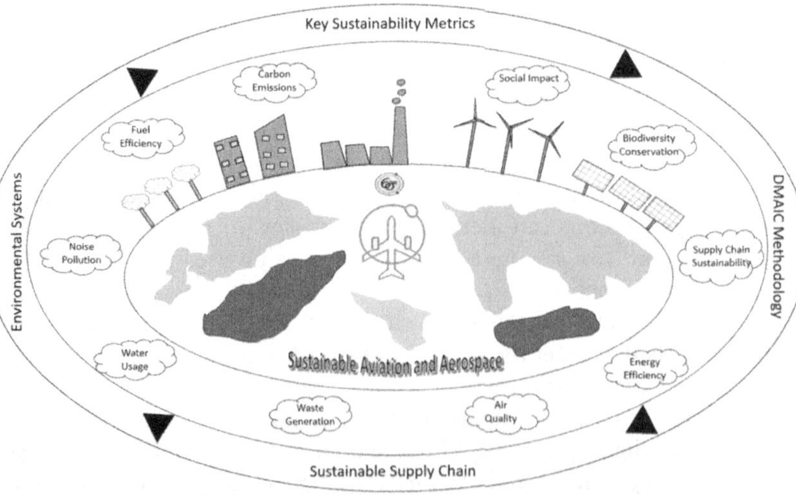

Figure 14.11 Sustainability and Collaborative Management Model

The sustainability and collaborative management model framework is anchored by four structural approach cornerstones:

- *The Identification of Key Sustainability Metrics,*
- *The Incorporation of Sustainability Into the DMAIC Methodology,*
- *The Integration of an Environmental Management System,* and
- *The Development of Sustainable Supply Chain Practices*

The Identification of Key Sustainability Metrics

Key sustainability metrics in the aviation and aerospace industries are crucial for assessing environmental impact, resource efficiency, and overall sustainability performance.

- *Carbon emissions* – tracking and reducing carbon emissions is a primary focus for sustainability in aviation and aerospace. Common metrics include CO_2 emissions, CO_2 emissions per passenger-kilometer or ton-kilometer, and emissions intensity per aircraft or flight.
- *Fuel efficiency* – monitoring fuel consumption and improving fuel efficiency helps reduce carbon emissions and operating costs. Common metrics are fuel burn per seat-kilometer, fuel efficiency per revenue ton-kilometer, and fuel consumption per aircraft movement.
- *Noise pollution* – aircraft noise can have significant environmental and community impacts. Common metrics include noise levels measured in decibels (dB) and tracking noise complaints from communities around airports.
- *Water usage* – monitoring water consumption in aviation and aerospace manufacturing processes, maintenance facilities, and airport operations is essential for sustainable water management. Common metrics include total water consumption and water usage per unit of production.
- *Waste generation* – aviation and aerospace operations generate various types of waste, including hazardous materials and solid waste. Common metrics include total wase generated, waste diverted from landfills through recycling and reuse, and waste generation per unit of production.
- *Air quality* – monitoring emissions of nitrogen oxides (NOx), sulfur oxides (Sox), particulate matter (PM), and other pollutants from aircraft engines and ground support equipment is essential for assessing air quality impacts.
- *Energy efficiency* – improving energy efficiency in aircraft design, manufacturing processes, and airport operations helps reduce greenhouse gas emissions and operating cost. Common metrics include energy consumption per unit of production and energy intensity per aircraft movement.
- *Supply chain sustainability* – assessing and improving the sustainability performance of suppliers in the aviation and aerospace industries is critical for reducing environmental impacts throughout the supply chain. Common metrics include supplier compliance with environmental regulations, carbon footprint of supply chain activities, and supplier engagement in sustainability initiatives.
- *Biodiversity conservation* – protecting biodiversity in areas surrounding airports and aerospace facilities is essential for minimizing environmental impacts. Common metrics include the preservation of habitats, biodiversity offset measures, and conservation efforts.

- *Social impact* – assessing and mitigating social impacts such as community displacement, labor rights, and health and safety hazards associated with aviation and aerospace operations is crucial for sustainable development. Common metrics include community engagement, employee satisfaction, and adherence to labor standards.

By tracking and improving these sustainability metrics within the collaborative model, aviation and aerospace industries can minimize their environmental footprint, enhance resource efficiency, and contribute to a more sustainable future.

The Incorporation of Sustainability Into the DMAIC Methodology

Incorporating the DMAIC methodology into the sustainability and collaborative model in aviation and aerospace industry directly contributes to the organizations systemically address environmental impacts, enhance efficiency, and drive continuous improvement initiatives. Here is how sustainability can be integrated into each phase of the DMAIC methodology:

- *Define* – clearly articulate the sustainability objectives and goals, such as reducing carbon emissions, minimizing waste generation, or improving energy efficiency. Also, engage stakeholders, including customers, employees, regulators, and communities, to understand their sustainability priorities and concerns. Use sustainability metrics to measure the current environmental performance of aviation and aerospace operations.
- *Measure* – collect data on key sustainability metrics identified in the Define phase, such as carbon emissions, fuel consumption, waste generation, and water usage. Assess the environmental impact of aviation and aerospace activities through its entire life cycle, from raw material extraction to end of life disposal. Compare sustainability performance metrics with industry benchmarks and best practices to identify areas for improvement.
- *Analyze* – use root cause analysis techniques such as Ishikawa diagrams or Pareto analysis to identify the underlying causes of environmental impacts and resources inefficiencies. Evaluate the environmental, social, and economic impacts of potential improvement opportunities. Rank order these opportunities based on their potential to address key sustainability issues and achieve organizational goals.
- *Improve* – collaborate cross-functionally to develop and implement initiatives to reduce carbon emissions, minimize waste, optimize resource use, and improve energy efficiency. Pilot tests new technologies, processes, or practices to assess their effectiveness and feasibility before full-scale implementation. Integrate sustainability considerations into aircraft design, manufacturing processes, and supply chain management practices to minimize environmental impacts throughout the product life cycle.
- *Control* – establish regular monitoring and reporting mechanisms to track progress towards sustainability goals and identify deviations from targets. Take corrective actions to address any deviations from sustainability targets and continuously improve performance. Foster a culture of sustainability by providing training and awareness programs for employees and engaging stakeholders in sustainability initiatives.

By integrating sustainability into the DMAIC methodology within their collaborative management model, aviation and aerospace organizations can systemically identify, prioritize, and implement initiatives to improve environmental performance, enhance resource efficiency, and achieve long-term sustainability objectives.

Developing Sustainability Supply Chain Practices

Developing sustainable supply chain practices in the aviation and aerospace industry collaborative management model involves integrating environmental, social, and economic considerations into procurement processes, supplier relationships, and logistical operations. The following are methods that have proved effective in integrating this practice.

- *Supplier selection and evaluation* – establish sustainability criteria for selecting suppliers, such as environmental management systems creation, compliance with OSHA regulations, and ethical labor practices. Conduct comprehensive supplier assessments to evaluate their sustainability performance, including their carbon footprint, waste management practices, and social responsibility initiatives.
- *Supplier engagement and collaboration* – collaborate with all tiers of suppliers to identify opportunities for improving sustainability performance throughout the supply chain. Provide guidance and support to suppliers in implementing sustainable practices, such as energy efficiency improvements, waste reduction initiatives, and responsible sourcing of raw materials.
- *Transparency and traceability* – promote transparency and traceability in the supply chain by tracking the origin and environmental impact of materials, components, and products. Implement systems and technologies, such as blockchain and RFID, to enhance visibility and traceability of supply chain activities and ensure compliance with sustainability standards.
- *Material selection and design for supportability* – encourage the use of environmentally friendly materials and components in aircraft manufacturing and maintenance processes. Collaborate with suppliers and designers to incorporate principles of a circular economy, such as recycling and remanufacturing, into product design and development.
- *Energy efficiency and emissions reduction* – prioritize suppliers that offer energy-efficient and low-emission products and technologies, such as lightweight materials, fuel-efficient engines, and renewable energy solutions. Work with suppliers to implement measures for reducing greenhouse gas emissions, such as optimizing transportation, using alternative fuels, and improving efficiency in manufacturing processes.
- *Waste reduction and recycling* – implement waste reduction and recycling programs throughout the supply chain to minimize the environmental impact of waste generation. Collaborate with suppliers to identify opportunities for recycling materials and components, such as aluminum, carbon fiber, and electronics, to reduce landfill and conserve natural resources.
- *Social responsibilities and labor practices* – ensure that suppliers adhere to ethical labor practices, including fair wages, safe working conditions, and respect for human rights. Conduct audits and assessments to monitor compliance with social responsibility standards and address any instances of labor exploration or discrimination in the supply chain.

- *Risk management and resilience* – identify and assess sustainability risks in the supply chain, such as resource scarcity, regulatory changes, and geopolitical instability. Develop strategies to mitigate these risks, such as diversifying suppliers, building resilience through supplier collaboration, and developing contingency plans for supply chain disruptions.

By integrating sustainable supply chain practices into aviation and aerospace operations, organizations can reduce environmental impacts, enhance social responsibility, mitigate risks, and create long-term value for stakeholders. This approach not only contributes to environmental stewardship but also strengthens resilience, innovation, and competitiveness.

Integrating an Environmental Management System

Integrating an environmental management system (EMS) in the aviation and aerospace collaborative management model is crucial for effectively managing environmental risks, reducing environmental impacts, and ensuring compliance with regulations. The following are some methods that have proved effective in integrating an EMS into an aviation and aerospace organization's collaborative management model.

- *Establishment of environmental policy* – develop a comprehensive environmental policy that aligns with the organization's overall objectives and commitment to sustainability. The policy should articulate the organization's commitment to compliance with environmental regulations, pollution prevention, continuous improvement, and stakeholder engagement.
- *Identification of environmental aspects and impacts* – conduct a thorough assessment of all environmental aspects and impacts associated with aviation and aerospace activities, including aircraft manufacturing, maintenance, repair, operations, and end-of-life disposal.
- *Legal and regulatory compliance* – ensure compliance with relevant environmental laws, regulations, and industry standards applicable to aviation and aerospace operations. Stay updated on changes in environmental regulations and incorporate them into the EMA to maintain compliance.
- *Set objectives and targets* – establish measurable objectives and targets to address significant environmental aspects and impacts identified. Objectives and targets should be achievable, relevant to the organization's environmental policy, and aligned with its overall strategic goals.
- *Implementation and operation* – develop and implement procedures and processes to manage environmental aspects and impacts effectively. Provide training and awareness program to employees to ensure they understand their roles and responsibilities in environmental management. Integrate environmental considerations into procurement processes, supplier management, and product design to minimize environmental impacts throughout the supply chain.
- *Monitoring and measurement* – establish a system for monitoring and measuring key environmental performance indicators, such as energy consumption, carbon emissions, waste generation, water usage. Regularly collect and analyze data to track progress towards environmental objectives and targets.

- *Evaluation of compliance and performance* – conduct periodic audits and reviews to evaluate the effectiveness of the EMS and ensure compliance with environmental requirements. Identify areas for improvement and take corrective actions to address non-conformities and improve environmental performance.
- *Communication and stakeholder engagement* – communicate environmental performance, objective, and achievements transparently to stakeholders, including employees, customers, regulators, and the public. Engage stakeholders in the development and implementation of environmental initiatives and seek feedback to improve sustainability practices.

By integrating an EMS into aviation and aerospace collaborative management model, organizations can effectively manage environmental risks, improve resource efficiency, and demonstrate their commitment to sustainability. This approach not only helps minimize environmental impacts but also enhances operational efficiency, reduces cost, and strengthens reputation and stakeholder relationships.

SUMMARY

The chapter began with a discussion of how the application of Lean Six Sigma principles in aviation and aerospace can lead to more efficient processes, reduced time to market, improved product quality, and continuous improvement. It then addressed how the application of LSS in system design offers a compelling case for improving quality and reducing cost. The point was then made that institutionalizing LSS in the aviation and aerospace organizational domain causes a cultural shift that enhances overall performance. The chapter then explained how employing methodologies like Design for Six Sigma (DFSS), Define, Measure, Explore, Develop, and Implement (DMEDI), and Define, Measure, Analyze, Design, and Verify (DMADV) can improve system velocity and precision and enhance the system design process. The chapter then explained why building a continuous cycle of improvement with aviation and aerospace is crucial for staying competitive and meeting customer demand. An overarching LSS Body of Knowledge framework and roadmap was then presented that standardizes the principles, methodologies, and tools required for LSS certification. The chapter concluded with a discussion of how designing a sustainability and collaborative model within aviation and aerospace promotes operational efficiency, and collaborative decision-making.

LEAN SIX SIGMA AT WORK!

ISO 14000 at ALC, Inc.

ALC's new leadership is environmentally conscious. Using ISO 14000 as a guide, they have taken many positive actions to reduce their organization's environmental impact.

To improve recycling of metal shavings and scrap, they quickly purchased a "puck-making" machine. This machine compresses scrap metal into a more easily reusable shape. Vacuums at each chip-making machine capture the chips directly into a barrel. When full, workers transfer chips and shavings to the "puck-making" machine, which compresses the chips and shavings into recyclable discs of metal. This enables nearly 100% of the shavings and scrap metal to be recycled.

A study of the shipping area resulted in significant changes to how parts are shipped. The new method greatly reduces part damage during shipment. These changes reduced the amount of packing material by 40%. Made from recycled materials, the new packing is reuseable and recyclable.

Grinders, lathes, mills, and drills all use coolant to dissipate heat during operation. In the past, this coolant was disposed of through a waste hauler. Under the new management, systems were put in place to clean and reuse the coolant.

Office paper usage has declined through improved processes and computerization. Scrap office paper is no longer thrown out but is shredded and recycled.

Policies about energy usage have been put in place. Lights, fans, and other equipment must be turned off when not in use. The HVAC system has been updated and is now maintained regularly, allowing it to operate with greater efficiency.

Many of these changes paid for themselves through the selling of recyclable materials, lower energy consumption, and material reuse. Positive changes are happening all the time at ALC Inc. Through environmentally sound changes, the focus is on improving overall organizational effectiveness.

ISO 14000
Section 1: Scope
Section 2: Normative References
Section 3: Definitions
Section 4: Environmental Management System Requirements

4.1 General Requirements
4.2 Environmental Policy
4.3 Planning
 4.3.1 Environmental Aspects
 4.3.2 Legal and Other Requirements
 4.3.3 Environmental Management Program(s)
4.4 Implementation and Operation
 4.4.1 Structure and Responsibility
 4.4.2 Training, Awareness, and Competence
 4.4.3 Communication
 4.4.4 Environmental Preparedness and Response
4.5 Checking and Corrective Action
 4.5.1 Monitoring and Measurement
 4.5.2 Nonconformance and Corrective and Preventive Action
 4.5.3 Records
 4.5.4 Environmental Management System Audit
4.6 Management Review

CHAPTER 14 DISCUSSION QUESTIONS

1 Define and briefly describe the following:
 a Lean Six Sigma
 b Design for Lean Six Sigma (DFLSS)
 c Define, measure, explore, develop, implement (DMEDI)
 d Define, measure, analyze, design, and verify (DMADV)
 How are they alike, and how are they different?
2 Figure 14.3 presents a Lean Six Sigma educational process. Select 5 of the 11 activities that you consider the most critical components to consider during the educational process and elaborate on why you selected them.
3 What do you see as the most important differentiator between the White Belt, Green Belt and Black Belt levels of LSS certification? Provide a rationale for your decision.
4 Which of the 11 LSS central building blocks do you consider the most critical for ensuring proper program development? Provide a rationale for your recommendation.
5 Which of the four sustainability and collaborative management model structural approach cornerstones do you consider the most important for a Lean Six Sigma program's long-term success? Support your answer with a rationale.

BIBLIOGRAPHY

Akbulut-Bailey, Asli Yagmur, Jaideep Motwani, and Everett M. Smedley. "When lean and six sigma converge: A case study of a successful implementation of lean six sigma at an aerospace company." *International Journal of Technology Management* 57.1/2/3 (2012): 18–32.

Cherrafi, Anass, et al. "Green and lean: A Gemba–Kaizen model for sustainability enhancement." *Production Planning & Control* 30.5–6 (2019): 385–399.

Dhallin, Arthur J. *The Identification, Validation, and Modeling of Critical Parameters in Lean Six Sigma Implementations.* Diss. University of Southern California, 2011.

Garre, Parthasarathy, et al. "Applying lean in aerospace manufacturing." *Materials Today: Proceedings* 4.8 (2017): 8439–8446.

Gerger, Atakan, and Ali Rıza Firuzan. "Use of six sigma method as a process improvement technique: A case study in aerospace industry." *Academic Journal of Science* 6.1 (2016): 191–202.

Gupta, Mahesh, et al. "Integrating theory of constraints, lean and six sigma: A framework development and its application." *Production Planning & Control* (2022): 1–24.

Kısakürek, İrem. *Six Sigma Methodology Restructuring the Training and Development Process of the Organization and Application.* Diss. Marmara Universitesi (Turkey), 2005.

Lee, Seanan C. "A literary survey on the challenges of adopting lean in aerospace production and aviation maintenance." *Journal of Aviation Technology and Engineering* 12.1 (2023): 4.

Luskin, Paul. *A Systems Engineering Methodology for Fuel Efficiency and Its Application to a Tactical Wheeled Vehicle Demonstrator.* Diss. Massachusetts Institute of Technology, 2010.

Manos, Anthony, and Chad Vincent, eds. *The Lean Handbook: A Guide to the Bronze Certification Body of Knowledge.* Quality Press, 2010.

Manville, Graham, Thanos Papadopoulos, and Patrizia Garengo. "Twenty-first century supply chain management: A multiple case study analysis within the UK aerospace industry." *Total Quality Management & Business Excellence* 32.7–8 (2021): 869–885.

Oppenheim, Bohdan W. *Lean for Systems Engineering with Lean Enablers for Systems Engineering.* Vol. 82. John Wiley & Sons, 2011.

Siviy, Jeannine M., M. Lynn Penn, and Robert W. Stoddard. *CMMI and Six Sigma: Partners in Process Improvement.* Pearson Education, 2007.

Spanyi, Andrew. *Operational Leadership.* Business Expert Press, 2010.

Stadnicka, Dorota. "Lean education in the faculty of mechanical engineering and aeronautics of Rzeszow University of Technology, Poland." *Lean Education: An Overview of Current Issues* (2017): 125–147.

Thomas, Andrew J., et al. "Implementing lean six sigma to overcome the production challenges in an aerospace company." *Production Planning & Control* 27.7–8 (2016): 591–603.

Yadav, Vishwas, et al. "Green lean six sigma for sustainability improvement: A systematic review and future research agenda." *International Journal of Lean Six Sigma* 14.4 (2023): 759–790.

Zhang, Min. *Using Six Sigma to Achieve Sustainable Manufacturing: A Case Study in Aviation Company*. Diss. Concordia University, 2014.

Index

Note: Page numbers in *italics* indicate figures, and page numbers in **bold** indicate tables on the corresponding page.

Made in the USA
Monee, IL
13 September 2026

62980170R00201